Y0-AGJ-662

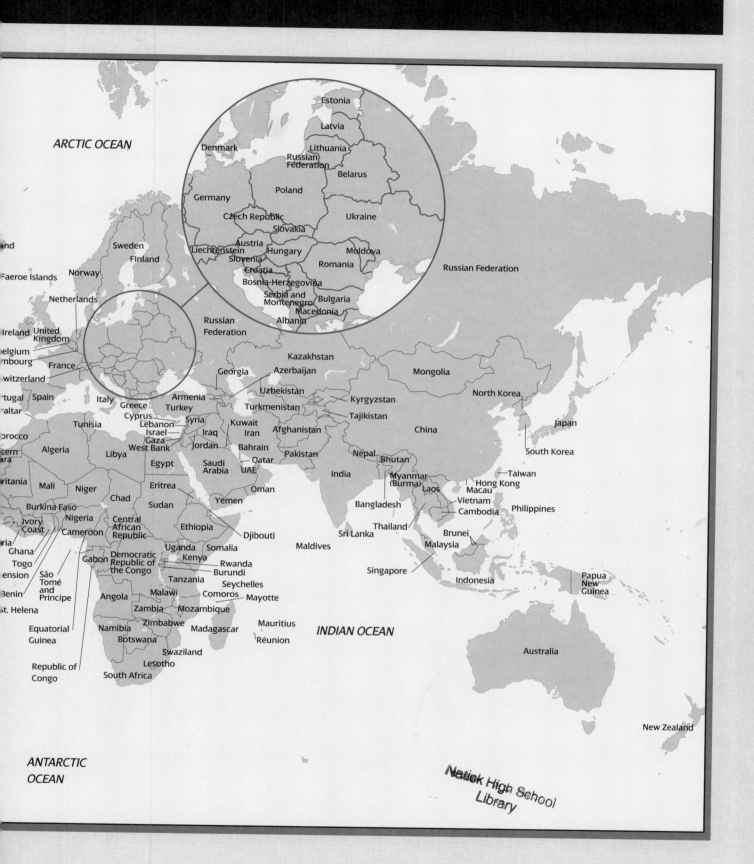

ARCTIC OCEAN

Estonia
Latvia
Denmark
Lithuania
Russian
Federation
Belarus
Germany
Poland
Czech Republic
Ukraine
Slovakia
Austria
Liechtenstein Hungary Moldova
Slovenia
Croatia Romania
Bosnia-Herzegovina
Serbia and Bulgaria
Montenegro
Macedonia
Albania

Sweden
Finland
Norway
Faeroe Islands
Netherlands
Ireland United
Kingdom
Belgium
mbourg
Switzerland France
Russian
Federation

Russian Federation

Kazakhstan
Georgia Azerbaijan
Uzbekistan Mongolia
Armenia
Turkey Kyrgyzstan North Korea
Cyprus
Lebanon Syria Turkmenistan Tajikistan
Israel Kuwait Japan
Gaza Iraq Iran Afghanistan China
West Bank Jordan South Korea
Bahrain Pakistan
Egypt Qatar Nepal
Saudi UAE Bhutan Taiwan
Arabia India Hong Kong
Eritrea Oman Myanmar Macau
Yemen (Burma) Laos Vietnam
Sudan Bangladesh Cambodia Philippines
Ethiopia Thailand
Djibouti Sri Lanka Brunei
Uganda Somalia Maldives Malaysia
Kenya
Rwanda Singapore
Burundi Indonesia Papua
Tanzania New
Seychelles Guinea
Comoros Mayotte
Mauritius
Zambia INDIAN OCEAN
Zimbabwe Madagascar Réunion
Mozambique
Australia
Swaziland
Lesotho
South Africa
New Zealand

Italy
Greece
Tunisia
Spain
Portugal
Gibraltar
Morocco
Algeria
Libya
Western
Sahara
Mauritania
Mali
Niger
Chad
Central
African
Republic
Burkina Faso
Nigeria
Ivory
Coast
Cameroon
Ghana
Togo
Benin
São
Tomé
and
Príncipe
Gabon
Democratic
Republic of
the Congo
Angola
Malawi
Equatorial
Guinea
Namibia
Botswana
Republic of
Congo
St. Helena
Ascension

ANTARCTIC
OCEAN

Natick High School
Library

WORLD AND ITS PEOPLES

SUB-SAHARAN AFRICA, AUSTRALASIA, AND THE PACIFIC

11

INDEXES

Natick High School
Library

Marshall Cavendish
Reference
New York

For **MARSHALL CAVENDISH**
Publisher: Paul Bernabeo
Project Editor: Stephanie Driver
Production Manager: Alan Tsai
Indexer: Cynthia Crippen, AEIOU, Inc.

For **BROWN REFERENCE GROUP**
Consultant Editor: Clive Carpenter
Deputy Editors: Graham Bateman, Derek Hall, Peter Lewis, Briony Ryles
Cartography: Encompass Graphics Ltd
Picture Research: Martin Anderson, Andrew Webb
Managing Editor: Tim Harris

For **A GOOD THING, INC.**
Page Production: Howard Petlack

© 2011 Marshall Cavendish Corporation

Published by Marshall Cavendish Reference
An imprint of Marshall Cavendish Corporation

All rights reserved.

No part of this publication may be reproduced, stored in a retrieval system or transmitted, in any form or by any means, electronic, mechanical, photocopying, recording, or otherwise, without the prior permission of the copyright owner. Request for permission should be addressed to the Publisher, Marshall Cavendish Corporation, 99 White Plains Road, Tarrytown, NY 10591. Tel: (914) 332-8888, fax: (914) 332-1888.

Website: www.marshallcavendish.us

This publication represents the opinions and views of the authors based on personal experience, knowledge, and research. The information in this book serves as a general guide only. The author and publisher have used their best efforts in preparing this book and disclaim liability rising directly and indirectly from the use and application of this book.

Other Marshall Cavendish Offices:
Marshall Cavendish International (Asia) Private Limited, 1 New Industrial Road, Singapore 536196 • Marshall Cavendish International (Thailand) Co Ltd. 253 Asoke, 12th Flr, Sukhumvit 21 Road, Klongtoey Nua, Wattana, Bangkok 10110, Thailand • Marshall Cavendish (Malaysia) Sdn Bhd, Times Subang, Lot 46, Subang Hi-Tech Industrial Park, Batu Tiga, 40000 Shah Alam, Selangor Darul Ehsan, Malaysia

Marshall Cavendish is a trademark of Times Publishing Limited

All websites were available and accurate when this book was sent to press.

Library of Congress Cataloging-in-Publication Data

World and its peoples. Sub-Saharan Africa, Australasia, and the Pacific / [set consultants, Rudi van Aarde .. et al.].
   v. cm.
  Includes bibliographical references and index.
   ISBN 978-0-7614-7912-3 (set) -- ISBN 978-0-7614-7914-7 (v. 1) -- ISBN 978-0-7614-7915-4 (v. 2) -- ISBN 978-0-7614-7916-1 (v. 3) -- ISBN 978-0-7614-7917-8 (v. 4) -- ISBN 978-0-7614-7918-5 (v. 5) -- ISBN 978-0-7614-7919-2 (v. 6) -- ISBN 978-0-7614-7920-8 (v. 7) -- ISBN 978-0-7614-7921-5 (v. 8) -- ISBN 978-0-7614-7922-2 (v. 9) -- ISBN 978-0-7614-7923-9 (v. 10) -- ISBN 978-0-7614-7925-3 (v. 11)
   1. Africa, Sub-Saharan--Encyclopedias. 2. Australasia--Encyclopedias.
3. Pacific Area--Encyclopedias. I. Aarde, Rudi van. II. Marshall Cavendish Corporation.
   DT351.W895 2011
   903--dc22
                                                     2010002116

Printed in Malaysia (T)

14 13 12 11 10   1 2 3 4 5

PHOTOGRAPHIC CREDITS
Front cover: Danilo Donadoni/ AGE Fotostock; Photos.com (right); Shutterstock: Jiri Haureljuk (left).
Title page: Wikimedia Commons: Hans Hillewaert (Lycaon)

CONTENTS

COMPARATIVE TABLES

    Geography   1446

    Population   1450

    Autonomous Regions   1453

    Cities   1456

    Family Life   1460

    Trade   1464

    Transportation   1469

    Communication   1476

GLOSSARY   1480

FURTHER RESEARCH   1489

THEMATIC INDEXES   1493

    Place-Names Index   1493

    Ethnic and Religious Index   1513

    Landscape and Climate Index   1517

    Historical and Biographical Index   1519

    Cultural and Artistic Index   1529

    Economic Index   1536

COMPREHENSIVE INDEX   1539

ADVISORY BOARD

SET CONSULTANTS

Rudi van Aarde, Conservation Ecology Research Unit, Department of Zoology and Entomology, University of Pretoria, South Africa
Sharad Master, School of Geosciences, University of Witwatersrand, Johannesburg, South Africa
Peter Mitchell, Professor of African Archaeology, St. Hugh's College, University of Oxford, England
Ceri Peach, School of Geography, University of Oxford, England
John Rennie Short, Department of Geography and Public Policy, University of Maryland Baltimore County

VOLUME CONSULTANTS

Claude Ardouin, Africa Section, Department of Africa, Oceania, and the Americas, British Museum, London, England

Holly Barker, Department of Anthropology, University of Washington, Seattle

Alice Bellagamba, Department of Human Sciences for Education, University of Milan-Bicocca, Italy

Carol Berger, Department of Anthropology, McGill University, Montreal, Quebec, Canada; Institute of Social and Cultural Anthropology, University of Oxford, England

Frank Bongiorno, Menzies Centre for Australian Studies, School of Arts and Humanities, King's College, University of London, England

Marina Carter, School of History, Classics, and Archaeology, University of Edinburgh, Scotland

Anne Chambers, Department of Anthropology, Southern Oregon University, Ashland

Keith Chambers, Department of Anthropology, Southern Oregon University, Ashland

Katherine Boris Dernbach, Department of Anthropology, University of California, San Diego, La Jolla

Jan-Georg Deutsch, Faculty of History, University of Oxford, England

Bob Forrester, Mbabane, Swaziland

Getie Gelaye, Department of African and Ethiopian Studies, Asia-Africa-Institute, Hamburg University, Germany

Andrew S. Goudie, School of Geography and the Environment, Oxford University Centre for the Environment, England

Richard Grant, Department of Geography and Regional Studies, University of Miami, Coral Gables, Florida

Guy G. Guthridge, Office of Polar Programs (formerly United States Antarctic Program), National Science Foundation, Arlington, Virginia

Joan Haig, The Lembani Trust, Lusaka; Department of History, University of Zambia, Lusaka

David Hayward, Geology and Environmental Science, School of Geography, University of Auckland, New Zealand

Marie Jorritsma, Department of Art History, Visual Arts, and Musicology, University of South Africa (UNISA)

Matthew Kirwin, Department of Political Science, College of Social Science, Michigan State University, East Lansing

Hélène Neveu Kringelbach, African Studies Centre, University of Oxford, England

Kwame Amoah Labi, Institute of African Studies, University of Ghana, Legon

Lamont Lindstrom, Department of Anthropology, University of Tulsa, Oklahoma

Marieme S. Lo, Department of Global Gender Studies, College of Arts and Sciences, State University of New York at Buffalo

Cluny Macpherson, School of Social and Cultural Studies, Massey University, Auckland, New Zealand

Ignatius A. Madu, Department of Geography, University of Nigeria, Nsukka

Enrico Magnani, Researcher, UN Mission for the Referendum in Western Sahara (MINURSO), Laayoune, Western Sahara

Christine Matzke, Department of African Studies, Institute of Asian and African Studies, Humboldt University, Berlin, Germany

Georgina Numbasa, Environmental Science and Geography, School of Natural and Physical Sciences, University of Papua New Guinea, National Capital District

Martin and Harriet Ottenheimer, Department of Sociology, Anthropology, and Social Work, Kansas State University, Manhattan, Kansas

Rebecca Peters, Center for Scientific Studies and Investigation, Angola Catholic University, Luanda, Angola; Department of Anthropology, Brown University, Providence, Rhode Island

Innocent Pikirayi, Department of Anthropology and Archaeology, University of Pretoria, South Africa

Nancy J. Pollock, formerly Departments of Anthropology and Development Studies, Victoria University, Wellington, New Zealand

Max Quanchi, Humanities Program, Queensland University of Technology, Brisbane, Australia

Maano Ramutsindela, Department of Environmental and Geographic Science, University of Cape Town, Rondebosch, South Africa

Konstantin Richter, University Jean Piaget, Cape Verde

David Andrew Roberts, Faculty of Arts and Sciences, School of Humanities, University of New England, Armidale, New South Wales, Australia.

Cyrus Samimi, Department of Geography and Regional Research, University of Vienna, Austria; Department of Geography, Friedrich-Alexander University of Erlangen-Nuremberg, Germany

Gerhard Seibert, Center for African Studies, Institute of Labor Science and Enterprise, Lisbon, Portugal

Sylvester Sennabulya, Uganda Institute of Information and Communications Technology, Kampala, Uganda

Glenn R. Summerhayes, Department of Anthropology, Gender, and Sociology, University of Otago, Dunedin, New Zealand

Bairu Tafla, Department of African and Ethiopian Studies, Asia-Africa-Institute, Hamburg University, Germany

Mussie Tesfagiorgis, University of Hamburg, Germany

Justin Willis, Department of History, University of Durham, England; formerly British Institute in Eastern Africa, Nairobi, Kenya and London, England

Janet Wilson, English and Postcolonial Studies, School of the Arts, University of Northampton, England

SET CONTENTS
BY COUNTRY

COUNTRY	VOLUME	PAGE	COUNTRY	VOLUME	PAGE
American Samoa	9	1192	Mayotte	6	798
Angola	5	610	Micronesia	8	1064
Antarctica	10	1418	Mozambique	6	800
Australia	10	1358	Namibia	7	926
Benin	3	330	Nauru	8	1074
Botswana	7	902	New Caledonia	8	1084
Burkina Faso	3	350	New Zealand	9	1210
Burundi	5	628	Nigeria	1	94
Cameroon	1	50	Niue	9	1236
Cape Verde	2	180	Norfolk Island	10	1416
Central African Republic	5	646	Northern Mariana Islands	8	1086
Comoros	6	750	Palau	8	1088
Congo, Democratic Republic of the	5	662	Papua New Guinea	8	1098
Congo, Republic of	5	682	Pitcairn	9	1238
Cook Islands	9	1194	Reunion	6	816
Djibouti	4	470	Rwanda	5	698
Eritrea	4	482	Saint Helena	7	938
Equatorial Guinea	1	68	Samoa	9	1240
Ethiopia	4	496	São Tomé and Príncipe	1	130
Fiji	8	1038	Senegal	2	250
French Polynesia	9	1196	Seychelles	6	818
French Southern Territories	10	1434	Sierra Leone	2	268
Gabon	1	78	Solomon Islands	8	1124
Gambia	2	192	Somalia	4	540
Ghana	3	368	South Africa	7	940
Guam	8	1052	Swaziland	7	974
Guinea	2	204	Tanzania	6	828
Guinea-Bissau	2	218	Togo	3	410
Ivory Coast	3	390	Tokelau	9	1256
Kenya	4	518	Tonga	9	1258
Kiribati	9	1198	Tuvalu	9	1274
Lesotho	7	914	Uganda	4	554
Liberia	2	230	U.S. Pacific Island Territories	9	1286
Madagascar	6	760	Vanuatu	8	1136
Malawi	6	774	Wallis and Futuna	9	1290
Marshall Islands	8	1054	Zambia	6	843
Mauritius	6	788	Zimbabwe	7	986

COUNTRY COVERAGE BY VOLUME

1: NIGERIA AND THE GULF OF GUINEA

Cameroon	50
Equatorial Guinea	68
Gabon	78
Nigeria	94
São Tomé and Príncipe	130

2: WEST AFRICAN COAST

Cape Verde	180
Gambia	192
Guinea	204
Guinea-Bissau	218
Liberia	230
Senegal	250
Sierra Leone	268

3: CENTRAL WEST AFRICA

Benin	330
Burkina Faso	350
Ghana	368
Ivory Coast	390
Togo	410

4: EASTERN AFRICA

Djibouti	470
Eritrea	482
Ethiopia	496
Kenya	518
Somalia	540
Uganda	554

5: CONGO BASIN AND ANGOLA

Angola	610
Burundi	628
Central African Republic	646
Congo, Democratic Republic of the	662
Congo, Republic of	682
Rwanda	698

6: EASTERN CENTRAL AFRICA AND THE INDIAN OCEAN

Comoros	750
Madagascar	760
Malawi	774
Mauritius	788
Mayotte	798
Mozambique	800
Reunion	816
Seychelles	818
Tanzania	828
Zambia	843

7: SOUTHERN AFRICA

Botswana	902
Lesotho	914
Namibia	926
Saint Helena	938
South Africa	940
Swaziland	974
Zimbabwe	986

8: WESTERN PACIFIC

Fiji	1038
Guam	1052
Marshall Islands	1054
Micronesia	1064
Nauru	1074
New Caledonia	1084
Northern Mariana Islands	1086
Palau	1088
Papua New Guinea	1098
Solomon Islands	1124
Vanuatu	1136

9: NEW ZEALAND AND POLYNESIA

American Samoa	1192
Cook Islands	1194
French Polynesia	1196
Kiribati	1198
New Zealand	1210
Niue	1236
Pitcairn	1238
Samoa	1240
Tokelau	1256
Tonga	1258
Tuvalu	1274
U.S. Pacific Island Territories	1286
Wallis and Futuna	1290

10: AUSTRALIA AND ANTARCTICA

Australia	1358
Norfolk Island	1416
Antarctica	1418
French Southern Territories	1434

Geography

The world's longest river, the Nile, originates in sub-Saharan Africa, and the region contains one of the largest groups of lakes in the world, the Great Lakes of Africa. Australia is, by convention, regarded as a continent. The many islands of the Pacific Ocean are part of the region variously known as Australasia and Oceania.

This set treats the part of Africa, the second-largest continent, that lies to the south of the Sahara Desert. It also includes Australia, New Zealand, and the islands of the Pacific Ocean region: together these lands form the region that is known as either Oceania or Australasia. This set also treats the ice-covered continent of Antarctica.

The nations of these regions vary greatly in size. The smallest is Nauru, an island in the Pacific Ocean with an area of about 100 square miles (261 sq. km), and small dependent territories, The largest is Australia, which is the sixth-largest nation in the world.

The table on the following page ranks the countries and the dependent territories of the region by size.

The continents and island nations treated in this volume are largely formed from plateaus, above which mountain ranges rise, mainly at the fringes of the plateau regions. One table lists the major mountain ranges, while another lists the highest points in the various nations and dependent territories of the regions. Sub-Saharan Africa and Australia contain considerable deserts. As a result of the extensive desert areas, major rivers are

MOUNTAIN RANGES OF THE REGIONS

Range	Length in miles	Length in km	Location in the region	Highest peak in range
Great Dividing Range	2,250	3,600	Australia	Mount Kosciuszko
Transantarctic Mountains	2,200	3,500	Antarctica	Mount Fitzpatrick
Central New Guinea range*	1,250	2,000	Papua New Guinea	Ngga Pulu
Ethiopian Highlands	900	1,450	Ethiopia, Eritrea	Ras Dejen (Ras Dashen)
Malagasy Range	850	1,370	Madagascar	Maromokoto
Drakensberg Range	800	1,290	South Africa, Lesotho Swaziland, Mozambique	Nevado de Colima Thabana Ntlenyana
Antarctic Peninsula range	800	1,290	Antarctica	Mount Jackson
Southern Alps	310	500	New Zealand	Mount Cook

* Maximum extent

MAJOR LAKES OF THE REGIONS

Lake	Area in sq. miles	Area in sq. km	Character	Location
Lake Victoria	26,828	69,484	Freshwater	Uganda, Kenya, Tanzania
Lake Tanganyika	12,700	32,900	Freshwater	Tanzania, Congo, Zambia, Burundi
Lake Malawi or Lake Nyasa	11,430	29,600	Freshwater	Malawi, Tanzania, Mozambique
Lake Vostok	6,058	15,690	Freshwater (under ice)	Antarctica
Lake Eyre	3,688*	9,500*	Freshwater (often dry)	Australia
Lake Volta	3,275	8,482	Reservoir	Ghana
Lake Turkana	2,473	6,405	Alkaline	Kenya, Ethiopia
Lake Torrens	2,200*	5,700*	Freshwater (often dry)	Australia
Lake Kariba	2,150	5,580	Reservoir	Zambia, Zimbabwe
Lake Albert	2,046	5,299	Freshwater	Uganda, Congo
Lake Mweru	1,980	5,120	Freshwater	Zambia

* Maximum extent

NATIONS OF SUB-SAHARAN AFRICA AND AUSTRALASIA BY SIZE

Nation	Area in sq. miles	Area in sq. km	Nation	Area in sq. miles	Area in sq. km
Congo, Democratic Republic	905,354	2,344,856	Swaziland	6,704	17,363
Angola	481,354	1,246,700	Gambia	4,127	10,689
South Africa	472,854	1,224,691	Cape Verde	1,557	4,033
Ethiopia	435,184	1,127,121	Reunion	969	2,510
Tanzania	364,881	945,037	Mauritius	788	2,040
Nigeria	356,411	923,103	Comoros	719	1,862
Namibia	318,250	824,269	São Tomé and Príncipe	386	1,001
Mozambique	309,496	801,590	Seychelles	176	455
Zambia	290,586	752,614	Saint Helena	159	411
Somalia	246,201	637,657	Mayotte	145	376
Central African Republic	240,324	622,436			
Madagascar	226,658	587,041	Australia	2,988,901	7,741,220
Kenya	224,961	582,646	Papua New Guinea	178,704	462,840
Botswana	224,606	581,730	New Zealand	104,454	270,534
Cameroon	183,568	475,440	Solomon Islands	10,954	28,370
Zimbabwe	150,872	390,757	New Caledonia	7,172	18,576
Congo, Republic of	132,047	342,000	Fiji	7,055	18,272
Ivory Coast	123,854	320,783	Vanuatu	4,707	12,190
Burkina Faso	105,839	274,122	French Polynesia	1,544	4,000
Gabon	103,347	267,667	Samoa	1,093	2,831
Guinea	94,926	245,857	Tonga	289	748
Uganda	93,065	241,038	Kiribati	277	717
Ghana	92,098	238,533	Micronesia	271	701
Senegal	75,951	196,712	Northern Mariana Islands	184	477
Malawi	45,747	118,484	Palau	177	458
Eritrea	45,405	117,600	Wallis and Futuna	106	274
Benin	43,484	112,622	Niue	100	259
Liberia	43,000	111,370	Cook Islands	92	237
Sierra Leone	27,699	71,740	Pitcairn	92	237
Togo	21,925	56,785	American Samoa	77	199
Guinea-Bissau	13,948	36,125	Marshall Islands	70	181
Lesotho	11,720	30,355	Norfolk Island	13	35
Equatorial Guinea	10,831	28,051	Tuvalu	9	24
Burundi	10,745	27,830	Nauru	8	21
Rwanda	10,169	26,338	Tokelau	5	13
Djibouti	8,957	23,200			

LARGEST DESERTS IN THE REGIONS

Desert	Area in sq. miles	Area in sq. km	Location in the region
Australian Desert	3,250,000	8,000,000	Australia
Kalahari Desert	200,000	520,000	Botswana
Namib Desert	120,000	310,000	Namibia, Angola

restricted in places, although some major waterways flow through the arid regions. The major waterways of the region are listed in another table. Much of Africa is formed by plateaus, above which rise mountain ranges, mainly at the fringes. Australia too is largely low-lying plateaus, with mountains confined to the east. One table ranks the major mountain chains of the regions, while another lists the highest points in each of the regions' nations and territories.

LONGEST RIVERS IN THE REGIONS

River	Length in miles	Length in km	Location in the region
Nile*	4,145	6,670	Rwanda, Uganda, Ethiopia
Congo-Lualaba	2,920	4,700	Congo (Democratic Republic), Congo
Niger*	2,600	4,181	Nigeria
Zambezi	2,200	3,540	Angola, Zambia, Zimbabwe, Mozambique
Ubangi-Ulele	1,400	2,250	Congo (Democratic Republic), Congo
Kasai	1,338	2,153	Congo (Democratic Republic)
Orange	1,300	2,100	Lesotho, South Africa, Namibia
Shabeelle	1,130	1,820	Ethiopia, Somalia
Limpopo	1,100	1,800	Botswana, South Africa, Zimbabwe, Mozambique
Senegal*	1,020	1,641	Guinea, Senegal
Murray-Darling-Condamine	2,282	3,672	Australia
Murrumbidgee	923	1,485	Australia

* not all the course of these waterways flows through the region

HIGHEST POINTS BY NATION AND DEPENDENCY

Nation	Highest point	Height in feet	Height in meters
Angola	Morro de Moco	8,596	2,620
Benin	an unnamed point in Atacora Massif	2,235	681
Botswana	Mount Otse	4,885	1,489
Burkina Faso	Mont Tena	2,457	749
Burundi	Mount Heha	8,760	2,670
Cameroon	Fako (on Mount Cameroon)	13,435	4,095
Cape Verde	Mount Fogo (Pico do Cano)	9,281	2,829
Central African Republic	Mount Ngaoui	4,659	1,420
Comoros	Mount Kartala	7,746	2,361
Congo, Democratic Republic	Mount Ngaliema	16,763	5,110
Congo, Republic	Mount Nabeba	3,219	981
Djibouti	Musa Ali Terara	6,765	2,062
Equatorial Guinea	Pico de Basilé	9,868	3,008
Eritrea	Soira	9,902	3,018
Ethiopia	Ras Dejen (Ras Deshen)	15,157	4,620
Gabon	Mount Iboudji	5,167	1,575
Gambia	an unnamed point	174	53
Ghana	Mount Afadjato	2,887	880
Guinea	Mount Nima	5,747	1,752
Guinea-Bissau	an unnamed point in Boé Hills	984	300
Ivory Coast	a point on Mount Nimba	5,747	1,752
Kenya	Mount Kenya	17,057	5,199
Lesotho	Thabana Ntlenyana	11,425	3,482
Liberia	Mount Wuteve	4,531	1,380
Madagascar	Maromokoto (Tsaratanana Massif)	9,436	2,876

HIGHEST POINTS BY NATION AND DEPENDENCY (continued)

Nation	Highest point	Height in feet	Height in meters
Malawi	Sapitwa	9,849	3,002
Mauritius	Piton de la Petite Rivière Noire	2,711	826
Mayotte	Benara	2,165	660
Mozambique	Monte Binga	7,992	2,436
Namibia	Konigstein Peak (Brandberg)	8,550	2,606
Nigeria	Chappal Waddi (Mount Waddi)	7,936	2,419
Reunion	Piton des Neiges	10,066	3,069
Rwanda	Mount Karisimbi	14,826	4,519
Saint Helena	Queen Mary's Peak (Tristan da Cunha)	7,087	2,160
São Tomé and Príncipe	Pico de São Tomé	6,640	2,024
Senegal	an unnamed point in Fouta Djallon	1,906	581
Seychelles	Morne Seychellois	2,972	906
Sierra Leone	Bintimani Peak	6,390	1,948
Somalia	Surud Ad (Shimbiris)	7,927	2,408
South Africa	Injasuti	11,182	3,408
Swaziland	Emlembe	6,113	1,862
Tanzania	Mount Kilimanjaro	19,340	5,894
Togo	Mont Agou	3,235	986
Uganda	Ngaliema (secondary peak)	16,763	5,110
Zambia	an unnamed point in Mafinga Hills	7,549	2,301
Zimbabwe	Mount Inyangani	8,503	2,592
American Samoa	Lata Mountain	3,169	966
Australia	Mount Kosciuszko	7,316	2,230
Cook Islands	Mount Te Manga	2,142	653
Fiji	Tomaniivi	4,672	1,424
French Polynesia	Mount Orohena	7,352	2,241
Guam	Mount Lamlam	1,332	406
Kiribati	an unnamed point on Banaba	266	81
Marshall Islands	an unnamed point on Likiep	32	10
Micronesia	Dolohmwar	2,595	791
Nauru	an unnamed point	200	61
New Caledonia	Mount Panié	5,340	1,628
New Zealand	Mount Cook	12,315	3,754
Niue	an unnamed point	223	68
Norfolk Island	Mount Bates	1,047	319
Northern Mariana Islands	Agrihan	3,165	965
Palau	Mount Ngerchelchuus	794	242
Papua New Guinea	Mount Wilhelm	14,793	4,509
Pitcairn	Palawa Valley Ridge	1,139	347
Samoa	Silisili	6,096	1,858
Solomon Islands	Mount Makarakomburu	8,028	2,447
Tokelau	an unnamed point	15	5
Tonga	an unnamed point on Kao	3,389	1,033
Tuvalu	an unnamed point	17	6
Vanuatu	Mont Tabwémasana	6,158	1,877
Wallis and Futuna	Mount Singavi	2,510	765

Population

Much of sub-Saharan Africa and Australia is sparsely populated. Only a few regions, such as the Rand in South Africa and western Nigeria, are densely peopled.

Africa and Australasia both contain some of the world's most sparsely populated areas. The central deserts of Australia, a country whose peoples mainly live along the coastal fringes, and the semideserts and savannas of western Africa and deserts of southern Africa are home to relatively few people. Large metropolitan areas are limited to eastern Australia, for example the cities of Sydney and Melbourne, and relatively isolated major centers of population in sub-Saharan Africa, such as the southwestern states of Nigeria and the Rand mining and industrial region of South Africa.

NATIONS AND DEPENDENCIES OF THE REGIONS BY POPULATION DENSITY

Nation	Persons per sq. mile	Persons per sq. km	Nation	Persons per sq. mile	Persons per sq. km
Mauritius	1,610	622	Congo, Democratic Republic	64	25
Mayotte	1,283	495	Somalia	35	14
Comoros	931	359	Saint Helena	35	14
Reunion	807	312	Zambia	34	13
Rwanda	803	310	Angola	32	13
Burundi	686	265	Congo, Republic	26	10
Seychelles	472	182	Central African Republic	16	6
Nigeria	393	152	Gabon	15	6
São Tomé and Príncipe	358	138	Botswana	8	3
Gambia	331	128	Namibia	6	2
Cape Verde	327	126			
Uganda	318	123	Nauru	1,263	481
Malawi	286	110	Tuvalu	1,067	400
Ghana	254	98	Guam	742	287
Togo	243	94	American Samoa	740	286
Benin	180	70	Marshall Islands	729	282
Sierra Leone	179	69	Micronesia	399	154
Ethiopia	170	66	Northern Mariana Islands	375	145
Lesotho	161	62	Tonga	353	136
Kenya	156	60	Kiribati	336	130
Senegal	149	58	Tokelau	300	115
Burkina Faso	144	56	Cook Islands	213	83
Swaziland	142	55	French Polynesia	168	65
Ivory Coast	138	53	Samoa	164	63
Guinea-Bissau	111	43	Norfolk Island	146	54
South Africa	103	40	Wallis and Futuna	126	49
Tanzania	103	40	Fiji	119	46
Cameroon	102	39	Palau	112	43
Guinea	95	37	Solomon Islands	45	17
Equatorial Guinea	94	36	New Zealand	41	16
Liberia	81	31	Vanuatu	41	16
Madagascar	78	30	New Caledonia	34	13
Eritrea	78	30	Papua New Guinea	29	11
Zimbabwe	77	30	Niue	16	6
Djibouti	71	28	Australia	7	3
Mozambique	66	26	Pitcairn	3	1

NATIONS AND DEPENDENCIES OF THE REGIONS BY POPULATION

Nation	Date	Population	Nation	Date	Population
Nigeria	2006	140,003,000	Equatorial Guinea	2001	1,015,000
Ethiopia	2007	73,919,000	Swaziland	2007	954,000
Congo, Democratic Republic	2004	58,300,000	Reunion	2006	782,000
South Africa	2007	48,502,000	Comoros	2009	669,000
Tanzania	2005	37,394,000	Djibouti	2000	638,000
Kenya	2008	35,112,000	Cape Verde	2009	509,000
Uganda	2008	29,593,000	Mayotte	2007	186,000
Ghana	2009	23,417,000	São Tomé and Príncipe	2001	138,000
Mozambique	2007	20,530,000	Seychelles	2005	83,000
Cameroon	2007	18,675,000	Saint Helena	2008	5,600
Madagascar	2004	17,594,000			
Ivory Coast	2002	17,065,000	Australia	2009	21,875,000
Angola	2005	15,566,000	Papua New Guinea	2001	5,191,000
Burkina Faso	2009	15,224,000	New Zealand	2008	4,269,000
Malawi	2008	13,066,000	Fiji	2007	837,000
Zimbabwe	2002	11,635,000	Solomon Islands	2007	495,000
Senegal	2007	11,343,000	French Polynesia	2007	260,000
Zambia	2000	9,886,000	New Caledonia	2009	246,000
Guinea	2003	9,030,000	Vanuatu	2001	195,000
Somalia	2005	8,600,000	Samoa	2006	179,000
Rwanda	2002	8,129,000	Guam	2000	155,000
Benin	2006	7,841,000	Tonga	2006	102,000
Burundi	2004	7,384,000	Micronesia	2007	108,000
Togo	2006	5,337,000	Kiribati	2005	93,000
Sierra Leone	2004	4,977,000	Northern Mariana Islands	2000	69,000
Central African Republic	2003	3,895,000	American Samoa	2000	57,000
Eritrea	2005	3,622,000	Marshall Islands	1999	51,000
Liberia	2008	3,476,000	Palau	2005	19,900
Congo, Republic	2005	3,397,000	Cook Islands	2006	19,600
Lesotho	2008	1,881,000	Wallis and Futuna	2008	13,400
Namibia	2001	1,830,000	Nauru	2002	10,100
Botswana	2006	1,773,000	Tuvalu	2002	9,600
Guinea-Bissau	2009	1,548,000	Norfolk Island	2006	1,900
Gabon	2003	1,521,000	Niue	2006	1,600
Gambia	2003	1,365,000	Tokelau	2006	1,500
Mauritius	2008	1,269,000	Pitcairn	2006	50

POPULATION DENSITY

Australia is an example of great differences of population density across a nation. Australia has a population density of 7 people per square mile (3 per square km), but the empty center region of Australia is virtually uninhabited. By contrast, some of the small island nations of the Pacific region have considerable population densities: in Nauru there are 1,263 people per square mile (481 per square km) and in Tuvalu, where much of the population is concentrated on one island, the density is 1,067 per square mile (400 per square km). Such high population densities are unusual in sub-Saharan Africa, except around major cities where more diverse economies allow greater employment opportunities, and in small island territories, such as Mayotte, Mauritius, Reunion, and the Comoros. However, the small nations of Rwanda and Burundi, both largely agricultural countries, have high population densities: 803 people per square mile (310 per square km) in Rwanda and 686 per square mile (269 per square km) in Burundi.

NATIONAL POPULATION

The countries of the sub-Saharan African region range in size of population from Nigeria, which with more than 140 million people (in 2006) is the eighth most populous country in the world, to small

ANNUAL CHANGE IN POPULATION IN THE NATIONS OF THE REGION

Nation	Annual percentage growth/decline	Nation	Annual percentage growth/decline
Burundi	3.3	Zimbabwe	1.5
Mayotte	3.3	Reunion	1.3
Congo, Democratic Republic	3.2	Namibia	1.0
Ethiopia	3.2	Seychelles	1.0
Burkina Faso	3.1	Mauritius	0.8
São Tomé and Príncipe	3.1	Cape Verde	0.6
Benin	3.0	Swaziland	0.5
Madagascar	3.0	Saint Helena	0.4
Comoros	2.8	South Africa	0.3
Congo, Republic	2.8	Lesotho	0.1
Rwanda	2.8		
Somalia	c. 2.8	Solomon Islands	2.4
Equatorial Guinea	2.7	Northern Mariana Islands	2.3
Gambia	2.7	Kiribati	2.2
Kenya	2.7	Marshall Islands	2.1
Liberia	2.7	Papua New Guinea	2.1
Senegal	2.7	Nauru	1.7
Togo	2.7	Tuvalu	1.6
Uganda	2.7	Tonga	1.5
Eritrea	2.6	Fiji	1.4
Guinea	2.6	French Polynesia	1.4
Malawi	2.4	Guam	1.4
Sierra Leone	2.3	Vanuatu	1.4
Cameroon	2.2	Samoa	1.3
Angola	2.1	American Samoa	1.2
Ivory Coast	2.1	Australia	1.2
Gabon	2.0	New Caledonia	1.1
Guinea-Bissau	2.0	New Zealand	0.9
Nigeria	2.0	Palau	0.4
Tanzania	2.0	Wallis and Futuna	0.3
Botswana	1.9	Norfolk Island	0.0
Djibouti	1.9	Pitcairn	0.0
Ghana	1.9	Tokelau	-0.01
Mozambique	1.8	Niue	-0.03
Zambia	1.6	Micronesia	-0.3
Central African Republic	1.5	Cook Islands	-3.3

island sovereign states and dependent territories, such as Seychelles. While sub-Saharan Africa contains nine nations with more than 20,000,000 inhabitants, Oceania has only one with a population of more than 20,000,000, Australia. The majority of Oceanian states are small territories with fewer than 100,000 people. A table in this section ranks the countries and dependencies of sub-Saharan Africa and Oceania by population size. The figures in this table are taken from the latest national census or are official government or United Nations (UN) estimates. Because not all the figures are from the same year, the comparison cannot be exact.

Economic and social factors influence population growth rates. States with higher standards of living tend to have lower birthrates, but the populations of some southern African countries have low growth rates because of migration to South Africa and death through HIV/AIDS. A table ranks the regions' territories by yearly change in population density.

Autonomous Regions

Some countries have systems of government that are federal or quasi-federal in nature, in which particular regions have a degree of autonomy from one another. These regions are known by different names, for example, state, county, or community, among others, depending on the country.

STATES OF NIGERIA

State	Land area sq. miles	Land area sq. km	Population (2006 figure)	Capital
Abia	2,440	6,320	2,834,000	Umuahia
Adamawa	14,254	36,917	3,168,000	Yola
Akwa Ibom	2,734	7,081	3,920,000	Uyo
Anambra	1,870	4,844	4,182,000	Akwa
Bauchi	17,698	45,837	4,676,000	Bauchi
Bayelsa	4,160	10,773	1,703,000	Yenagoa
Benue	13,150	34,059	4,912,000	Makurdi
Borno	27,115	70,228	4,151,000	Maiduguri
Cross River State	7,782	20,156	2,889,000	Calabar
Delta State	6,833	17,698	4,098,000	Asaba
Ebonyi	2,189	5,670	2,174,000	Abakaliki
Edo	6,873	17,802	3,218,000	BeninCity
Ekiti	2,453	6,353	2,384,000	Ado-Ekiti
Enugu	2,765	7,161	3,257,000	Enugu
Gombe	7,246	18,768	2,354,000	Gombe
Imo	2,135	5,530	3,935,000	Owerri
Jigawa	8,940	23,154	4,349,000	Dutse
Kaduna	17,781	46,053	6,067,000	Kaduna
Kano	7,773	20,131	9,384,000	Kano
Katsina	9,341	24,192	5,793,000	Katsina
Kebbi	14,209	35,800	3,239,000	Birnin Kebbi
Kogi	11,519	29,833	3,278,000	Lokoja
Kwara	14,218	36,825	2,371,000	Ilorin
Lagos	1,292	3,345	9,014,000	Ikeja
Nassarawa	10,470	27,117	1,863,000	Lafia
Niger	29,484	76,363	3,950,000	Minna
Ogun	6,472	16,762	3,728,000	Abeokuta
Ondo	5,639	14,606	3,441,000	Akure
Osun	3,572	9,251	3,424,000	Oshogbo
Oyo	10,986	28,454	5,592,000	Ibadan
Plateau State	11,936	30,913	3,179,000	Jos
Rivers State	4,277	11,077	4,185,000	Port Harcourt
Sokoto	10,028	25,973	3,697,000	Sokoto
Taraba	21,032	54,473	2,301,000	Jalingo
Yobe	17,568	45,502	2,322,000	Damaturu
Zamfara	15,352	39,762	3,260,000	Gusau
Federal Capital Territory	2,824	7,315	1,405,000	Abuja

REGIONS OF ETHIOPIA

Region	Land area sq. miles	Land area sq. km	Population (2007 figure)	Capital
Addis Ababa City	205	530	2,738,000	Addis Ababa
Afar Region	37,339	96,708	1,411,000	Asayita
Amhara Region	61,458	159,174	17,214,000	Bahir Dar
Benishangul-Gumuz	19,031	49,289	671,000	Asosa
Dire Dawa City	468	1,213	343,000	Dire Dawa
Gambela Peoples	9,962	25,802	307,000	Gambela
Harari People	120	311	183,000	Harer
Oromiya	136,297	353,007	27,158,000	Adama and Addis Ababa (which is outside the region)
Somali Region	107,819	279,252	4,439,000	Jijiga
Southern Nations, Nationalities, and Peoples	43,376	112,343	15,043,000	Awasa
Tigray	19,336	50,079	4,314,000	Mekele

ISLANDS OF THE UNION OF THE COMOROS

Island	Comorian name of island	Land area sq. miles	Land area sq. km	Population (2009 figure)	Capital
Anjouan	Ndzouani or Nzwani	164	424	284,000	Mutsamudu
Grande Comore	Ngazidja	443	1,148	342,000	Moroni
Mohéli	Moili or Mwali	112	290	44,000	Fombon

TANZANIAN AUTONOMOUS STATE

Island	Land area sq. miles	Land area sq. km	Population (2002 figure)	Capital
Zanzibar	951	2,460	982,000	Zanzibar

PROVINCES OF SOUTH AFRICA

Province	Land area sq. miles	Land area sq. km	Population (2001 figure)	Capital
Eastern Cape	65,483	169,600	6,437,000	Bisho
Free State	49,992	129,480	2,707,000	Bloemfontein
Gauteng	7,262	18,810	8,837,000	Johannesburg
KwaZulu-Natal	35,591	92,180	9,426,000	Pietermaritzburg
Limpopo	47,599	123,280	5,273,000	Pietersburg
Mpumalanga	30,259	78,370	3,123,000	Nelspruit
Northern Cape	139,692	361,800	823,000	Kimberley
North-West Province	44,861	116,190	3,669,000	Mmabatho
Western Cape	49,950	129,370	4,524,000	Cape Town

AUTONOMOUS REGION OF PAPUA NEW GUINEA

Region	Land area (sq. miles)	Land area (sq. km)	Population (2000 figure)	Capital
Bougainville	3,590	9,300	175,000	Buka

THE FEDERATED STATES OF MICRONESIA

State	Land area (sq. miles)	Land area (sq. km)	Population (2000 figure)	Capital
Chuuk	49	127	54,000	Weno (formerly Moen)
Kosrae	42	110	8,000	Tofol
Pohnpei	133	345	34,000	Kolonia
Yap	46	119	11,000	Colonia

PROVINCES OF THE SOLOMON ISLANDS

Province	Land area sq. miles	Land area sq. km	Population (2007 figure)	Capital
Central Province	238	615	26,000	Tulagi
Choiseul	1,482	3,837	24,000	Taro Island
Guadalcanal	2,060	5,336	73,000	Honiara
Honiara City	8.5	22	59,000	Honiara
Isabel	1,597	4,136	25,000	Buala
Makira-Ulawa	1,231	3,188	38,000	Kirakira
Malaita	1,631	4,225	149,000	Auki
Rennell and Bellona	259	671	3,000	Tigoa
Temotu	334	865	23,000	Lata
Western Province	2,114	5,475	76,000	Gizo

STATES AND TERRITORIES OF AUSTRALIA

Name	Status	Land area sq. miles	Land area sq. km	Population (2006 figure)	Capital
Australian Capital Territory	territory	910	2,358	351,000	Canberra
New South Wales	state	309,130	800,642	7,100,000	Sydney
Northern Territory	territory	520,902	1,349,129	225,000	Darwin
Queensland	state	668,207	1,730,648	4,407,000	Brisbane
South Australia	state	379,724	983,482	1,623,000	Adelaide
Tasmania	state	26,410	68,401	503,000	Hobart
Victoria	state	87,806	227,416	5,428,000	Melbourne
Western Australia	state	976,790	2,529,875	2,237,000	Perth

TERRITORIAL CLAIMS IN ANTARCTICA

Some of these claims—the British, Argentine, and Chilean—overlap. Most nonclaimant nations do not recognize Antarctic territorial claims.

Name of territorial claim	Nation making the claim	Area (sq. miles)	Area (sq. km)
Adélie Land*	France	166,800	432,000
Antártica	Chile	482,600	1,250,000
Argentine Antarctica	Argentina	373,000	966,000
Australian Antarctic Territory	Australia	2,333,500	6,043,700
British Antarctic Territory	United Kingdom	695,000	1,800,000
Peter I Island	Norway	70	180
Queen Maud Land	Norway	No inland limit to the claim has been made; no estimate of the area can be given	
Ross Dependency	New Zealand	282,000	730,000

* Claimed as part of the French Southern and Antarctic Lands

Cities

Sub-Saharan Africa contains some of the world's fastest-growing cities, a small number of which were seats of African polities before the colonial era, which began in the late sixteenth century. However, most sub-Saharan African cities, like those of Oceania, have existed for fewer than 150 years, often much less. In modern times, despite the rapid growth of urbanization, these regions do not contain any of the 20 largest cities on Earth.

Before the arrival of Europeans in sub-Saharan Africa from the sixteenth century, some regions of the continent were the sites of African civilizations, empires, and kingdoms. Some of these cities have disappeared; others still exist but have been surpassed as local centers by cities founded in the colonial era—for example, M'Banza Kongo, in modern Angola. This city was the national capital of the powerful kingdom of Kongo. Most of the important cities of northern Nigeria are early foundations, which developed as capitals of the region's sultanates and emirates. However, the overwhelming majority of cities in sub-Saharan Africa are relatively modern foundations.

Most large metropolitan areas in sub-Saharan Africa were founded by European colonists as they opened up the continent for trade and colonial exploitation. The majority of the larger cities are along or near the coast, the point of contact between European colonial powers and the interior of the continent. Some were developed as ports, for example Douala in Cameroon and Durban in South Africa. Others were centers of colonial administration, such as Accra in Ghana and Dakar in Senegal. A number of sub-Saharan African colonies had more than one administrative center founded by colonial powers. For example, Matadi, along the coast, was the original colonial capital of the Belgian Congo, now the Democratic Republic of the Congo (DRC), while in Ivory Coast, French colonists administered the country from Grand-Bassam and Bingerville before moving the capital to Abidjan in the 1930s.

In modern times, a number of African countries have built new national capitals, in some cases more centrally located within their respective nations. They include Lilongwe in Malawi and Dodoma in Tanzania. Yamoussoukro, in Ivory Coast, is a different case: the city was developed around the birthplace of the nation's founding president.

Urban development in sub-Saharan Africa was relatively slow in the first half of the twentieth century, although coastal ports grew, as did centers of mining, such as Johannesburg, in South Africa, Elisabethville (now Lubumbashi) in the Belgian Congo (modern DRC), and the Copperbelt towns of Northern Rhodesia, now Zambia. The great wave of urbanization on the continent occurred from the 1960s onward, largely corresponding with the period when many territories gained national independence. This era was characterized by a drift to the cities by people in search of employment opportunities. For example, Nairobi, the national capital of Kenya, grew from a population of 380,000 in 1965 to 2,511,000 in 1989.

The cities of Oceania are also of modern foundation. The original inhabitants of Australia, New Zealand, Papua New Guinea, and the Pacific Islands were not urban dwellers, and cities in this region date from European settlement (in Australia, from 1788) and European colonization. Throughout the region, settlement is predominantly in coastal areas. In part, this reflects the history of the development of the various territories of the region, but, in the case of Australia, it highlights climatic and other determinants that effectively restrict widespread settlement to the more fertile, milder, and better-watered regions along the eastern coast and in the far southwest of the continent. However, substantial reserves of minerals attract settlement to some of the more extreme inland areas of Australia, for example, Mount Isa in Queensland, and Kalgoorlie and Boulder in Western Australia.

URBAN POPULATION

The greatest rates of urbanization in sub-Saharan Africa have been in modern times. This has been particularly notable in countries with large coastal cities or states that are rich in mineral resources. However, while the population of some states, such as Gabon, South Africa, and the Republic of the Congo, are predominantly urban, other African nations are still overwhelmingly rural and agricultural. Sub-Saharan African nations whose economies and populations are still rural include Rwanda, Burundi, Burkina Faso, and Tanzania.

Higher levels of urbanization occur in many of the nations of the Pacific Ocean region, particularly in some of the small dependent and independent island territories where there are few urban centers. Such territories are often dominated by a single principal urban center, for example Papeete in French Polynesia, Nouméa in New Caledonia, and Suva in Fiji. On some small island territories, almost all the population is concentrated in a single settlement. For example, Burnt Pine on Norfolk Island, an external Australian territory, contains 89 percent of the territory's population.

LARGEST METROPOLITAN AREAS OF THE REGIONS

City	Nation	Date	Source	Population within city limits	Population of metropolitan area
Lagos	Nigeria	2006	Nigerian national census	527,000	7,938,000
Kinshasa	Congo, Democratic Rep.	2004	Congolese census authority	7,274,000	7,274,000
Johannesburg	South Africa	2001	South African census	1,009,000	6,420,000
Kano	Nigeria	2006	Nigerian national census	365,000	3,849,000
Durban	South Africa	2001	South African census	537,000	3,090,000
Abidjan	Ivory Coast	2002	Ivorian government estimate	2,878,000	3,000,000
Nairobi	Kenya	2006	Kenyan government estimate	2,948,000	2,948,000
Accra	Ghana	2000	Ghanaian national census	1,659,000	2,906,000
Cape Town	South Africa	2001	South African census	827,000	2,872,000
Addis Ababa	Ethiopia	2007	Ethiopian national census	2,738,000	2,738,000
Ibadan	Nigeria	2006	Nigerian national census	1,339,000	2,551,000
Dakar	Senegal	2007	Senegalese national census	2,243,000	2,446,000
Dar es Salaam	Tanzania	2002	Tanzanian national census	2,336,000	2,336,000
Luanda	Angola	2005	Angolan government estimate	2,262,000	2,262,000
Harare	Zimbabwe	2002	Zimbabwean national census	1,445,000	1,881,000
Kampala	Uganda	2008	Ugandan census authority	1,480,000	1,790,000
Pretoria	South Africa	2001	South African census	525,000	1,787,000
Maputo	Mozambique	2007	Mozambican national census	1,099,000	1,775,000
Kaduna	Nigeria	2006	Nigerian national census	770,000	1,521,000
Douala	Cameroon	2001	Cameroonian census authority	1,495,000	1,495,000
Ouagadougou	Burkina Faso	2006	Burkinabé national census	1,475,000	1,475,000
Antananarivo	Madagascar	2001	Madagascan census authority	1,403,000	1,403,000
Lomé	Togo	2005	Togolese census authority	921,000	1,377,000
Lubumbashi	Congo, Democratic Rep.	2004	Congolese census authority	1,284,000	1,284,000
Yaoundé	Cameroon	2001	Cameroonian census authority	1,248,000	1,248,000
Port Harcourt	Nigeria	2006	Nigerian national census	541,000	1,228,000
Mbuji-Mayi	Congo, Democratic Rep	2004	Congolese census authority	1,214,000	1,214,000
Brazzaville	Congo, Republic	2005	Congolese national census	1,174,000	1,174,000
Kumasi	Ghana	2000	Ghanaian national census	1,170,000	1,170,000
Sydney	Australia	2009	Australian census authority	157,000	4,400,000
Melbourne	Australia	2009	Australian census authority	71,000	3,892,000
Brisbane	Australia	2009	Australian census authority	956,000	1,946,000
Perth	Australia	2009	Australian census authority	12,000	1,603,000
Auckland	New Zealand	2008	New Zealand national census	438,000	1,313,000
Adelaide	Australia	2009	Australian census authority	17,000	1,172,000
Gold Coast	Australia	2009	Australian census authority	472,000	559,000
Newcastle	Australia	2009	Australian census authority	142,000	531,000
Canberra	Australia	2009	Australian census authority	324,000	395,000
Wellington	New Zealand	2008	New Zealand national census	193,000	382,000
Christchurch	New Zealand	2008	New Zealand national census	369,000	382,000
Wollongong	Australia	2009	Australian census authority	184,000	284,000
Port Moresby	Papua New Guinea	2000	Papua New Guinean census	254,000	254,000
Sunshine Coast	Australia	2009	Australian census authority	88,000	238,000
Hobart	Australia	2009	Australian census authority	48,000	209,000
Hamilton	New Zealand	2008	New Zealand national census	139,000	197,000
Suva	Fiji	2007	Fijian national census	74,000	194,000
Geelong	Australia	2009	Australian census authority	172,000	172,000

NATIONS OF THE REGIONS BY URBANIZATION

Nation	Percentage of urban population	Percentage of rural population	Nation	Percentage of urban population	Percentage of rural population
Djibouti	83	17	Madagascar	29	71
Gabon	81	19	Mayotte	29	71
Botswana	66	34	Tanzania	24	76
Reunion	65	35	Burkina Faso	19	81
Congo, Republic	63	37	Eritrea	19	81
Cape Verde	62	38	Malawi	19	81
South Africa	61	39	Ethiopia	18	82
Seychelles	59	41	Rwanda	18	82
Cameroon	57	43	Uganda	14	86
Guinea	49	51	Burundi	9	91
Equatorial Guinea	48	52			
Mauritius	48	52	Nauru	100	0
São Tomé and Príncipe	47	53	Guam	93	7
Senegal	47	53	Northern Mariana Islands	91	9
Liberia	45	55	Australia	89	11
Ivory Coast	44	56	Norfolk Island	89	11
Nigeria	44	56	New Zealand	87	13
Saint Helena	43	57	Palau	81	19
Zambia	43	57	Cook Islands	72	28
Benin	42	58	Marshall Islands	71	29
Central African Republic	40	60	New Caledonia	62	38
Angola	38	62	French Polynesia	56	44
Ghana	38	62	Fiji	52	48
Namibia	37	63	Tuvalu	46	54
Sierra Leone	37	63	Kiribati	44	56
Zimbabwe	37	63	Tonga	43	57
Mozambique	35	65	Niue	38	62
Congo, Democratic Rep.	34	66	Samoa	34	66
Swaziland	34	66	American Samoa	33	67
Gambia	33	67	Micronesia	26	74
Kenya	33	67	Vanuatu	25	75
Togo	33	67	Solomon Islands	18	82
Comoros	32	68	Wallis and Futuna	18	82
Lesotho	32	68	Papua New Guinea	17	83
Guinea-Bissau	30	70	Pitcairn	0	100
Somalia*	30–40	60–70	Tokelau	0	100

* Estimate: there has been no census in Somalia since 1963.

MAJOR CITIES

In modern times, sub-Saharan Africa and Australia contain many large cities. A table ranks the major metropolitan areas of the region. In the table, the most recent national census figures are given; where no recent census figures are available, national government or United Nations (UN) estimates are given. Unofficial estimates, which often give higher population figures, are not recorded. In some cases, the population of the city (that is, the area within the city limits) is considerably lower than that for the city and its contiguous suburbs. In the case of Johannesburg, for example, some 1,009,000 people lived within the city limits in 2001, but the city was the center of a metropolitan area that was home to 6,420,000 people. Australian cities are even more notable examples of this phenomenon: the Sydney metropolitan area had a population of 4,400,000 in 2009, although the area within the city limits, the historic center and the downtown commercial area, was home to

DOMINANT CITIES IN THE NATIONS OF THE REGION

Nation	Largest metropolitan area	Percentage of population residing in area	Nation	Largest metropolitan area	Percentage of population residing in area
Angola	Luanda	14.5	Seychelles	Victoria	30.2
Benin	Cotonou	11.2	Sierra Leone	Freetown	15.9
Botswana	Gaborone	17.4	Somalia*	Mogadishu	c. 8.0–9.0
Burkina Faso	Ouagadougou	9.7	South Africa	Johannesburg	14.2
Burundi	Bujumbura	5.1	Swaziland	Manzini	8.1
Cameroon	Douala	8.0	Tanzania	Dar es Salaam	6.8
Cape Verde	Praia	24.6	Togo	Lomé	25.8
Central African Republic	Bangui	19.2	Uganda	Kampala	6.0
Comoros	Moroni	6.0	Zambia	Lusaka	11.0
Congo, Republic	Brazzaville	34.6	Zimbabwe	Harare	16.2
Congo, Democratic Rep.	Kinshasa	12.5			
Djibouti	Djibouti	67.4	American Samoa	Tafuna	14.9
Equatorial Guinea	Malabo	9.2	Australia	Sydney	20.1
Eritrea	Asmara	13.8	Cook Islands	Avarua	72.4
Ethiopia	Addis Ababa	3.7	Fiji	Suva	23.2
Gabon	Libreville	43.5	French Polynesia	Papeete	50.8
Gambia	Banjul	38.4	Guam	Hagatna	17.4
Ghana	Accra	15.4	Kiribati	Bairiki-Betio-South Tarawa	43.0
Guinea	Conakry	15.3	Marshall Islands	Delap-Uliga-Darrit	31.4
Guinea-Bissau	Bissau	24.9	Micronesia	Weno	13.0
Ivory Coast	Abidjan	17.6	Nauru	Denigomudu	22.8
Kenya	Nairobi	8.4	New Caledonia	Nouméa	66.7
Lesotho	Maseru	10.5	New Zealand	Auckland	30.8
Liberia	Monrovia	29.1	Niue	Alofi	37.5
Madagascar	Antananarivo	8.9	Norfolk Island	Burnt Pine	89.0
Malawi	Lilongwe	15.1	Northern Mariana Islands	San Antonio	18.8
Mauritius	Beau Bassin-Rose Hill	15.1	Palau	Koror	53.8
Mayotte	Mamoudzou	28.5	Papua New Guinea	Port Moresby	4.9
Mozambique	Maputo	8.6	Pitcairn	Adamstown	100.0
Namibia	Windhoek	12.8	Samoa	Apia	34.1
Nigeria	Lagos	5.7	Solomon Islands	Honiara	11.9
Reunion	Saint-Denis	21.6	Tokelau	Atafu	34.7
Rwanda	Kigali	7.4	Tonga	Nuku'alofa	33.3
Saint Helena	Jamestown	42.9	Tuvalu	Vaiaku-Fongafale	46.9
São Tomé and Príncipe	São Tomé	39.1	Vanuatu	Port-Vila	14.9
Senegal	Dakar	21.6	Wallis and Futuna	Mata-Utu	8.2

* There has been no census in Somalia since 1963.

only 157,000 people. Australia is a largely urban society but one in which geography has determined that there should be a number of large centers rather than the single large city that tends to develop in smaller nations.

While development and economic activities are among the principal spurs to urban growth, other factors are also at work. These include civil war, which uproots many people from their homes in rural areas. As a result of civil war, countries such as Guinea-Bissau and Liberia have an unusually high percentage of urban population, compared with neighbors. The countries and territories of the regions are ranked according to the extent of urbanization in a table. The degree to which a single major urban area dominates the life of a nation or territory is shown in the table above.

Family Life

In much of Africa, improvements in health care and water supply have prolonged life expectancy, but in some nations, particularly in southern Africa, HIV/AIDS has greatly reduced life expectancy. The birthrate in many African countries is among the highest in the world. By contrast, except in some poorer, mainly agricultural Pacific Island territories, people live longer, and birthrates are considerably lower, in the wealthier nations of Oceania.

In most of Africa, society is patriarchal, and each family is a unit, with well-defined traditional roles assigned to different family members. In sub-Saharan Africa, families tend to be large, and many of the countries in the region have some of the highest birthrates in the world. Women are traditionally expected to cultivate land and to raise children. In many societies, men are agriculturalists, often herding livestock. In some African nations, however, industry, particularly mining, is important, and male workers may leave home to work, sometimes in another country. Large numbers of men from Swaziland, Lesotho, and Zimbabwe work in mines and other facilities in South Africa.

LIFE EXPECTANCY AT BIRTH

Nation	Female life expectancy (in years)	Male life expectancy (in years)	Overall life expectancy (in years)
Saint Helena	81.5	75.5	78.4
Reunion	77.8	70.8	74.2
Mauritius	77.7	70.5	74.0
Seychelles	77.9	68.3	73.0
Cape Verde	75.1	68.3	71.6
São Tomé and Príncipe	69.7	66.4	68.0
Comoros	65.9	61.1	63.5
Madagascar	64.9	60.9	62.9
Mayotte	65.2	60.7	62.9
Botswana	62.0	61.7	61.9
Eritrea	63.9	59.7	61.8
Equatorial Guinea	62.1	60.4	61.2
Ghana	60.8	59.0	59.9
Benin	60.2	57.8	59.0
Senegal	60.9	57.1	59.0
Togo	60.9	56.6	58.7
Kenya	58.1	57.6	57.9
Guinea	58.6	55.6	57.1
Ivory Coast	56.3	54.6	55.5
Ethiopia	58.0	52.9	55.4
Gambia	57.3	53.4	55.4
Congo, Democratic Republic	56.2	52.6	54.4
Congo, Republic	55.4	52.9	54.2
Gabon	54.6	52.5	53.5
Cameroon	54.1	52.5	53.3
Burkina Faso	54.9	51.0	53.0
Uganda	53.8	51.7	52.7
Burundi	53.0	51.2	52.1
Tanzania	53.5	50.6	52.0

LIFE EXPECTANCY AT BIRTH (continued)

Nation	Female life expectancy (in years)	Male life expectancy (in years)	Overall life expectancy (in years)
Namibia	50.9	51.6	51.2
Rwanda	51.8	49.3	50.5
Somalia*	c. 52.0	c. 48.0	49.0–50.0
South Africa	48.1	49.8	49.0
Guinea-Bissau	49.8	46.1	47.9
Nigeria	47.3	45.8	46.5
Zimbabwe	45.2	46.4	45.8
Central African Republic	44.5	44.4	44.5
Malawi	43.6	44.1	43.8
Djibouti	44.9	41.9	43.4
Liberia	43.0	40.7	41.8
Mozambique	40.5	41.8	41.2
Sierra Leone	43.6	38.9	41.2
Lesotho	39.5	41.2	40.4
Zambia	38.5	38.7	38.6
Angola	39.2	37.2	38.2
Swaziland	32.2	31.6	31.9
Australia	84.1	79.3	81.6
New Zealand	82.4	78.4	80.4
Wallis and Futuna	81.3	75.2	78.2
Guam	81.2	75.0	78.0
French Polynesia	79.3	74.3	76.7
Northern Mariana Islands	79.5	74.1	76.7
New Caledonia	78.1	73.0	75.0
Cook Islands	77.1	71.5	74.2
American Samoa	76.8	70.8	73.7
Solomon Islands	76.1	71.1	73.7
Samoa	74.8	69.0	71.9
Marshall Islands	73.3	69.2	71.2
Palau	74.5	68.1	71.2
Micronesia	72.0	69.1	70.9
Fiji	74.3	68.2	70.7
Tonga	73.4	66.2	70.7
Tuvalu	71.7	67.0	69.3
Papua New Guinea	68.7	60.9	66.3
Nauru	68.0	60.9	64.2
Vanuatu	65.7	62.4	64.0
Kiribati	60.1	66.5	63.2

Note: No information is available for Niue, Norfolk Island, Pitcairn, and Tokelau. * The last census in Somalia was in 1963.

Throughout the second half of the twentieth century, there was considerable movement of population in sub-Saharan Africa. The population of urban areas greatly increased and, with it, social changes occurred. In cities, established networks of support, through extended families and village communities, are weakened, and the nuclear family, of parents and their children, becomes more important.

At the same time, improvements in health care, associated with better provision of a safe supply of drinking water, more medical facilities, and immunization programs, have helped bring about an increase in life expectancy. In some African states, life expectancy is a decade more than it was half a century ago. However, high rates of HIV/AIDS infection have drastically lowered life expectancy in some nations of southern Africa. Swaziland, with the highest rate of HIV/AIDS infection in the world, has the lowest life expectancy: 31.9 years. People in Angola, Zimbabwe, Zambia, South Africa, Malawi, and Lesotho also have low life expectancy for the same reason.

AGE STRUCTURE OF THE POPULATION

Nation	Percentage under 15	Percentage 15 to 65	Percentage over 65
Angola	43.5	53.8	2.7
Benin	39.8	50.5	9.7
Botswana	22.9	68.6	8.5
Burkina Faso	46.2	51.3	2.5
Burundi	46.2	51.3	2.5
Cameroon	41.1	55.7	3.2
Cape Verde	35.2	58.4	6.4
Central African Republic	40.9	55.0	4.1
Comoros	42.2	54.7	3.1
Congo, Democratic Republic	46.9	50.6	2.5
Congo, Republic	45.9	51.3	2.8
Djibouti	43.3	53.0	3.7
Equatorial Guinea	42.0	53.8	4.2
Eritrea	42.8	53.6	3.6
Ethiopia	46.1	51.2	2.7
Gabon	42.1	54.0	3.9
Gambia	46.3	50.9	2.8
Ghana	37.3	59.1	3.6
Guinea	42.8	53.7	3.5
Guinea-Bissau	40.8	56.1	3.1
Ivory Coast	40.6	56.5	2.9
Kenya	42.3	55.1	2.6
Lesotho	34.8	53.1	5.0
Liberia	44.1	60.2	2.8
Madagascar	43.5	53.5	3.0
Malawi	45.8	51.5	2.7
Mauritius	22.5	70.4	7.1
Mozambique	44.3	52.8	2.9
Namibia	35.9	60.2	3.9
Nigeria	41.7	55.3	3.0
Rwanda	42.1	55.5	2.4
São Tomé and Príncipe	23.6	70.4	6.0
Senegal	42.2	54.8	3.0
Seychelles	22.8	70.1	7.1
Sierra Leone	44.5	52.3	3.2
Somalia*	c. 45.0	c. 53.0	2.0–3.0
South Africa	28.9	65.7	5.4
Swaziland	39.4	56.9	3.7
Tanzania	43.0	54.1	2.9
Togo	41.5	55.7	2.8
Uganda	50.0	47.9	2.1
Zambia	45.1	52.6	2.3
Zimbabwe	43.9	52.2	3.9
Australia	18.6	67.9	13.6
Fiji	30.3	64.9	4.8
Kiribati	37.6	58.9	3.5
Marshall Islands	38.6	57.5	3.9
Micronesia	34.8	62.3	2.9
Nauru	34.7	63.2	2.1
New Zealand	20.7	66.5	12.8
Palau	22.9	70.9	6.2
Papua New Guinea	36.9	59.0	4.1
Samoa	37.6	56.7	5.7
Solomon Islands	39.5	57.0	3.5
Tonga	32.8	62.9	4.3
Tuvalu	29.2	65.6	5.2
Vanuatu	30.7	65.3	4.0

* The last census in Somalia was in 1963.

FAMILY SIZE

Nation	Number of children per woman	Nation	Number of children per woman
Uganda	6.8	Ghana	3.7
Somalia*	c. 6.5	Zimbabwe	3.7
Burkina Faso	6.3	Swaziland	3.2
Burundi	6.3	Cape Verde	3.1
Congo, Democratic Republic	6.2	Lesotho	3.1
Angola	6.1	Namibia	2.7
Ethiopia	6.1	Botswana	2.6
Sierra Leone	5.9	Reunion	2.5
Congo, Republic	5.8	South Africa	2.4
Liberia	5.8	Seychelles	1.9
Malawi	5.6	Mauritius	1.8
Benin	5.5	Saint Helena	1.6
Mayotte	5.5		
São Tomé and Príncipe	5.4	Samoa	4.2
Rwanda	5.3	Kiribati	4.0
Equatorial Guinea	5.2	Marshall Islands	3.6
Guinea	5.2	Papua New Guinea	3.6
Mozambique	5.2	Solomon Islands	3.5
Zambia	5.2	American Samoa	3.3
Djibouti	5.1	Micronesia	2.9
Madagascar	5.1	Nauru	2.9
Gambia	5.0	Tuvalu	2.9
Nigeria	5.0	Fiji	2.7
Senegal	5.0	Cook Islands	2.5
Comoros	4.8	Guam	2.5
Togo	4.8	Vanuatu	2.5
Eritrea	4.7	Tonga	2.3
Gabon	4.7	New Caledonia	2.2
Guinea-Bissau	4.7	New Zealand	2.1
Kenya	4.6	French Polynesia	1.9
Tanzania	4.5	Wallis and Futuna	1.9
Cameroon	4.4	Australia	1.8
Central African Republic	4.1	Palau	1.8
Ivory Coast	4.1	Northern Mariana Islands	1.2

Note: No data are available for Niue, Norfolk Island, Pitcairn, and Tokelau.

* There has not been a census in Somalia since 1963.

In contrast. Australia and New Zealand have high life expectancy (more than 80 years) and small families. These nations have advanced Western standards of living and modern health care that, as in Europe, is largely free. The small dependent territories of the region are also characterized by better health care and higher living standards than many other developing nations. Only Papua New Guinea, the Solomon Islands, and Vanuatu resemble sub-Saharan African states demographically. The more developed territories of the hemisphere generally have lower birthrates.

A table in this section ranks the nations and territories of the regions by life expectancy. Another table in this section details the age breakdown of the independent nations of sub-Saharan Africa and of Oceania—data for some of the dependent territories is not available. A third table in this section ranks the various nations and other territories of these two regions according to average family size. The large family size in some African nations reflects several factors, including the necessity for the work of many children to contribute to the support of the family unit, as well as the lack of family planning and the continuance of traditional social norms.

Trade

The economies of the countries of sub-Saharan Africa and of Oceania largely depend upon the export of primary products, petroleum, minerals, and agricultural products. However, the economies of Australia, South Africa, and Nigeria are more diverse.

MAJOR TRADING PARTNERS FOR EXPORTS

Nation	Main destinations of exports	Nation	Main destinations of exports
Angola	China, United States, France	Sierra Leone	Belgium, United States, India
Benin	China, India, Japan	Somalia*	United Arab Emirates, Yemen, Saudi Arabia
Botswana	Great Britain, South Africa, Switzerland	South Africa	United States, Japan, Great Britain
Burkina Faso	Singapore, Belgium, China	Swaziland	South Africa, United States, Great Britain
Burundi	Switzerland, Great Britain, Pakistan	Tanzania	India, Japan, China
Cameroon	Spain, Italy, France	Togo	Ghana, Burkina Faso, Germany
Cape Verde	Japan, Spain, Portugal	Uganda	Sudan, Kenya, Switzerland
Central African Republic	Japan, Belgium, China	Zambia	China, South Africa, Congo (Democratic Rep.)
Comoros	France, Turkey, India	Zimbabwe	South Africa, Congo (Democratic Rep.),
Congo, Democratic Rep.	China, Belgium, Finland		Botswana
Congo, Republic	United States, China, Taiwan		
Djibouti	Somalia, United Arab Emirates, Yemen	American Samoa	Indonesia, India, Australia
Equatorial Guinea	United States, China, Spain	Australia	Japan, China, South Korea
Eritrea	Italy, Sudan, China	Cook Islands	Australia, Japan, New Zealand
Ethiopia	Germany, Saudi Arabia, Netherlands	Fiji	United States, Great Britain, Australia
Gabon	United States, China, France	French Polynesia	France, Japan, United States
Gambia	India, Japan, China	Guam	Japan, Singapore, Great Britain
Ghana	Netherlands, Ukraine, Great Britain	Kiribati	United States, Japan, Belgium
Guinea	India, Spain, Russia	Marshall Islands	United States, Japan, Australia
Guinea-Bissau	India, Nigeria, Pakistan	Micronesia	Japan, United States, Guam
Ivory Coast	Germany, United States, Netherlands	Nauru	South Africa, South Korea, Canada
Kenya	Great Britain, Netherlands, Uganda	New Caledonia	France, Japan, Spain
Lesotho	United States, South Africa, Belgium	New Zealand	Australia, United States, Japan
Liberia	India, United States, Poland	Niue	New Zealand, Fiji, Cook Islands
Madagascar	France, United States, Germany	Norfolk Island	Australia, New Zealand
Malawi	South Africa, Egypt, Zimbabwe	Northern Mariana Islands	United States, Japan, Guam
Mauritius	Great Britain, France, United States	Palau	United States, Great Britain, Australia
Mayotte	France, Mauritius, South Africa	Papua New Guinea	France, Japan, United States
Mozambique	Netherlands, South Africa, Zimbabwe	Pitcairn	N/A
Namibia	South Africa, China, United States	Samoa	Australia, American Samoa, New Zealand
Nigeria	United States, India, Brazil	Solomon Islands	China, Thailand, South Korea
Reunion	France, Japan, Comoros	Tokelau	No exports
Rwanda	China, Thailand, Germany	Tonga	United States, Japan, New Zealand
Saint Helena	South Africa, Great Britain, Tanzania	Tuvalu	Germany, Italy, Fiji
São Tomé and Príncipe	Japan, Netherlands, Belgium	Vanuatu	Thailand, India, Japan
Senegal	Mali, India, France	Wallis and Futuna	Italy, Croatia, United States
Seychelles	Great Britain, France, Mauritius		

* Estimated: there are no recent official data.

The nations of sub-Saharan Africa include some of the world's increasingly important producers of oil: Nigeria, Gabon, Angola, and Equatorial Guinea. The discovery and exploitation of oil in Equatorial Guinea transformed the economy of that country but have not been translated into a higher standard of living for its people. The majority of sub-Saharan African states depend upon the export of oil and other minerals, for example bauxite in Guinea, copper in Zambia, and diamonds in Namibia. A feature of the late twentieth century and early twenty-first century was the

rapid expansion of those economies based on the exploitation and export of oil rather than the extraction of and sale of metal ores and precious stones.

Some countries in the region have been economically damaged by civil war and political instability. The mineral-rich Democratic Republic of the Congo greatly suffered through civil wars in 1996–1997 and 1998–2003. The economies of Sierra Leone and Liberia, both dependent upon mineral exports, collapsed owing to civil war. Zimbabwe's once strong economy

MAJOR TRADING PARTNERS FOR IMPORTS

Nation	Main sources of imports	Nation	Main sources of imports
Angola	Portugal, China, United States	Seychelles	Saudi Arabia, Singapore, France
Benin	China, United States, France	Sierra Leone	China, Ivory Coast, United States
Botswana	Great Britain, South Africa, United States	Somalia*	Djibouti, India, Kenya
Burkina Faso	Ivory Coast, France, Togo	South Africa	Germany, China, United States
Burundi	Saudi Arabia, Uganda, Belgium	Swaziland	South Africa, Japan, Great Britain
Cameroon	France, Nigeria, China	Tanzania	China, India, South Africa
Cape Verde	Portugal, Netherlands, Spain	Togo	China, Netherlands, France
Central African Republic	South Korea, France, Cameroon	Uganda	United Arab Emirates, Kenya, India
Comoros	Brazil, France, China	Zambia	South Africa, United Arab Emirates, China
Congo, Democratic Rep.	South Africa, Belgium, Zambia	Zimbabwe	South Africa, China, Botswana
Congo, Republic	France, South Korea, China		
Djibouti	Saudi Arabia, India, China	American Samoa	Australia, Samoa, New Zealand
Equatorial Guinea	United States, Spain, Ivory Coast	Australia	China, United States, Japan
Eritrea	India, Saudi Arabia, Italy	Cook Islands	New Zealand, Fiji, United States
Ethiopia	China, Saudi Arabia, India	Fiji	Singapore, Australia, New Zealand
Gabon	France, United States, Belgium	French Polynesia	France, Singapore, New Zealand
Gambia	China, Senegal, Ivory Coast	Guam	Singapore, South Korea, Japan
Ghana	China, Nigeria, India	Kiribati	Australia, Fiji, Japan
Guinea	China, France, Netherlands	Marshall Islands	United States, Japan, Australia
Guinea-Bissau	Portugal, Senegal. France	Micronesia	United States, Japan, Australia
Ivory Coast	Nigeria, France, China	Nauru	South Korea, Australia, United States
Kenya	India, United Arab Emirates, China	New Caledonia	France, Singapore, Australia
Lesotho	China, Taiwan, India	New Zealand	Australia, China, United States
Liberia	South Korea, Singapore, Japan	Niue	New Zealand, Fiji, Japan
Madagascar	China, Bahrain, France	Norfolk Island	Australia, New Zealand
Malawi	South Africa, China, India	Northern Mariana Islands	United States, Japan, China
Mauritius	India, France, South Africa	Palau	United States, Singapore, Japan
Mayotte	France, Seychelles, China	Papua New Guinea	Australia, Singapore, China
Mozambique	South Africa, Netherlands, China	Pitcairn	N/A
Namibia	South Africa, United States, China	Samoa	New Zealand, Fiji, Singapore
Nigeria	China, Netherlands, United States	Solomon Islands	Singapore, Australia, Fiji
Reunion	France, Bahrain, Germany	Tokelau	New Zealand
Rwanda	Kenya, Uganda, China	Tonga	Fiji, New Zealand, United States
Saint Helena	Great Britain, South Africa, Spain	Tuvalu	Fiji, Japan, China
São Tomé and Príncipe	Portugal, Belgium, Japan	Vanuatu	Australia, United States, Japan
Senegal	France, Great Britain, China	Wallis and Futuna	France, Australia, New Zealand

* Estimated: there are no recent official data.

declined because of economic mismanagement. Other states in the region have agricultural economies and export products such as cocoa, coffee, or timber. The majority of the small states of Oceania also rely upon agricultural exports, although New Caledonia is rich in ferronickels, Papua New Guinea has a variety of rich mineral deposits, and the tiny nation-state of Nauru formerly relied upon the export of phosphates. The much larger and more diverse economies of Australia and New Zealand center on the export of primary products but both countries also have important industrial and service sectors.

One table in this section lists the principal destinations of exports from the nations of the sub-Saharan Africa and Oceania, while another lists the main import partners of the same countries and territories. In a third table, the leading trading nations of sub-Saharan Africa and of Oceania are ranked according to the value of their exports, while in another the leading trading nations of these two regions are ranked according to the value of their imports. Finally, the states of these regions are ranked by their trade balance, the difference in value of exports and imports.

BALANCE OF TRADE SURPLUSES AND DEFICITS

Nation	Year	Balance in million U.S.$	Nation	Year	Balance in million U.S.$
Nigeria	2008	36,400	Madagascar	2008	-1,220
Equatorial Guinea	2008	12,610	Uganda	2008	-1,550
Gabon	2008	6,910	Mauritius	2008	-2,140
Congo, Republic	2008	6,300	Reunion	2000	-2,200
Angola	2008	5,730	Senegal	2008	-2,750
Ivory Coast	2008	4,010	Tanzania	2008	-3,410
Zambia	2008	1,210	Ghana	2008	-4,380
Congo, Democratic Rep.	2008	900	South Africa	2008	-4,500
Botswana	2008	400	Ethiopia	2008	-4,780
Saint Helena	2004	-26	Kenya	2008	-5,890
Guinea-Bissau	2006	-67	Liberia	2008	-5,940
São Tomé and Príncipe	2008	-82			
Central African Republic	2008	-91	Papua New Guinea	2008	2,600
Swaziland	2008	-100	American Samoa	2004	136.8
Comoros	2008	-111	Tokelau	2002	-1
Gambia	2008	-190	Niue	2004	-8.8
Guinea	2008	-190	Tuvalu	2004	-11.9
Burundi	2008	-260	Solomon Islands	2006	-19
Mayotte	2005	-335	Nauru	2008	-20
Malawi	2008	-341	Kiribati	2004	-45
Sierra Leone	2006	-344	Marshall Islands	2008	-60
Somalia	2008	-498	Wallis and Futuna	2004	-60.8
Seychelles	2008	-527	Cook Islands	2005	-75.8
Rwanda	2008	-540	Palau	2004	-101.4
Benin	2008	-584	Vanuatu	2006	-116
Eritrea	2008	-587	Northern Mariana Islands	2008	-116.2
Mozambique	2008	-600	Tonga	2006	-117
Zimbabwe	2008	-600	Micronesia	2004	-118.7
Namibia	2008	-710	Samoa	2006	-193
Togo	2008	-730	Guam	2004	-656
Cape Verde	2008	-785	New Caledonia	2008	-660
Burkina Faso	2008	-861	French Polynesia	2005	-1,489
Cameroon	2008	-890	New Zealand	2008	-1,700
Lesotho	2008	-927	Fiji	2006	-1,900
Djibouti	2006	-1,220	Australia	2008	-2,500

Source: CIA World Factbook. There are no data for Norfolk Island or Pitcairn.

LEADING EXPORTERS IN THE REGIONS

Nation	Year of data	Value of exports in million U.S.$	Principal exports
South Africa	2008	86,100	Gold, diamonds, machinery, agricultural products (wine and fruit)
Nigeria	2008	83,100	Petroleum and petroleum products, cocoa, rubber
Angola	2008	72,600	Crude and refined petroleum, diamonds, coffee, timber
Equatorial Guinea	2008	15,820	Petroleum and petroleum products, cocoa, timber
Ivory Coast	2008	11,960	Petroleum, cocoa, coffee, timber, cotton
Gabon	2008	9,740	Crude oil, timber, manganese, uranium
Congo, Republic	2008	9,000	Petroleum, timber, sugar, cocoa, coffee, diamonds
Congo, Democratic Rep.	2008	6,100	Diamonds, gold, cobalt, petroleum, timber, coffee
Zambia	2008	5,630	Copper, cobalt, gemstones, electricity, tobacco, flowers
Ghana	2008	5,440	Gold, cocoa, timber, tuna, bauxite, manganese, diamonds
Cameroon	2008	5,250	Crude oil, timber, cocoa, bauxite, coffee, cotton
Botswana	2008	4,900	Diamonds, copper, nickel, soda ash, meat, textiles
Kenya	2008	4,880	Vegetables and cut flowers, tea, coffee, refined petrol, cement
Namibia	2008	2,790	Diamonds, copper, gold, zinc, lead, uranium, meat
Mozambique	2008	2,690	Aluminum, shrimp, cashews, cotton, sugar, fruit, electricity
Tanzania	2008	2,490	Gold, coffee, cashews, manufactured goods, cotton
Mauritius	2008	2,360	Clothing and textiles, sugar and molasses, cut flowers, fish
Uganda	2008	2,030	Coffee, tea, fish, cotton, cut flowers, gold
Senegal	2008	1,900	Fish, groundnuts, refined petroleum, phosphates, cotton
Swaziland	2008	1,760	Soft drink concentrates, sugar, wood pulp, cotton, refrigerators
Ethiopia	2008	1,440	Coffee, qat, gold, leather products, live animals, oilseeds
Madagascar	2008	1,320	Vanilla, shellfish, coffee, sugar, cotton, cloth
Zimbabwe	2008	1,320	Platinum, cotton, tobacco, gold, ferro-alloys, textiles
Guinea	2008	1,200	Bauxite and aluminum, gold, diamonds, coffee, fish
Liberia	2008	1,200	Rubber, timber, iron, diamonds, cocoa, coffee
Togo	2008	1,000	Cotton, phosphates, re-exported goods
Lesotho	2008	953	Clothing and footwear, wool, mohair, livestock
Burkina Faso	2008	809	Cotton, livestock, gold
Benin	2008	776	Cotton, textiles, cashews, palm products
Malawi	2008	679	Tobacco, tea, sugar, cotton, coffee, groundnuts, clothing
Seychelles	2008	425	Canned tuna, frozen fish, cinnamon, copra
Djibouti	2006	340	Re-exported goods, live animals, hides
Reunion	2000	300	Sugar, rum and molasses, perfume essence, lobsters
Somalia	2008	300	Livestock, bananas, hides
Rwanda	2008	219	Coffee, tea, hides, tin ore
Sierra Leone	2006	216	Diamonds, rutile, cocoa, coffee, fish
Central African Republic	2008	147	Diamonds, timber, coffee, cotton, tobacco
Guinea-Bissau	2006	133	Cashews, shrimp, groundnuts, palm kernels, timber
Australia	2008	189,900	Coal, iron ore, gold, crude oil, natural gas, meat, wool, wheat
New Zealand	2008	30,800	Dairy products, meat, fruits, vegetables, fish, coal, timber
Papua New Guinea	2008	5,700	Copper, gold, nickel, petroleum, timber, coffee, cocoa, palm oil
New Caledonia	2008	1,340	Ferronickels and nickel ore, fish
Fiji	2006	1,200	Sugar, clothing, gold, molasses, timber, copra, fish
American Samoa	2004	446	Canned tuna
Solomon Islands	2006	237	Tuna and other fish, timber, cocoa, copra and palm oil
French Polynesia	2005	211	Cultured pearls, coconut products, mother-of-pearl, vanilla
Samoa	2006	131	Coconut products, fish, taro, automotive parts, clothing

Source: CIA World Factbook.

LEADING IMPORTERS IN THE REGIONS

Nation	Year	Value of imports in million U.S.$	Principal imports
South Africa	2008	90,600	Machinery and equipment, chemicals, petroleum, food
Nigeria	2008	46,400	Machinery, vehicles, chemicals, consumer goods, iron, steel
Angola	2008	15,250	Machinery and equipment, vehicles, medicine, food, textiles
Kenya	2008	10,077	Machinery, vehicles, petroleum, vehicles, iron, steel
Ghana	2008	9,820	Capital equipment, petroleum and petroleum products, food
Ivory Coast	2008	7,950	Capital goods, food, petroleum, fuels, lubricants
Liberia	2008	7,140	Fuels, chemicals, machinery and equipment, food
Ethiopia	2008	6,220	Machinery and equipment, petroleum, food, manufactures
Tanzania	2008	5,900	Consumer goods, machinery, vehicles, raw materials, oil
Congo, Democratic Rep.	2008	5,200	Food, mining and other machinery, vehicles, fuel
Senegal	2008	4,650	Food, consumer goods, petroleum, machinery, vehicles
Botswana	2008	4,500	Food, machinery, electrical goods, vehicles, textiles, petroleum
Mauritius	2008	4,500	Manufactures, capital equipment, food, petroleum, chemicals
Zambia	2008	4,420	Machinery and vehicles, manufactures, chemicals, petroleum
Cameroon	2008	4,360	Machinery, electrical equipment, vehicles, fuel, food
Uganda	2008	3,580	Capital equipment, vehicles, petroleum, medicines, cereals
Namibia	2008	3,500	Food, petroleum, machinery, vehicles, chemicals
Mozambique	2008	3,290	Machinery, vehicles, fuel, chemicals, metal products, food
Equatorial Guinea	2008	3,210	Equipment for the oil industry, consumer goods, food
Gabon	2008	2,830	Machinery and vehicles, food, chemicals, construction materials
Congo, Republic	2008	2,700	Capital equipment, construction materials, food
Reunion	2000	2,500	Manufactures, food, machinery and vehicles, raw materials
Zimbabwe	2008	1,920	Machinery, vehicles, manufactures, chemicals, petroleum
Lesotho	2008	1,880	Food, building materials, vehicles, petroleum, medicines
Swaziland	2008	1,860	Vehicles, machinery and equipment, food, petroleum, chemicals
Togo	2008	1,730	Capital equipment, food, petroleum products
Burkina Faso	2008	1,670	Capital goods, food, petroleum
Djibouti	2006	1,560	Petroleum, food, vehicles, chemicals, consumer goods
Guinea	2008	1,390	Petroleum, manufactured goods, metals, textiles, cereals
Benin	2008	1,360	Capital equipment, petroleum, food
Malawi	2008	1,020	Food, petroleum, semimanufactured goods, consumer goods
Seychelles	2008	952	Petroleum, food, consumer goods, industrial machinery
Cape Verde	2008	887	Food, consumer goods, vehicles and manufactures, petroleum
Somalia	2008	798	Petroleum, qat, food, manufactured goods
Rwanda	2008	759	Food, machinery and vehicles, steel, petroleum, cement
Eritrea	2008	601	Machinery, petroleum, food, manufactures
Sierra Leone	2006	560	Food, machinery and vehicles, fuels, chemicals
Mayotte	2005	341	Food, machinery, vehicles, metals
Australia	2008	192,400	Petroleum, road vehicles, intermediate goods, consumer goods
New Zealand	2008	32,500	Machinery, electrical and transportation equipment, fuel, textiles
Fiji	2006	3,100	Manufactures, machinery, vehicles, petroleum, food, chemicals
Papua New Guinea	2008	3,100	Machinery for mining, vehicles, food, manufactures, fuels
New Caledonia	2008	2,000	Machinery and vehicles, fuels, chemicals, food
French Polynesia	2005	1,700	Petroleum and fuels, food, chemicals, machinery and vehicles
Guam	2004	701	Petroleum and petroleum products, food, manufactures
Samoa	2006	324	Machinery, industrial supplies, food
American Samoa	2004	309	Fish and materials for canneries, food, petroleum

Source: CIA World Factbook.

Transportation

In sub-Saharan Africa, only South Africa and some of the islands in the Indian Ocean have advanced transportation systems. In Oceania, Australia and New Zealand have expressways, major ports, and large airports.

The coasts of Africa have been centers of international trade for centuries. There were early links across the Indian Ocean, and East African ports such as Mombasa and Zanzibar developed. From the sixteenth century, Portuguese explorers, and later mariners from other European countries, established trading centers and, eventually, colonies along the Atlantic and Indian ocean coasts. This led to the foundation of a number of ports, many in natural harbors, such as Lourenço Marques (now Maputo) in Mozambique and Cape Town, South Africa. Some European colonies, however, struggled with a lack of natural, sheltered anchorages; for example, the Gold Coast (modern Ghana) had no natural harbors and, today, Ghana relies upon the modern, large, artificial harbor at Tema.

The Suez Canal links the Mediterranean Sea and the Indian Ocean through the Red Sea. Opening in 1869, the canal eliminated the need for shipping to make the long journey around the Cape of Good Hope at the southern tip of Africa. In modern times, however, large oil tankers and other bulk vessels must still make the journey around southern Africa,

PORTS

Many ports line the shores of the Indian and Atlantic oceans, most exporting the primary products of African nations. The largest are in southern Africa, the region with the most developed mining and agricultural activities and the most advanced economies. The two busiest ports in Africa are both in South Africa: Richards Bay (near Durban) and Saldanha Bay (near Cape Town). Both ports may be considered as large outports of their longer-established neighbors. Richards Bay is a deepwater port that can handle the largest bulk carriers; it exports coal and anthracite (both major South African exports) as well as other minerals. Saldanha Bay mainly exports iron ore from the Northern Cape. Other ports have greatly expanded in modern times through the export of oil, for example, Port Harcourt in Nigeria, Port-Gentil in Gabon, Luanda in Angola, and Malabo in Equatorial Guinea. Sub-Saharan Africa also has a number of landlocked nations that must rely upon ports in neighboring states for the export of their primary products. Uganda, for example, depends upon the Kenyan port of Mombasa.

NATIONS OF THE REGIONS WITH NAVIGABLE WATERWAYS

Nation	Principal waterways	Length in miles	Length in km
Congo, Democratic Rep.	Congo, Lualaba	9,323	15,000
Nigeria	Niger	5,345	8,609
Central African Republic	Ubangi, Sangha	1,740	2,800
Zambia	Zambezi*	1,398	2,250
Gabon	Ogooué	994	1,600
Angola	Cuanza*	808	1,300
Guinea	Niger*	808	1,300
Ghana	Volta	804	1,293
Congo, Republic	Congo	696	1,120
Senegal	Senegal*§	622	1,000
Ivory Coast	Komoé*	609	980
Papua New Guinea	Fly, Sepik	6,837	11,000
Australia	Murray-Darling*§	1,243	2,000

* Navigable only by shallow boats. § Great seasonal variations in navigability.
Note: Lakes Tanganyika (Tanzania), Victoria (Kenya, Uganda, and Tanzania), Kivu (Rwanda), Volta (Ghana), Kariba (Zambia and Zimbabwe), and Malawi/Nyasa (Malawi and Mozambique) are also important navigable waterways.

MAJOR PORTS OF THE REGIONS

BY GOODS HANDLED

Port	Nation	Year	Goods handled (short tons)	Goods handled (metric tons)
Richards Bay*	South Africa	2007	93,140,000	84,500,000
Saldanha Bay*	South Africa	2007	48,170,000	43,700,000
Durban	South Africa	2007	46.180,000	41,900,000
Dampier*	Australia	2007	147,600,000	133,900,000
Port Hedland*	Australia	2007	144,070,000	130,700,000
Newcastle*	Australia	2007	102,840,000	93,300,000
Hay Point*	Australia	2007	88,730,000	80,500,000
Gladstone*	Australia	2007	83,110,000	75,400,000

BY CONTAINERS HANDLED

Port	Nation	Year	TEUs (standard containers) handled
Durban	South Africa	2007	2,512,000
Cape Town	South Africa	2007	784,000
Melbourne	Australia	2007	2,257,000
Brisbane	Australia	2007	943,000
Auckland-Tauranga	New Zealand	2007	841,000
Sydney	Australia	2007	809,000

MAIN PORT OF OTHER MAJOR NATIONS OF THE REGIONS

Nation	Port	Type of port
Angola	Luanda	Handles general cargo and exports minerals
Cameroon	Douala	Exports oil and handles general cargo
Congo, Democratic Republic	Matadi	Handles general cargo and exports minerals
Congo, Republic	Pointe-Noire	Exports oil and handles general cargo
Gabon	Port-Gentil	Exports oil and handles general cargo
Ghana	Tema	Handles general cargo
Ivory Coast	Abidjan	Handles general cargo and containers
Kenya	Mombasa	Handles general cargo
Madagascar	Toamasina	Handles general cargo
Mozambique	Maputo	Handles general cargo and exports minerals
Namibia	Walvis Bay	Handles general cargo and exports minerals
Nigeria	Apapa (Lagos)	Handles general cargo and containers
Senegal	Dakar	Handles general cargo
Tanzania	Dar es Salaam	Handles general cargo
Togo	Lomé	Exports phosphates and handles general cargo
Fiji	Suva	Handles general cargo
Papua New Guinea	Lae	Handles general cargo and exports minerals

Source: American Association of Port Authorities (AAPA) World Port Rankings 2007, Institute of Shipping Economics and Logistics
* Ports exporting minerals. Other ports handle general cargo.

HIGHWAY SYSTEMS OF THE REGIONS BY LENGTH

Nation	Length of highways (miles)	Length of highways (km)	Nation	Length of highways (miles)	Length of highways (km)
South Africa	225,619	363,099	Djibouti	1,904	3,065
Nigeria	120,050	193,200	Equatorial Guinea	1,260	2,028
Kenya	110,458	177,765	Cape Verde	839	1,350
Congo, Democratic Republic	95,379	153,497	Reunion	754	1,214
Zimbabwe	60,438	97,267	Mauritius	724	1,165
Burkina Faso	57,473	92,495	Comoros	547	880
Zambia	56,818	91,440	Seychelles	285	458
Ivory Coast	49,710	80,000	São Tomé and Príncipe	199	320
Tanzania	49,020	78,891	Saint Helena	123	198
Uganda	43,959	70,746	Mayotte	58	93
Madagascar	40,801	65,663			
Ghana	38,662	62,221	Australia	505,157	812,972
Angola	31,956	51,429	New Zealand	58,145	93,576
Cameroon	31,069	50,000	Papua New Guinea	12,179	19,600
Guinea	27,557	44,348	New Caledonia	3,493	5,622
Namibia	26,245	42,237	Fiji	2,138	3,440
Ethiopia	22,661	36,469	French Polynesia	1,609	2,590
Mozambique	18,890	30,400	Samoa	1,452	2,337
Botswana	16,030	25,798	Marshall Islands	1,260	2,028
Central African Republic	15,104	24,307	Solomon Islands	845	1,360
Somalia	c. 13,700	c. 22,000	Vanuatu	665	1,070
Congo, Republic	10,743	17,289	Guam	649	1,045
Benin	9,942	16,000	Tonga	423	680
Malawi	9,601	15,451	Kiribati	416	670
Rwanda	8,704	14,008	Northern Mariana Islands	333	536
Senegal	8,436	13,576	Cook Islands	199	320
Burundi	7,657	12,322	Micronesia	149	240
Sierra Leone	7,021	11,300	American Samoa	137	221
Liberia	6,586	10,600	Wallis and Futuna	99	160
Gabon	5,698	9,170	Niue	75	120
Togo	4,673	7,520	Norfolk Island	50	80
Lesotho	4,406	7,091	Palau	37	60
Eritrea	2,492	4,010	Nauru	15	24
Gambia	2,325	3,742	Tuvalu	5	8
Swaziland	2,233	3,594	Pitcairn	4	6
Guinea-Bissau	2,147	3,455	Tokelau	0	0

In modern times, much of the world's cargo is shipped in containers known as TEUs—TEU stands for 20-feet equivalent units, the standard size of a container unit. Sub-Saharan Africa has only one of the world's 50 largest container ports, Durban. The region also has just one of the world's 50 largest general cargo ports, Richards Bay.

By contrast, Australia has a number of major ports that export bulk mineral cargo. These include Dampier and Port Hedland in northern Western Australia, both of which export iron ore, and Newcastle in New South Wales, which is the world's largest exporter of coal. These three ports are ranked among the world's 50 largest ports. At the same time, the ports of Melbourne, Sydney, Brisbane, Port Adelaide, and Fremantle (the port of Perth) have become significant container ports. Sea travel and trade are obviously important throughout the Pacific region, and the small island-nations of the South Pacific are dependent upon their ports to export minerals, such as ferronickels from New Caledonia and agricultural produce, such as sugar from Fiji.

A table ranks the major ports of sub-Saharan Africa and of the Australasian-Oceanian region, both by number of container units and tonnage of all cargo handled in a year.

NAVIGABLE WATERWAYS

Sub-Saharan Africa contains some of the world's major waterways: the Nile, Congo, and Niger rivers. The Congo, in particular, receives many tributaries, which are locally important for navigation. In contrast, the major waterway of southern Africa, the Orange River, is not important for navigation, largely because it is subject to seasonal variations in flow and does not offer an economically attractive route. Similarly, Angola has many waterways but, mainly owing to seasonal variations, only the Cuanza River is navigable. The Congo is important for the transportation of goods and, locally, passengers. However, the waterway and its major tributaries do not offer an uninterrupted navigational system because of rapids. People and goods must be disembarked to go around the obstacle on land. In places, this is achieved by railroad links. For example, navigation along the upper Congo, known as the Lualaba, is blocked by the Boyoma Falls. At this point, where goods have to be transferred to another boat, the city of Kisangani grew. Downstream, in the lowest stretches of the waterway, waterfalls and rapids make the Congo impassable to shipping below Kinshasa, the national capital of the Democratic Republic of the Congo.

In places, the great rivers of Africa have been dammed to provide hydroelectric power. Examples include the Kariba Dam on the Zambezi and the Cahora (or Cabora) Bassa Dam on the same river. These and other barrages, such as those on the Niger and Volta rivers, impede navigation. At the same time, the shallowness of many of the region's rivers, such as the Senegal River, greatly restricts the usefulness of river systems for navigation. However, sub-Saharan Africa has a number of major lakes that are important for transportation. In particular, the so-called Great Lakes of eastern Africa form a significant part of the transportation network of the region. They include Lake Kivu in Rwanda and the Democratic Republic of the Congo; Lake Victoria in Uganda, Kenya, and Tanzania; Lake Tanganyika in Tanzania, Burundi, the Democratic Republic of the Congo, and Zambia; and Lake Malawi in Malawi, Mozambique, and Tanzania. Lake Malawi, which is known as Lake Nyasa in Tanzania and Mozambique, does not lie within Tanzania, however; the international border runs along Tanzania's lake shore.

By contrast to sub-Saharan Africa, Australasia has few major waterways, and many of those that do exist experience large seasonal differences in flow. For example, Australia's longest waterway, the Murray-Darling, is of little importance for navigation for this reason. The nation's most important rivers for transportation are the major rivers of the east and southeast whose estuaries are locally significant.

A table ranks the nations of sub-Saharan Africa and of the Australasian-Oceanian region by the length of navigable waterways.

NATIONS WHOSE PAVED HIGHWAYS ARE MORE THAN 10 PERCENT OF THE TOTAL

Nation	Percentage of highway that is paved	Nation	Percentage of highway that is paved
Mauritius	100	Ethiopia	19.1
Reunion	100	Rwanda	19
Seychelles	95.8	Zimbabwe	19
Saint Helena	84.6	Mozambique	18.7
Mayotte	77.6	Ghana	16
Comoros	76.4	Nigeria	15
Cape Verde	69	Namibia	12.8
São Tomé and Príncipe	67.8	Somalia	c. 11.7
Malawi	45	Madagascar	11.6
Djibouti	40	Central African Republic	11.5
Botswana	32.6	Angola	10.4
Togo	31.6	Burundi	10.4
Swaziland	30	Gabon	10.2
Senegal	29.2	Cameroon	10
Guinea-Bissau	27.9		
Uganda	23	New Zealand	65.8
Zambia	22	Australia	57.4
Eritrea	21.8		
South Africa	20.2	Apart from Australia and New Zealand, few	
Lesotho	19.8	of the nations of Oceania record the mileage	
Gambia	19.3	of paved and unpaved roads separately.	

HIGHWAYS

In some of the small countries and territories of the Indian Ocean, all, or almost all, of the highways are paved, but in most nations of sub-Saharan Africa, more of the highway network is unpaved than paved. For example, owing to their size, both the Democratic Republic of the Congo and Kenya have large road networks but only 1.8 percent and 5 percent, respectively, of these systems are paved. The most developed highway systems are in the nations with the largest economies, such as South Africa and Nigeria. Nevertheless, even states that have achieved some prosperity through the exploitation of minerals, such as Gabon (which has rich reserves of oil), do not have modern systems of paved highways. Gabon, for example, has only 5,698 miles (9,170 km) of roads, of which only 582 miles (937 km) are paved.

Throughout much of sub-Saharan Africa, highways may become seasonally impassable owing to floods or heavy rain. At the same time, in some countries the condition of many highways is poor. In Liberia, Sierra Leone, Ivory Coast, and particularly the Democratic Republic of the Congo, civil war and neglect have resulted in a stark deterioration in the condition of roads. In Zimbabwe, economic mismanagement has resulted in a collapse in the nation's infrastructure and what was once one of Africa's best highway systems has been greatly damaged. At the same time, there is much cause for optimism in the development of transportation systems in Africa, where some major projects are funded by China.

Both Australia and New Zealand have modern highway systems, including expressways. The transportation networks of these two countries are maintained to a high standard. Fast modern roads connect the main cities as well as carrying traffic between the major metropolitan areas and their satellite towns. Nevertheless, not all of the road networks of these countries is paved. Australia has 505,157 miles (812,972 km) of roads, of which only 212,166 miles (341,448 km) are paved, and many Australian roads in the countryside are unpaved. The road systems of Papua New Guinea and the Solomon Islands resemble those of many sub-Saharan African nations: they are limited, not continuous, and mostly unpaved.

The highway systems of the nations and territories of both regions are ranked in tables by length of the system and by the extent of paved roads.

RAILROADS, SUBWAYS, LIGHT RAILROADS

Only a minority of the nations and territories of the region have railroad systems; in some cases, such as Sierra Leone, railroad systems have been closed because they were uneconomical. In some other nations, such as the Democratic Republic of the Congo, Angola, and Eritrea, much of the system is inoperable because of damage inflicted by civil war. In other cases, such as Nigeria and Tanzania, part of the rail network is unused or underused owing to economic reasons. Railroads in most of Africa are mainly concerned with the transportation of goods rather than passengers. Some lines were constructed purely for the transportation of minerals, such as iron ore and copper, to

RAILROAD NETWORKS OF THE REGIONS

Nation	Length of railroad system in miles	Length of railroad system in km	Nation	Length of railroad system in miles	Length of railroad system in km
South Africa	12,972	20,872	Guinea	520	837
Congo, Democratic Rep.*	3,193	5,138	Gabon	506	814
Tanzania	2,293	3,690	Malawi	495	797
Nigeria*	2,178	3,505	Benin	471	758
Mozambique	1,941	3,123	Ethiopia	434	699
Zimbabwe	1,912	3,077	Ivory Coast	410	660
Kenya	1,727	2,778	Burkina Faso	387	622
Angola*	1,715	2,761	Togo	353	568
Namibia	1,634	2,629	Liberia §	305	490
Zambia	1,341	2,157	Eritrea	190	306
Uganda	773	1,244	Swaziland	187	301
Cameroon	613	987	Djibouti	62	100
Ghana	592	953	Lesotho	1.6	2.6
Senegal	563	906			
Congo, Republic	556	894	Australia	23,527	37,855
Botswana	552	888	New Zealand	2,566	4,128
Madagascar	531	854	Fiji	371	597

Source: CIA World Factbook   *Only in partial use   §Not currently in operation

NUMBER OF AIRPORTS AND RUNWAYS PER NATION

Nation	Number of international airports with scheduled flights	Total number of paved runways	Nation	Number of international airports with scheduled flights	Total number of paved runways
Angola	1	30	Seychelles	1	9
Benin	1	1	Sierra Leone	1	1
Botswana	3	10	Somalia	3	7
Burkina Faso	1	2	South Africa	8	146
Burundi	1	1	Swaziland	1	1
Cameroon	3	11	Tanzania	3	9
Cape Verde	2	8	Togo	1	2
Central African Republic	1	2	Uganda	1	5
Comoros	1	4	Zambia	3	9
Congo, Democratic Rep.	1	26	Zimbabwe	3	20
Congo, Republic	1	6			
Djibouti	1	3	American Samoa	1	3
Equatorial Guinea	2	5	Australia	18	325
Eritrea	1	4	Cook Islands	1	1
Ethiopia	1	16	Fiji	1	4
Gabon	3	10	French Polynesia	1	47
Gambia	1	1	Guam	1	4
Ghana	1	7	Kiribati	1	4
Guinea	1	1	Marshall Islands	1	4
Guinea-Bissau	1	3	Micronesia	3	6
Ivory Coast	1	7	Nauru	1	1
Kenya	3	16	New Caledonia	1	12
Lesotho	1	3	New Zealand	6	41
Liberia	1	2	Niue	1	1
Madagascar	1	27	Norfolk Island	1	1
Malawi	2	6	Northern Mariana Islands	1	3
Mauritius	1	2	Palau	1	1
Mayotte	1	1	Papua New Guinea	1	21
Mozambique	3	23	Pitcairn	0	0
Namibia	1	20	Samoa	1	2
Nigeria	8	36	Solomon Islands	1	2
Reunion	1	2	Tokelau	0	0
Rwanda	1	4	Tonga	1	5
Saint Helena*	1	2	Tuvalu	1	1
São Tomé and Príncipe	1	2	Vanuatu	1	3
Senegal	1	9	Wallis and Futuna	1	2

ports for export. Commuting into major metropolitan areas is almost exclusively by road.

Australia and New Zealand have comprehensive railroad systems. Like the nations of sub-Saharan Africa, Australia has lines that were built just to export minerals; typically, these connect mines with a port and are often not linked to the rest of the nation's railroad system.

Both Sydney and Melbourne have commuter railroads that, in part, resemble subways. There are also plans for rapid light transit railroads in Perth, Brisbane, and Gold Coast. Most passenger journeys are over short distances, although tourists take long-distance rail journeys (such as on the Ghan, the railroad that links Adelaide with Darwin). Nevertheless, because of the great distances involved, railroads in Australia are not an alternative to air travel.

Apart from those in Australia and New Zealand, there are no other passenger railroads in the Australasia-Oceania region. Fiji, however, has a light railroad that transports sugarcane. A table ranks the railroad systems of the nations of sub-Saharan Africa and Oceania.

PRINCIPAL AIRPORTS OF THE REGIONS

City and nation	Name of airport	Year	Number of passengers handled in year
Johannesburg, South Africa	O.R. Tambo International	2008	18,502,000
Cape Town, South Africa	Cape Town International	2008	8,079,000
Addis Ababa, Ethiopia	Bole International	2008	6,296,000
Lagos, Nigeria	Murtala Muhammed International	2008	5,137,000
Nairobi, Kenya	Jomo Kenyatta International	2008	5,105,000
Durban, South Africa	Durban International	2008	4,459,000
Plaisance/Port Louis, Mauritius	Seewoosagur Ramgoolam International	2008	2,610,000
Abuja, Nigeria	Nnamdi Azikiwe International	2008	2,354,000
Dakar, Senegal	Léopold Sédar Senghor Yoff International	2008	2,205,000
Saint-Denis, Reunion	Roland Garos Airport	2003	1,465,000
Dar es Salaam, Tanzania	Julius Nyerere International	2006	1,249,000
Mombasa, Kenya	Mombasa Moi International	2006	1,007,000
Sydney, Australia	Sydney Airport	2008	32,701,000
Melbourne, Australia	Melbourne Airport	2008	23,943,000
Brisbane, Australia	Brisbane Airport	2008	18,298,000
Auckland, New Zealand	Auckland Airport	2008	13,000,000
Perth, Australia	Perth Airport	2008	8,952,000
Adelaide, Australia	Adelaide Airport	2008	6,619,000
Christchurch, New Zealand	Christchurch International	2008	5,908,000
Wellington, New Zealand	Wellington International	2008	5,178,000
Gold Coast, Australia	Gold Coast Airport	2008	4,323,000
Cairns, Australia	Cairns Airport	2008	3,777,000
Canberra, Australia	Canberra International	2008	2,853,000
Hobart, Australia	Hobart International	2008	1,758,000
Darwin, Australia	Darwin International	2008	1,562,000
Melbourne, Australia	Avalon Airport	2008	1,400,000
Townsville, Australia	Townsville Airport	2008	1,366,000

Source: Airports Council International, World Air Traffic Statistics

AIR TRANSPORTATION

Since the mid-twentieth century, air travel has expanded rapidly. Industrialization, commercial development, and urbanization have combined to encourage the construction and development of new airports and air transportation facilities in both regions. A table lists the nations of sub-Saharan Africa and Oceania and details the number of airports and paved runways in each. Some of these nations, such as Australia, South Africa, the Democratic Republic of the Congo, and Nigeria, cover a large geographical area and, as a result, air transportation is often the only feasible means of rapid travel between major cities. Consequently, air travel is the preferred method of distance travel. However, only Australia, South Africa, New Zealand, and Nigeria have major airports that handle large numbers of passengers, and none of the airports in either region ranks among the 30 largest airports in the world in terms of either passenger numbers or in terms of cargo handled.

Many of the smaller and some of the larger nations of sub-Saharan Africa and Oceania have a single international airport. Domestic services radiate from these airports. Some nations have a national carrier, and few African countries have competitive systems or have privatized the state airline.

A table ranks the largest airports in sub-Saharan Africa and Oceania in terms of passengers carried. The major Australian airports are much busier than most airports in Africa. Some airports both in Africa and in Australasia mainly handle tourists, for example, Gold Coast Airport in Australia, Seewoosagur Ramgoolam International (Mauritius), and Roland Garos (Reunion).

Communication

Many of the nations of sub-Saharan Africa have inadequate communication systems. In many, the telephone network is out of date and does not cover much of the country beyond the main cities. As a result, the number of mobile cellular phones in the region has greatly increased. In contrast, Australia and New Zealand and some of the Pacific Island countries have modern communication systems.

NUMBER OF MOBILE CELLULAR PHONES IN THE REGIONS

Country	Number of people per cellular phone	Date	Country	Number of people per cellular phone	Date
Seychelles	1.1	2007	Malawi	12.4	2007
South Africa	1.1	2007	Rwanda	12.9	2007
Botswana	1.3	2007	Djibouti	14.2	2007
Gabon	1.3	2007	Somalia	c. 14.3	2006
Mauritius	1.4	2007	Comoros	16.7	2007
Reunion	1.4	2006	Gambia	17.8	2007
Namibia	2.2	2007	Burundi	29.5	2006
Ivory Coast	2.4	2007	Central African Republic	30.0	2007
Swaziland	2.5	2006	Guinea	47.5	2005
Congo, Republic	2.6	2007	Eritrea	51.7	2007
Senegal	2.8	2007	Ethiopia	61.6	2007
Togo	2.8	2007			
Ghana	3.1	2007	Australia	0.9	2008
Kenya	3.1	2007	New Zealand	0.9	2008
Cape Verde	3.4	2007	New Caledonia	1.3	2008
Nigeria	3.5	2007	Fiji	1.4	2008
Zambia	3.7	2007	French Polynesia	1.4	2008
Mayotte	3.9	2005	Samoa	1.4	2008
Tanzania	4.0	2008	Guam	1.6	2004
Benin	4.1	2007	Palau	1.7	2008
Lesotho	4.1	2007	Norfolk Island	2.0	2009
São Tomé and Príncipe	4.5	2007	Tonga	2.0	2008
Equatorial Guinea	4.6	2007	Niue	2.4	2007
Angola	4.7	2007	Cook Islands	2.9	2008
Cameroon	4.7	2007	Northern Mariana Islands	3.4	2004
Guinea-Bissau	5.2	2007	Micronesia	4.4	2008
Liberia	6.2	2007	Tuvalu	4.8	2008
Mozambique	6.2	2007	Vanuatu	5.4	2008
Sierra Leone	6.4	2007	Nauru	6.7	2002
Uganda	7.0	2007	Papua New Guinea	8.7	2008
Madagascar	8.0	2007	Marshall Islands	11.6	2008
Congo, Democratic Republic	8.8	2007	American Samoa	25.9	2004
Burkina Faso	9.5	2007	Solomon Islands	35.4	2008
Zimbabwe	9.5	2007	Kiribati	93.0	2008

NUMBER OF TELEPHONE LINES IN THE REGIONS

Country	Number of people per telephone line	Date	Country	Number of people per telephone line	Date
Saint Helena	2.4	2008	Burundi	211.0	2006
Reunion	2.6	2005	Congo, Republic	213.6	2005
Mauritius	3.6	2007	Tanzania	226.6	2008
Seychelles	3.6	2007	Mozambique	306.4	2007
Cape Verde	7.1	2006	Central African Republic	324.6	2007
South Africa	10.5	2007	Guinea-Bissau	336.5	2007
Botswana	13.0	2006	Rwanda	353.4	2006
Namibia	13.3	2007	Guinea	356.9	2005
Gambia	17.8	2007	Liberia	496.6	2002
São Tomé and Príncipe	17.9	2007	Congo, Democratic Rep.	6,010.3	2006
Mayotte	18.6	2008			
Swaziland	21.7	2006	Norfolk Island	0.8	2004
Ivory Coast	23.4	2007	Niue	1.6	2008
Zimbabwe	33.7	2007	Australia	2.3	2008
Comoros	35.2	2006	Guam	2.4	2008
Lesotho	35.5	2007	New Zealand	2.4	2008
Senegal	42.2	2007	Palau	2.7	2008
Gabon	56.3	2007	Northern Mariana Islands	2.8	2008
Djibouti	59.1	2005	Cook Islands	2.9	2008
Togo	65.0	2007	New Caledonia	3.9	2008
Benin	71.3	2007	Tonga	4.0	2008
Malawi	75.7	2007	French Polynesia	4.8	2008
Ethiopia	84.0	2007	Tokelau	5.0	2008
Ghana	84.5	2007	Wallis and Futuna	5.0	2008
Somalia	c. 86.0	2007	American Samoa	5.5	2008
Nigeria	89.2	2007	Nauru	5.6	2008
Eritrea	96.6	2006	Samoa	6.2	2008
Equatorial Guinea	101.5	2005	Tuvalu	6.4	2008
Zambia	107.5	2007	Fiji	6.5	2008
Madagascar	131.3	2007	Marshall Islands	11.6	2008
Kenya	132.5	2007	Micronesia	12.4	2008
Cameroon	142.6	2006	Vanuatu	18.8	2008
Angola	158.5	2006	Kiribati	23.3	2008
Burkina Faso	158.6	2006	Pitcairn	50.0	2009
Uganda	182.3	2007	Solomon Islands	61.9	2008
Sierra Leone	207.4	2002	Papua New Guinea	86.5	2008

TELEPHONE SYSTEMS

Throughout Australasia, there is access to an advanced multipurpose telecommunications system. Similar conditions exist in the large cities of southern Africa, some of the small Indian Ocean territories, and some states in the South Pacific. In Australia and New Zealand, an extensive system of fiber-optic cables, coaxial cables, microwave radio relays, and satellites carry telephone communication in every part of the country. In both nations, the cellular phone network covers all but very remote areas. In both Australia and New Zealand, the telecommunications network is privately owned and operated. However, in New Zealand, the main provider, Telecom New Zealand, was in public ownership until it was privatized in the early 1990s.

In many countries of sub-Saharan Africa, the telephone system is undergoing modernization and expansion. In some countries, however, the network is little better than rudimentary. In much of Africa, telecommunications is state-owned, although networks have been privatized in some countries. Zimbabwe's telecommunications network is contracting, while civil wars have destroyed much of the infrastructure in some other

countries. In the majority of African states, the inadequacy of the main line network has led to the rapid growth in popularity of mobile cellular phones. Some African states have levels of cell phone ownership comparable to Latin American nations. A few, for example in eastern and central Africa, still have low levels of cell phone ownership both for economic reasons and because areas of the continent do not have a signal.

Some of the small countries of the South Pacific have relatively high rates of cellular phone ownership, although in some very small territories there are few phones, in part because ownership is not perceived as being useful. However, one of the most recent countries to join the cell phone network, Norfolk Island, now has a moderate level of ownership. The inhabitants of the island held a referendum in 2007 to allow cell phones, having previously rejected them as "anti-social."

The development of the cell phone network was spectacular through the first decade of the twenty-first century. In Australia, New Zealand, Mauritius, Reunion, and a few other states, most adults have a cellular phone, and in most countries in the regions, there are more cellular phones than fixed line phones. A table ranks the states of the regions according to the number of people to each mobile cellular telephone.

RADIO AND TELEVISION IN THE REGIONS

Country	Number of radio broadcast stations	Number of television broadcast stations	Country	Number of radio broadcast stations	Number of television broadcast stations[a]
Angola	34	6	Seychelles[a]	4	11
Benin	36	6	Sierra Leone	11	2
Botswana	25	2	Somalia	14	4
Burkina Faso	31	3	South Africa[a]	605	556
Burundi	5	1	Swaziland[a]	12	19
Cameroon	14	1	Tanzania	25	3
Cape Verde[a]	34	8	Togo[a]	15	5
Central African Republic	7	1	Uganda[a]	42	9
Comoros	6	1	Zambia	28	9
Congo, Democratic Republic	16	4	Zimbabwe[a]	45	16
Congo, Republic	9	1			
Djibouti	3	1	American Samoa	5	1
Equatorial Guinea	8	1	Australia	615	105
Eritrea	4	2	Cook Islands	2	1
Ethiopia[a]	11	25	Fiji	43	2
Gabon[a]	21	8	French Polynesia[a]	18	24
Gambia	5	1	Guam	16	3
Ghana	89	7	Kiribati	3	1
Guinea	8	6	Marshall Islands	4	2
Guinea-Bissau	5	1	Micronesia	6	3
Ivory Coast	14	14	Nauru	1	1
Kenya	48	8	New Caledonia[a]	6	31
Lesotho	5	1	New Zealand	418	41
Liberia[a]	12	8	Niue	2	1
Madagascar[a]	17	37	Norfolk Island[a]	4	3
Malawi[a]	29	1	Northern Mariana Islands[a]	8	3
Mauritius[a]	13	5	Palau	6	1
Mayotte	6	3	Papua New Guinea	55	3
Mozambique	41	4	Pitcairn	1	0
Namibia	45	2	Samoa	7	2
Nigeria[a]	130	18	Solomon Islands	3	1
Reunion[a]	57	35	Tokelau	1	0
Rwanda	10	2	Tonga	6	3
Saint Helena[a]	4	3	Tuvalu	2	0
São Tomé and Príncipe	7	2	Vanuatu	7	1
Senegal	29	4	Wallis and Futuna Islands	1	2

[a] includes relays and repeaters.

INTERNET ACCESS IN THE REGIONS

Country	Internet country code	Percentage of population with Internet access	Date	Country	Internet country code	Percentage of population with Internet access	Date
Seychelles	.sc	38.5	2007	Angola	.ao	0.6	2006
Reunion	.re	33.3	2007	Madagascar	.mg	0.6	2006
Mauritius	.mu	27.0	2007	Burkina Faso	.bf	0.5	2006
Saint Helena	.sh	17.9	2007	Guinea	.gn	0.5	2006
São Tomé and Príncipe	.st	16.7	2007	Congo, Democratic Rep.	.cd	0.4	2007
Zimbabwe	.zw	11.6	2007	Ethiopia	.et	0.4	2007
South Africa	.za	10.5	2005	Central African Republic	.cf	0.3	2006
Gabon	.ga	9.5	2007	Sierra Leone	.sl	0.3	2007
Kenya	.ke	8.5	2007	Liberia	.lr	0.02	2003
Gambia	.gm	7.3	2007	Mayotte	.yt	n/a	n/a
Cape Verde	.cv	7.2	2007				
Senegal	.sn	7.2	2007	New Zealand	.nz	76.9	2008
Nigeria	.ng	7.1	2007	Australia	.au	71.4	2008
Uganda	.ug	6.8	2007	Niue	.nu	55.6	2002
Togo	.tg	6.0	2006	Norfolk Island	.nf	45.5	2002
Namibia	.na	5.5	2007	Tuvalu	.tv	43.5	2008
Zambia	.zm	5.1	2007	Guam	.gu	41.7	2005
Benin	.bj	5.0	2007	New Caledonia	.nc	32.3	2006
Swaziland	.sz	4.4	2006	French Polynesia	.pf	25.0	2008
Botswana	.bw	4.0	2006	Cook Islands	.ck	18.5	2002
Lesotho	.ls	3.7	2007	Northern Mariana Islands	.mp	14.5	2003
Eritrea	.er	3.3	2007	Micronesia	.fm	13.9	2008
Comoros	.km	3.1	2007	Fiji	.fj	9.5	2008
Ghana	.gh	2.8	2007	Vanuatu	.vu	8.7	2008
Guinea-Bissau	.gw	2.4	2006	Tonga	.to	8.3	2008
Congo, Republic	.cg	2.1	2007	Wallis and Futuna	.wf	6.7	2002
Ghana	.gh	2.8	2007	Samoa	.ws	5.0	2008
Cameroon	.cm	1.9	2007	Marshall Islands	.mh	4.3	2008
Ivory Coast	.ci	1.8	2006	Nauru	.nr	3.0	2003
Djibouti	.dj	1.7	2006	Kiribati	.ki	2.2	2008
Rwanda	.rw	1.2	2007	Papua New Guinea	.pg	2.1	2008
Malawi	.mw	1.1	2007	Solomon Islands	.sb	1.6	2006
Somalia	.so	1.1	2007	American Samoa	.as	n/a	n/a
Tanzania	.tz	1.1	2007	Palau	.pw	n/a	n/a
Mozambique	.mz	1.0	2007	Pitcairn	.pn	n/a	n/a
Burundi	.bi	0.8	2006	Tokelau	.tk	n/a	n/a
Equatorial Guinea	.gq	0.8	2007				

RADIO, TELEVISION, AND INTERNET

In the small nations of the South Pacific region, the size of the population restricts the domestic provision of radio and, particularly, television networks. However, satellite television stations are widely available. In some sub-Saharan African countries, the number of television and radio stations is restricted because of censorship, and the authorities keep control of the dissemination of news. Only in South Africa, Nigeria, Australia, New Zealand, and a few other countries are there many commercial radio and television stations. A table details the number of radio and television broadcast stations.

Internet access is restricted in the poorer nations of sub-Saharan Africa, although some countries, such as Kenya, Gabon, and Senegal, have relatively high levels of Internet access by regional standards. Internet access is also important in remote communities, where it provides a link with the outside world. Both Australia and New Zealand have rates of Internet access comparable to North America. The table ranks states according to the percentage of people with Internet access.

Glossary

A

a cappella singing unaccompanied by instruments

Aboriginal a member of the indigenous people of a region, commonly used to describe one of the original inhabitants of Australia

abstraction (**abstract art**) art that does not represent any recognizable matter and exists for its own sake

àdir Yoruba dyed fabric

adobe dried clay or mud, widely used as a building material throughout Africa

afofo a local African alcoholic beverage

ágógó an iron bell, in Ghana

agriculturalist a settled (sedentary) farmer who makes his or her living by cultivating crops

aguardente an alcoholic drink

AIDS acquired immune deficiency syndrome, a disease that damages the body's natural immune system, making it more prone to attack by other diseases; AIDS is caused by HIV infection

àkàrà fried bean cake, in western Africa

alafin king, in Nigeria

Allah the Islamic name for God

alloucou musical style of the Bete people, in Ivory Coast

alluvium fine sediment transported or deposited by flowing water

almaami West African Muslim rulers

aloalo a funerary sculpture, in Madagascar

àmàlà paste or porridge made from yam flour, in West Africa

amarula a South African cream liqueur made with sugar, cream, and the fruit of the African Marula tree (*Sclerocarya birrea*)

ampesi a Ghanaian meal of either boiled yam, plantain, cocoyam, or cassava served with other dishes

ancestor worship the religious practice of worshipping the spirits of dead ancestors

andesite the most common volcanic rock after basalt

Anglican a protestant church founded in England in the sixteenth century, which includes the Church of England and other churches throughout the world in communion with it

animism belief system that attributes conscious life to plants and inanimate objects

anorthosite a form of igneous rock

anticyclone a center of high atmospheric pressure

ANZAC abbreviation for Australian and New Zealand Army Corps

àpàlà (**talking drum**) a drum, the pitch of which can be altered to mimic the tonal qualities of different African languages

apartheid (Afrikaans: "separateness") the system of ethnic segregation introduced by South Africa's Nationalist government in 1948

aquifer a layer of water-bearing rock

arak (**arrake** or **arrack**) an alcoholic beverage that is distilled from fermented fruit, grain, sugarcane, or the sap of coconut palms

Archean the earlier of the two divisions of the Precambrian, from about 3.8 to 2.5 billion years ago

arid dry and usually hot

aroids members of the flowering plant family Araceae, which contains food plants such as taro

artesian source of water that rises from below ground because of natural underground pressure

assembly as a legislature or parliament, a meeting of representatives convened to discuss government proposals and enact laws

athieke steamed manioc or cassava, in Senegal

atoll oceanic coral island, often ring- or horseshoe-shaped and surrounding a lagoon

attiéké a food made from manioc or cassava by fermentation, in the Ivory Coast

Austronesian a language family spoken in Southeast Asia and the countries of the Pacific Basin

autonomy the condition of being self-governing, usually granted to a subdivision of territory belonging to a larger state

axatse a musical instrument made from a gourd, in West Africa

B

baasto a spaghetti-like pasta from Somalia

babariga a large flowing robe, in West Africa

bagasse pulp extracted from the juice of the sugarcane

Bahá'i Faith a faith founded in Iran in 1863, which emphasizes the spiritual unity of all humankind

bai community house, in Palau

balafon a percussion instrument, similar to the xylophone

baleen whales species of whales that capture food by sieving it from the water through bony plates (baleen) in their mouths

balele a music and dance tradition from Equatorial Guinea

bandiri a musical tradition from Nigeria

banksias members of the genus Banksia, Australian trees and shrubs that have characteristic brightly colored, bottlebrush-shaped flower heads

baobab any of several trees of the genus Adansonia, which typically have a broad swollen trunk that stores water

barracouta a long, slender food fish common on the coasts of Australia, New Zealand, and southern Africa

basalts dark fine-grained igneous rocks

basinyi Chopi dancers, in Mozambique

bas relief a form of sculpture in which figures are carved in a flat surface and project only slightly from the background rather than standing freely

bauxite the ore that is smelted to make aluminum

bêche-de-mer boiled, dried, and smoked flesh of sea cucumbers

benachin (**Jollof rice**) a West African dish of rice, fish (or other meat), with vegetables

betel the dried leaves of the Asian pepper plant (*Piper betle*), which are mostly chewed with an Areca or betel nut (*Areca catechu*), used as a mild stimulant and for medicinal properties

betel nut (Areca nut or **buai)** fruit of the palm Areca catechu

bilharzia *see* **schistosomiasis**

biltong a form of cured meat that originated in South Africa

biodiversity the diversity of plant and animal life in a particular habitat (or in the world as a whole)

birthrate the number of births, usually expressed as the annual number of live births per 1,000 population

bissap a drink made from hibiscus leaves

bourzwa (**red snapper**) a prized tropical marine fish valued for its flesh

bridewealth a gift given by the groom to the family of his bride, a common marriage practice among African peoples

bryophytes plants that have stems and leaves but lack true vascular tissue and roots, such as mosses

bùbá (*ágbada*, *boubou*, or *bubu*) a flowing wide-sleeved robe worn in much of West Africa

bushmeat the general term for wild animals that are killed for human consumption

bwiti a political-religious cult that developed among the Fang people of Gabon in the early twentieth century

C

cachupa a stew of corn, beans, and fish or meat from Cape Verde

calabash a dried gourd

calcareous rocks rocks made wholly or partly of calcite

caldera volcanic crater

caliph (Arabic: "successor") a political and spiritual leader of the Muslim people

calligraphy in Islam, the art form of creating elaborate, decorative scripts of religious texts

Cambrian the period 545 through 495 million years ago

capital city the city where the government of a country or state is located

capital goods goods used in the production of other goods

cash crop a crop grown for sale rather than for subsistence

cassava *see* **manioc**

Cenozoic era the geologic era from 65 million years ago to the present

central business district (**CBD**) the part of a town or city, usually in the center, where retail stores, offices, and cultural activities are concentrated

cereal a cultivated grass selectively bred to produce edible grain, for example wheat, corn, rice, and barley

china clay (**kaolin**) a fine, usually white, clay used in ceramics and as an absorbent and as a filler

chlorinated fluorocarbons (**chloroflurocarbons** or **CFCs**) organic compounds used as aerosol propellants and refrigerant gases, which are known to cause depletion of the ozone layer in the atmosphere above Antarctica

Christianity a religion based on the teachings of Jesus Christ, originating in the first century CE from Judaism

cibi a Fijian war dance, originally performed before or after battle

clan a social group made up of several extended families or lineages; clan members often trace their descent from a common ancestor

clubmoss any of about up to 400 species of primitive vascular plants that constitute the family Lycopodiaceae; they are evergreen plants with needle-like leaves, plus cone-like clusters of small leaves

coalition an alliance of different interests to achieve a mutual purpose

coladeira a music genre from Cape Verde

Cold War the period of rivalry between communist countries led by the Soviet Union and Western nations led by the United States; 1945-1991

collectivization the merging of smaller, family farms into big, state-run units

colonialism the control of a foreign territory by a state or people for the purposes of settlement and economic expansion

colony a territory under the sovereignty of a foreign power

Commonwealth a loose grouping of states that were once part of the British Empire, with the British monarch at its head

communism a social and economic system that is based on the communal ownership of property; all means of production in this system are owned by the state

constitutional monarchy a form of government with a hereditary head of state or monarch and a constitution

consumer goods goods that are acquired for immediate use, such as foodstuffs, radios, computers, televisions, and washing machines

continental climate the climatic type characteristic of large landmasses, with hot summers and cold winters

continental drift the theory that the continents move gradually over the planet's surface

continental plate one of the divisions of the lithosphere

copra the dried white kernel of the coconut from which coconut oil is extracted

coup d'etat a change of government by unconstitutional means, usually involving a rebellion by the armed forces

creole a language that developed from a combination of other languages

craton the stable, central part of a continental plate

cultural group a people who are identifiable as having a common culture and way of life

cyclone a center of low atmospheric pressure, the opposite of anticyclone; tropical cyclones are known as hurricanes and typhoons

D

dayurids a family of insectivorous and carnivorous marsupials mostly mouse- and shrew-like, but including the cat-sized quolls and larger Tasmanian devil

death rate the number of deaths, usually expressed as the annual number of deaths per 1,000 population

deforestation the clearing of trees in a forest region

degradation (of land) a process that reduces soil fertility

democracy a form of government in which policy is made by the people (direct democracy) or on their behalf by their elected representatives (indirect democracy)

dengue fever an acute tropical viral disease transmitted to humans by the mosquito *Aedes aegypti*

dependency a territorial unit under the jurisdiction of another state, but not formally annexed to it

depressions low-pressure weather systems

dervish a member of a Muslim order given to religious practices that induce trances

desert a very arid area with less than 10 inches (250 mm) of rain annually. Such areas may be hot or cold.

desertification the creation of desertlike conditions through land degradation

Devonian the period 417 through 354 million years ago

diaspora people living outside their ancestral homeland

Difaqane a Sotho-Tswana word meaning "scattering" referring to the wars and migrations that affected southern Africa from 1819

diphtheria a bacterial disease of the upper respiratory tract

diptocarps (**dipterocarps**) tall, tropical rain forest trees of the family Dipterocarpaceae

dodo fried ripe plantain, in West Africa

doline a rounded depression formed by water erosion or the collapse of caves in a limestone region

dolomites sedimentary carbonate rocks

domoda (**domodah**) peanut stew, popular in Gambia

Dreamtime the Aboriginal understanding of the world, which explains the origins of the land and its people

drift deposits unstratified deposits of glacial material

drought an extended period in which rainfall is substantially lower than average, and the water supply is insufficient to meet demand

dumboy cassava or manioc, boiled then mashed, a staple Liberian dish

dune a mound or ridge of wind-blown sand

E

Easter a Christian festival marking the resurrection of Jesus Christ, observed on a Sunday in March or April each year

ecosystem a community of plants and animals, and the environment in which they live and react with each other

Eid al-Adha the Muslim Feast of Sacrifice

Eid al-Fitr the Muslim festival that marks the end of the month of Ramadan

Eid-e-Milad-un-Nabi anniversary of the birth of the Prophet Muhammad

El Nino occasional shift of the region of warmest sea-surface temperature (above 82°F or 27.5°C) in the Pacific Ocean from the western Pacific to the central and eastern Pacific

electorate the persons qualified to vote in an election

emir an Arab leader

emirate the territory ruled by an emir

endemic species found nowhere else

ensete a member of the banana family, a root crop grown in Ethiopia

eon one of three very large divisions of geological time: Phanerozoic (the most recent), Proterozoic, and Archean (the latter two eons are together known as the Cryptozoic eon)

epicontinental sea a shallow sea that extends over part of a continental shelf

epiphytes plants that live on other plants but are not parasitic

era one of four large periods of geological time: Cenozoic (the most recent), Mesozoic, Paleozoic, and Neoproterozoic or Precambrian (the most ancient). Eras are shorter than eons and are divided into periods.

escarpment a steep slope or cliff

ethnic group a group of people sharing a social or cultural identity based on language, history, religion, descent, customs, or common descent or kinship

eucalypts (**gum trees**) woody plants belonging to three closely related genera (Eucalyptus, Corymbia, and Angophora), which dominate the tree flora of Australia

Eunoto a rite of passage ceremony among the Maasai of Kenya and Tanzania, marking the initiation of young men into adulthood

exports goods and services sold to other countries, bringing in foreign exchange

F

fady the term for a taboo among the Merina people of Madagascar

faience a ceramic glazed material

fale afolau Samoan guesthouses

fault a fracture or crack in the Earth along which there has been movement of the rock masses

federal republic a form of constitutional government in which power is shared between two levels, a central or federal government and a tier of provincial or state governments

ferrinho a musical instrument from Cape Verde

fetish an object that people believe contains spirits or has magical powers

fiafia a Pacific island expression meaning a celebration with dancing and singing

filariasis a parasitic infection spread by mosquitoes and caused by threadlike parasitic worms that damage the human lymphatic system

fjord a deep, narrow, steep-walled, U-shaped valley that was carved by a glacier and is now occupied by the sea

fjords long, deep inlets of the sea with steep sides

flash flood a localized flood of considerable volume that results from sudden heavy rainfall upstream

fluvial water-carried

fly the part of a flag that is farthest from the flagpole

FNLA Frente Nacional de Libertação de Angola, or National Front for the Liberation of Angola

fokontany originally, a traditional Malagasy village; a basic administrative subdivision of Madagascar

fossil fuel any fuel, such as coal, oil, and natural gas, formed beneath the Earth's surface from organisms that died millions of years ago, under conditions of heat and pressure

free port a port, or part of a part, where goods are imported and reexported without duty being levied

fufu (*foutou*) a thick paste or porridge usually made by boiling starchy root vegetables such as cassava or yams

fynbos natural shrubland or heathland that occurs in a small belt of the Western Cape of South Africa

G

GDP *see* **gross domestic product**

Ge'ez an ancient Semitic language related to Amharic

Gelede annual ceremonies held by the Yoruba people to celebrate the power of women and appease local witches

ghee clarified butter

ghetto a slum area in a city that is occupied by an ethnic minority

gibber plain a large plain that is covered by loose rock fragments (gibber)

glacial a period of time when glaciers and ice sheets formed and spread

glaciation the process of glacier and ice sheet growth and their effect on the landscape

glacier a thick mass of ice that forms on land from an accumulation and recrystallization of snow great enough to remain through the summer and grow year by year

glaciology the study of glaciers

gneiss granite in which the mineral content and structure has been changed by heat

Gondwana (**Gondwanaland**) supercontinent that mainly included South America and Africa

grand mosque the principal mosque in a city

granites igneous rocks formed from slow cooling of igneous intrusions

grave goods items that are buried with a body in a grave

greenstone a tough, dark type of basalt rock that once was solid deep-sea lava

greywacke a sedimentary rock consisting of fragments of quartz, feldspar, and other minerals, set in a muddy base

griot a storyteller, singer, and musician

gross domestic product (**GDP**) the total value of all the goods and services produced in a country in a fixed term, usually one year

groundnut an alternative name for the peanut, a staple food and major cash crop for many peoples of sub-Saharan Africa

groundwater water that has percolated into the ground from the Earth's surface

guano mass accumulations of bird feces, which were a valuable source of nitrates for agriculture and gunpowder

guest worker a foreign laborer who is working temporarily in a country

gum trees *see* **eucalypts**

gumbe a musical genre from West Africa

H

hajj the annual pilgrimage to the city of Mecca in Saudi Arabia to pray at Islam's holiest shrine, the Kaaba, and undertake other religious duties

hangi a social gathering and meal, in New Zealand

Hansen's disease *see* **leprosy**

hapu Maori word for descent group or clan; modern meaning: a section of a tribe or a subtribe

harmattan a dry and dusty West African trade wind that blows south from the Sahara

head of state the highest office of state, in which the holder personally represents the state in key functions such as declaring war or dissolving the legislature

hei-tiki (*tiki*) a Maori term for a human figure carved in greenstone as a neck ornament

hepatitis a severe viral infection, existing in several types, that causes inflammation of the liver

heroic era in the history of Antarctic exploration, the period that extended from the end of the nineteenth century through the early 1920s

HIV human immunodeficiency virus, the virus that causes AIDS

homeland in apartheid South Africa, a region created by the government to accommodate black African peoples

hominid early human

Homo sapiens modern humans

hunter-gatherers people who obtain their food by hunting wild animals and gathering berries, fruits, and other food from wild plants

hydrocarbons any of numerous organic compounds that contain only carbon and hydrogen, such as methane, and important constituents of coal, crude oil, and natural gas

I

ice age a long period of geological time in which cold climatic conditions prevail and snow and ice are present throughout the year

ice cap a mass of ice and snow that permanently covers a large area of land

ice cores cylindrical sections of ice removed from a glacier or an ice sheet in order to study climate patterns of the past

ice sheet a large area of ice, usually over about 20,000 square miles (50,000 sq. km)

ice shelf ice that is attached to land but projects out to sea

iceberg a massive floating body of ice broken away from a glacier. Only about 10 percent of an iceberg is above the surface of the water.

iconoclasm the destruction of religious images

iconoclast an opponent of icons

igneous intrusions places where magma welled up to the surface along faults

igneous rocks rocks formed from volcanic activity

imam an Islamic religious official who leads a congregation in prayer and addresses social and religious matters

immigrants foreigners who enter a country to settle there

impi an armed body of men among the Zulu

imports goods and services purchased from other countries

Incwala the "first fruits" festival of the Zulu and the Swazi at which the king is honored and the people ask for blessings from their ancestors

infibulation the custom of female circumcision (also called female genital mutilation)

inselberg a rocky upland that rises sharply from a plain; a steep, isolated hill found in arid or semiarid landscapes

Interahamwe the Hutu militias, trained by the Rwandan military in 1993-1994 to destroy the country's Tutsi population

interglacial a period of milder global climate between glacials, when ice sheets and glaciers retreat

intermediate goods raw materials that are transformed into other goods

isicathamiya an unaccompanied singing style that evolved among migrant Zulu workers in hostels in KwaZulu-Natal

Islam a religion based on the revelations of God to the prophet Muhammad in the seventh century CE, which are contained in the Koran

iwi Maori word for a set of people bound together by descent from a common ancestor or ancestors; modern meaning: tribe

J

jade a hard green stone

jihad (Arabic: "struggle") in Islam, the struggle a person undertakes to submit to Allah. It may involve armed struggle and so often translates as "holy war."

jobwa a stick dance from the Marshall Islands

Judaism a religion based in Israelite traditions from 1200 BCE and practiced by Jews

Jurassic the period 206 through 142 million years ago

K

kabaka the ruler of the kingdom of Buganda

kaban a form of lute, in Somalia

kachasu a form of homemade beer, in Zambia

kanga a brightly colored and patterned two-piece cotton garment traditionally worn by Swahili women

kaolin *see* **china clay**

karakia Maori prayers

karst a bare limestone landscape formed by chemical weathering of the rock

kastom a pidgin word used to refer to traditional culture, including religion, economics, art, and magic in the Pacific islands

kava (**ava** or **yaqona**) refers to both the plant (*Piper methysticum*) and the beverage produced from its roots, popular in Fiji

kente a fabric woven from narrow strips by the Asante, regarded as the national dress of Ghana

kikoi a cloth worn wrapped around the waist of Swahili men

kimberlite a rock formation in South Africa in which diamonds are found

kinship a system of rights and obligations among a group of people culturally defined as related to one another by birth or marriage; also the social network defined by these relations

kopjes rocky outcrops that emerge from the surrounding grassland or scrub

kora a 21-string harp made from a gourd (calabash) and a rosewood pole, used in West Africa

Koran the holy book of the Islamic faith. It consists of verses (suras) and is regarded by Muslims as a direct transcription of the Word of God (Allah) recited to Muhammad by the angel Jibril (Gabriel).

kraal a group of traditional beehive-shaped homes, in South Africa

L

lali Fijian word for a bell or drum

lap-lap a waistcloth or loincloth, in the South Pacific

laterites deposits of iron and alumina that form a hard layer in soils from which other soluble material has been washed out by weathering caused by heavy tropical rainfall

Laurasia the ancestor of the North American and European continents

leached deprived of minerals by water percolating through the soil

leprosy (**Hansen's disease**) an infectious disease that is characterized by disfiguring skin sores, nerve damage, and progressive debilitation

lichen a close symbiotic association between a fungus and an alga

lineage an extended family group that shares a common ancestor

linear dunes sand dunes that are straight or slightly sinuous, typically much longer than they are wide

lingua franca commonly understood language

lithosphere Earth's thin outer layer

litunga a Lozi king

living fossil an organism that has persisted, essentially unchanged, since its first appearance millions of years ago, often with no obvious living relative

LNG liquefied natural gas

lost-wax method a method of casting metal objects by using two molds in easily workable wax

lovo an earth oven, in Fiji

lu pulu Polynesian dish of corned beef cooked with taro leaves

lu sipi Polynesian dish of lamb or beef cooked with taro leaves

luluai chief or village elder

lunette dune a crescent-shaped sand dune

M

madrasa an Islamic theological school

maffé a West African stew with meat simmered in a sauce thickened with ground peanuts

magma molten rock material beneath the surface of the ground

magnetosphere the region surrounding the Earth, in which the behavior of charged particles is controlled by the planet's magnetic field

mahdi (Arabic: "guided one") in Islam, a holy messiah, or liberator

mahi-mahi (**dolphinfish**) a large food and game fish found in tropical and subtropical waters

makwaya a dance accompanied by a drum and palm leaf rattles attached to the legs, in South Africa

malaria an infectious disease caused by parasites that enter the human bloodstream through Anopheles mosquito bites

malu a tattoo typical of Samoan women that covers the legs from just below the knee to the upper thighs

mana a supernatural force or power that may be ascribed to persons, spirits, or inanimate objects

manioc (**cassava**) a plant (*Manihot esculenta*) grown in the tropics for its fleshy rootstock

mantle the layer extending from the base of Earth's crust to the core

marabout an Islamic holy man or mystic

marae a traditional Maori tribal meeting place or place of worship

masquerade a festival in which masks and costumes are worn

Mau Mau a secret society founded in 1948-1949 among the Kikuyu, Meru, and Embu peoples of Kenya to fight against British colonial rule

mbalax a form of popular music with complex percussion rhythms, in Gambia and Senegal

mbaqanga a style of five-part harmony singing, in South Africa

mbira (or **thumb piano**, **lamellaphone**, **sanza**) a musical instrument made of tuned metal strips attached to a resonating chamber; the keys are plucked with the thumbs; used in Africa

Mediterranean climate a climatic type characterized by dry warm summers and mild wetter winters

megadunes long, undulating waves on the surface of an ice sheet

megaliths large stones or rocks

meke any traditional style of dance from Fiji

melktert a South African dessert made from milk

meningitis a serious inflammation of the membranes covering the brain and spinal cord

Mesolithic Middle Stone Age

Mesozoic period between 248 to 65 million years ago

mestiços a Portuguese term used to denote a person of mixed European and African descent

metamorphosed rocks rocks changed through heat, chemical action, or pressure

meteorology the science that deals with the study of the atmosphere in relation to the weather and climatic situation

metropolitan district the city and its suburbs, which may spread over more than the city's administrative area

Mfecane (Nguni: "crushing") the term used by the Bantu peoples to refer to the wars and migrations that affected southern Africa from 1819

mganda a warlike dance performed by the Tonga of Zambia

microclimate small-scale local climatic variations

migration the permanent shift of people from one country, region, or from another part of the same country, for economic, political, religious, or other reasons

military dictatorship a government staffed and controlled by members of the armed forces

military regime a government staffed and controlled by the armed forces

minaret a slender tower attached to a mosque, from which calls to prayer are sung five times each day

miombo woodland in southern Africa that is characterized by the presence of trees belonging to the genus Brachystegia

missionary a person who tries to convert others to his or her religious beliefs

mokorotlo the characteristic cone-shaped, woven hat worn by Sotho men

monarchy a form of rule involving a hereditary head of state

mopane (**mopani**) a tree (*Colophospermum mopane*) that grows in hot, dry, low-lying areas of southern Africa, and the habitat it dominates

moraines rock material deposited by glaciers

morna a music and dance genre from Cape Verde

mosque an Islamic place of worship

multiparty republic a system in which several political parties compete for the votes of the people in an election

municipality (**municipal district**) a town or city that has some measure of local government

---

N

natural resources raw materials created by Earth's natural processes, including mineral deposits, soil, water, timber, and plants and animals

nebkha mound of soil or sand, blown by wind, that forms in the lee of bushes and trees

Neogene the last 24 million years

Neolithic New Stone Age period c. 3300-2900 BCE

ngasech celebration of a first-born child in Palau

nggwalndu an ancestral figure in the form of a statue, in New Guinea

ngil a society that existed among communities of the Fang people in precolonial times. Its members had political and judicial power and often punished or executed people found guilty of witchcraft.

ngloik any performance art in Palau

ngoma drums used by the Bantu peoples of central, eastern, and southern Africa

nguzu-nguzu a carving mounted on the prow of Polynesian canoes and widely believed to give protection

Nilotic relating to certain ethnic groups found mainly in southern Sudan, Uganda, Kenya, and northern Tanzania

nomad (adjective: **nomadic**) a person who follows a wandering lifestyle, usually living either by herding livestock or trading

nshima (*nsima*) a staple food in Zambia and Malawi made from ground corn

nongovernmental organization (**NGO**) any nonprofit, voluntary citizens' group that is organized on a local, national, or international level

nunatak an isolated mountain peak protruding through glacial ice

O

oba a king of the Yoruba people

ocher a red or yellow pigment

official language the language used by governments, schools, courts, and other official institutions of a particular country

oil palm palm trees of the genus Elaeis native to tropical regions, with dark fleshy fruits containing a kernel from which palm oil is extracted for use in soaps, margarine, lubricants, and other products

one-party state a political system in which there is no competition with the government party at elections, as in communism and military dictatorships, and all but the government party is banned

open-cast mining the mining of minerals and coal from immediately below the surface of the land by first removing the overlying layer

opposition (government) the major political party not in power at a particular time

Ordovician the period from 495 through 443 million years ago

orographic rain rain that results when near-saturated warm maritime air is forced to rise when confronted by a coastal mountain barrier

orisa (or *orisha*) in the Yoruba religion, one of a pantheon of several hundred deities

orogeny the process of mountain formation

Orthodox Church a branch of the Christian Church that recognized the Patriarch of Constantinople as its head and split with the Roman Catholic Church in 1054

Outback in Australia, a general term for the areas that are far away from towns and cities, especially the desert areas in central Australia

ozone layer a band of enriched oxygen (ozone) found in the upper atmosphere

P

Pacific Plate the tectonic plate that lies beneath the Pacific Ocean

pack ice a large area of broken, floating ice

Paleolithic Old Stone Age

Paleozoic period between 545 and 248 million years ago

palusami a Fijian dish made with taro leaves, coconut milk, and corned beef

parliamentary democracy a political system in which the legislature is elected by the adult members of the population, and the government is formed by the party that commands a majority

party an organized group seeking political power to implement an agreed set of policies

pastoralism a way of life based on tending herds of animals, such as sheep, goats, cattle, or camels

pastoralist a person who lives by herding livestock such as cattle or sheep, often as part of a nomadic or seminomadic life

pataka Maori storehouse

pe'a the traditional male tattoo of Samoa

per capita per person

Permian period between 290 to 248 million years ago

petroglyphs rock paintings and engravings

phytoplankton microscopic, drifting plants, mostly algae, which are found in marine and freshwater ecosystems and form part of the plankton

piassava a palm fiber

pijin (pidgin) a language spoken in the Solomon Islands

pipi any of various edible shellfish from Australia and New Zealand

plankton the community of microscopic plants (phytoplankton) and animals (zooplankton) that float at or near the surface of freshwater or saltwater habitats

plantain a form of banana that has to be cooked before being eaten

plateau a large area of level, elevated land

polasisi the blinds or screens of a Samoan house formed of braided coconut leaves

polygamy having multiple spouses, of which polygyny is the most common form

polygyny the practice of marrying more than one wife

potjiekos a South African stew prepared in a large cast iron pot

PPP *see* **purchasing power parity**

Precambrian period before 600 million years ago

Presbyterian Church a Protestant church in which lay members of the congregation are involved in the church's administration

president a head of state, elected in some countries directly by votes and in others by members of the legislature

prime minister the chief executive in a parliamentary democracy

privatization redistribution of state-owned property

productivity output per hour worked

protectorate a state or territory under the control of a stronger foreign nation

Protestant a term used to describe a number of Christian churches that have rejected the authority of the pope and the Roman Catholic Church

protozoans microscopic single-celled animals

purchasing power parity (PPP) a formula that allows comparison between living standards in different countries

Q

qat (**khat**) a plant (*Catha edulis*) and its leaves, which are traditionally chewed as a mild stimulant

Quaternary period the most recent one million years of geological time

R

rain forest dense forest that grows in tropical zones with abundant rainfall all year round

Ramadan the ninth month of the Islamic calendar during which Muslims fast during daylight hours

rangatira a Maori chief

ravitoto a pork stew with ground manioc, or cassava, leaves from Madagascar

razana ancestors (Madagascar)

refugee a person who is forced to leave his or her country for either political or economic reasons

reliquary a container used to hold the remains of a person

republic a form of government with a nonhereditary head of state

rhyolite a volcanic rock

rift valley an elongated valley formed between two fault lines

rite of passage a ceremony, such as initiation into adulthood or marriage, that marks the passage of a person from one stage of life into another

robusta coffee a type of coffee that, compared to arabica coffee, is easier to grow and cheaper to produce, but lower in quality

rondavel (*rondawel*) a traditional round or oval African house made with materials that can be found locally

Roman Catholic Church the largest of the Christian churches, acknowledging the pope as its spiritual head on Earth

rougailles a traditional dish from Mauritius made from tomatoes and sausages, or other meats

S

sabar a Senegalese high-stepping and high-energy dance that accompanies the drumming of the *sabar*, a type of drum

sago the starch extracted from the pith of the stem of the sago palm (*Metroxylon sagu*)

Sahel a semidesert region south of the Sahara

salinity salt concentration

salt lake a body of water that has no outlet to the sea and contains in solution a high concentration of salts

sandstone common sedimentary rock formation composed mainly of quartz

savanna tropical grassland dominated by various species of perennial grasses interspersed with varying numbers of shrubs and low trees

sawei an exchange system in Micronesia where goods are exchanged between island and atolls

schist a metamorphic rock in which the constituent minerals are arranged in parallel

schistosomiasis (or **bilharzia**) a parasitic disease of humans, caused by flatworms carried by certain species of snails

scree weathered rock fragments on slopes formed by shattering frost

seamounts mountains that rise from the ocean floor but do not reach the water's surface

sediment layers of rock, gravel, sand, silt, or organic material that have been laid down by water, ice, or wind, and cover the bedrock

sedimentary rocks rocks laid down in layers

semba a form of traditional music originating from Angola

shantytown an area of impermanent housing, usually made from scrap materials, on the outskirts of large cities, often where poor migrants live

Sharia (Arabic: "divine law") Islamic law

shebeen an illegal township bar in South Africa

sheikh an Islamic chief

Shia Islam (noun and adjective: **Shiite**) the branch of Islam that forms a minority of Muslims worldwide but a majority in Iran, Iraq, and Bahrain. Shiites believe that descendants of Muhammad's grandson Ali are the rightful leaders of Islam.

shield a plateau, a geologically stable region of older rock

shifting cultivation a farming method (once termed "**slash and burn**" agriculture) that involves clearing an area of forest for temporary crop growing

siapo Samoan cloth made from bark

silimba a xylophone-like instrument from Zambia

sleeping sickness (or **African trypanosomiasis**) a parasitic disease in humans transmitted through the bite of the tsetse fly

solpugids (**sun spiders**) scorpion-like insects with large mouth pincers

sorghum a genus (Sorghum) of grasses, several of which are grown for grain or as fodder plants

South Pole (geographic) the southernmost point of the Earth's axis; the intersection between Earth's surface and its axis of rotation

South Pole (magnetic) the point (in the south) on the Earth's surface where Earth's magnetic field points directly into the ground. Because of changes in Earth's magnetic field, the magnetic South Pole constantly shifts and is not the same as the geographic South Pole.

state the primary political unit of the modern world, usually defined by the possession of sovereignty over a territory and its people

stele (plural: **stelae**) a carved obelisk or pillar

sub-Antarctic the region just outside the Antarctic Circle

subduction the geological process in which a heavier tectonic plate meets and sinks beneath a lighter tectonic plate

subsistence farming a type of agriculture in which all the crops grown are eaten by the farmer and his family, leaving nothing to sell for profit

subtropical the climatic zone between the tropical and the temperate zones; there are marked seasonal changes of temperature, but it is never very cold

Sufism a branch of Islam whose adherents follow a path of strict self-discipline and devote themselves to prayer in an attempt to know Allah directly through mystical experience

Sunni one of the two principal branches of Islam (the other is Shia). It is made up of people who believe in the legitimacy of the first of the four caliphs who followed the prophet Muhammad as the leaders of Islam. Shiites believe that only descendants of the Prophet's grandson Ali are rightful leaders.

supercontinent a former landmass from which smaller continental blocks have broken away, for example, the former northern supercontinent Laurasia and the former southern supercontinent Gondwanaland

Surrealism art in which actuality was fused with dreams and the unconscious experience

sweet potato a plant (*Ipomoea batatas*) grown for its starchy, sweet tasting tuberous roots

syncretism the combination of elements of different religions

T

Tabaski the Wolof term, used throughout West Africa, for the Islamic festival of Eid al-Adha, the commemoration of Abraham's willingness to sacrifice his son Isaac

taboo a restriction or prohibition, established by convention in a culture

tangata a Maori term for the indigenous people of New Zealand

tapa bark cloth

tapu a Polynesian concept of sacredness from which the word taboo is derived

taro (**taro tru**) the edible corm of the tropical plant *Colocasia esculenta*

tectonic activity activity associated with the movement of the plates that form the lithosphere

teff (**taff, taf**) a cereal crop (*Eragrostis tef*) native to northeastern Africa

temperate the climate in the mid-latitudes, between the warm tropics and the cold polar regions; temperatures are generally mild, with marked seasons such as summer, fall, and winter

temperature range the difference between maximum and minimum temperatures

terra-cotta a hard, fired, and waterproof ceramic clay used in pottery and building construction

terranes areas of old, stable rock

tiki wood and stone carvings of humanlike forms; also, Maori mythology refers to Tiki as the first man

timbila a form of xylophone

toothed whales species of whales that capture food by grabbing it with their teeth

township government-built shantytowns put up in the apartheid era in South Africa to house people evicted from "white" towns

trade winds normally easterly winds over the equatorial Pacific Ocean

Trekboer (Afrikaans: "migrant farmer") an Afrikaner farmer who settled inland in the eighteenth and nineteenth centuries

trevallys a number of species of edible fish

trypanosomiasis *see* **sleeping sickness**

tsetse fly an insect that carries parasites, which pass directly to both people and cattle

tuberculosis a serious bacterial infection of the lungs

typhoons tropical atmospheric disturbances that are characterized by severe winds and heavy rain

U

Umhlanga an annual ceremony performed by unmarried girls to pay homage to the Queen Mother of the Swazi people

United Nations (UN) a world organization of states, formed in 1945, to which nearly every independent state in the world belongs

urbanization the process by which the proportion of a country's population living in towns and cities grows, while the rural population declines; the process of city formation and growth

V

vernacular a spoken rather than written language

volcano a vent in the surface of the Earth through which magma and associated gases and ash erupt

Voortrekker (Afrikaans: "pioneer") an Afrikaaner who took part in the Great Trek (1836-1845)

W

waiata Maori word for song

wattle-and-daub a building technique that uses clay plastered on a latticework made of sticks

welfare state a social and economic system based on the state provision of, and responsibility for, such things as health care, pensions, and unemployment benefits

whanau in Maori, a family consisting of the nuclear family and their blood relatives; an extended family

wharenui Maori meeting house where the spirits of ancestors are believed to reside

Y

yavusa the largest kin-based political unit in the Fijian system

yaws a chronic, infectious, bacterial disease of the skin

yellow fever an acute viral disease carried by mosquitoes

Z

zimbabwe a house or enclosure

Further Research

WORLD GEOGRAPHY, HISTORY, AND CULTURAL EXPRESSION

Boyle, Kevin, and Juliet Sheen. *Freedom of Religion and Belief: A World Report*. New York: Routledge, 1997.

Brown, James H., and Mark V. Lomolino. *Biogeography*. Sunderland, MA: Sinauer Associates Publishers, 1998.

Butzer, Karl W. *Geomorphology from the Earth*. Reading, MA: Addison-Wesley Educational Publishers, 1976.

Chilvers, Ian. *A Dictionary of Twentieth Century Art*. New York: Oxford University Press, 1999.

Clark, Audrey N. *Longman Dictionary of Geography: Human and Physical*. New York: Longman, 1985.

The Europa World Year Book 2005. London: Europa Publications, 2005.

Gran, Peter. *Beyond Eurocentrism: A New View of World History*. Syracuse, NY: Syracuse University Press, 1998.

Hughes, J. Donald, ed. *The Face of the Earth: Environment and World History*. Armonk, NY: M. E. Sharpe, 2000.

Kraemer, Hendrik. *World Cultures and World Religions*. Philadelphia: Westminster Press, 1960.

Lydolph, Paul E. *Weather and Climate*. Lanham, MD: Rowman and Littlefield, 1985.

National Geographic Family Reference Atlas. Washington, D.C.: National Geographic Society, 2004.

Oliver, John E., and W. Fairbridge, eds. *The Encyclopedia of Climatology*. New York: Van Nostrand Reinhold, 1987.

Robbins, Keith. *The World since 1945: A Concise History*. Oxford, UK: Oxford University Press, 1998.

The Statesman's Yearbook 2004: The Politics, Cultures, and Economies of the World. New York: St. Martin's Press, 2004.

Strahler, Arthur N., and Alan H. Strahler. *Modern Physical Geography*. 3rd ed. Hoboken, NJ: John Wiley and Sons, 1987.

Times Atlas of the World: Comprehensive Edition. New York: Crown Publishers, 1999.

Trewartha, Glenn T., and Lyle H. Horn. *An Introduction to Climate*. 5th ed. New York: McGraw-Hill, 1980.

Walker, R. B. J. *Culture, Ideology, and World Order*. Boulder, CO: Westview Press, 1986.

TRAVEL LITERATURE

Atkinson, Lee, et al. *Frommer's Australia 2010*. Hoboken, NJ: Frommers, 2009.

Bainbridge, James. *South Africa, Lesotho, and Swaziland*. London: Lonely Planet, 2009.

Balseiro, Isabel, and Tobias Hecht, eds. *South Africa: A Traveler's Literary Companion*. Berkeley, CA: Whereabouts Press, 2009.

Blond, Becca et al. *Lonely Planet Madagascar and Comoros*. London: Lonely Planet Publications, 2008.

Briggs, Philip. *Ethiopia*. Chalfont St. Peter: Bradt Travel Guides, 2009.

Briggs, Philip. *Ghana*. Chalfont St. Peter: Bradt Travel Guides, 2007.

Cole, Geert. *South Pacific and Micronesia*. London: Lonely Planet Publications, 2006.

de Bruyn, Pippa. *Frommer's South Africa*. Hoboken, NJ: Frommers, 2007.

Fitzpatrick, Mary. *East Africa*. London: Lonely Planet, 2009.

Fodor's. *Tahiti and French Polynesia*. New York: Fodor's, 2008.

Ham, Anthony. *West Africa*. London: Lonely Planet Publications, 2006.

Irwin, Aisling, and Colum Wilson. *Cape Verde Islands*. Chalfont St. Peter: Bradt Travel Guides, 2009.

Lambkin, David. *National Geographic Traveler: South Africa*. Washington, DC: National Geographic Society, 2009.

Lobello, Rick Louis. *Guide to Rwanda's Volcanoes National Park: Home to Critically Endangered Mountain Gorillas*. Scotts Valley, CA: CreateSpace, 2009.

Masters, Tom. *Mauritius, Reunion and Seychelles*. London: Lonely Planet Publications, 2007.

McIntyre, Chris, and Susan McIntyre. *Zanzibar*. Chalfont St. Peter: Bradt Travel Guides, 2009.

McKinnon, Rowan, Dean Starnes, and Jean-Bernard Carillet. *Papua New Guinea and Solomon Islands*. London: Lonely Planet Publications, 2008.

Mudd, Tony, Paul Whitfield, and Laura Harper. *The Rough Guide to New Zealand*. New York: Rough Guides, 2008.

Osborn, Ian. *The Rough Guide to Fiji*. New York: Rough Guides, 2008.

Rough Guides. *The Rough Guide to First-Time Africa*. New York: Rough Guides, 2007.

Rubin, Jeff. *Antarctica*. London: Lonely Planet Publications, 2008.

Smith, Rolf. *National Geographic Traveler: Australia*. Washington, DC: National Geographic Society, 2008.

Smitz, Paul. *Samoan Islands and Tonga*. London: Lonely Planet Publications, 2006.

Trillo, Richard. *The Rough Guide to West Africa*. New York: Rough Guides, 2008.

West, Ben. *Cameroon*. Chalfont St. Peter: Bradt Travel Guides, 2008.

Williams, Lizzie. *Namibia Handbook*. Bath: Footprint Handbooks, 2009.

Williams, Lizzie. *Nigeria*. Chalfont St. Peter: Bradt Travel Guides, 2008.

SUB-SAHARAN AFRICA: GEOGRAPHY

Adams, William, Andrew Goudie, and Antony Orme, eds. *The Physical Geography of Africa*. New York: Oxford University Press, 1999.

Aryeetey-Attoh, Samuel, et al. *Geography of Sub-Saharan Africa*. Upper Saddle River, NJ: Prentice Hall, 2009.

Beckwith, Carol, and Angela Fisher. *Faces of Africa*. Washington, DC: National Geographic Society, 2004.

Chrétien, Jean-Pierre. *The Great Lakes of Africa: Two Thousand Years of History*. New York: Zone Books, 2006.

Col, Roy, and Harm J. de Blij. *Africa South of the Sahara: A Regional Geography*. New York: Oxford University Press, 2006.

Heine, Bernd, and Derek Nurse, eds. *A Linguistic Geography of Africa*. New York: Cambridge University Press, 2008.

Schluter, Thomas. *Geological Atlas of Africa*. Heidelberg: Springer, 2008.

Sinclair, Ian, et al. *Birds of Africa South of the Sahara: A Comprehensive Illustrated Field Guide*. London: Random House Struik, 2008.

SUB-SAHARAN AFRICA: HISTORY

Arnold, Guy. *Historical Dictionary of Civil Wars in Africa*. Lanham, MD: The Scarecrow Press, 2007.

Arnold, Guy. *Africa: A Modern History*. London: Atlantic Books, 2005.

Collins, Robert O. *Historical Dictionary of Pre-Colonial Africa*. Lanham, MD: The Scarecrow Press, 2001.

Collins, Robert O., and James M. Burns. *A History of Sub-Saharan Africa*. New York: Cambridge University Press, 2007.

Connah, Graham. *Forgotten Africa: An Introduction to Its Archaeology*. New York: Routledge, 2004.

Coombes, Annie E. *History after Apartheid: Visual Culture and Public Memory in a Democratic South Africa*. Durham, NC: Duke University Press, 2003.

Davidson, Basil. *West Africa before the Colonial Era: A History to 1850*. New York: Longman, 1998.

Ehret, Christopher. *The Civilizations of Africa: A History to 1800*. Charlottesville: University of Virginia Press, 2002.

Ingram, Scott. *History's Villains: Idi Amin*. Farmington Hills, MI: Blackbirch Press, 2003.

Lester, Alan. *From Colonization to Democracy: A New Historical Geography of South Africa*. London: I. B. Tauris, 1998.

Lindsay, Lisa A. *Captives as Commodities: The Transatlantic Slave Trade*. Upper Saddle River, NJ: Prentice Hall, 2007.

Marcus, Harold G. *A History of Ethiopia*. Berkeley: University of California Press, 2002.

Maxon, Robert M. *East Africa: An Introductory History*. Morgantown: West Virginia University Press, 2009.

Mockler, Anthony. *Haile Selassie's War*. Oxford: Signal Books, 2003.

Pavitt, Nigel. *Kenya: A Country in the Making, 1880–1940*. New York: W. W. Norton, 2008.

Prunier, Gerard. *Africa's World War: Congo, the Rwandan Genocide, and the Making of a Continental Catastrophe*. New York: Oxford University Press, 2008.

Reef, Catherine. *This Our Dark Country: The American Settlers of Liberia*. New York: Clarion Books, 2002.

Robinson, David. *Muslim Societies in African History*. New York: Cambridge University Press, 2004.

Shillington, Kevin. *History of Africa*. New York: Palgrave Macmillan, 2005.

Visona, Monica B., Robin Poynor, Herbert M. Cole, and Preston Biler. *A History of Art in Africa*. Upper Saddle River, NJ: Prentice Hall, 2007.

SUB-SAHARAN AFRICA: GENERAL AND CURRENT AFFAIRS

Akindes, Francis. *The Roots of the Military-Political Crises in Côte d'Ivoire*. Uppsala: Nordic Africa Institute, 2005.

Aligwekwe, Pauline E. *The Continuity of Traditional Values in the African Society: The Igbò of Nigeria*. Bloomington, IN: Xlibris, 2008.

Apter, Andrew. *The Pan-African Nation: Oil and the Spectacle of Culture in Nigeria*. Chicago: University of Chicago Press, 2005.

Barsby, Jane. *Kenya—Culture Smart!: The Essential Guide to Customs and Culture*. London: Kuperard, 2007.

Beckwith, Carol, Angela Fisher, and Graham Hancock. *African Ark: People and Ancient Cultures of Ethiopia and the Horn of Africa*. New York: Harry N. Abrams, 1990.

Cameroon Country Study Guide. Washington, DC: International Business Publications, 2003.

Falola, Toyin. *Culture and Customs of Nigeria*. Westport, CT: Greenwood Press, 2008.

Iliffe, John. *The African AIDS Epidemic: A History*. Athens: Ohio University Press, 2006.

Lamin, Sylvester Amara. *Women and Development in Sierra Leone*. Frederick, MD: PublishAmerica, 2007.

Lewis, Ioan. *Understanding Somalia and Somaliland: Culture, History, Society*. New York: Columbia University Press, 2008.

Little, Peter D. *Somalia: Economy without State*. Bloomington: Indiana University Press, 2003.

Magubane, Peter. *Vanishing Cultures of South Africa*. New York: Rizzoli, 1998.

Matateyou, Emmanuel. *An Anthology of Myths, Legends, and Folktales from Cameroon: Storytelling in Africa*. New York: Edwin Mellen Press, 1997.

Rake, Alan. *African Leaders*. Lanham, MD: The Scarecrow Press, 2001.

Rotberg, Robert I., ed. *Battling Terrorism in the Horn of Africa*. Washington, DC: Brookings Institution Press, 2005.

Salm, Steven J., and Toyin Falola. *Culture and Customs of Ghana*. Westport, CT: Greenwood Press, 2002.

Simpson, Andrew, ed. *Language and National Identity in Africa*. New York: Oxford University Press, 2008.

Sirleaf, Ellen Johnson. *This Child Will Be Great: Memoir of a Remarkable Life by Africa's First Woman President*. New York: Harper, 2009.

Smith, Ian. *Bitter Harvest: Zimbabwe and the Aftermath of Its Independence*. London: John Blake, 2008.

Woodward, Peter. *The Horn of Africa: Politics and International Relations*. London: I. B. Tauris, 2002.

AUSTRALASIA: GEOGRAPHY

Egerton, Louise, and Jiri Lochman. *Wildlife of Australia*. London: Orion, 2010.

Hillstrom, Kevin, and Laurie Collier Hillstrom. *Australia, Oceania, and Antarctica: A Continental Overview of Environmental Issues*. Santa Barbara, CA: ABC-CLIO, 2003.

Johnson, David. *The Geology of Australia*. Cambridge: Cambridge University Press, 2004.

McGonigal, David, ed. *Antarctica: Secrets of the Southern Continent*. Richmond Hill, ON: Firefly Books, 2008.

Roy, Tui De, and Mark Jones. *New Zealand: A Natural History*. Richmond Hill, ON: Firefly Books, 2006.

Sturman, Andrew P., and Nigel J. Tapper. *The Weather and Climate of Australia and New Zealand*. New York: Oxford University Press, 2006.

Vernon, J. E. N. *A Reef in Time: The Great Barrier Reef from Beginning to End*. Cambridge, MA: Harvard University Press, 2010.

Shirihai, Hadoram. *The Complete Guide to Antarctic Wildlife: Birds and Marine Mammals of the Antarctic Continent and the Southern Ocean*. Princeton, NJ: Princeton University Press, 2008.

AUSTRALASIA: HISTORY

Brooking, Tom. *The History of New Zealand*. Westport, CT: Greenwood Press, 2004.

Dorney, Sean. *Papua New Guinea: People, Politics, and History since 1975*. North Sydney, Australia: Random House, 2000.

Griffin, James, Hank Nelson, and Stewart Firth. *Papua New Guinea: A Political History*. London: Pan Books, 1999.

Gurney, Alan. *The Race to the White Continent: Voyages to the Antarctic*. New York: W. W. Norton, 2002.

Isaacs, Jennifer. *Australian Dreaming: 40,000 Years of Aboriginal History*. Chatswood, NSW: New Holland Publishing Australia, 2006.

King, Michael. *Nga Iwi o Te Motu: 1,000 Years of Maori History*. Auckland: Raupo Publishing (NZ), 1997.

Macintyre, Stuart. *A Concise History of Australia*. New York: Cambridge University Press, 2004.

Phillips, Jock, and Terry Hearn. *Settlers: New Zealand Immigrants from England, Ireland, and Scotland 1800–1945*. Auckland: Auckland University Press, 2008.

Thomas, Nicholas. *Cook : The Extraordinary Voyages of Captain James Cook*. New York: Walker, 2004.

Waiko, John Dademo. *A Short History of Papua New Guinea*. Victoria, Australia: Oxford University Press, 1993.

AUSTRALASIA: GENERAL AND CURRENT AFFAIRS

Australia Country Study Guide. Washington, DC: International Business Publications, 2009.

Corazza, Jago. *The Last Men: Journey among the Tribes of New Guinea*. Vercelli, Italy: White Star Publishers, 2008.

Kleinert, Sylvia, and Margo Neale, eds. *The Oxford Companion to Aboriginal Art and Culture*. New York: Oxford University Press, 2001.

Mcintosh, Tracey. *Culture and Customs of New Zealand*. Westport, CT: Greenwood Press, 2009.

Reed, A. W., and Buddy Mikaere, eds. *Taonga Tuku Iho: An Illustrated Encyclopedia of Maori Culture*. Auckland: New Holland Publishers (NZ), 2002.

OCEANIA: GEOGRAPHY

Bennetts, Peter, and Tony Wheeler. *Time and Tide: The Islands of Tuvalu*. London: Lonely Planet Publications, 2001.

Darwin, Charles. *The Voyage of the Beagle: Journal of Researches into the Natural History and Geology of the Countries Visited during the Voyage of H.M.S. Beagle Round the World*. New York: Modern Library, 2001.

Fitzpatrick, Judith M. *Endangered Peoples of Oceania: Struggles to Survive and Thrive*. Westport, CT: Greenwood Press, 2000.

Howe, Kerry, R. *Nature, Culture, and History: The "Knowing" of Oceania*. Honolulu: University of Hawaii Press, 2000.

Oliver, Douglas L. *The Pacific Islands*. Honolulu: University of Hawaii Press, 1989.

Strathern, Andrew J., et al. *Oceania: An Introduction to the Cultures and Identities of Pacific Islanders*. Durham, NC: Carolina Academic Press, 2002.

West, Barbara A. *Encyclopedia of the Peoples of Asia and Oceania*. New York: Facts on File, 2008.

Whistler, Arthur W. *Plants in Samoan Culture*. Honolulu: University of Hawaii Press, 2005.

OCEANIA: HISTORY

D'Arcy, Paul. *The People of the Sea: Environment, Identity, and History in Oceania*. Honolulu: University of Hawaii Press, 2008.

Fischer, Steven Roger. *A History of the Pacific Islands*. New York: Palgrave Macmillan, 2002.

Howe, K. R., Brij V. Lal, and Robert C. Kiste, eds. *Tides of History: The Pacific Islands in the Twentieth Century*. Honolulu: University of Hawaii Press, 1994.

Irwin, Geoffrey. *The Prehistoric Exploration and Colonisation of the Pacific*. New York: Cambridge University Press, 1994.

Kirch, Patrick Vinton. *On the Road of the Winds: An Archaeological History of the Pacific Islands before European Contact*. Berkeley: University of California Press, 2002.

Kirk, Robert W. *Pitcairn Island, the Bounty Mutineers, and Their Descendants: A History*. Jefferson, NC: McFarland, 2008.

Lal, Brij V. *Broken Waves: A History of the Fiji Islands in the Twentieth Century*. Honolulu: University of Hawaii Press, 1992.

Maretu. *Cannibals and Converts: Radical Change in the Cook Islands*. Translated by Marjorie Tuainekore Crocombe. Suva: IPS Publications, 2001.

Oliver, Douglas L. *Polynesia: In Early Historic Times*. Honolulu: Bess Press, 2002.

Wiest, Andrew A., and Gregory Louis Mattson. *The Pacific War: Campaigns of World War II*. Osceola, WI: Motorbooks International, 2001.

OCEANIA: GENERAL AND CURRENT AFFAIRS

Bonnemaison, Joel, ed. *Arts of Vanuatu*. Honolulu: University of Hawaii Press, 1996.

D'Alleva, Anne. *Arts of the Pacific Islands*. New York: Harry N. Abrams, 1998.

Eimke, Andrea, and Susanne Kuchler. *Tivaivai: The Social Fabric of the Cook Islands*. London: British Museum Press, 2009.

Fischer, H. *Sound-Producing Instruments in Oceania*. Boroko: Institute of Papua New Guinea Studies, 1986.

Stevenson, Robert Louis. *A Footnote to History: Eight Years of Trouble in Samoa*. Charleston, SC: BiblioBazaar, 2009.

Trompf, Garry. *The Religions of Oceania*. New York: Routledge, 1995.

White, Geoffrey M. *Identity through History: Living Stories in a Solomon Islands Society*. New York: Cambridge University Press, 2003.

PERIODICALS AND OTHER MEDIA

Antarctic Journal of the United States. National Science Foundation. www.nsf.gov/od/opp/antarct/journal/start.jsp

Australian Archaeology. Australian Archaeological Association. www.australianarchaeologicalassociation.com

The Economist. London. www.economist.com

Journal of Pacific Studies. University of the South Pacific, Fiji. www.usp.ac.fj/editorial/jpacs_new/index.html

The Journal of Geology. University of Chicago Press. www.journals.uchicago.edu/loi/jg

The Journal of Pacific History. London. www.tandf.co.uk/journals/titles/00223344.asp

Journal of the Polynesian Society. The Polynesian Society. www.jps.auckland.ac.nz

Micronesian Journal of the Humanities and Social Sciences. Albury, Australia. marshall.csu.edu.au/MJHSS

Oceania. Sydney, Australia. www.arts.usyd.edu.au/publications/oceania/oceania1.htm

People and Culture in Oceania. Japanese Society for Oceanic Studies. http://wwwsoc.nii.ac.jp/jsos/mco-e.html

ELECTRONIC RESOURCES

Australian History. www.australianhistory.org

BBC World Service. www.bbc.co.uk/worldservice (world news in several languages from the British Broadcasting Service).

British Antarctic Survey. www.antarctica.ac.uk

Country Studies, Federal Research Division, Library of Congress. http://countrystudies.us (for information about the countries of the regions).

Geographia.com. www.geographia.com

Newspapers Online. www.newspapers.com

New Zealand History Online. www.nzhistory.net.nz

Pacific Remote Islands Marine National Monument www.fws.gov/pacificremoteislandsmarinemonument

United States Antarctic Program. www.usap.gov

The World Bank. www.worldbank.org/

The World Factbook. CIA. www.odci.gov/cia/publications/factbook/index.html

THEMATIC INDEXES

Place-Names Index

Numbers in **boldface** refer to volume numbers; those in *italic* refer to illustrations:

A

Abemama Atoll **9:**1203, *1207*
Abidjan **3:**294, 329, 363, 394, *394,* 400, *403,* 405, *407,* 409
  architecture **3:**398–399, 405
  climate **3:**304
  history **3:**395, 396, 405
  as "Paris of Africa" **3:**398, 405
  population **3:**405
  university **3:**403
Abomey *see* Danhome
Abuja **1:**103, 104, 119, 123
  architecture **1:**107, *113*
  population **1:**10, 119
  slum demolition **1:**118
Accra **3:**308, 381, 383–384, 423
  climate **3:**304, 305
  history **3:**313, 319, *320,* 329, 373, 374, 383
  Nkrumah memorial **3:***374*
  population **3:**294, 383
Achuago site **8:**1029
Adal (Adel) **4:**462, 464, 467, 540
Adamawa State **1:**11, 42, 47, 57
Adamstown **9:**1163, *1239*
Addis Ababa **4:**438, 439, 445, 475, 479, 480, 512, 512–513, 517
  climate **4:***447*
  cultural activity **4:**506, 507
  history **4:**502, 512, 514
Adelaide **10:**1381, 1393, 1397, 1415
  history **10:**1348, 1350, 1357, 1358
Admiralty Islands **8:**1015, 1027
Afadjato, Mount **3:**295, *296*
Afars and Issas, French Territory of **4:**470, 475, 479, 480

Ajache *see* Porto-Novo
Akagera National Park **5:***594, 700*
Aksum (city) **4:**452, 454, 459, 508, 517
Albert, Lake **6:**739
Aldabra Island **6:**649, 729
  giant tortoise **6:**736, *818*
Alice Springs **10:**1307, *1343, 1362*
  climate **10:**1321, 1322
Alo **9:**1162, 1186, 1290
Alofi **9:**1160, 1162, 1290
  cyclone damage **9:**1168, 1236
American Samoa **9:**1192–1193
  cyclone hazard **9:**1168
  geography **9:**1158, 1163, 1192
  history **9:**1174, 1187, 1192, 1245, 1252
  peoples **9:**1189–1190, 1191, 1193
Amundsen-Scott South Pole Station **10:**1326, 1328, *1429*
Angola **5:**610–627
  art and architecture **5:**619–620, 622, 624
  climate **5:**582, 588–589, *591,* 610, 624
  cultural expression **5:**619–621
  daily life **5:**622–623
  economy **5:**611–612, 625–627
  education **5:**623, 625
  family and society **5:**623
  festivals and ceremonies **5:**621
  flag **5:**612
  flora and fauna **5:**592–595
  food and drink **5:***620,* 621
  geography **5:**580–584, 610
  geology **5:**586–587, 625
  government and political parties **5:**612, 614
  health and welfare **5:**623

history
  chronology **5:**613
  Congo Wars **5:**618, 670, 678, 705
  modern **5:**610, 615–618, 669
  precolonial **5:**597–599, 600–604, 608
  independence **5:**614, 616, 624, 625
  languages **5:**607, 619
  literature **5:**619
  music **5:**620–621
  peoples **5:**607, 608, 612, 619, 622
  population **5:**610–611
  religion **5:**612, 622
  resources **5:**610, 622, 625–626
  transportation and communication **5:**612, 624, 627
Anjouan Island **6:**728, 736, 750, 753, 754, 755, 758, 798
Annobón **1:**10, 15, 17, 21, 68, 76, 138
  local government **1:**72
Antananarivo **6:**728, 742, *765,* 769, 771
  architecture **6:**767, 771
Antarctica **10:**1329, 1418–1433
  chronology **10:**1422
  climate **10:**1314, 1326–1328, 1336, 1337, 1418, 1425
  climate change **10:**1328, 1339, 1418, 1425, 1428, 1430
  daily life **10:**1428–1429
  economy **10:**1430–1433
  flora and fauna **10:**1336–1339, 1418, 1432
  geography **10:**1302–1303, 1312–1315, 1418, 1430
  geology **10:**1319–1320
  government **10:**1419, 1423
  history **10:**1352–1354, 1418, 1424–1425

population **10:**1419
  resources **10:**1302, 1419, 1430–1431, 1432
  territorial claims **10:**1419, *1420–1421,* 1423
  transportation **10:**1419, *1428,* 1433
Antarctic Ocean **10:**1411
Antarctic Peninsula **10:**1311, 1314, 1319, 1320, 1418, 1424, 1433
Antisirabé **6:***769, 770*
Antsiranana (formerly Diego Suaraz) **6:**728, 742
Apapa **1:**124
Apia **9:**1163, 1167, 1251, 1252, 1254
  history **9:**1174, 1187, 1245, 1252
Apolima Strait **9:**1162–1163
Arabia **4:**452–453, 454, 459, 462, 551
Argentina **10:**1426, 1433
Arnhem Land **10:**1300, 1304, 1305, 1343, 1344, 1356
Arusha **6:**837, 838, 839, 841
Ascension **7:**872, 880, 938
Asmara **4:**439, 445, *490,* 491, 493
  Italian influences **4:**487, 490, 493
Assab **4:**439, 465, 487, 495
Assal, Lake **4:**436, 438, *472*
Atafu Atoll **9:**1161, 1256
Atakora Mountains (Massif) **3:**295, 304, 339, 347
Atherton Plateau **10:**1309, 1310
Auckland **9:**1159, 1229, 1235
  cathedrals **9:**1123
  festivals **9:**1221
  history **9:**1185, 1229
Australasia **10:**1300
Australia **8:**1034, 1035; **9:**1183, 1185, 1279, 1284; **10:**1358–1415
  art and architecture **10:**1318, 1374–1376, 1381, 1396, 1401, 1405

Australia (continued)
climate **10:**1305, 1321–1325, 1329, *1406*, 1408, 1410, 1411
climate change **10:**1325, 1371
climatic hazards **10:**1323–1324
cultural expression **10:**1372–1383
daily life **10:**1384–1394
economy **10:**1358, 1360, 1369, 1371, 1406–1416
education **10:**1370, 1392–1393, 1397, 1398, 1401, 1405, 1406
family and society **10:**1387–1393
federation **10:**1350–1351, 1358, 1365, 1368, 1388, 1395, 1401, 1406
festivals and ceremonies **10:***1356, 1357,* 1380–1381, 1397
flag **10:**1359
flora and fauna **10:**1329–1335, 1374
food and drink **10:**1383
geography **10:**1300–1301, 1304–1311
geology **10:**1316–1318
government and political parties **10:**1360, 1364, 1368, 1371, 1407
health and welfare **10:**1370, 1390–1391, 1406, 1407, 1408
history
British First Fleet landing **10:**1344, 1346, 1347, 1358, 1372, 1380, 1383, 1385, 1387, 1404
chronology **10:**1363
colonial **10:**1347–1351, 1358
European explorers **10:**1344–1346
modern **10:**1365–1371, 1388–1389, 1398, 1400–1401, 1402, 1404–1405, 1406
languages **10:**1356, 1362, 1372
literature **10:**1372–1373, 1379
music **10:**1377–1378, 1381
Nauru **8:**1074, 1079, 1080, 1081, 1083
Papua New Guinea **8:**1098, 1104, 1105, 1117, 1118, 1122

peoples **10:**1340–1343, 1355–1357, 1362, 1368, 1370, 1371, 1378, 1384, 1387, 1388–1389, 1397, 1403, 1405
population **10:**1359–1360, 1387
religion **10:**1350, 1362, 1384–1386
resources **10:**1306, 1358, 1409–1410
Solomon Islands **8:**1133, 1134
states and territories **10:**1362, 1388
transportation and communication **10:**1360, 1398, 1399, 1401, 1405, *1413,* 1415
Australian Alps **10:**1311, 1323, 1325
Australian Capital Territory **10:**1356, 1396
see also Canberra
Austral Islands **9:**1163
Awasa **4:***496,* 515
Ayers Rock **10:**1307, 1413, 1418

B

Babelthuap Island **8:**1015, 1032, 1093, 1096
Bafing River **2:**148
Bafoulabé **2:**148
Bairiki **9:**1161, 1207
Bakassi Peninsula **1:**56, 65
Bakau **2:***192,* 201
Baker Island **9:**1263, 1286
Bakoye River **2:**148
Bakrlavento Islands **2:**153
Bamako **3:**350, 395
Bamenda **1:***50,* 60
Banaba Island **9:**1198, 1202, 1203, 1284
Banana (port) **5:**605, 681
Banfora **3:***352,* 367
Bangui **5:**583, 652, 654, 657, 661
architecture **5:**654
climate **5:***591*
history **5:**604
Bani River **1:**8
Banjul **2:**150, 173, 192, 197, 201, 203
architecture **2:***197,* 198, *200*
history **2:**150, 173, 192, 197, 201
Bani River **1:**8
Barotseland **6:**739, 746, 844, 849
Bass Strait **10:**1301, 1311, 1342

Basutoland *see* Lesotho
Bata **1:**76, 77
Bathurst *see* Banjul
Bechuanaland *see* Botswana
Beira **6:**726, 733, 785, 808, 810, 815
history **6:**740, 741, 745
Belgian Congo **5:**606, 633, 662, 667, 668, 671, 672, 703, 704, 712
see also Congo Free State
Benguela **5:**582, *611,* 615
Benin **3:**330–349
art and architecture **1:**33–34, *35,* 106; **3:**338–339, *344*
climate **3:**302–305, 330
cultural expression **3:**338–340
daily life **3:**341–343
economy **3:**336–337, 343, 346–349
education **3:**343, 347
family and society **3:**341–342
festivals and ceremonies **3:**339
flag **3:**332
flora and fauna **3:**306–309
food and drink **3:**339–340
geography **3:**292–299, 330
geology **3:**300–301
government and political parties **3:**330, 331, 334, 335–337, 346, 347
health and welfare **3:**342–343
history
chronology **3:**333
colonial **3:**321–326, 328, 335
early **1:**27, 31, 49; **3:**313, 322
modern **3:**330, 335–337
slave trade **3:**321
independence **3:**330, 335, 346
literature **3:**338
music **3:***338,* 339
peoples **3:**327–329, 332, 335, 338, 339, 341, 345, 346
population **3:**331
religion **3:**332, 335, 339, 341, *343*
resources **3:**330, 347–348
transportation and communication **3:**331, 335, *346,* 349
Benin City **1:**33, 34, 35, 38
Benue River **1:**8, 10, 11, 12, 13, 14, 19, 65, 129

Berbera **4:**440, 446, 540, 544, 553
Biafra **1:**48, *102,* 103; **3:**324, 396
Bijagós Archipelago **2:**151, 160, 173, 223, 227
Bikini Atoll **8:***1018,* 1059
Bimbia **1:**46
Bingerville **3:**395, 405
Bintimani Peak (Loma Mansa) **2:**152
Bioko **1:**15, 17, 21, 25, 68, *70,* 74, 75
history **1:**26, 73, 138
local government **1:**72
Malabo **1:**76, 77
Bismarck Archipelago **8:**1012, 1014, 1015
charting **8:**1033
early Melanesians **8:**1026
German claims **8:**1103, *1105*
World War II **8:**1105
Bismarck Sea **8:**1012
Bissau **2:**151, 169, 173, *220,* 222, 223, *224,* 225, 227, *228, 229*
Black Mountain **10:**1396
Black Volta **3:**292, 294, 355
Blantyre **6:**727, 781, 784, 786
Blue Mountains **10:**1310, 1311, 1348
Blue Nile River **4:**439, 456, 515
Boa Vista island **2:**153, 191
Bobo-Dioulasso **3:**297–298, 358, 359, 362, 367
Boer republics *see* Orange Free State; Transvaal
Bolama **2:**173, 227
Boma **5:**580, 606
Bomi Lake **2:***232*
Bondi Beach **10:**1404, *1405*
Bong Mountains **2:**154, 247
Bonny **1:**20, 27, 129
Bonny River **1:**8
Boosaaso **4:**440, 553
Bora Bora **9:***1159,* 1163, 1181, 1186
Bosumtwi, Lake **3:**295, *368*
Botany Bay **10:**1346, *1347,* 1404, 1405
Botswana **7:**902–913
art and architecture **7:***902,* 908–909
climate **7:**878–881, 884–885, 902
cultural expression **7:**908–909
daily life **7:**910
economy **7:**902, 903, 907, 912–913, 936

family and society **7**:910
festivals, food, and drink **7**:909
flag **7**:904
flora and fauna **7**:882–885, 913
geography **7**:870–873, 902
geology **7**:876–877
government and political parties **7**:903–904, 906, 921
health, welfare, and education **7**:910
history
 chronology **7**:905
 modern **7**:896, 897, 902, 907
 precolonial **7**:886, 888, 889, 902
independence **7**:902, 906, 907, 909, 911
languages **7**:905, 908
literature **7**:908
music **7**:909
peoples **7**:900, 901, 902, 904, 910
population **7**:903
religion **7**:905, 910
resources **7**:902, 912
transportation and communication **7**:904, 913
Bouaké **3**:297, 399, 400, 403, *409*
Bouar **5**:646, 652
Bougainville **8**:1012, 1015, 1020, 1035, 1113, 1118, 1120, 1124
 rebellion **8**:1098, 1105, 1119
Boundou region **2**:151
Bounty Bay **9**:*1238*
Bouvet Island **10**:1315, 1328, 1337, 1423, 1426
Boyoma Falls **5**:580, 583, 604
Brava Island **2**:153, 190
Brazil, Portuguese slave trade **5**:598, *601*, 602, 624
Brazzaville **1**:90; **5**:580, 583, 584, 677, 692, 693, 694, 695, 697
 climatic hazards **5**:590–591
 cultural expression **5**:689, 690
 history **5**:604, 682, 687, 688, 694
Brisbane **10**:1310, 1381, 1387, 1398, 1415
 history **10**:1347, 1348, 1398
Britain *see* Great Britain
British Cameroon **1**:50, 55, 56,

60, 62, 63, 64
British Central African Protectorate **6**:745, 774, 779, 780, 784
British East Africa Protectorate **4**:466, 469, 518, 523–525, 527, 533, 535, 536, 546
British Federation of Rhodesia and Nyasaland **6**:774, 779, 844, 849–850, 855; **7**:986, 991–992, 999
 see also Malawi; Zambia
British Indian Ocean Territory **6**:724, *728*, 729, 749, 826
British New Guinea *see* Papua New Guinea
British Somaliland **4**:440, 465, 487, 493, 502, 512, 540, 546, 548, 551, 552
Broken Hill **10**:1350, 1409
Bujumbura **5**:639, 641, 642, 643, 645, 703, 713
Bulawayo **7**:990, 995, 996
Burkina Faso **3**:350–367
 art and architecture **3**:357–358, *359*, 363, 367
 Benin border dispute **3**:336
 climate **3**:302–305, 350
 cultural expression **3**:357–359
 daily life **3**:360–362
 economy **3**:352, 364–367
 education **3**:362
 emigrants to Ivory Coast **3**:402
 family and society **3**:360–361
 festivals and ceremonies **3**:358–359, 367
 flag **3**:351
 flora and fauna **3**:306–309
 food and drink **3**:359
 geography **3**:292–299, 350
 geology **3**:300–301
 government and political parties **3**:351, 354
 health and welfare **3**:342, 356, 361–362
 history
  chronology **3**:353
  early kingdoms **3**:310–312, 314–318, 319, 322, 324, 326, 350, 355, 357, 359
  French rule **3**:318, 350, 355, 357, 360, 363, 364
  modern **3**:350, 355–356, 359, 364
 independence **3**:350, 354, 355, 364
 literature **3**:357

music **3**:358
name change **3**:355
 see also Upper Volta
peoples **3**:323, 327–329, 350, 352, 355, 357, 360
population **3**:351
religion **3**:352, 359, 360, 361, 363
resources **3**:350, 365
transportation and communication **3**:352, *362*, 363, *364*, 367
Burley Griffin, Lake **10**:1395, 1396
Burundi **5**:628–645
 art and architecture **5**:636–637, 642
 climate **5**:589, 590, 628
 cultural expression **5**:636–638
 daily life **5**:639–641
 economy **5**:630, 643–645
 education **5**:641, 643
 family and society **5**:639
 festivals and ceremonies **5**:638
 flag **5**:630
 flora and fauna **5**:592, 593, 595
 food and drink **5**:638
 geography **5**:580, 582, 585, 628
 geology **5**:586–587
 government and political parties **5**:630, 632, 635, 643
 health and welfare **5**:640–641, 643
 history
  chronology **5**:631
  colonial *see* German East Africa; Ruanda-Urundi
  Congo Wars **5**:678, 705
  modern **5**:628, 633–635, 705
  precolonial **5**:599, 628
 independence **5**:628, 632, 633, 634, 638, 645
 languages **5**:630, 636
 literature **5**:636
 music **5**:*636*, 637–638
 peoples **5**:599, 609, 628, 630, 632, 634–635, 636
 population **5**:629, 643, 644
 religion **5**:630, 634, 638, 639
 resources **5**:628, 643
 transportation and communication **5**:630, 642, *643*, 645

Butare **5**:*700*, 703, 706, 711, 712, 713
Butaritari Atoll **9**:1203

C

Cabinda **5**:582, 619, 622, 626
 history **5**:604, 610, 618
Cabo Blanco **1**:38
Cacheu **2**:169, 173, 218, 223, 227
Caheu River **2**:151
Calabar (city) **1**:27, 107, 129
Caledon River **7**:868, 870, 871, 923
Cameroon **1**:50–67
 art and architecture **1**:59, *62*, 63
 climate **1**:18–21, 50
 cultural expression **1**:57–59
 daily life 60–61
 economy **1**:52, 56, 64–67
 education **1**:61
 family and society **1**:60
 festivals and ceremonies **1**:59
 flag **1**:51
 flora and fauna **1**:22–25
 food and drink **1**:59
 geography **1**:10, 11, 12, 13–15, *16*, 18, 50
 geology **1**:16
 government and political parties **1**:52, 54
 health and welfare **1**:60–61
 history
  chronology **1**:53
  colonial period *see* French Cameroon; Kamerun
  early **1**:27
  modern **1**:50, 55–56
  nineteenth-century **1**:45–46
 independence **1**:50, 55, *58*, 62
 music **1**:59
 peoples **1**:45, 47–49, 50, 52, 57
 population **1**:10, 52
 refugee camps **5**:657
 religion **1**:52, 60
 resources **1**:50, 64–65
 transportation and communication **1**:52, 62, 67
Cameroon, Mount **1**:14, 17, 18, *19*, 21, 50, 59
Cameroon Mountains **1**:25
Campbell Islands **10**:1302
Canary Islands **2**:256, 264–265

Canberra **10:**1311, 1376, 1393,
1395–1396
national capital **10:***1365,*
1366, 1367, 1369,
1395–1396, 1401
Canterbury **9:**1165
Canterbury Plains
9:1159–1160, 1168, 1230
Cape Bojador **2:**169
Cape Coast **3:**321, 373, 381
Cape Colony **7:**890–893, 894,
896, 898, 902, 907, 911,
919, 923, 940, 945, 951,
962, 964, 967
Cape Fold Mountains **7:**870,
872, *876,* 879
Cape Mesurado **2:**235
Cape of Good Hope **7:**890, 892
Cape Palmas **2:**150, 185
Cape Town **7:**872, 963, 972,
973
climate **7:**880, 881
cultural life **7:**952, 954
history **7:**890, 891, 940, 962,
963, 967
region **7:**868, 870, 872
university **7:**951
Cape Verde **2:**180–191
art and architecture
2:186–187
climate **2:**156, 159, 180, 188,
190
cultural expression
2:186–187
daily life **2:**188
economy **2:**181, 188,
190–191
family and society **2:**188
flag **2:**182
flora and fauna **2:**160–163
food and drink **2:**187
geography **2:**148–153, 180,
186
geology **2:**155
government and political
parties **2:**182, 184
health and welfare **2:**188
history
chronology **2:**182
modern **2:**180, 185, 223
Portuguese rule **2:**166,
169, 172, 173, 179, 180,
185, 186, 189, 190, 223
independence **2:**180, 184,
185, 222, 223
literature **2:**186
music **2:**187
peoples **2:**179, 180, 182, 185,
186, 188
population **2:**181

religion **2:**179, 182, 188
resources **2:**180, 190–191
transportation and
communication **2:**182,
191
Cape Verde Archipelago **2:**153,
155, 156–159, 172, 173,
180
Cape Verde Islands **1:**38; **2:**153
Cape York Peninsula **10:**1300,
1309, 1310
Cap-Vert Peninsula **2:**150, 260,
263
Caroline Islands **8:**1029, 1031,
1032, 1033, 1034, 1035,
1054, 1059, 1064, 1069,
1086, 1093, 1094, 1098
see also Micronesia
Carpentaria, Gulf of **10:**1300,
1305, *1307,* 1309, 1310,
1345, 1350
Casamance region **2:**150, 172,
173, 258, 260, 261
separatist movement **2:**150,
172, 173, 256, 265
Casamance River **2:**150, 169
Central African Republic **1:**67;
5:646–661
art and architecture **5:**654
climate **5:**589, 590, *591,* 646
cultural expression
5:653–655
daily life **5:**656–657
economy **5:**647, 659–661
education **5:**657, 658, 659
family and society
5:656–657
festivals and ceremonies
5:655
flag **5:**648
flora and fauna **5:**592, 593
food and drink **5:**655
geography **5:**580–585, 646
geology **5:**586–587
government and political
parties **5:**648, 650, 659
health and welfare **5:**657
history
chronology **5:**648
colonial *see* Ubangi-Shari
modern **5:**646, 651–652,
658
independence **5:**646, 650,
651, 652, 655
languages **5:**648, 653
lingua franca **5:**607, 651, 653
literature **5:**653–654
peoples **5:**608–609, 648,
653, 656
population **5:**647

religion **5:**648, 655, 656
resources **5:**646, 652, 659
transportation and
communication **5:**648,
658, 659, 661
Central Deserts **10:**1304,
1306–1307
Central Kalahari Game
Reserve **7:**885
Chad **1:**30, 46, 56, 66, 67;
5:652, 657, 670, 678, 694,
705
Chad, Lake **1:**11, 24, 29, 50, 128
desertification **1:**8
Kanem kingdom **1:**28, 36
Chad Basin National Park **1:**24
Chagos Islands **6:**729, 749
Chalbi Desert **4:**441, 445
Chatham Islands **9:**1160
Chavuma Falls **6:**724
China
Angola **5:**625, 627
Central African Republic
5:659
Congo, Democratic Republic
of the **5:**681
Gabon **1:**84, 91, 92, 93
Gambia **2:**203
Guinea **2:**209, 214, 217
Guinea-Bissau **2:**222
Congo, Republic **5:**688, 690,
695, 696, 697
Choiseul Island **8:**1016, 1130
Christchurch **9:**1160, 1210,
1223, 1230
architecture **9:**1219, 1230
Arts Festival **9:**1221
climate **9:**1168
history **9:**1184, 1185, 1230
Christmas Island **9:**1161,
10:1411
Chuuk lagoon **8:***1066,* 1068,
1069
Cidade Velha **2:**169, 186, 189
Ciskei **7:**947, 948
Comoros **6:**750–759
art and architecture **6:**756
climate **6:**732–733, 750
cultural expression **6:**755
daily life **6:**756
economy **6:**751, 759
education **6:**756
flag **6:**752
flora and fauna **6:**736, *757*
geography **6:**728–729, 750
geology **6:**731
government and political
parties **6:**752, 754, 755
history
chronology **6:**753

modern **6:**745, 750, 754,
759
precolonial **6:**740, 750
independence **6:**750, 755
islands of union **6:**753, 754
literature **6:**756
music **6:**756
peoples **6:**748, 750, 752
population **6:**751, 759
religion **6:**752, 756, 757, 758
resources **6:**750, 759
transportation and
communication **6:**752,
759
see also Mayotte
Conakry **2:***152,* 158, *204, 208,*
209, 212, 214, 217
history **2:**209, 214
Congo *see* Congo, Democratic
Republic of ; Congo,
Republic of
Congo Basin, European
intervention **5:**600–602,
603
Congo-Brazzaville *see* Republic
of the Congo
Congo, Democratic Republic of
1:46; **5:**662–681
art and architecture **5:**672
Burundi **5:**642, 643, 645
climate **5:**589–591, 662
cultural expression
5:671–673, 689, 690, 706
daily life **5:**674–676
economy **5:**664, 678–681
education **5:**676
family and society **5:**675
festivals and ceremonies
5:673
flag **5:**664
flora and fauna **5:**592–593,
595
food and drink **5:**673
geography **5:**580–585, 662
geology **5:**586–587
government and political
parties **5:**661, 664, 670
health and welfare **5:**657,
675–676
history
chronology **5:**661
colonial *see* Belgian
Congo; Congo Free State
Congo Wars **5:**618, 670,
678, 705
modern **5:**617, 618, 652,
662, 667–670, 698
precolonial **5:**597–599,
600, 608, 662
as Zaire **5:**662, 669–670

Hutu refugees **5:**670, 705, 709, 713
independence **5:**662, 668, 673, 678
languages **5:**664, 671
lingua franca **5:**607, 671
literature **5:**671–672
music **5:**655, 672–673, 689, 690, 706
peoples **5:**607, 608, 664, 667, 671, 673
population **5:**663, 664
religion **5:**664, 674–675
resources **5:**583, 596, 662, 668, 679
transportation and communication **5:**664, 677, 679, 681
Congo Free State **5:**604, 605–606, 662, 667, 677, 694
see also Belgian Congo
Congo, Republic of the **1:**90; **5:**682–697
art and architecture **5:**689
climate **5:**589, 590, 682
cultural expression **5:**689–691
daily life **5:**692–693
economy **5:**684, 695–697
education **5:**693, 694
family and society **5:**692
festivals and ceremonies **5:**690–691
flag **5:**683
food and drink **5:***690*, 691
geography **5:**580, 582, 583, 584, 682
geology **5:**586–587
government and political parties **5:**684, 686
health and welfare **5:**657, 692–693
history
chronology **5:**685
colonial *see* Middle Congo
modern **5:**682, 687–688, 695
precolonial **5:**600, 608
independence **5:**682, 687, 691, 694
languages **5:**684, 689
lingua franca **5:**607, 684, 689
literature **5:**689
music **5:**689, 690
peoples **5:**607, 608, 609, 684, 692
population **5:**683, 692
religion **5:**684, 692

resources **5:**682, 695, 696
transportation and communication **5:**684, 694, 695, 697
Congo River **5:**580, 582, 583, 584, 585, 589, 592, 593, 594, 597, 599, 660, 661, 677, *682*, 694
exploration **5:**600, 603, 604, 605
navigation **5:**604, 606, 677, 681
Cook, Mount **9:**1158, 1159, 1165
Cook Islands **9:**1194–1195
climate change threat **9:**1169
climate hazards **9:**1168, 1169
geography **9:**1160, 1194
history **9:**1175, 1180, 1181, 1188, 1194, 1215
independence **9:**1217
migrants to New Zealand **9:**1225, 1229
peoples **9:**1189, 1191, 1195
religion **9:**1189, 1195
Cook Strait **9:**1158, 1159, 1228
Coral Sea **8:**1012
Coral Sea Island Territory **10:**1310
Corubal River **2:**151
Costa da Pimenta **2:**169
Côte d'Ivoire *see* Ivory Coast
Cotonou **3:**304, 337, 341, 344, 345, 349
architecture **3:**338, *344*
history **3:**323, 325, 329, 330, 335, 344
population **3:**294, 344
Courland (Latvia) **2:**171, 192
Cristal Mountains **1:**15
Crozet Islands **10:**1315, 1337, 1434
Cuba **5:**610, 617, 625; **7:**931
Cunene River **5:**582, 583; **7:**874, 883, *928*

D

Dahomey *see* Benin
Dakar **2:**150, 159, 179, 261, 263, 267; **3:**335, 395
architecture **2:***257*, 258, *265*
festivals **2:**259
history **2:**169, 173, 209, 250, 255, 263
universities **2:***256*, 262
Daloa **3:**297, 403
Danakil Desert **4:**438, *440*, 445, 467
Danhome **3:**321, 322–323, 324, 328
cities **3:**344, 345

cultural expression **3:**338, 339
French rule **3:**323, 325–326, 330, 335, 338, 344, 346, 415
name change **3:**330
see also Benin
Danhome, Republic of **3:**335–336
Dar es Salaam **6:**726, 837, 838, 839, 843, 859
Darwin **10:**1305, 1350, 1367, 1394
climate **10:**1323, 1324
Deception Island **10:**1424
Denmark, Gold Coast **3:**314, 320, 321, 324, *329*, 368, 377, 383
D'Entrecasteaux Islands **8:**1015, 1104
Diego Garcia **6:***728*, 729, 749
Diégo-Suarez *see* Antsiranana
Dimlang, Mount **1:**11
Djibouti **4:**470–481
art and architecture **4:**476
climate **4:**438, 444, 446, 447, 470, 480
cultural expression **4:**476–477
daily life **4:**478
economy **4:**471, 480–481
flag **4:**472
flora and fauna **4:**448–451
geography **4:**436, 438, 470
geology **4:**442–443
government and political parties **4:**470, 471, 474
history
chronology **4:**473
colonial *see* French Somaliland
history, modern **4:**475, 480, 545
independence **4:**470, 475, 477, 480
literature **4:**476
music **4:**476–477
peoples **4:**467, 472, 474, 476, 478, 480, 546
population **4:**470
religion **4:**470, 472
resources **4:**470, 480
transportation and communication **4:**471, 481
Djibouti (city) **4:**475, 476, 477, 478, 479, 481, 502
history **4:**438, 465, 470, 479, 502
population **4:**479

Dodoma **6:**726, 733, 838
Dogoli **4:**465, 487
Douala (city) **1:**59, 60, 63, 67
history **1:**45, 46, 62, 63
population **1:**14, 63
Drakensberg Escarpment **5:**582–583; **7:**870–871, *873*, 879, 882, 895, 896
Drake Passage **10:**1320
DRC *see* Congo, Democratic Republic of
Ducie Island **9:**1163, 1238
Dunedin **9:**1160, 1168, 1184, 1185, *1223*
Octagon **9:***1212*
Durban **7:**870, 880, 895, *951*, 964, 973
Dutch East Indies *see* Indonesia
Dutch Republic *see* Netherlands

E

East Antarctic Mountains **10:**1314
East Cameroon. *see* French Cameroon
Easter Island **9:**1181
Eastern Cape Province **7:**870, 871, 883, 892, 900, 957, 958
Ebeye **8:**1059, 1061
Edie Creek **8:**1104
Efaté Island **8:**1145
Egbeda **1:**120
Egypt **4:**452, 453, 459, 465, 466, 487, 508
Eighty Mile Beach (Australia) **10:**1306
Elem 27
Elgon, Mount **4:**439, 440–441, 443, 446
Elisabethville *see* Lubumbashi
Ellice Islands *see* Tuvalu
Elmina **3:**313, 315, 319, 320, 321, 324
Elobey Islands **1:**75
Enewetak atoll **8:**1059
England *see* Great Britain
Entebbe **4:**436, 447, *561*, 567, 571
Israeli airport rescue (1976) **4:**560
Enugu **1:**20
Epupa Falls **7:***928*
Equatorial Guinea **1:**68–77
art and architecture **1:**74
climate **1:**18, 21, 68
cultural expression **1:**74
daily life **1:**75
economy **1:**70, 73, 77

Equatorial Guinea (*continued*)
  education **1**:75
  festivals and food **1**:74
  flag **1**:69
  flora and fauna **1**:22–25
  geography **1**:10, 15, 17, 68
  government and political
    parties **1**:68, 70, 72
  health and welfare **1**:75
  history
    chronology **1**:71
    modern **1**:73
  independence **1**:73, 76
  literature **1**:74
  music **1**:74
  peoples **1**:47–49, 70, 73, 74,
    75
  population **1**:70
  religion **1**:70, 75
  resources **1**:68, 77, 92
  transportation and
    communication **1**:70
  see also Bioko
Erebus, Mount **10**:1314, *1319*,
    1433
Eritrea **4**:482–495
  art and architecture **4**:487,
    489–490, 493
  climate **4**:444, 445, 447, 482
  cultural expression
    4:489–490
  daily life **4**:491–492
  economy **4**:483, 494–495
  flag **4**:484
  flora and fauna **4**:448–451
  geography **4**:436, 439, 482
  geology **4**:442–443
  government and political
    parties **4**:483–484, 486,
    488
  history
    chronology **4**:485
    modern **4**:465, 482,
      487–488, 489, 492, 493,
      494, 501–502, 503, 504,
      514, 546
  independence **4**:482, 486,
    487, 488, 493, 495, 496,
    504
  literature **4**:489
  music **4**:490
  peoples **4**:467–468, 484, 491
  population **4**:483
  religion **4**:484, 490, 491
  resources **4**:482, *494*, 495
  transportation and
    communication **4**:484,
    495
Escravos River **1**:8
Espiritu Santo **8**:1136, 1141

Ethiopia **4**:496–517
  art and architecture **4**:454,
    456, 506, 513
  climate **4**:444–445, 447, 496
  cultural expression
    4:505–507
  daily life **4**:508–511
  economy **4**:498, 514–517
  education **4**:511, 513
  family and society **4**:509
  festivals and ceremonies
    4:507, 508
  flag **4**:497
  flora and fauna **4**:448–451
  food and drink **4**:507
  geography **4**:436–440, *442*,
    496
  geology **4**:442–443
  government and political
    parties **4**:498, 500, 502,
    503, 509
  health and welfare **4**:510
  history
    chronology **4**:499
    colonial *see* Eritrea; Italian
      Somaliland
    early **4**:452–456,
      459–460, 463–464
    modern **4**:465, 496,
      501–504, 512, 513, 514
  literature **4**:505–506
  music **4**:506–507
  peoples **4**:467–468, 498,
    509, 546
  population **4**:498
  religion **4**:498, 505, 508,
    512
  resources **4**:496, 515
  transportation and
    communication **4**:481,
    498, 513, 517
Etosha National Park **7**:883,
    883
Eyre, Lake **10**:1309, *1321*,
    1322, 1343
Eyre Peninsula **10**:1304, 1308

F

Fakaofo Atoll **9**:1161, 1256,
    1257
Fako Peak **1**:14, 17, 50
Falkland Islands **10**:1315,
    1423, 1426
Fernando Poo *see* Bioko
Fiji **8**:1038–1051; **9**:1123,
    1162, 1169, 1180
  art and architecture
    8:1045–1046
  chronology **8**:1041
  climate **8**:1019–1022, 1038

  cultural expression
    8:1045–1046
  daily life **8**:1047–1048
  economy **8**:1038, 1039,
    1049, 1050–1051
  education **8**:1048
  family and society **8**:1045,
    1047–1048
  festivals, food, and drink
    8:1045, 1046
  flag **8**:1040
  flora and fauna **8**:1023–1025
  geography **8**:1014, 1016, 1038
  geology **8**:1017–1018
  government and political
    parties **8**:1039, 1042, 1050
  health and welfare **8**:1048
  history
    colonial **8**:1034–1035
    early **8**:1026–1027, 1033
    modern **8**:1034, 1038,
      1042, 1043–1044, 1045
  independence **8**:1038, 1043,
    1044, 1046, 1049
  languages **8**:1040, 1045
  literature **8**:1045
  music **8**:1046
  New Zealand **9**:1180, 1225
  peoples **8**:1036, 1037, 1040,
    1042, 1043, 1044, 1045,
    1047
  population **8**:1039
  religion **8**:1040, 1043, 1046,
    1047
  resources **8**:1038, 1050–1051
  Tongo **9**:1265
  transportation and
    communication
    8:1039–1040, 1048, 1051
  Tuvalu **9**:1274
Fiordland **9**:1166
Fiordland National Park
    9:1172
Flinders Island **10**:1301
Flinders Mountains **10**:1304,
    1308, 1309
Fogo Island **1**:24; **2**:153, 190
Fongafale **9**:1279, 1280, 1283
Fouta Djallon **2**:164, 166,
    167–168, 209
  French control **2**:172–173,
    209
  peoples **2**:176
  slave trade **2**:171
France **1**:30; 39, 83; **3**:312,
    314, 320, 329, 373, 383;
    4:465, 487, 501, 502, 546;
    5:603, 604, 659, 682
  Afars and Issas **4**:470, 475,
    479, 480

  cultural influence **5**:689, 690
  Gabon **1**:46, 78, 83, 90, 91
  Mossi system **3**:318, 350
  New Caledonia **8**:1084–1085
  Pacific exploration **9**:1181
  Polynesia **9**:1186, 1196,
    1290
  semi-independent colonies
    3:395
  southern Africa **7**:890
  West African coast **2**:167,
    168, 169, 170–171, 204,
    263, 268, 280
  Western Pacific **8**:1032, 1033,
    1034, 1037, 1084–1085,
    1136, 1141, 1145, 1147
  see also Danhome; French
    headings; Ivory Coast;
    Middle Congo; Senegal;
    Togoland; Upper Volta
Franceville **1**:88
Free State **7**:868, 871, 889,
    893, 971
  people **7**:900
Freetown **2**:276, *278*, 280, 283
  history **2**:169, 173, 174–175,
    268, 273, 274, 275, 279,
    280
Fremantle **10**:1305, 1403
French Cameroon **1**:50, 55, 56,
    60, 63
  economy **1**:64
  literature **1**:57–58
  Yaoundé **1**:62
French Community **3**:355,
    395, 415
French Congo *see* Middle Congo
French Equatorial Africa **1**:46;
    5:694, 695
Gabon **1**:78, 83, 90, 91
  see also Middle Congo;
    Ubangi-Shari
French Guinea **2**:172, 173,
    184, 204, 209, 211, 214
French Indian Ocean islands
    6:724, 741, 742, 745, 816,
    825, 826
French Polynesia **9**:1158,
    1196–1197
  climate **9**:1166, 1167
  flora and fauna **9**:1170, 1173
  geography **9**:1163, 1196
  history **9**:1175, 1180, 1181,
    1186, 1196
  peoples **9**:1189, 1190–1191,
    1196
  religion **9**:1191, 1196
French Somaliland **4**:465, 470,
    479
  see also Djibouti

French Southern Territories
6:762; **10:**1315, 1423,
1426, 1434–1435
French Sudan **2:**173, 250, 255,
263; **3:**355
see also Mali
French West Africa **2:**173, 209,
250, 255; **3:**350, 355, 415,
424
Dakar **2:**263
Ivory Coast **3:**390, 395, 406
see also Guinea; Senegal
Funafuti Atoll **9:***1262, 1274,
1276,* 1278, 1279, 1283
Futa Tooro **2:**164, 166, 167,
168, 171, 172, 176
Futuna *see* Wallis and Futuna

G
Gabon **1:**78–93; **2:**173
art and architecture **1:**85–86
climate **1:**18, 21, 78
cultural expression **1:**85–87
daily life **1:**88–89
economy **1:**78, 79, 83–84,
88, 90, 91–93
education **1:**88, 90
family life **1:**89
flag **1:**79
flora and fauna **1:**22–25
food and drink **1:**87
geography **1:**10, 15, 17, 78
government and political
parties **1:**80, 82, 83, 84
health and welfare **1:**88–89
history
chronology **1:**81
French rule **1:**46, 78, 83,
90, 91
modern **1:**83–84
nineteenth-century
1:45–46
independence **1:**78, 83, 90
literature **1:**85
music **1:**86–87
peoples **1:**45–46, 47–49, 80,
85
population **1:**79
religion **1:**80, 85, 88
resources **1:**78, 91–92
transportation and
communication **1:**80, 90,
91, 93
Gabon River **1:**90
Gaborone **7:**873, 911, 913
Gagnoa **3:**297, *392*
Galmudug **4:**545, 547, 552
Gambia **2:**192–203
art and architecture **2:***197,*
198–199, 201

climate **2:**156–157, 192
cultural expression
2:198–199
daily life **2:**200
economy **2:**192, 193, 200,
201, 202–203
family and society **2:**199,
200
festivals and ceremonies
2:198, 199, 203
flag **2:**193
flora and fauna **2:**160–163
food and drink **2:**199
geography **2:**148–153, 192
geology **2:**154
government and political
parties **2:**194, 196, 197,
201
health and welfare **2:**200
history
British rule **2:**173, 192,
197, 198, 201, 203
chronology **2:**195
early **2:**164–168, 171, 192
modern **2:**197, 201, 250,
256
independence **2:**192, 197
literature **2:**198
music **2:**199
peoples **2:**176, 178, 194, 198,
200, 201
population **2:**193, 202
religion **2:**194, 198, 199, 200,
201
resources **2:**192, 202
Senegal **2:**192, 197, 250, 256
transportation and
communication **2:**194, 203
Gambia River **2:**150, 169, 170,
171, 172, 192, *194,* 197,
201, 202, 203
slave trade **2:**192, 197, 198
Gambier Islands **9:**1163, 1186
Gamburtsev Mountains
10:1312, 1314
Gamji Gate (Kaduna) **1:**121
Garlep Dam and Reservoir
7:868
Gauteng Province **7:**882, 888,
900, 973
gold mine **7:***969,* 971
Geba **2:**169, 173
Geba River **2:**151, 227
Gedi (settlement) **4:**457, *460*
German Cameroon *see*
Kamerun
German East Africa **4:**465,
466, 523; **5:**604, 609, 628,
633, 642, 651, 698, 703,
706, 709, 712; **6:**743, 744,

745, 828, 833, 838, 839,
849
see also Burundi; Tanzania
German New Guinea
8:1103–1104, *1105,* 1111,
1117, 1118
German Samoa **9:***1186,* 1187,
1192, 1216, 1240, 1245,
1249, 1252, 1254
see also Western Samoa
German South-West Africa
7:896, 897, 901, 903, 926,
931, 932, 934, 945
Windhoek **7:**935
see also Namibia
Germany **3:**324
Nauru **8:**1074, 1079, 1080
Polynesia **9:**1186, 1187
Solomon Islands **8:**1124,
1129
see also Caroline Islands;
Togoland
Ghana **1:**38, 39, 49; **2:**164,
171, 172, 241; **3:**368–389
art and architecture
3:377–378, 383–384, 385
climate **3:**302–305, 368
cultural expression
3:377–379, 383–384
daily life **3:**380–382
economy **3:**370, 375,
386–389
education **3:**382
family and society
3:380–381
festivals and ceremonies
3:379
flag **3:**369
flora and fauna **3:**306–309
food and drink **3:**379
geography **3:**292–299, 368
geology **3:**300–301
government and political
parties **3:**370, 372
health and welfare **3:**342,
381–382
history
chronology **3:**371
colonial *see* Gold Coast
early **3:**310–314
modern **3:**373–376,
386–387
independence **3:**368, 373,
374, 375, 385, 386
Ivory Coast **3:**396
literature **3:**374, 377
music **3:**378–379
peoples **3:**311, 327–329, 370,
377, 380, 381
population **3:**370

religion **3:**370, 377, 379,
380, 384
resources **3:**348, 368, 388
transportation and
communication **3:**367,
370, 373, 383, 385, 389
Gibson Desert **10:**1304, 1306
Gilbert Islands *see* Kiribati
Gitega **5:**642, 645
Glorioso Islands **6:**762;
10:1434
Goede Reede (Ila da Pama)
2:170
Gold Coast (Australia)
10:1310, 1398, 1399, 1413
architecture **10:**1376
Gold Coast (West Africa) **2:**171,
172, 174, 176; **3:**312, 315,
319, 322
British rule **3:**320, 321,
324–325, 326, 330, 355,
368, 373, 374, 375, 377,
383, 385, 386, 410, 415,
424
European forts **3:**313, 320,
321, 324, 325, 326, 368,
377, 383
see also Ghana
Gombe **1:**42, 47
Gonder **4:***463,* 464, 517
Gorée Island **2:**170, 171, 172,
250, 258, 262, 263
festival **2:**259
Grand-Bassam **3:**398, 405
Grande Comore **6:***751, 752,*
753, 754, 755, 758
Granville Town *see* Freetown
Grassfields (Cameroon) **1:**57, 59
Great Britain **1:**33, 39; **2:**180,
263, 273; **4:**458, 465, 501,
512
Ashanti conflict **3:**314–315,
321, 324, 326, 368, 373,
385
Basutoland **7:**914, 919, 923,
924
Bechuanaland **7:**902, 907,
911
Cape Verde **2:**180
Eritrea **4:**482, 487, 488, 489,
493, 494, 502
Fiji **8:**1043–1044, 1045,
1046, 1047, 1050
Gambia **2:**173, 192, 197, 198,
201, 203
Gilbert and Ellice Islands
9:1161–1162, 1203, 1204,
1208, 1278, 1279
Kenya *see* British East Africa
Protectorate

Great Britain (*continued*)
New Guinea **8:**1098, 1102, 1103, 1104, 1117, 1118
New Zealand and Polynesia **9:**1179, 1181, 1182–1185, 1186, 1187, 1188, 1191, 1194, 1198, 1209, 1212, 1216, 1217, 1221, 1224, 1229, 1230, 1236, 1238, 1256, 1258, 1262, 1263, 1290
Northern Rhodesia **6:**849–850, 856
Pacific exploration **9:**1181, 1194
Polynesia **9:**1186, 1187, 1188, 1198, 1236, 1238, 1256, 1258, 1262, 1263, 1290
Prince Edward Islands **7:**868
Saint Helena **7:**872, 938
Senegal **2:**250, 263
Sierra Leone freed slave settlement **2:**174–175, 179, 268, 273, 275, 280, 281
slave trade **2:**169, 204, 250, 268, 280
slave trade ban **1:**35, 42, 45, 46, 68, 76; **2:**172, 173, 192, 197, 268, 273; **3:**322–323, 324, 325; **6:**744
Solomon Islands **8:**1124, 1128, 1129, 1131, 1133, 1134, 1141
South Africa **7:**945–946, 963, 967
see also Cape Colony; Natal
Southern Rhodesia **7:**986, 991–993, 994, 997, 1000
Swaziland **7:**974, 978, 979, 983
Togoland **3:**410, 415, 423, 424
Uganda **4:**554, 559, 562, 567, 568
West Africa **2:**170, 171, 172, 173, 273
see also Gold Coast
Western Pacific **8:**1032, 1033, 1034, 1035, 1037, 1038, 1043, 1074, 1079, 1136
Zulu kingdoms **7:**895–896
see also Australia; British *headings*; Kiribati; Nigeria; Sierra Leone; Southern Rhodesia; Tuvalu
Great Dyke **7:**875, 876
Great Escarpment *see* Drakensberg Escarpment

Great Victoria Desert **10:**1304, 1306
Guadalcanal **8:**1016, 1027, 1124, 1134
Honiara **8:**1133
petroglyphs **8:**1130
Guam **8:**1052–1053
history **8:**1032, 1034, 1035, 1052
peoples **8:**1037, 1053
Guiers, Lake **2:**148
Guinea **2:**204–217; **3:**313, 323, 396
art and architecture **2:**211–212
climate **2:**157–158, 204
cultural expression **2:**211–212
daily life **2:**213
economy **2:**204, 205, 206, 215–217
education **2:**213, 214
family and society **2:**213
festivals and ceremonies **2:**212
flag **2:**206
flora and fauna **2:**160–163
food and drink **2:**212
geography **2:**148, 151–152, 204
geology **2:**154
government and political parties **2:**204, 206, 207, 210, 215, 220
health and welfare **2:**213
history
chronology **2:**207
colonial *see* French Guinea
early **2:**164–168, 171, 172
modern **2:**204, 209–210, 255
independence **2:**204, 207, 209–210, 223, *223*, 225, 227
literature **2:**211
music **2:**212
peoples **2:**176, 178, 204, 206, 211, 213
population **2:**205
religion **2:**204, 206, 211, 212, 213
resources **2:**204, 215, 216
transportation and communication **2:**206, *215*, 217
Guinea, Gulf of
climate **1:**18–21
coast **3:**294, 302, 305, 309, 344, 345, 405, 423
early trade **1:**34

flora and fauna **1:**22–25
geography **1:**8, 10, 12–15
geology **1:**16–18
history **1:**26–47, 68
islands **1:**10, 15, *17*, 21, 25, 68, 76, 129–139
oil exploration **1:**135, 137
peoples **1:**47–49
Portuguese power **1:**38–39
transatlantic slave trade **1:**39, 45
Guinea-Bissau **1:**38; **2:**218–229
art and architecture **2:**186, *220, 222*, 225
climate **2:**157–158, 218
cultural expression **2:**186, 224–225, 277
daily life **2:**226
economy **2:**219–220, 228–229
education **2:**226
family and society **2:**226
festivals and ceremonies **2:**225
flag **2:**219
flora and fauna **2:**160–163
food and drink **2:**225
geography **2:**148, 151, 218
geology **2:**154
government and political parties **2:**185, 218, 222
health and welfare **2:**226
history
chronology **2:**221
colonial **2:**173, 180, 184, 185, 218
early **2:**164, 164–168, 171
independence movement **2:**180, 222, 227, 228
modern **2:**215, 218, 223
independence **2:**218
literature **2:**224
music **2:**225, 277
peoples **2:**176, 178–179, 220, 226
population **2:**219
religion **2:**220, 225, 226
resources **2:**218, 228
transportation and communication **2:**220, 229
Gulf of *see key word*

H
Hamersley Mountains **10:**1304, 1305, 1306, 1409
Harare **7:**875, 990, 995, 999, 1000
climate **7:**811, 880, 999

cultural life **7:**994, 996
university **7:**998, 999
Harer **4:**462, 508
Havannah Harbour **8:**1141, 1145
Heard Island **10:**1315, 1328, 1337, 1411, 1423, 1426
Henderson Island **9:**1163, 1176, 1238
Herbertshöhe *see* Kokopo
Hlane Royal National Park **7:***974*
Hluhluwe-Umfolozi game preserve **7:**883
Hobart **10:***1359*, 1394
Honiara **8:**1016, 1128, 1129, 1130, 1133
crime and riots **8:**1132, 1133, 1134
Hoorn Islands **9:**1162, 1290
Horn of Africa **4:**436, 438, 448, 452, 462, 487, 546, 551
Howland Island **9:***1288*
geography **9:**1163, 1286
Huambo **5:**583, 589, 615, 617, 623
reconstruction **5:**620
Hunter River and Valley **10:**1310, 1402
Huon Peninsula **8:**1015, 1026, 1103
Hwange National Park **7:***875*

I
Ibadan **1:**13, 20, 120
Ifat **4:**462, 464
Ife (Ile-Ife) **1:**27, 31, 32, 106
Ila da Palma **2:**170
Indian Ocean **6:**724, 732–734; **7:**870
Antarctica **10:**1411, 1423, 1426
East Africa **4:**438, 443, 449, 457, 459, 469, 475, 481, 535, 547
Portuguese-Dutch rivalry **7:**890
southern Africa **7:**870, 883, 890
trade routes **6:**740, 741, 748
tsunami **6:**826
Indian Ocean islands **6:**724, 726, 729, 741, 745, 816, 825, 826
climate **6:**732–733, 734
endemic species **6:**735, 736–737
European annexation **6:**745
French colonies **6:**741, 742, 788

peoples **6:**746, 748
slave trade **6:**744
volcanism **6:**731
see also British Indian Ocean
    Territory; Comoros;
    Madagascar; Mauritius;
    Reunion; Seychelles
Indonesia (formerly Dutch East
    Indies) **8:**1033, 1034,
    1103; **9:**1180; **10:**1300,
    1308, 1344, 1345
Interahamwe **5:**698, 705, 712
Inyanga Mountains **7:**870, 875
Israel (ancient) **4:**452
Israel (modern) **4:**560
Italian Somaliland **4:**482, 487,
    488, 493, 502, 512, 540,
    546, 548, 551, 552
Ivory Coast **2:**173, 178, 239;
    3:390–409
    art and architecture
        3:398–399, 405
    climate **3:**302–305, 390
    cultural expression
        3:398–400
    daily life **3:**401–403
    economy **3:**386, 392, 402,
        406–408
    education **3:**403
    family and society
        3:401–402
    festivals and ceremonies
        3:400
    flag **3:**391
    flora and fauna **3:**306–309
    food and drink **3:**400
    geography **3:**292–299, 390
    geology **3:**300–301
    government and political
        parties **3:**392, 394, 404
    health and welfare
        3:402–403, 407
    history
        chronology **3:**393
        early kingdoms **3:**310, 311,
            312, 321, 390
        French control **3:**324, 325,
            326, 355, 364, 390, 395,
            396, 397, 398, 400, 406
        modern **3:**390, 395–397
    independence **3:**395–396,
        404, 406
    Liberian rebels **2:**239
    literature **3:**398
    music **3:**399–400
    peoples **3:**311, 323, 327–329,
        392, 398, 401, 407
    population **3:**391
    religion **3:**392, 401, 402, 404
    resources **3:**390, 407

    transportation and
        communication **3:**367,
        392, 404, 405, 409

J

Jamaica **2:**268, 273; **4:**502
James Island **2:**171
Japan **8:**1034, 1035, 1052,
    1054, 1059, 1064, 1069,
    1073, 1074, 1079, 1080,
    1086, 1093, 1094, 1098,
    1105, 1117, 1118, 1124,
    1129, 1133; **9:**1198, 1203,
    1208
Jarvis Island **9:**1163, 1286
Jesus, Fort **4:***518*, 535
Jinja **4:**441, 570, 571
Johannesburg **7:**871, 882, 952,
    964, 965–966, 972, 973
Johnston Atoll **9:**1163, 1286,
    1288
Juan de Nova Island **6:**762
Jubba River **4:**440, 553
Julio Escudero Station **10:**1429

K

Kaarta territory **2:**168
Kaduna **1:**10, 121
Kaduna River **1:**8, 121
Kainji Lake National Park **1:**24
Kainji Reservoir **1:**8, 10
Kakadu National Park
    10:1305, *1325*
Kalabari **1:**27
Kalahari Desert **5:**583, 590;
    7:868, 870, 872–873, 874,
    878–879, 883, 884
Kaloum Peninsula **2:**152, 214
Kamabalda **10:**1409
Kamerun (German Cameroon)
    1:46, 50, 55, 57, 59, 60,
    62, 63, 64, 83
Kampala **4:**441, 457, 535, 567,
    571
    architecture **4:**562
    climate **4:***447*
    history **4:**560, 567
Kankan **2:***206*, 217
Kano **1:**10, 20, 21, 29, 106, 122
Kansala (city) **2:**166
Kapingamarangi **8:**1030, 1037
Kapsiki Peak **1:**11, *12*
Kariba, Lake **6:**724, 727, 746,
    857, 858; **7:**883
Kariba Dam **6:**850, 857;
    7:1002, *1003*
Karisimbi, Mount **5:**585
Karoo **7:**870, 872, 877, 885,
    891
Karre Mountains **5:**584

Karthala, Mount, eruption of
    6:*751*
Kasai **5:**603, 604, 669
Kasai River **5:**583
Katanga provinces **5:**596, 599,
    605–606, 668, 669, 673,
    679; **6:**739
Katsina (city) **1:**10
Katsina (Hausa state) **1:**36, 37,
    42, 47
Kavango River **7:**883
Kawa **1:**29
Kenya **4:**518–539; **5:**705
    art and architecture
        4:526–527
    climate **4:**444, 445–446,
        447, 518
    cultural expression
        4:526–528
    daily life **4:**529–532
    economy **4:**520, 536–539
    education **4:**532
    family and society **4:**530, 531
    festivals and ceremonies
        4:528
    flag **4:**519
    flora and fauna **4:**448–451
    food and drink **4:**528
    geography **4:**436–441, *443*,
        518
    geology **4:**442–443
    government and political
        parties **4:**469, 518, 520,
        522, 536, 537
    health and welfare **4:**531
    history
        chronology **4:**521
        colonial *see* British East
            Africa Protectorate
        modern **4:**468, 469, 518,
            523–525
        precolonial **4:**453,
            457–458, 460, 518
    independence **4:**518, 523,
        525, 536
    literature **4:**526
    music **4:**527
    peoples **4:**457–458, 467,
        468–469, 520, 526, 528,
        530, 534, 546
    population **4:**520
    religion **4:**520, 529
    resources **4:**518, 537
    transportation and
        communication **4:**520,
        534, 539
Kenya, Mount **4:**439, 440,
    443, 446, 451, 469, 523
Kerguelen Islands **10:**1315,
    1337, 1434

Keur Massar **2:**262
Kgalagadi Transfrontier Park
    7:885
Kibara Mountains **5:**583
Kigali **5:**642, 705, 706, 708,
    709, 711, 712, 713, 715
Kigali Memorial Center **5:***704*,
    712
Kilimanjaro, Mount **6:**726,
    730, *731*, 733, 736, 843
    European explorers **6:**744
Kilimanjaro National Park
    6:*836*
Kilwa **6:**740–741, 743, 828
Kimberley
    mine **7:**893, 898, 971
    siege **7:**898
Kimberley Mountains **10:**1304,
    1305
King Jimmy's Watering Place
    2:280
Kinshasa **5:**580, 583, *669*,
    675, 677, 681, 697
    architecture **5:**672
    climate **5:**590, 592
    cultural exchanges **5:**671
    history **5:**604, 606, 667, 670,
        677, 694
    music scene **5:**590, 673,
        689, 690
Kiowa Island **8:**1047
Kiribati **9:**1198–1209
    art and architecture **9:***1202*,
        1204
    climate **9:**1167
    climate change threat
        9:1169, 1203
    cultural expression
        9:1204–1205
    cyclones **9:**1166
    daily life **9:**1206
    economy **9:**1199, 1208–1209
    family and society **9:**1206
    festivals, food, and drink
        9:1205
    flag **9:**1199
    flora and fauna **9:**1173
    geography **9:**1161, 1163,
        1198, 1204
    geology **9:**1165
    government and political
        parties **9:**1200, 1202
    history
        chronology **9:**1201
        modern **9:**1198, 1203,
            1208
    independence **9:**1202, 1203
    languages **9:**1191, 1200,
        1204
    literature **9:**1204

Kiribati (*continued*)
  music **9:**1204–1205
  peoples **9:**1189, 1190, 1198, 1200, 1204
  population **9:**1199
  religion **9:**1190, 1200, 1206, 1207
  resources **9:**1198, 1209
  transportation and communication **9:**1200, 1209
Kiritimati **9:**1161
Kisangani **5:**580, 583, 669, 677, 681, 688
Kisumu **4:**436, 445
Kivu, Lake **5:**585, *586, 698*, 713, 714
Klira Dam **4:**569
Kokopo **8:**1103, 1116, 1117
Kolonia **8:**1019, 1072
Konigstein Peak **7:**874, 926
Koror **8:**1015, *1090*, 1093, 1096
Kosciuszko, Mount **10:**1311
Kosrae **8:**1031, 1064, 1069, 1070, 1071
Koudougou **3:**362, 367
Kribi **1:**67
Kruger National Park **7:**871, *880, 882*, 883, 889
Kukawa **1:**30
Kumasi **3:**295, *370*, 381, 385, 389
  history **3:**314, 315, 324, 385
  Peace Pole **3:***379*
Kumbi (city) **2:**164
Kwajalein **8:**1059
KwaZulu-Natal **7:**870–871, *873, 879*, 964
  climate **7:**881
  family life **7:***958*
  flora and fauna **7:**883
  history **7:**895
  peoples **7:**888, 889, 900, 951, 957
  tourism **7:***972*
Kwinana **10:**1305, 1403

L

La Digue Island **6:**729, *820*
Lae **8:**1113, 1121
Lagos **1:**13, 20, 21, 103–104, 119, 123–124, 129; **3:**294, 324
  architecture **1:***107*
  history **1:**34, 38, 43, 100, 123–124
  population **1:**13, 123
Lake *see key word*
Lalibela **4:**439, 456, 506, 517

Lambaréné **1:**88
Lami **8:**1049
Lamu **4:**441, 457, *527*, 538
Langue de Barbarie National Park **2:***165, 168*
Lau Islands **8:**1027
Lebombo Mountains **7:**870, 871
Léopoldville *see* Kinshasa
Lesotho **7:**914–925
  art and architecture **7:**920–921, 923
  climate **7:**878, 879, 914, 923
  cultural expression **7:**920–921
  daily life **7:**922
  economy **7:**915, 924–925, 936
  family and society **7:**922
  festivals, food, and drink **7:**921
  flag **7:**915
  geography **7:**868–871, 914
  government and political parties **7:**915–916
  health, welfare, education **7:**922
  history
    chronology **7:**917
    modern **7:**907, 914, 918, 919, 923, 924
    precolonial **7:**896, 914
  independence **7:**914, 918, 919, 923
  languages **7:**916, 920
  literature **7:**920
  music **7:**921
  peoples **7:**900, 916, 920, 921, 922
  population **7:**915
  religion **7:**916, 922
  resources **7:**914, 924
  transportation and communication **7:**916, 923, 925
Liberia **2:**230–249; **3:**396
  art and architecture **2:**240–241
  climate **2:**157–158, 159, 230
  cultural expression **2:**240–241
  daily life **2:**243–245
  economy **2:**231, 237, 238, 247–249
  education **2:**245, 246
  family and society **2:**243–244
  festivals and ceremonies **2:**241
  flag **2:**231
  flora and fauna **2:**160–163
  food and drink **2:**241

geography **2:**148, 152–153, 230
geology **2:**154
government and political parties **2:**231, 234
health and welfare **2:**244–245, 246
history
  chronology **2:**233
  founding **2:**170, 172, 174, 175, 176, 179, 230–236, 240, 246
  modern **2:**237–239, 240, 247, 268
independence **2:**230, 236
literature **2:**240
music **2:**241
peoples **2:**178, 179, 232, 239, 243
population **2:**230
religion **2:**232, 243
resources **2:**230, 247–248
Sierra Leone **2:**239, 240, 268
transportation and communication **2:**232, 246, 249
Libreville **1:**15, 21, 46, 78, 84, 85, 86–87, *89*, 90
Likiep Island **8:**1016
Likoma Island **6:**781, 782
Lilongwe **6:**727, 781, 784, 785
Limpopo Province **7:**872, 888, 900
Limpopo River **7:**951
Limpopo Valley **7:**872, 886, 887
Line Islands *see* Kiribati
Little America station **10:**1424, 1429
Liverpool (Australia) **10:**1404
Livingstone (city) **6:**849, 851, 859
Lobamba **7:**974, 978, 981, 983
Lobito **5:**582, *609*
Lofty Ranges, Mount **10:**1397
Lomé **3:**304, *324*, 415, 420, 423
  architecture **3:**418
  history **3:**423, 424
Louisiade Archipelago **8:**1015, *1099*, 1104
Lourenço Marques *see* Maputo
Loyalty Islands **8:**1016, 1084
Lualaba River **5:**580, 583, 681
Luanda **5:**582, 589, 623, 624, 625
  architecture **5:**620, 624
  climate **5:***591*, 624
  Cuca sign **5:**621
  history **5:**598, 599, 602, 610, 615, 617, 624

housing **5:**622
  population **5:**582, 624
  ruling elite **5:**623
Luangwa River **6:**734, 736
Lubango **5:**582, *612, 621*
Lubumbashi **5:**583, 671, 672, *674*
Lüderitz Bay **7:**897
Luganville **8:***1136*, 1140, 1141, 1145, 1146
Lulua River **5:**583
Lusaka **6:**727, 848, 849, 855, 859
  art scene **6:**851
Lyell Range **9:**1160
Lyttelton Harbor **9:***1210*, 1230, 1235

M

Macdonnell Mountains **10:**1307
Madagascar **6:**760–773
  art and architecture **6:**767
  climate **6:**732–734, 760
  cultural expression **6:**766–768
  daily life **6:**769–770
  economy **6:**761, 772–773
  education **6:**770
  festivals and food **6:**768
  flag **6:**762
  flora and fauna **6:**735–737
  geography **6:**724, 728, *729*, 760
  geology **6:**730–731
  government and political parties **6:**762, 764
  history
    chronology **6:**763
    modern **6:**745, 755, 760, 765, 772
    precolonial **6:**740, 742, 745, 750, 760, 771
  independence **6:**760, 765
  literature **6:**766
  music **6:**766, *767*, 768
  peoples **6:**742, 748, 760, 762–763, 766, 769
  population **6:**760–761
  religion **6:**742, 763, 765, 769–770
  resources **6:**760, 773
  transportation and communication **6:**762, 773
Madang **8:**1103, 1113, 1116
Madina do Boé **2:**223, 227
Mafeking (now Mafikeng) **7:**902, 911
  siege of **7:**898, *899*

Mafia Island **6**:726, 740
magnetic South Pole *see* South Pole
Mahé Island **6**:729, 826
Mailu **8**:1028
Majuro **8**:1059, 1061, 1062
Makira **8**:1033, 1129
Malabo **1**:15, 75, 76, 77
Malaita Island **8**:1016, 1130, 1131, 1132
Malan, Daniel **7**:946
Malawi **6**:774–787
  art and architecture **6**:780–781
  climate **6**:732, 733, 734, 774
  cultural expression **6**:780–781
  daily life **6**:782–783
  economy **6**:775, 785–787
  family and society **6**:782, 785
  festivals and food **6**:781
  flag **6**:775
  geography **6**:724, 727, 736, 774
  geology **6**:731
  government and political parties **6**:776, 778
  health and education **6**:782–783, 785
  history
    chronology **6**:777
    modern **6**:745, 774, 779, 780, 784, 849
    precolonial **6**:739, 747, 774
  independence **6**:774, 779, 784
  lingua franca **6**:748
  literature **6**:780
  music **6**:781
  peoples **6**:746, 747, 776, 778, 780, 782: **7**:896
  population **6**:774–775
  religion **6**:776, 782
  resources **6**:774, 785–786
  transportation and communication **6**:776, *785*, 787
Malawi (Nyasa), Lake **4**:438; **6**:724, 727, 731, 736, 739, 744–745, 746, 774, 781, 782
  ferry service **6**:*785*, 787
  fishing **6**:786, 842
  tourism **6**:*776*, 787
Mali **1**:8, 27, 36; **2**:148, 154, 168, 192, 267; **3**:323, 395
  Burkina Faso war **3**:355
  early history **3**:310, 311, 312, 313

formation **2**:250
medieval Ghana Empire **3**:368, 374
see also French Sudan
Malindi **4**:457, *458*, 535, 538; **6**:740
Malolotja Nature Reserve **7**:*984*
Maloti Mountains **7**:871, 923
Mandara Mountains **1**:11, 45
Manukau Harbour **9**:1229
Manzini **7**:980, 983
Mapungubwe **7**:886, 887, 889, 951
Maputo **6**:726, 733, *808*, 810, *811*, 812, 815
  artists collective **6**:808
  history **6**:805, 812, 813
Marampa **2**:273, 281
Mariana Arc **8**:1018
Marianas **8**:1032, 1035
  see also Northern Mariana Islands
Marion Island **7**:868
Markala Dam **1**:8
Marquesas Islands **9**:1158, 1163, 1175, 1176, 1180, 1186, 1189, 1196
Marshall Islands **8**:1054–1063
  art and architecture **8**:1060
  climate **8**:1019–1022, 1054
  cultural expression **8**:1060
  daily life **8**:1061
  economy **8**:1056, 1063
  family and society **8**:1061
  festivals and food **8**:1060
  flag **8**:1055
  flora and fauna **8**:1023–1025
  geography **8**:1014, 1016, 1054
  geology **8**:1017–1018
  government and political parties **8**:1056, 1058, 1061
  history
    chronology **8**:1057
    colonial **8**:1034–1035
    early **8**:1029, 1030–1031
    modern **8**:1034, 1054, 1059, 1069
  independence **8**:1054, 1058, 1059
  languages **8**:1056, 1059
  literature **8**:1060
  music **8**:1059
  nuclear bomb tests **8**:1059, 1060, 1063
  peoples **8**:1036, 1056, 1061
  population **8**:1054
  religion **8**:1056, 1061
  resources **8**:1054, 1063

transportation and communication **8**:1056, 1063
Mascarenes *see* Mauritius; Reunion
Mascarin Peak **7**:868
Maseru **7**:871, 923, 925
Masina **2**:168
Massangano **5**:599, 602
Massawa **4**:439, 445, 465, 482, 493
  architecture **4**:490
  history **4**:487, 488, 501
Matadi **5**:580, 590, 600, 677, 681
Mata-Utu **9**:1162
Matavanu, Mount **9**:1163
Mauritania **2**:148, 154, 164–168, 256; **3**:368, 374
  geology **2**:154
  history, early **2**:164–168
Mauritius **6**:788–797
  art and architecture **6**:794
  climate **6**:732–733, 788
  cultural expression **6**:794
  daily life **6**:795
  economy **6**:788, 790, 797
  family and society **6**:795
  festivals and food **6**:794
  flag **6**:790
  flora and fauna **6**:737
  geography **6**:724, 729, 788
  geology **6**:731
  government and political parties **6**:788, 790, 792
  history
    chronology **6**:791
    modern **6**:741, 745, 749, 788, 793, 796
  independence **6**:788, 793, 796
  lingua franca **6**:748, 794
  literature **6**:794
  music **6**:794
  peoples **6**:*746*, 748, 749, 790, 793, 794, 795
  population **6**:789
  religion **6**:790, 795, 796
  resources **6**:788, 797
  Seychelles **6**:818, 823, 826
  transportation and communication **6**:796, 797
Mayotte **6**:729, 755, 758, 798–799
Mbabane **7**:980, 983
Mbini **1**:15, 22, 68, 73, 75, 76, 77
McDonald Islands **10**:1328, 1411, 1423, 1426

McMurdo scientific station **10**:1314, 1327, 1428, 1429, 1433
Melanesia **8**:1014, 1026–1028, 1034
Melbourne **10**:1309, 1365, 1387, *1388*, 1395, 1400–1401, 1405, 1408, 1415
  architecture **10**:1376, 1401
  climate **10**:1324
  cultural life **10**:1374, 1401
  football club **10**:1382
  geography **10**:1311
  history **10**:1348, 1349, 1350, 1357, 1400–1401, 1405
  holidays **10**:1381
  housing **10**:1394, 1401
  population **10**:1311, 1400, 1401
  religion **10**:1384
  universities **10**:1393, 1401
Micronesia **8**:1064–1073
  art and architecture **8**:1070
  climate **8**:1019–1022, 1064
  cultural expression **8**:1070
  daily life **8**:1071
  economy **8**:1065, 1073
  family and society **8**:1071
  festivals and food **8**:1070
  flag **8**:1065
  flora and fauna **8**:1023–1025
  geography **8**:1014, 1016, 1064
  geology **8**:1017–1018
  government and political parties **8**:1065, 1068
  health, welfare, and education **8**:1071
  history
    chronology **8**:1067
    colonial *see* Caroline Islands
    early **8**:1029–1031, 1064
    modern **8**:1069, 1073
  independence **8**:1064, 1068, 1069, 1073
  languages **8**:1066, 1070
  music **8**:1070
  peoples **8**:1029–1031, 1036, 1037, 1066, 1071
  population **8**:1064, 1071
  religion **8**:1066, 1071
  resources **8**:1064, 1073
  transportation and communication **8**:1066, 1073
Middle Congo (French Congo) **1**:46, 90; **5**:580, 604, 651, 653, 658, 682, 687, 692, 694, 695

Midway Islands **9:**1286, *1289*
  geography **9:**1163, 1288
Milo River **2:***206*
Mindelo **2:***182,* 185, 189, 190,
  191
Moçambique **6:**741, 808, *809,*
  810
Mogadishu **4:**440, *462,* 465,
  504, 540, 545, 548, 551
  civil war damage **4:**547, 551
Mohéli Island **6:**729, 736, 750,
  753, 754, 755, 758, 798
Mole-Dagbon (people) **3:**380
Mombasa **4:**441, *518,* 535,
  536, 539
  climate **4:***447*
  history **4:**457, 459, 460, 467,
    523, 533, 535
Mono River **3:**348, 426
Monrovia **2:**152, 158, 159, 175,
  235, 237, 239, 240, 246,
  249
Moorea Island **9:**1163, 1176
Moroni (Comoros) **6:**728–729,
  754, 758
Mortlock Islands **8:**1070
Moshi **6:**837, 843
Mouhoun River **3:**292, 294
Mount *see key word*
Mount Lofty Ranges **10:**1307,
  1397
Mozambique **6:**800–815; **7:**999
  art and architecture
    6:807–808
  climate **6:**732–734, 800
  cultural expression
    6:807–809
  daily life **6:**810–811
  economy **6:**802, 806, 813–815
  family and society **6:**810–811
  festivals and food **6:**809
  flag **6:**802
  flora and fauna **6:**735
  geography **6:**724–728, 736,
    800
  geology **6:**730, 731
  government and political
    parties **6:**802, 804, 806
  health and education **6:**810,
    811
  history
    chronology **6:**803
    colonial. **5:**599
    modern **6:**745, 800,
      805–806, 812, 813
    precolonial **6:**739,
      740, 741, 747, 800;
      7:886
  independence **6:**800, 804,
    812, 813

lingua franca **6:**748
literature **6:**807
music **6:**808–809
peoples **6:**746, 747, 748,
  802, 810; **7:**896
population **6:**801–802
religion **6:**802, 810
resources **6:**800,
  813–814
transportation and
  communication **6:**785,
  802, 815
Zimbabwe guerrillas **7:**992
Mozambique Channel **6:**724,
  728
Mpumalanga Province **7:**888,
  900, 971
Mungo, Lake **10:**1340–1341,
  1342
Mutsamudu **6:**754, 758
Mwanza **6:**727, 838
Mweru, Lake **5:**585, 590

N

Nacala **6:**726, 785
Nairobi **4:**469, 533–534, *534,*
  538, 539
  architecture **4:**527
  history **4:**533
  population **4:**441, 533
  slums **4:***530,* 534
Nakambe River **3:**292, 294
Nakoué, Lake **3:**294
Nakuru, Lake **4:**451
Nalubaale Dam **4:**436, 441,
  569, 570
  power station **4:**562
Namib Desert **5:**588, 589, 594,
  595; **7:**870, 874–875, 880,
  881, 884, 926, 931
Namibia **5:**583, 589, 595;
  7:926–937
  art and architecture
    7:932–933, 935
  climate **7:**878–881, 884, 926,
    935
  cultural expression
    7:932–933
  daily life **7:**934
  economy **7:**928, 936–937
  festivals, food, and drink
    7:933
  flag **7:**927
  flora and fauna **5:**595;
    7:882–885, *926*
  geography **5:**583, 589;
    7:868, 870, 872–875, 926
  government and political
    parties **7:**928, 930
  health, welfare, and

education **7:**934
history
  chronology **7:**929
  colonial *see* German
    South-West Africa
  modern **7:**926, 931, 932,
    935, 947
  precolonial **7:**889, 890,
    891, 926
  Second Congo War **5:**670,
    678, 705
  independence **7:**926, 930,
    931, 932, 934, 935, 936
  languages **7:**928, 932
  literature **7:**932
  music **7:**933
  peoples **7:**901, 926, 928,
    933, 934, 935
  population **7:**927–928
  religion **7:**928, 934
  resources **7:**926, 936
  transportation and
    communication **7:**928,
    935, 937
Nampula **6:**810, 815
Nanumea Atoll **9:**1279
Napier **9:**1159
Natal **7:**892, 893, 894, 896,
  898, 940, 945, 956, 962,
  964
Nauru **8:**1074–1083
  art and architecture **8:**1080
  climate **8:**1019–1022, 1074
  cultural expression **8:**1080
  daily life **8:**1081
  economy **8:**1075, 1083
  family **8:**1081
  festivals and food **8:**1080
  flag **8:**1075
  flora and fauna **8:**1023–1025
  geography **8:**1014, 1016, 1074
  geology **8:**1017–1018
  government and political
    parties **8:**1075, 1078, 1079
  health, welfare, and
    education **8:**1081
  history
    chronology **8:**1077
    early **8:**1074
    modern **8:**1035, 1074,
      1079
  independence **8:**1074, 1079,
    1080
  languages **8:**1075, 1076,
    1080
  literature **8:**1080
  music **8:**1080
  peoples **8:**1036, 1076, 1081
  population **8:**1075
  religion **8:**1076, 1081

resources **8:**1014, 1074,
  1079, 1083
transportation and
  communication **8:**1075,
  1083
Nauru Island **9:**1279, 1284
Nazinon River **3:**292, 294
Ndakarou *see* Dakar
Ndar Island **2:**170
Ndogo, Lake **1:**78
Ndola **6:**727, 857
Nelson **9:**1160, 1184, 1221
Netherlands **1:**38–39;
  9:1180–1181, 1258, 1263
  Angola **5:**601–602, 624
  central African slave trade
    5:598, 601
  Gold Coast **3:**313, 320–321,
    324, 368, 377, 383
  slave trade **2:**171, 250, 268,
    280
  West Africa **2:**170, 171, 172,
    263
  Western Pacific **8:**1032,
    1033, 1034, 1038, 1103
New Britain **8:**1012, 1015,
  1027, 1103, 1107, 1117
  dance **8:**1109
  religion **8:**1085
New Caledonia **8:**1084–1085;
  9:1164, 1174, 1290
  flora and fauna **8:**1023–1025
  geography **8:**1012, 1016,
    1084
  government **8:**1085
  history **8:**1026–1027, 1033,
    1034, 1084, 1141
  Lapita site **8:**1026
  peoples **8:**1036, 1037, 1085
Newcastle **10:**1402, *1408,*
  1413, 1415
  history **10:**1347, 1350
Newcombe, John **10:**1382
New Georgia Island **8:**1027,
  1124
New Guinea *see* Papua New
  Guinea
New Hebrides *see* Vanuatu
New Ireland **8:**1015, 1027,
  1033, 1103, 1107, 1110
  dance **8:**1109
  traditional art **8:**1106
New Plymouth **9:**1184, 1185
New South Wales **10:**1365,
  1366, 1380, 1398, *1408,*
  1411
  Aboriginal Australians
    10:1355
  climate **10:**1325
  federation **10:**1388

geography **10:**1309, 1310, 1311
history **10:**1346, 1347, 1348, 1349, 1350, 1358, 1404
resources **10:**1385, 1409, 1411
rugby **10:**1382
theater **10:**1379
university **10:**1393
see also Canberra; Melbourne; Sydney
New Zealand **8:**1034, 1074, 1079; **9:**1179, 1210–1235
art and architecture **9:**1219, 1230
climate **9:**1166, 1167–1169, 1210
Cook Islands **9:**1194
cultural expression **9:**1218–1222
daily life **9:**1223–1227
economy **9:**1212, 1231–1235
family and society **9:**1224–1225
festivals and ceremonies **9:***1191, 1217,* 1221, 1222
flag **9:**1211
flora and fauna **9:**1170–1172, 1177, 1185
food and drink **9:**1222
geography **9:**1158–1160, 1210
geology **9:**1164–1166
government and political parties **9:**1185, 1212, 1214, 1216, 1217
health, welfare, and education **9:**1226–1227, 1233
history
chronology **9:**1213
early **9:**1174, 1177–1179, 1210
modern **9:**1179, 1180, 1181, 1182–1185, 1187, 1188, 1191, 1210, 1215–1217, 1231
independence **9:**1210, 1215, 1216, 1231
languages **9:**1189, 1218
literature **9:**1218
music **9:**1220
Niue **9:**1236
peoples **9:**1189, 1190, 1191, 1210, 1212, 1224, 1225
population **9:**1212
religion **9:**1123, 1182, 1184, 1189, 1212
resources **9:**1210, *1232,* 1233–1234
Samoa **9:**1240, 1245, 1252
Tokelau **9:**1256

transportation and communication **9:**1212, 1229, 1230, 1233, 1235
Tuvalu **9:**1274, 1279
Ngorongoro Conservation Area **6:**735
Ngulu *see* Barotseland
Niari Valley **5:**584, 696
Niger **3:**336, 355
geology **2:**154
Niger Delta **1:**8, 13, 20, 22, 23
militants **1:**127
oil fields **1:**104, 127
slave trade **1:**43
Nigeria **1:**94–129; **2:**174, 176; **3:**323, 325, 329, 396
art and architecture **1:**106–107, 119
climate **1:**18–21, 94
cultural expression **1:**105–111, 129
economy **1:**97, 104, 125–129
education **1:**117, 120
family and society **1:**114–115
festivals and ceremonies **1:**110, *114*
flag **1:**94
flora and fauna **1:**22–25
food and drink **1:**111
geography **1:**8–14, 18, 19, 94
government and political parties **1:**97, 99, 101
military regimes **1:**103, 104, 116, 125, 126, 129
health and welfare **1:**116
history
Bakassi dispute **1:**56, 65
British Cameroon **1:**55
British rule **1:**30, 42, 43–44, 100–101, 112, 120, 121, 122, 123
chronology **1:**98
early **1:**27–32, 36–37
historic Benin Empire **3:**322, 330, 337
modern **1:**100–104, 112
modern Benin **3:**336, 337
housing **1:**118
independence **1:**102–104
music **1:**108, 129
peoples **1:**31, 40–42, 47–49, 97, 101, 104, 114; **2:**176
population **1:**10, 97, 104
religion **1:**40, 41–42, 97, 112, 114, 121
resources **1:**94, 127
transportation and communication **1:**97, 120, 121, 126, 129

Niger River **1:**8, 10, 12–13, 19, 27, 129; **2:**152, 168, 176, 216; **3:**306, 307, 311, 335, 336, 346
British trade **1:**43
early trade centers **3:**314
Northern Mossi **3:**316
trade route **1:**34, 43
Niger River Valley **3:**298, 325, 329
Nile River **4:**239, 436, 438, 441, *441,* 454, 562; **5:**583
search for source **4:**458, 466
source **5:**582, 585, 603, *629;* **6:**744
see also Blue Nile River
Nimba, Mount **2:**151, 152–153, 162, 204, 216, 247; **3:**296
Niokolo Koba National Park **2:***260*
Niokolo region **2:**151
Nioro territory **2:**168
Niue **9:**1236–1237
climate **9:**1167
cyclone **9:**1168, 1236
geography **9:**1160, 1236
geology **9:***1165*
history **9:**1174, 1188, 1215, 1236, 1258
independence **9:**1217, 1236
migrants to New Zealand **9:**1225, 1229, 1236
peoples **9:**1189, 1237
religion **9:**1189, 1237
Njimi **1:**28, 29
Nokoué, Lake **3:**294, 339
Norfolk Island **9:**1188, 1238; **10:**1310, 1416–1417
first settlement **10:**1347, 1348
Northern Cape Province **7:**872, 951, 971
Northern Mariana Islands **8:**1086–1087
climate **8:**1019–1022, 1086
flora and fauna **8:**1023–1025
geography **8:**1015, 1086
geology **8:**1017–1018
government **8:**1087
history
colonial **8:**1034–1035
early **8:**1029–1031, 1086
modern **8:**1034, 1069, 1086
peoples **8:**1037, 1087
Northern Rhodesia *see* Zambia
Northern Territory **10:**1318, 1350, 1396
Aboriginal Australians **10:**1359, *1386,* 1387

agriculture **10:**1411
climate **10:**1322–1323, 1324
geography **10:**1300, 1304, 1305, 1306, 1307
resources **10:**1409
see also Alice Springs
North Island **9:**1158–1159, 1165, 1231, 1234
climate **9:**1166
flora and fauna **9:**1170, 1172
history **9:**1182, 1185
Maori **9:**1177, 1178, 1179, 1189
see also Auckland; Wellington
Northland **9:**1159, 1165, 1168, 1229
North-West Province **7:**872, 889, 957
Nouméa **8:**1016, 1084
Ntamo **5:**677, 694
Ntibantunganya, Sylvestre **5:**635
Nujoma, Samuel **7:**930, 931
Nuku'alofa **9:**1160, 1174, *1258,* 1264, 1268, *1269,* 1270
riots **9:**1258, *1263,* 1264, 1270, 1271
Nukufetau Atoll **9:**1279
Nukunonu Atoll **9:**1161, 1256
Nukuoro **8:**1029, 1037, *1066*
Nullarbor Plain **10:**1304, 1306, *1317,* 1318
Nun River **1:**8
Nyanza **5:**703, 706, 712, 713
Nyasa, Lake *see* Malawi (Nyasa), Lake
Nyasaland *see* Malawi
Nyos, Lake **1:**14, *16,* 17
Nzwani *see* Anjouan Island

O

Obock **4:**470, 475, 479
Oceania **10:**1300
Oeno Island **9:**1163, 1238
Ogaden **4:**440, 444, 467, 502, 546
Ogooué River **1:**15, 45, 46
Okavango Delta **7:**883, *904, 910*
Okavango River **7:**874
Oktika **1:**27
Oman **4:**458, 459, 460, 518, 526, 527, 535, 536; **6:**741, 743, 744, 748, 828, 834
Onitsha **1:**8
Orange Free State **7:**893, 894, 898, 903, 940, 945, 962, 967
Orange River **7:**868, 870, 872, 874, 883, 891, 893, 897, 936

Oribi Gorge Nature Reserve
7:883
Otago **9**:1160, 1165, *1227*
  Gabriel's Gully **9**:*1185*
  gold rush **9**:1184, 1185, 1215
  Presbyterian First Church
    9:1223
  wine production **9**:*1235*
Ouagadougou **3**:292, 353,
  358, 367
  fairs and festivals **3**:357,
    359, 363, 367
  history **3**:311, 316, 318, 326,
    350, 355, 363
  markets **3**:361, 363
  population **3**:297, 353
  public buildings **3**:*354*, 363
  rainfall **3**:303, 305
  universities **3**:362, 363
Ouidah **3**:313, 321, *342*
Oupay, Mount **1**:11
Owen Falls Dam *see* Nalubaale
  Dam
Owen Stanley Range **8**:1015,
  1123
Oyo **1**:31, 32, 42, 43, 106, 120
Oyo-Ile **1**:27

P

Pacific Island groups **8**:1014
  see also United States Pacific
    Islands Territories
Pagan, Mount **8**:1015
Pago Pago **9**:1163, 1187, 1192
Paichuk **8**:1068, 1069
Palau **8**:1088–1097
  art and architecture **8**:1094
  climate **8**:1019–1022, 1088
  cultural expression **8**:1094
  daily life **8**:1095
  economy **8**:1089, 1097
  festivals and food **8**:1094
  flag **8**:1089
  flora and fauna **8**:1023–1025
  geography **8**:1015, 1088
  geology **8**:1017–1018
  government **8**:1090, 1092
  history
    chronology **8**:1091
    colonial **8**:1034–1035
    early **8**:1029, 1031
    modern **8**:1034, 1069,
      1088, 1093, 1094
  independence **8**:1093, 1097
  languages **8**:1090, 1094
  literature **8**:1094
  music **8**:1094
  peoples **8**:1036–1037, 1090
  population **8**:1088, 1095
  religion **8**:1090, 1093, 1095

resources **8**:1088, 1097
transportation and
  communication **8**:1090,
  1097
Palmyra Atoll **9**:1163, 1288
Papua, Gulf of **8**:1012, 1015,
  1107, 1117, 1118, 1120
Papua New Guinea
  8:1098–1123
  art and architecture
    8:1106–1107
  climate **8**:1019–1020, 1098,
    1118
  cultural expression
    8:1106–1110
  daily life **8**:1111–1116
  economy **8**:1100, 1118–1123
  education **8**:1116
  family and society
    8:1112–1113, 1115
  festivals and ceremonies
    8:1108, 1109
  flag **8**:1100
  flora and fauna
    8:1023–1025, 1028
  food and drink **8**:1110
  geography **8**:1012,
    1014–1015, 1016, 1098
  geology **8**:1017–1018
  government and political
    parties **8**:1100, 1102
  health and welfare
    8:1114–1115
  history
    chronology **8**:1101
    early **8**:1026, 1027, 1028,
      1098
    modern **8**:1033, 1034,
      1035, 1098, 1103–1105,
      1117, 1118, 1141
  independence **8**:1098, 1105
  languages **8**:1036, 1098,
    1100, 1106, 1116
  literature **8**:1106
  music **8**:1108–1109
  peoples **8**:1026, 1036–1037,
    1100, 1106, 1112
  population **8**:1098–1099
  religion **8**:1100, 1111
  resources **8**:1098, 1118,
    1120–1121
  transportation and
    communication **8**:1100,
    1122
Pate **6**:741, 743
Pelew Islands *see* Palau
Pemba **4**:460; **6**:726, 733, 748
  history **6**:740, 741, 743, 834
Pentecost Island **8**:1143
Perth **10**:1324, 1387, 1403, 1415

geography **10**:1304–1305
history **10**:1357, 1358
Philippines **8**:1033, 1034,
  1035, 1064
Phoenix Islands *see* Kiribati
Phophonyane Falls **7**:*975*
Pico do Cano **2**:153, 180
Pietermaritzburg **7**:962, 964
Pilbara region **10**:1304, 1305
Pitcairn **9**:1176, 1188,
  1238–1239; **10**:1416
  geography **9**:1163, 1238
  population **9**:1191, 1238
Plenty, Bay of **9**:1159, 1165, 1185
Pohnpei **8**:1016, 1019, 1064,
  1069, 1070, 1072
Pointe-Noire **5**:584, 658, 687,
  690, 692, 693, 694, 695,
  696, 697
Polynesia **8**:1014
  climate **9**:1166–1169
  flora and fauna **9**:1170,
    1172–1173, 1177
  geography **9**:1158, *1159*,
    1160, 1163
  geology **9**:1164, 1165
  see also French Polynesia;
    Tonga
Port-aux-Français **10**:1315,
  1434, 1435
Port Elizabeth **7**:870, 883, 951,
  973
Port-Gentil **1**:15, *80*, 84, *85*,
  87, 88, *89*, 90, *91*
  oil industry **1**:92
Port Harcourt **1**:13, 127
Port Jackson *see* Sydney
  Harbour
Port Louis **6**:729, 745, 796,
  797
Port Moresby **8**:1015, 1020,
  1028, 1104, 1105, 1107,
  1108, 1116, 1117
  manufacturing **8**:1121
  transportation and
    communication **8**:1122
  urbanization **8**:1113
Port Natal *see* Durban
Porto-Novo **3**:294, 341, 344,
  345
  architecture **3**:*337*, 338, 339
  history **3**:322, 323, 325, 326,
    330, 335, 345
Port Phillip Bay **10**:1311, 1347,
  1400
Portugal **1**:46, 68, 78
  Angola **5**:583, 602, 603,
    604, 610, 614, 615–616,
    616, 617, 618, 619, 620,
    621, 622, 624, 682

Benin **1**:34
Cape Verde **2**:166, 169, 172,
  173, 179, 180, 185, 186,
  189, 190, 223
central West Africa **3**:292,
  313, 314–315, 319, 321,
  330, 345, 368, 380
colonial expansion **2**:173
colonial guerrilla
  insurrections **2**:223
dictatorship **2**:185, 223
eastern African coast **4**:518,
  535, 536, 551
Ethiopia **4**:458, 459–460,
  464, 496
Guinea **2**:210
Guinea-Bissau *see*
  Portuguese Guinea
Indian Ocean islands **6**:739,
  741, 742, 745, 750, 774,
  788, 816, 818, 828
Kongo kingdom **5**:598, 599,
  600–602, 603, 608, 610,
  674
Lagos **1**:38, 123
Pacific exploration **8**:1031,
  1064, 1086
São Tomé and Príncipe **1**:26,
  38, 49, 130, 135, 137, 138
slave trade **1**:38, 123; **2**:169,
  204, 250, 263; **3**:324
slave trade ban **2**:172
southern Africa **7**:887, 889,
  890, 896, 926, 938, 940,
  986
West African coastal
  exploration **2**:165, 166,
  169, 170, 171, 172, 192,
  204, 227, 230, 246, 250,
  268
Portuguese East Africa **6**:800,
  812
  see also Mozambique
Portuguese Guinea **2**:173, 180,
  184, 185, 210, 222,
  224–225, 228
  formation **2**:223, 227
  independence *see* Guinea-
    Bissau
Portuguese West Africa *see*
  Angola
Port-Vila **8**:1140, 1141, 1143,
  1144, 1145, 1146
  art galleries **8**:1142
  tourism **8**:1147
Praia **2**:153, 159, 186–187,
  189, 191
Pretoria **7**:871, 882, *893*, 951,
  962
  history **7**:899, 962

university **7:**961, 962
Prince Charles Mountains
10:1314, 1432
Prince Edward Islands **7:**868
Príncipe *see* São Tomé and
Príncipe
Pukapuka *see* Cook Islands
Puntland **4:**440, 544, 545,
547, 550, 552, 553

Q

Queen Maud Land **10:**1314,
1425
Queensland **8:**1034, 1104,
1141; **10:**1365, 1394, 1411,
1413
climate **10:**1322–1323,
1325
federation **10:**1388
geography **10:**1300, 1306,
1307, 1309, 1310, 1318
history **10:**1347, 1349, 1350,
1351
indigenous peoples **10:**1300,
1355, 1387, 1398
resources **10:**1409, 1410,
1411
rugby **10:**1382
university **10:**1393
see also Brisbane; Gold Coast
Quelimane **6:**726, 741, 744

R

Rabaul **8:**1015, 1103, 1104,
1108, 1117
Rabi Island **8:**1047; **9:**1202
Raklura *see* Stewart Island
Ralik and Ratak *see* Marshall
Islands
Rand *see* Witwatersrand
Rapanui **9:**1189, 1191
Rarotonga Island **9:**1160, 1169,
1194
Red Sea **4:**449, 452, 453, 454,
459, 462, 465, 475, 479,
480, 487
fish resources **4:**481
Red Volta **3:**292, 294, 355
Republic of the Congo *see*
Congo, Republic of
Reunion **6:**731, 737, 748,
816–817
Rhodesia **7:**896, 992, 999,
1000, 1003
see also Zambia; Zimbabwe;
Southern Rhodesia
Ribeira Grande *see* Cidade Velha
Richard Toll (city) **2:**148
Rima River **1:**10
Rio Muni *see* Mbini

Rock Islands **8:**1015, 1031,
1090
Rodrigues Island **6:**729, 792
Roggeveld Mountains **7:**871
Roha *see* Lalibela
Rooiberg Mountains **7:**889
Ross, Mount **10:**1315
Ross Island **10:**1314, *1419,*
1429, 1433
Ross Sea **10:**1312, 1313, 1320,
1432
Ruanda *see* Rwanda
Ruanda-Urundi **5:**604, 609,
628, 633, 642, 698, 703,
706, 712, 713
Rufiji Valley **6:**726, 842
Rufisque **2:**263
Ruwenzori Mountains **4:**439,
441, 442, 446, 571; **5:***583,*
585, 587
Rwanda **4:**561; **5:**698–715,
700, 709
art and architecture **5:**706
Burundi **5:**642, 643, 645
climate **5:**589, 590, *591,* 698
cultural expression
5:706–708
daily life **5:**709–711
economy **5:**699–700,
713–715
education **5:***709,* 711
family and society **5:**710–711
festivals and ceremonies
5:707–708
flag **5:**699
flora and fauna **5:**592–595
food and drink **5:**708
geography **5:**580, 582, 585,
698, 713
geology **5:**586–587
government and political
parties **5:**700, 702
health and welfare **5:**711
history
chronology **5:**701
colonial *see* Ruanda-
Urundi
Congo Wars **5:**670, 678,
705
modern **5:**618, 670, 698,
703–705, 709
precolonial **5:**599
independence **5:**698, 703,
704, 708, 709, 712, 713
languages **5:**700, 705, 706
music **5:**706–707
peoples **5:**607, 609, 698, 700
population **5:**699, 713
religion **5:**700, 707–708,
709–710

resources **5:**698, 713–714
transportation and
communication **5:**700, 715

S

Saba (Arabia) **4:**452, 453, 454
Sahara Desert **2:**150, 156, 158;
5:590
caravan trade **2:**164,
165–166, 169
Saint Helena **7:**938–939
climate **7:**880, 938
flag **7:**938
flora and fauna **7:**885
geography **7:**872, 938
geology **7:**877
population **7:**939
Saint-Louis **2:**148, 150, *250,*
258
festival **2:**259
history **2:**170, 171, 172, *173,*
250, 263
Saint Mary's Island **2:**150, 173,
201
Saint Paul River **2:**152, 246,
248
Saint Vincent, Gulf of **10:**1308,
1397
Saipan **8:**1029, 1035
Salisbury *see* Harare
Sal Island **2:**153, 191
Salonga National Park **5:**592
Saloum River **2:**150
Samoa **8:**1026–1027, 1034,
1124, 1129; **9:**1240–1255
art and architecture
9:1246–1247
climate **9:**1166, 1167, 1240
cultural tradition
9:1246–1248
daily life **9:**1249–1251
economy **9:**1240–1241,
1253–1255
family and society
9:1249–1251
festivals and ceremonies
9:1247–1248
flag **9:**1242
flora and fauna **9:**1170, 1173
food and drink **9:**1248
geography **9:**1162–1163, 1240
geology **9:**1165
government and political
parties **9:**1190, 1241, 1244,
1253
health and education **9:**1251
history
chronology **9:**1243
early **9:**1174, 1175, 1176,
1180, 1240

modern **9:**1187, 1240,
1245, 1252
independence **9:**1244, 1245
languages **9:**1190, 1242,
1246
literature **9:**1246
music **9:**1247
natural disasters **9:**1168,
1253
partition **9:**1187
peoples **9:**1180, 1189–1190,
1191, 1242, 1249
population **9:**1240
religion **9:**1190, 1242, 1249
resources **9:**1240, 1254
transportation and
communication **9:**1242,
1255
see also American Samoa;
German Samoa; Western
Samoa
Sanaga River **1:**12, 65
Sanaga Valley **1:**14, 15
Sandhills Region **2:**150
Sangha River **5:**604, 661
Santa Cruz Islands **8:**1016,
1130
Santiago (São Tiago) Island
2:153, 169, 189, 190, 191
Santo Antão Island **2:**153, 190
São Nicolau Island **2:**153, 190
São Paulo de Luanda *see*
Luanda
São Tomé (city) **1:**15, 138
São Tomé and Príncipe
1:130–139
art and architecture **1:**136
climate **1:**18, 21, 130
cultural expression **1:**136
daily life **1:**137
economy **1:**132, 139
education **1:**137
flag **1:**131
flora and fauna **1:**22, 25
geography **1:**10, 15, 130
geology **1:**17
government and political
parties **1:**130, 132, 134,
135
history
chronology **1:**133
modern **1:**135
Portuguese settlement
1:26, 38, 49, 130, 135,
137, 138
independence **1:**130, 135
literature **1:**136
music **1:**136
peoples **1:**47, 49, 132, 138
population **1:**130

São Tomé and Príncipe
(*continued*)
religion **1**:132
resources **1**:92, 130, 139
transportation and
communication **1**:132,
138
São Tomé Island **5**:598, 602
São Vincente Island **2**:153,
180, 185, *188*, 189, *190*,
191
Savai'i Island **9**:1162–1163,
1240, *1250*, 1252
Ségou **3**:323
Sekondi **3**:373
Senegal **2**:250–267; **3**:329,
335, 395, 417
art and architecture
2:257–258, 259, *265*
chronology **2**:252
climate **2**:156–157, 159, 250,
260
cultural expression
2:257–259, 275; **5**:653
daily life **2**:260–261
economy **2**:252, 264–267
education **2**:*256*, 260, 262
family and society
2:261–262
festivals and ceremonies
2:258–259
flag **2**:252
flora and fauna **2**:160–163
food and drink **2**:259
geography **2**:148–151, 250
geology **2**:154
government and political
parties **2**:252, 254
health and welfare **2**:262
history
early **2**:164–168, 250, 263
French rule **2**:172–173,
209, 250, 255, 257, 263,
264
modern **2**:250, 255–256
independence **2**:250, 255
literature **2**:257; **3**:417
music **2**:258, 259
peoples **2**:176, 177, 178, 179,
252, 257, 258, 260, 261
population **2**:252, 261
religion **2**:250, 252, 257,
259, 260–261
resources **2**:250, 265
transportation and
communication **2**:252,
263, 267
Senegal River **2**:148, 150, 164,
165, 250
exploration **2**:169, 170

flooding **2**:148, 150
French settlement **2**:172, 263
Sentinel Peak **7**:*873*
Sepik River **8**:1015, 1107
Serengeti National Park **6**:735,
834, 843
Seychelles **6**:818–827
climate **6**:732–733, 818
cultural expression **6**:824
daily life **6**:825
economy **6**:819, 827
family and society **6**:825
festivals and food **6**:824
flag **6**:820
flora and fauna **6**:736, *818*
geography **6**:724, 729, 818
geology **6**:730, 731
government and political
parties **6**:819–820, 822,
823
health and education **6**:825
history
chronology **6**:821
modern **6**:745, 748, 818,
823
independence **6**:749, 818,
823
literature **6**:824
music **6**:824
peoples **6**:820, 825
population **6**:818–819
religion **6**:820, 825
resources **6**:818, 827
transportation **6**:820, 827
Shaba *see* Katanga province
Shabeelle River **4**:440, 515,
553
Shackleton Range **10**:1313
Shag Island **10**:1426
Sherbro Island **2**:171
Shire River **6**:736, 744
Shire Valley **6**:727, 734, 739
Sierra Leone **1**:38, 43, 73;
2:268–283; **3**:315
art and architecture **2**:186,
275–276, 280
chronology **2**:271
climate **2**:157–158, 268
cultural expression **2**:186,
275–277
daily life **2**:278–279
economy **2**:270, 281–283
education **2**:273, 279
family and society **2**:278
festivals and ceremonies
2:277
flag **2**:269
food and drink **2**:277
geography **2**:148, 152–153,
268

geology **2**:154
government and political
parties **2**:270, 272, *273*
health and welfare **2**:278, 279
history
British rule **2**:173,
174–175, 179, 268, 273,
275, 280, 281
early **2**:172, 268
founding **2**:174–175, 176,
179
modern **2**:268, 273–274
independence **2**:268, 272,
273, 280, 281
Liberia **2**:239, 240, 268
literature **2**:275
music **2**:276–277
peoples **2**:176, 177–178, 270,
275, 278
population **2**:269
religion **2**:174, 270, 277, 278
resources **2**:268, 281–282
transportation and
communication **2**:270,
280, 283
Sierra Leone Peninsula **2**:152,
169
Sigave **9**:1162, 1186, 1290
Simangaliso Wetlands Park
7:883
Simpson Desert **10**:1306
Singavi, Mount **9**:1162
Slave Coast **3**:321, 322, 325
Snowy Mountains **10**:1309,
1311, 1406
Society Islands **9**:175, 1163,
1176
history **9**:1181, 1186, 1196
Sofala *see* Beira
Sokoto **1**:10, 20, 30, 37, 40,
41–42, 45, 47, *96*, 101;
2:167
Sokoto Plains **1**:10, 20
Sokoto River **1**:10
Solomonic dynasty **4**:456,
463–464, 468, 501–502
Solomon Islands **8**:1124–1135;
9:1174, 1187, 1245
art and architecture
8:1130–1131
climate **8**:1019–1022, 1124
cultural expression
8:1130–1131
daily life **8**:1132
economy **8**:1125, 1134–1135
family and society **8**:1132
festivals, food, and drink
8:1131
flag **8**:1126
flora and fauna **8**:1023–1025

geography **8**:1012, 1015,
1016, 1124
geology **8**:1017–1018
government and political
parties **8**:1125, 1128
health, welfare, education
8:1132
history
chronology **8**:1127
early **8**:1027, 1032, 1033,
1124
modern **8**:1034, 1035,
1103, 1124, 1129, 1133,
1134, 1141
independence **8**:1124, 1129,
1131
languages **8**:1126, 1130, 1133
literature **8**:1130
music **8**:1131
peoples **8**:1036, 1124, 1126,
1129, 1130, 1134
population **8**:1125
provinces **8**:1126, 1128
religion **8**:1126, 1132
resources **8**:1124, 1134
transportation and
communication **8**:1126,
1135
Solomon Sea **8**:1012
Somalia **4**:540–553
art and architecture **4**:548
climate **4**:444, 446, 447, 540
cultural expression
4:548–549
daily life **4**:550
economy **4**:542, 552–553
as failed state **4**:540, 545,
546, 547, 553
family and society **4**:550
festivals and ceremonies
4:549
flag **4**:541
flora and fauna **4**:448–451
food and drink **4**:549
geography **4**:436, 440,
442–443, 540
government **4**:540, 542, 544,
545
history
chronology **4**:543
colonial *see* British
Somaliland; Italian
Somaliland
early **4**:459, 462–463,
464, 540
Ethiopian war *see* Ogaden
modern history **4**:487,
546–547, 552
independence **4**:440, 540,
546, 547, 551

literature **4**:548

music **4**:549

peoples **4**:462, 467, 542, 546, 550

population **4**:541–542

religion **4**:464, 467, 540, 542, 545, 550

resources **4**:540, *552*, 553

transportation and communication **4**:542, 553

Somaliland **4**:464, 465, 466, 544, 550

autonomy **4**:544, 545, 547, 549, 552

economy **4**:544, 553

flag **4**:544

government **4**:545

Sotavento Islands **2**:153

South Africa **3**:396; **7**:940–973

art and architecture **7**:951, 966

chronology **7**:943

climate **7**:878, 879, 880, 881, 940

cultural expression **7**:950–955

daily life **7**:956–961

economy **7**:936, 942, 949, 967–973

education **7**:961, 968, 970

family and society **7**:957–958, 970

festivals and ceremonies **7**:954

flag **7**:942

flora and fauna **7**:882–885

food and drink **7**:955

formation **7**:907, 940

geography **5**:583, 589; **7**:868–873, 940

geology **7**:876–877

government and political parties **7**:942, 944, 949

new democratic era **7**:940, 947, 948–949, 954, 969–970

health and welfare **7**:959–960, 970

history

Angolan Civil War **5**:617, 625

Congo War **5**:670

European settlers **7**:890–896, 898–899, 940

modern **7**:940, 945–949, 967

languages **7**:943, 950, 957, 961

literature **7**:950

music **7**:952–953

peoples **7**:900, 901, 902, 942, 945, 946, 952, 957–958

population **7**:942

religion **7**:942–943, 954, 956, 958

resources **7**:893, 940, 962, 967, 971

transportation and communication **7**:942, 966, 971, 972, 973

South African Republic *see* Transvaal

South Australia **10**:1308, 1309, 1365

climate **10**:1322, 1324

federation **10**:1388

history **10**:1348, 1349, 1350, 1358

resources **10**:1409

see also Adelaide

Southern Alps **9**:1159, 1160, 1165, 1166, 1168, 1170, 1172

Southern Ocean **10**:1302, 1313, 1320, 1339, 1424, 1425, 1430

climate **10**:1328

fisheries **10**:1432–1433

Southern Rhodesia **7**:896, 986, 991, 991–993, 993, 994, 997, 999, 1000

see also Zimbabwe

South Georgia **10**:1315, 1328, 1337, 1338, 1339, 1423, 1426, 1430

exploration **10**:1354

South Island **9**:1158, 1159–1160, *1162*, 1165, 1228, 1229, 1231

agriculture **9**:1234

architecture **9**:1219

climate **9**:1166, 1168

flora and fauna **9**:1170, 1171

history **9**:1180, 1182, 1185, 1191

lifestyle **9**:1225

Maori settlement **9**:1177, 1178–1179

see also Christchurch

South Luangwa National Park **6**:859

South Orkney Islands **10**:1313, 1315, 1337

South Pole **10**:1313, 1320, 1336, 1352, 1353, *1354, 1423*, 1424, 1425, 1433

Amundsen-Scott Station **10**:1326, 1328, *1429*

South Sandwich Islands **10**:1313, 1315, 1337, 1423, 1426

South Shetland Islands **10**:1315, 1337

South West Africa *see* Namibia

Soviet Union

Angola **5**:617, 618, 625

Congo, Democratic Republic **5**:668

Congo, Republic **5**:687, 690

Ethiopia **4**:503–504, 514

Guinea **2**:204, 209, 210, 217

Guinea-Bissau **2**:223, 228

Katanga secession **5**:668

Namibia **7**:931

Somalia **4**:547

Soweto **7**:956, 957, 965, 966

uprising (1976) **7**:947, 954, 966

Spain

African colony **1**:68

Dutch war **5**:601

Equatorial Guinea **1**:72, 73, 75

exploration **2**:170

maritime exploration **1**:38–39, 46

Western Pacific **8**:1032–1033, 1034–1035, 1052, 1054, 1059, 1064, 1069, 1086, 1093, 1095

Spanish Guinea **1**:68, 72, 73, 75, 76

Stanley Falls *see* Boyoma Falls

Stanleyville *see* Kisangani

Stewart Island **9**:1158, 1231

Stirling **10**:1403

Stirling Mountains **10**:1305

Sturt Stony Desert **10**:1309

sub-Antarctic territories **10**:1302, 1315, 1423, 1424, 1426–1427

climate **10**:1326

tourism **10**:1433

see also French Southern Territories

Sudan **4**:453, 454, 455, 459, 465, 496

geology **5**:586–587

history **5**:652

linguistic groups **4**:457

Mahdi **4**:487, 501

Uganda **4**:561

Suez Canal **4**:465, 470, 479, 501, 546; **6**:796, 816

Sunshine Coast (Australia) **10**:1310, 1413

Surfers Paradise (Australia) **10**:1399

Suva **8**:1016, 1045, 1049

Swakopmund **7**:932, 933, 937

Swaziland **7**:974–985

art and architecture **7**:980

climate **7**:878, 879, 974

cultural expression **7**:980–981

daily life **7**:982

economy **7**:936, 975, 984–985

family and society **7**:982

festivals, food, and drink **7**:981, 983

flag **7**:976

flora and fauna **7**:882–885, *984*

geography **7**:870, 974

geology **7**:876

government and political parties **7**:974, 975, 978, 979, 984

health, welfare, and education **7**:979, 982

history

chronology **7**:977

modern **7**:907, 974, 979, 983

precolonial **7**:888–889, 896

independence **7**:974, 978, 979, 983

languages **7**:976, 980

literature **7**:980

music **7**:980–981

peoples **7**:900, 976, 980, 982

population **7**:975

religion **7**:976, 982

resources **7**:974, 985

transportation and communication **7**:976, 985

Sweden, Gold Coast **3**:320, 324, 368, 383

Sydney **10**:1310–1311, 1366, 1395, 1398, 1404–1405, 1415

art and architecture **10**:1374, 1376

festivals **10**:1381

history **10**:1344, 1347, 1348, 1349, 1350, 1357, 1372, 1401, 1404–1405

housing **10**:1394

population **10**:1311, 1404

religion **10**:1384

universities **10**:1393, 1405

Sydney Cove **10**:1380, 1387

Sydney Harbour **10**:1311, 1344, 1347, 1372, *1381*, 1404

T

Table Bay **7:**890

Table Mountain **7:***871*, 872, 885, 963

 Rhodes Memorial **7:**951

Tadjoura **4:***471*, 475, 476, 479

Tadjoura, Gulf of **4:**438, 479

Tagbaladougou Falls **3:**298

Tahiti **9:**1163, 1165, 1166

 flora and fauna **9:**1173

 history **9:**1181, 1186, 1196

 peoples **9:**1189, 1191

Takoradi **3:**373, 389

Tamale **3:**304, 305, *381*

Tamatave *see* Toamasina

Tana, Lake **4:***439*, 451, *515*

Tanami Desert **10:**1306

Tananarive *see* Antananarivo

Tanga **6:**726, 837

Tanganyika *see* Tanzania

Tanganyika, Lake **5:**580, 585, 642, 643; **6:**727, 731, 736, 746

 British explorers **5:**603

 European explorers **6:**744

 fishing **5:***628*, 638, 644; **6:**842, 858

 German railroad line **6:**833, 838, 839

Tanna Island **8:**1016, *1137*, 1141, 1143

Tanzania **4:**466, 523; **5:**586–587, 681; **6:**828–843

 art and architecture **6:**835, 839

 Burundi refugees **5:***638*, 641, 643, 645

 climate **6:**732–734, 828

 cultural expression **6:**756, 835–836

 daily life **6:**837

 economy **6:**830, 840–843

 family life **6:**837

 festivals and food **6:**836

 flag **6:**830

 flora and fauna **6:**735–736

 geography **6:**724, 726–727, 736, 828

 geology **6:**730, 731

 government and political parties **6:**830, 832

 health and education **6:**837

 history

  chronology **6:**831

  modern **6:**744, 745, 828, 833–834, 838, 839, 849–850

  precolonial **6:**739, 740–741, 747, 828

 independence **6:**828, 833, 839

 Kenya **4:**535, 538

 lingua franca **6:**748

 literature **6:**835

 music **6:**836

 peoples **6:**744, 746, 747–748, 830, 837: **7:**896

 population **6:**829, 834

 religion **6:**830, 837

 resources **6:**828, 841

 Rwanda **5:**705

 transportation and communication **6:**830, *840*, 843, 859

 Uganda **4:**560, 568

Taoué River **2:**148

Taranaki **9:**1159, 1184, 1185, 1221, 1233

Tarawa Atoll **9:**1161, 1203, 1204, 1205, 1206, 1207, 1279, 1284

Tasman Bay **9:**1160

Tasmania **10:**1304, 1309, 1311, 1381, 1400

 Aboriginal Australians **10:**1343, 1355

 climate **10:**1323, 1329

 federation **10:**1388

 flora and fauna **10:**1334

 history **10:**1345, 1346, 1347, 1348, 1349, 1387

 resources **10:**1410, 1411

 university **10:**1393

Tasman Sea **9:**1166

Ta'u Island **9:**1163, *1168*

Taupo, Lake **9:**1159, 1165

Tauranga **9:**1159, 1221, 1229, 1235

Tavurvur, Mount **8:***1018, 1100, 1123*

Tema **3:**294, 383, 384, *386*, 389

Terra Australis **9:**1180, 1181; **10:**1346, 1352, 1418

Thukela River **7:**895, 896

Thuli Parks and Wildlife Land **7:***986*

Tigray **4:**453, 454, 464, 468, 501, 504

 religion **4:**508

Timbo **2:**167, 172

Timbuktu **1:**8; **2:**168

Tinkisso Falls **2:**151

Tintenpalast **7:***930, 931*, 932, 935

Toamasina **6:**728, 742, 745

Togo **1:**49; **3:**410–427; **5:**618

 art and architecture **3:**417–418

Benin border dispute **3:**336

 climate **3:**302–305, 410

 cultural expression **3:**417–419

 daily life **3:**420–422

 economy **3:**344, 411, 424–427

 education **3:**422, 425

 family and society **3:**420–421

 festivals and ceremonies **3:**419

 flag **3:**411

 flora and fauna **3:**306–309

 food and drink **3:**419

 geography **3:**292–299, 410

 geology **3:**300–301

 government and political parties **3:**411, 414, 415–416

 health and welfare **3:**421–422, 425

 history

  chronology **3:**413

  colonial *see* Togoland

  early **3:**321

  modern **3:**410, 415–416, 424

 independence **3:**410, 415, 419, 423

 literature **3:**417

 music **3:**419

 peoples **3:**327–329, 410, 412, 417, 420, 421, 423

 population **3:**410–411

 religion **3:**412, 419, 420, 421

 resources **3:**410, 425–426

 transportation and communication **3:**412, 423, 427

Togo-Atakora Mountains **3:**294, 295

Togoland **3:***324*, 325, 326

 British-French partition **3:**373, 410, 415

 French region **3:**415–416, 417, 423, 424

Tokelau **9:**1256–1257

 climate change **9:**1169, 1256

 geography **9:**1161, 1256

 geology **9:**1165

 peoples **9:**1189, 1257

Tombo Island **2:**152, 214

Tombouctou **3:**311, 312

Tonga **8:**1026–1027; **9:**1258–1273

 art and architecture **9:**1265

 climate **9:**1167, 1258

 cultural expression **9:**1265–1267

 cyclone **9:**1168, 1271

 daily life **9:**1268–1269

 economy **9:**1258–1259, 1271–1273

 family and society **9:**1268

 festivals, food, and drink **9:**1267

 flag **9:**1260

 flora and fauna **9:**1173

 geography **9:**1160, 1258

 geology **9:**1165

 government and political parties **9:**1260, 1262, 1272

 health, welfare, education **9:**1268–1269

 history

  chronology **9:**1261

  early **9:**1174, 1175, 1176, 1180, *1188*, 1258

  modern **9:**1180, 1181, 1186–1187, 1258, 1263–1264

 independence **9:**1258, 1263, 1271

 language **9:**1260, 1265

 literature **9:**1265

 migrants to New Zealand **9:**1229

 music **9:***1259, 1265*, 1266–1267

 peoples **9:**1174, 1180, 1189, 1190, 1258, 1260, 1268

 population **9:**1259

 religion **9:**1186, 1190, 1260, 1268

 resources **9:**1258, 1272

 transportation and communication **9:**1260, 1273

Tongareva Island **9:**1160

Tongatapu Island **9:**1165, 1180, 1258, 1264, *1266*, 1267

Torres Strait **8:**1033; **10:**1300, 1310, 1342, 1344, 1345

Touba **2:**260, *262*

Transantarctic Mountains **10:**1313, 1318, 1320

Transkei **7:**947

Transvaal **7:**893, 894, 895, 896, 903, 907, 940, 945, 962, 964, 965, 967

 Second Anglo-Boer War **7:**898–899, 940, 962

 Swaziland **7:**974, 979

Tristan da Cunha island group **7:**872, 877, 880, 938

Trobriand Islands **8:**1015, 1104, 1109, 1113

Tromelin Island **6:**762; **10:**1434

Truk *see* Chuuk lagoon

Trust Territory of the Pacific
Islands *see* United States
Pacific Islands Territories
Tsodilo Hills **7:***904*, 908, *908*
Tuamotu Archipelago **9:**1163,
1180, 1181, 1186
Tubuai **9:**1163
Tulagi **8:**1129, 1133
Tumba, Lake **5:**583
Turkana, Lake **4:**439, 441, 451,
453, 469, 537
Tutuila Island **9:**1163, 1174,
1187, 1192
Tuvalu **9:**1274–1285
art and architecture **9:**1280
climate **9:**1274
climate change danger
9:1162, 1169, 1274, *1276*,
1279, 1284
cultural expression
9:1280–1281
daily life **9:**1282
economy **9:**1275, 1284–1285
family, health, education
9:1282
festivals, food, and drink
9:1281
flag **9:**1275
flora and fauna **9:**1173
geography **9:**1161–1162, 1274
geology **9:**1165
government **9:**1275, 1278
history
chronology **9:**1277
modern **9:**1180, 1181,
1188, 1203, 1274, 1279
independence **9:**1274, 1279,
1284
languages **9:**1276, 1280
literature **9:**1280
music **9:**1281
peoples **9:**1189, 1190, *1191*,
1276, 1280
religion **9:**1276, 1280, 1281,
1282
resources **9:**1274, 1284
transportation and
communication **9:**1276,
1285

U

Ubangi River **5:**583, 651, 658,
660, 661
Ubangi-Shari **5:**646, 651–652,
653, 658, 659, 687, 694
Uganda **4:**554–571; **5:**670, 698
Angola **5:**618
art and architecture **4:**562
Central African Republic
5:652
climate **4:**444, 446–447, 554
cultural expression
4:562–564
daily life **4:**565
economy **4:**535, 536, 556,
568–571
education **4:**566, 568
family and society
4:565–566
flag **4:**555
flora and fauna **4:**448–451
food and drink **4:**564
geography **4:**436, 440, 441,
554
geology **4:**442–443
government and political
parties **4:**556, 558, 561
health and welfare **4:**566,
569
history
chronology **4:**556
colonial **4:**457–458, 466,
523, 559, 562, 566, 567
modern **4:**554, 559–561,
568
independence **4:**554, 559,
568
literature **4:**562
music **4:**562–563
peoples **4:**457–458, 468,
469, 556, 559, 563–564,
565
population **4:**556
religion **4:**469, 556, 565
resources **4:**554, 569, *570*
transportation and
communication **4:**556,
567, 571
Tutsi exiles **5:**703, 704, 705,
708, 709
uKhahlamba-Drakensberg
Park **7:**882, 951
Uluru *see* Ayers Rock
Union Islands *see* Tokelau
Union of South Africa *see*
South Africa
United Kingdom *see* Great
Britain
United States **9:**1186, 1187,
1216, 1217
Angolan Civil War **5:**617, 625
Antarctica **10:**1423, 1424,
1425, 1429, 1430, *1432*
Australia **10:**1369, 1370
Liberia **2:**234–236, 237, 238
Western Pacific **8:**1034–1035,
1052, 1054, 1058, 1060,
1063, 1064, 1069, 1071,
1093, 1094, 1095
see also American Samoa

United States Pacific Islands
Territories **8:**1035, 1054,
1059, 1064, 1069,
1086–1087, 1093, 1097,
1098; **9:**1286–1289
geography **9:**1163, 1263,
1286–1289
United States Pacific Remote
Islands National Wildlife
Refuge **9:***1161*, 1286
Upolu Island **9:**1162, 1163,
1187, 1240, *1241*, *1242*
Upper Volta **3:**326, 350, 355,
357, 360, 363, 364
Mossi system **3:**318, 350
see also Burkina Faso
Urewera National Park **9:**1172
Urundi *see* Burundi
Usumbura *see* Bujumbura
Uvéa **9:**1162, 1174, 1186, 1290

V

Vaal River **7:**868, 870, 883,
888, 893, 896
Vaiaku **9:**1279, 1280, 1283
Vaitupu Atoll **9:**1279, 1281,
1285
Van Diemen's Land *see*
Tasmania
Vanuatu **8:**1136–1147
art and architecture
8:1142–1143
climate **8:**1019–1022, 1136
cultural expression
8:1142–1143
daily life **8:**1144
economy **8:**1137, 1146–1147
family and society **8:**1144
festivals, food, and drink
8:1143
flag **8:**1137
flora and fauna **8:**1023–1025
geography **8:**1012, 1014,
1016, 1136
geology **8:**1017–1018
government and political
parties **8:**1138, 1140
health, welfare, and
education **8:**1144
history
chronology **8:**1139
early **8:**1026–1027, 1033
modern **8:**1136, 1141, 1145
independence **8:**1136, 1140,
1141, 1145, 1146
languages **8:**1036, 1138, 1142
literature **8:**1142
music **8:**1143
peoples **8:**1036, 1138, 1142,
1144

population **8:**1137
religion **8:**1138, 1144
resources **8:**1136, 1146
transportation and
communication **8:**1138,
1147
Vella Lavella **8:**1130
Vereeniging **7:**868, 871
Victoria (Australian state)
10:1311, 1365, 1382, 1411
bushfires **10:**1324, 1408
federation **10:**1388
history **10:**1311, 1348, 1349,
1350, 1358, 1385, 1400,
1405, 1406
resources **10:**1410
see also Melbourne
Victoria (Malawi city) **6:**729,
733, *823*, 826
Victoria, Lake **4:**436, 438, 439,
441, 446, 451, 467, 468,
469, 559; **5:**603, *642*;
6:727, 736, 738, 739
European explorers **6:**744
fishing **6:**842
Kenya **4:**523, 528, 537–538
as Nile source **4:**466
Uganda **4:**562, 564, 567,
570, 571
Victoria Falls **6:**724, *726*, 727,
744, 855, 859; **7:**875
Victoria Land **10:**1314, *1315*
Vietnam War **10:**1369, 1370,
1380
Vinson, Mount **10:**1314
Virunga Mountains **5:**585,
587, *593*, 714
Virunga National Park **5:***591*,
715
Viti Levu **8:**1016, *1038*, *1042*,
1047, 1049, 1050
Volta, Lake **3:**292, 294, 295,
305, 375, *376*, 381, *382*,
388
Volta River **3:**292, 294, 295,
298, *299*, 307, 312, 388
Vostok Station **10:**1326–1327,
1429

W

Waigani **8:**1116, 1117
Waikato **9:**1165, 1185,
1233
Waikato River **9:**1159
Waitemata Harbour **9:**1229
Wake Island **9:**1286, *1288*
geography **9:**1163, 1289
Wallis and Futuna
9:1290–1291
geography **9:**1162, 1290

Wallis and Futuna (*continued*)
history **9:**1174, 1180, 1186, 1290
peoples **9:**1191, 1291
Walvis Bay **7:**874, 881, 926, 931, 937
population **7:**935
Weddell Sea **10:***1312*, 1313, 1314, 1327, 1352
Wellesley Islands **10:**1300
Wellington **9:**1159, 1228, 1229, 1235
architecture **9:**1219
Arts Festival **9:**1221
churches **9:**1223
history **9:**1184, 1185, 1228
immigrant population **9:**1225, 1228
Wellington Harbour **9:**1159, 1228
Wenger, Susanne **1:**106
West African coast
climate **2:**156–159
colonial division **2:**172–173, 250
early states **2:**164–168
first European intervention **2:**169–171, 250
flora and fauna **2:**160–163
freed slave settlements **2:**174–175
geography 148–153
geology **2:**154–155
peoples **2:**176–179
slave trade **2:**171, 180, 250
West Antarctic Mountains **10:**1314
West Cameroon *see* British Cameroon
Western Australia **10:**1304, 1305, 1365, 1393, 1409, 1411
Aboriginal Australians **10:**1355, 1356
federation **10:**1388
history **10:**1347, 1349, 1350, 1351, 1358, 1387, 1406
resources **10:**1306, 1409–1410, 1411
see also Perth
Western Cape Province **7:**871, 951, 955, 958, *967*, 971, 972

Western Pacific, colonial history **8:**1034–1035
Western Samoa **9:**1187, 1216, 1217, 1240, 1245
see also Samoa
Westland **9:**1160, 1166
Westland Tai Poutini National Park **9:**1172
White Nile River **4:***441*
White Volta 292: **3:***294*, 316, 355
Wilhelm, Mount **8:**1015
Wilkes Land coast **10:**1429
Willis Islets **10:**1310
Windhoek **7:**874, 897, 933, 934, 935
architecture **7:***930*, *931*, 932, *934*
Witwatersrand **7:**871, 876, 962, 964, 965
gold field **7:**893, 898, 965, 967, 971
university **7:**961, 966
Wollemia **10:**1331, *1332*
Wuteve, Mount **2:**153

Y

Yaméogo, Maurice **3:**355
Yamoussoukro **3:**297, 396, 404, 405
public buildings **3:**396, 399, *400*, 403
Yaoundé **1:**14, *58*, 59, 60, 62, *67*
Yap **8:**1029, 1064, 1069, 1070, 1071
Yasur, Mount **8:**1016, *1137*
Yule Island **8:**1028, 1104

Z

Zaire *see* Congo, Democratic Republic of
Zambezi River **6:**724, 726, 727, 734, 736, 738, 739, 741, 746, *844*, 849; **7:**875, 883, 896, 897
European explorers **6:**744
hydroelectric power **6:**724, 814, 857
Mozambican divide **6:**810
Zambezi Valley **7:**870, 879–880, 887, 998
Zambia **6:**844–859
Angolan peace accord **5:**618
art and architecture **6:**851,

855
climate **6:**732–734, 746, 844
cultural expression **6:**851–852
daily life **6:**853–854
economy **6:**846, 856–859
family and society **6:**853
festivals and food **6:**852
flag **6:**846
flora fauna **7:**882
geography **5:**583; **6:**724, 727, 736, 844
geology **5:**586–587; **6:**730, 731
government and political parties **6:**846, 848
health and education **6:**854, 855, 857
history
chronology **6:**847
colonial **7:**986, 991, 999
modern **5:**618: **6:**745, 774, 779, 844, 849–850, 855, 856
precolonial **5:**599: **6:**739, 741, 747
independence **6:**844, 850, 856
literature **6:**851, 855
music **6:**852
peoples **6:**727, 746–747, 844, 846; **7:**896
population **6:**845–846
religion **6:**846, 853
resources **6:**727, 844, 856, 857
transportation and communication **6:***840*, 846, 855, 859
Zimbabwe guerrillas **7:**992
Zamfara River **1:**10
Zanzibar **4:**458, 460, 465, 518, 525, 526, 546, 551; **5:**603; **6:**726, 733, 842
British protectorate **4:**466, 523, 535
cultural expression **6:**756, 836
government **6:**832
history **6:**740, 741, 743, 828
independence **6:**828, 834
Muslim traders **5:**599
peoples **6:**748, 853
slave trade **6:**744, 745
Tanganyika union *see*

Tanzania
Zealandia **9:**1164–1165
Zimbabwe **4:**504; **7:**986–1003
art and architecture **7:**995
climate **7:**878, 879–881, 986
cultural expression **7:**994–996
daily life **7:**997–998
diaspora **7:**997, 1002
economy **7:**986, 988, 993, 997, 1000–1003
family and society **7:**997–998
festivals, food, and drink **7:**996
flag **7:**988
flora and fauna **7:**882, 883, *987*
geography **7:**870, 872, 875, 986
geology **7:**876
government and political parties **7:**986, 988, 990, 993, 998, 1000–1001
health, welfare, and education **7:**998
history
British rule *see* Southern Rhodesia
chronology **7:**989
modern **7:**896, 986, 991–993
precolonial **7:**886–887, 889
Second Congo War **5:**670, 678, 705
independence **7:**986, 991, 992, 996, 997, 999, 1000
languages **7:**988, 994
literature **7:**994–995
music **7:**995–996
peoples **7:**900–901, 988, 994, 997
population **7:**987
religion **7:**988, 997
resources **7:**986, 1002
transportation and communication **7:**988, 1003
Zomba **6:**734, 781, 784
Zula, Gulf of **4:**454
Zululand **6:**744

Ethnic and Religious Index

Numbers in **boldface** refer to volume numbers; those in *italic* refer to illustrations:

A

Aboriginal Australians **10:**1307, 1355–1357, 1358, 1413
  contemporary life **10:**1383, 1388, 1390, 1392
  cultural expression **10:**1318, 1342, 1372–1375, 1377, *1378*, 1379, 1381, 1413
  discrimination **10:**1356, 1369–1370, 1371, 1373, 1388, 1406, 1455
  early history **10:**1340–1343, 1344, 1346, 1348, 1355, 1387–1388, 1398, 1399, 1402–1405
  kinship system **10:**1343
  population **10:**1355, 1362
  sacred places **10:**1307, 1318, *1341, 1343*
  spirituality **10:**1342, 1384, 1385, 1386, 1413
  "Stolen Generation" **10:**1371, 1373, 1388
Adamawa (people) **1:**47–49, 50
Adja (people) **3:**322, 328, 330, 340
Afar (people) **4:**467, 470, 474, 475, 476–478, 480, 491
African Americans **2:**174, 175, 179
  Liberia colonization **2:**230, 235–236, 246, 247
  Roots festival **2:**198, 199, 203
  Sierra Leone settlement **2:**174–175, 179, 268, 273, 275, 280
African churches **3:**341, 342, *343,* 401; **6:**802, 810, 853; **7:**900, 905, 910, 916, 922, 928, 934, 942, 997, 998
African religions **1:**8, 88, 97, 110, 112
  see also traditional beliefs
Afrikaaners (Boers) **7:**890–891, 892, 893, 894, 895, 901, 940, 958, 962, 964
  Basotho conflict **7:**919
  Great Trek **7:**892, 893, 901, 940, 946, 962
  Namibia **7:**926, 945

nationalism **7:**894, 899, 945–946, 956
  Zulu conflicts **7:**895, 896, 962
Afro-Brazilians **3:**329, 335, 338, 345
Afro-European Creoles **2:**179, 183, 185, 186
Akan (people) **3:**312–313, 314, 328, *377,* 378, 379, 380, 381, 401, 402
Americo-Liberians **2:**179, 230, 234, 235–236, 237, 238–239, 241, 243, 246
  as political elite **2:**240, 247
Amhara (people) **4:**464, 467–468, 509
ancestor veneration **6:**767, 768, 769–770; **8:**1111, 1132, 1143; **9:**1249
  Madagascar **6:**767, 768, 769–770
  Papua New Guinea **8:**1111
  Samoa **9:**1249
  Solomon Islands **8:**1132
  Vanuatu **8:**1143
Anglicanism
  Australia **10:**1350, 1362, 1384, 1385, 1401, 1402
  Botswana **7:**905, 910
  Burundi **5:**639
  Congo, DR. 674
  Ethiopia **5:**508
  Kenya **4:**520, 529
  Lesotho **7:**922
  Malawi **6:**782
  Namibia **7:**92, 9348
  New Zealand **9:**1182, 1184, 1212, 1219, 1223, 1230
  Nigeria **1:**112
  Papua New Guinea **8:**1104, 1111
  Rwanda **5:**700, 709
  Saint Helena **7:**939
  Seychelles **6:**820, 825, 826
  Solomon Islands **8:**1126, 1132
  South Africa **7:**939, 943, 956
  Swaziland **7:**976, 982
  Tanzania **6:**830, 837
  Uganda **4:**556, 559, 560, 565, *567*
  Vanuatu **8:**1138, 1143; **9:**1182
  Zambia **6:**846, 853
  Zimbabwe **7:**988, 997

animism **1:**57, 80, 132; **2:**200, 226, 243, 261, 277, 278; **5:**622, 639, 656, 692, 709
Annobones (people) **1:**75
Arabs **6:**739, 740–741, 742, 744, 748, 750, 758, 800, 818, 828, 834
Assembly of God churches **8:**1040, 1047, 1056, 1061
Australian Methodist Society **8:**1104
Awandji (people) **1:**46

B

Baganda (people) **4:**469, 559, 562, 565
Baghirmi (people) **1:**30
Baka Pygmies **1:**57
Bakweri (people) **1:**45, 46
Balante (people) **2:**166, 173, 178–179, 218, 224, 226, 261
Banda (people) **5:**609, 648, 656
Bantu (people) **5:**607, 609, 674; **6:**738–739, 740, 746, 747, 748, 800; **7:**914, 940, 986
Banyangs (people) **1:**46
Baptist churches **1:**60, 112; **5:**648, 651, 656, 674–675, 692
Basotho (people) **7:**871, 888–889, 896, 900, 918–923, 925, 957
Baule (people) **3:**395, 402, 498
Baya (people) **5:**609, 648, 651, 653, 656
Bemba (people) **3:**311; **6:**746, 846, 851, 853
Beti-Pahuin (people) **1:**45, 46, 48, 57, 59
Betsileo (people) **6:**742, 769
Bisa (people) **3:**360
Bobo (people) **3:**328, 360
Boers *see* Afrikaaners
British Christian Missionary Society **9:**11887
Bubi (people) **1:**74, 75, 76
Buddhism 1384, 1385
Bulala (people) **1:**29, 36
Burkinabé (people) **3:**397, 407
Bwiti (indigenous faith) **1:**88

C

Calabar (people) **1:**12, 49
cargo cult **8:**1141, 1143

Catholicism *see* Roman Catholicism
Chamorro (people) **8:**1032, 1052, 1086
Chewa (people) **6:**746, 778, 780, 781, 782, 852, 853
Chinese, ethnic **1:**75, 88, 91; **8:**1037, *1079,* 1080, 1134
Chiounda Mosque **6:**758
Chokwe (people) **5:**619, 622, 672
Christianity *see* missionaries; Protestantism; Roman Catholicism
Church of England *see* Anglicanism
Claretian order **1:**75
Congo (people) **2:**179, 243
Congregationalism
  Australia **10:**1384, 1385
  Kiribati **9:**1200, 1206, 1207
  Marshall Islands **8:**1056, 1061, 1071
  Nauru **8:**1081
  Polynesia **9:**1187, 1189, 1190, 1237, 1257
  Samoa **9:**1242, 1249
  Tuvalu **9:**1276, 1282
Coptic Christians **4:**459, 484, 490, 508
creation legends **1:**31, 36, 48
Creoles **6:**748, 793, 795, 817, 821, 825
  see also Afro-European Creoles; Krio
curandeiros (healers) **6:**810

D

Dagbon (people) **3:**314
Dan (people) **3:**398
Dioula (peoplo) **3:**313, 317
Douala (people) **1:**45, 46, 59
Dreamtime **10:**1372, 1377, 1386
Dutch Reformed Church **7:**943, 956, 997

E

Edo (people) **1:**33, 35; **3:**322
Église Évangélique du Gabon **1:**88
Ethiopian Orthodox Church **4:**455, 459, 464, 467, 468, 484, 490, 498, 502, 505–508, 512, 513

Ethiopian Orthodox Church
(*continued*)
Eritrea **4**:491, 492
liturgical text **4**:468, 511
Evangelical churches **3**:401, 420;
8:1047, 1111, 1126, 1132
Evangelical Church of
Polynesia **9**:1191
Ewe (people) **1**:47, 49; **3**:324,
328, 379, 380, 410, 417,
419, 420, 421, 423

F
Falashas (Jewish sect) **4**:508
Fang (people) **1**:45, 46, 47–48,
68, 70, 73–76, 85, 86, 88
female genital mutilation **2**:200,
213, 226, 244; **3**:342, 361,
381, 420; **4**:478, 492, 532,
550; **5**:656–657, 675
Fijians (people) **8**:1036, 1038,
1042, 1043, 1044, 1046,
1047–1048, 1051
Filipinos, ethnic **8**:1037, 1094,
1095
Fon (people) **3**:322, 328, 335,
338, 339, 340, 341, 417, 419
French Huguenots **7**:890, 901,
957, 963
Fula (people) *see* Fulani
Fulani (Fula) (people) **1**:10, 37,
40, 47, 50, 57, 101–103,
112, 128, 192; **2**:176–177,
198, 200, 204, 211, 212,
213, 218, 224, 226, 258;
3:310, 318, 322, 323, 329,
341, 355, 360; **5**:608, *653*

G
Gä (people) **3**:328, 329, 379,
380, 383
Ganda (people) *see* Baganda
Gio (people) **2**:239, 243
Golden Stool (Ashanti symbol)
3:314, 315, 378, 385
Gouro (people) **3**:398
Grebo (people) **2**:236, 240, 243
Guale (people) **8**:1129
Guan (Guang) (people) **3**:328
Gur (people) **3**:311, 320, 401
Gurma (people) **3**:323
Gurunsi (people) **3**:360

H
Hausa (people) **1**:10, 40, 47,
101, 102, 103, 112, 114,
117; **3**:317
cultural expression **1**:106, 108
Kano **1**:122
Haya (people) **6**:746–748, 837

Hehe (people) **6**:739, 833
Heke (people) **9**:1185
Herero (people) **7**:889, 932,
934, 935
genocide **7**:897, 901, 926, 933
Hima (people) **6**:747–748
Hinduism
Fiji **8**:1040, 1043, 1046–1048
Mauritius **6**:790, 793, 794,
795, 796
Reunion **6**:817
Seychelles **6**:820
South Africa **7**:956
Tanzania **6**:837
Hisbi Islam **4**:545
Hova (people) **6**:742, 766, 771
Hutu (people) **5**:599, 628, 630,
632, 713
Burundi violence **5**:634–635,
638, 639, 642, 643, 644
colonial policies **5**:609, 633,
642, 703, 704, 709, 711
Congo Wars **5**:670
language **5**:636
percentage in Rwanda **5**:706,
709
Rwandan genocide **5**:670,
698, 704–705, 709, 712
Rwandan government **5**:702

I
Ibibio (people) **1**:12, 49
Ibo (people) **1**:12, 47, *48*, 101,
102, 103, 112, 114, 115, 117
Igbo (people) *see* Ibo
I-Kiribati (people) **9**:1204,
1205, 1206
Ile-Ife *see* Ife
Imbangala (people) **5**:599
Indo-Fijians **8**:1037, 1038,
1042, 1043, 1044, 1045,
1046, 1047, 1048, 1050
Indonesians **6**:748, 750, 760,
766, 769, 816
Iru (people) **6**:747, 748
Islam **1**:36, 48, 49, 76; **5**:599
Australia **10**:1384, 1385
Benin **3**:332, 335, 339, 341,
342
Bono **3**:313
Burkina Faso **3**:352, 358,
359, 360, 361, 363
Burundi **5**:639
Cameroon **1**:52, 60, *61*
Central African Republic
5:648, 656
Comoros **6**:752, 755, 756,
757, 758
Congo, DR **5**:664, 674, 675
Congo, Rep. **5**:684, 692

Djibouti **4**:470, 472, 476,
477, 478
eastern Africa **4**:455, 456, 467
eastern Central Africa **6**:740,
741, 742, 747, 748
Eritrea **4**:484, 490, 491, 493
Ethiopia **4**:463, 464, 496,
498, 502, *503*, 505, 508,
510, 512
Fiji **8**:1040, 1043, 1046–1048
Fulani **1**:40–42, 45, 47
Fulani jihad **3**:310, 322, 323,
329
Gabon **1**:80, 88, *89*
Gambia **2**:194, 198, 199, 200
Ghana **3**:370, 379, 380
Guinea **2**:204, 206, 211–213
Guinea-Bissau **2**:225, 226
Hausa **1**:27, 36, 37, 40, 47
holidays **1**:59, 110; **3**:379,
400, 419
Ivory Coast **3**:390, 392, 397,
399, 401, 402, 406
Kanem-Bornu **1**:28, 29, 30
Kenya **4**:457, 460–461, 518,
520, 529
Liberia **2**:232, 243
Malawi **6**:782
Mauritius **6**:790, 795
Mayotte **6**:798, 799
Mossi Empire **3**:312, 318
Mozambique **6**:802, 810
Nigeria **1**:97, 101, 102, 104,
112–115, 119, 121, 122, 129
Rwanda **5**:700, 710, 712
Senegal **2**:250, 252, 257,
259, 260, 261, *262*
Sierra Leone **2**:270, 273,
277, 278
Sokoto **1**:10, 30
Somalia **4**:504, 529, 540,
542, 545, 547, 549, 550
Somalis **4**:440, 462, 464,
465, 467, 546, 548
South Africa **7**:956, 957
Swahilis **4**:459, *460*, 469
Swaziland **7**:976, 982
Tanzania **6**:830, 837
Togo **3**:412, 419, 420, 421
Uganda **4**:556, 560, 565
West African coast **2**:164–165,
166, 167–168, 172, 174,
177, 178
Zanzibar **6**:748
see also jihad; mosques;
Sharia; Sufism
Islamic brotherhoods
2:260–261
Issa (people) **4**:470, 474, 475,
476–477, 478

J
Jesuits **4**:464
Jews **7**:956, 957; **9**:1191, 1223;
10:1385
Ethiopia **4**:508
jihad **1**:30, 37
Fulani (1804) **1**:40, 42, 45,
47, 49, 112, 122
Somali **4**:465, 546, 548
Jola (people) **2**:258, 260, 261
Jolof (people) **2**:165–166, 250,
263
Jukun (people) **1**:47, 48

K
Kabye (Kabre) (people) **3**:328,
417, 420
Kalanga (people) **7**:908, 910
Kalenjin (people) **4**:468–469,
528, 530
Kassena (people) **3**:311, 358
Kele (people) **1**:46
Ketu (people) **1**:31
Khoisan (people) **7**:888, 891,
892, 901, 902, 908
Kikuyu (people) **4**:468, 469,
524, 525, 526, 530, 534;
6:746, 748
churches **4**:529
rain-making ceremony **4**:528
Kimbanguist church
5:674–675, 692
Kimbundu (people) **5**:607,
608, 612
King Fahd Mosque **2**:198, *200*,
201
King movement (Maori) **9**:1185
Kirdi (people) **1**:45, 57
Kong (people) **3**:310
Kongo (people) **5**:597, 607, 608,
667, 674, 687, 690, 692
art **5**:*599*, 600
Kono (people) **2**:178, 275, 278
Kotokoli (people) **3**:420
Kpelle (people) **2**:178, 213,
240, 243
Krio (Creole) (people) **2**:175, 179, 240,
273, 275, 278, 279, 280
Kru (people) **2**:178, 236, 237,
240, 243; **3**:401

L
Lebou (people) **2**:260, 263
Limba (people) **2**:275, 278
Lomwe (people) **6**:746, 747,
782, 810
London Missionary Society
6:766, 769; **8**:1104;
9:1186, 1188, 1206, 1245,
1249, 1279

Lozi (people) **6:**727, 746, 852, 853
Luba (people) **5:**583, 607, 674
Luhya (people) **4:**468, 526, 530
Luo (people) **4:**468, 469, 525, 526, 530
Lutheranism
  Australia **10:**1385, 1397
  Namibia **7:**928, 934
  Papua New Guinea **8:**1100, 1103, 1111
  Zimbabwe **7:**997

M

Maasai (people) **4:***467*, 468, 469, 523, 528, 534, *537*; **6:**739, 748, 837, 842
  decorative arts **4:**526, *527*
  social structure **4:**530
Makonde (people) **6:**746, 807
  sculpture **6:**748, 808, 835
Makua (people) **6:**746, 747, 807, 810
Malagasy (people) **6:**748, 766, 767, 768, 769
Malaitan (people) **8:**1124, 1129
Malinke (Malinga) (people) **2:**178, 211, 212, 213
Mande (people) **3:**360, 398, 401
Mandinka (Mandinga) (people) **2:**166, 176, 178, 198, 200, 201, 212, 226, 250, 260
Manjaca (people) **2:**115, 173, 226
Mano (people) **2:**239, 240, 243
Maori (people) **9:**1170, 1177–1179, 1180, 1191, 1209, 1226, 1228, 1231
  art and architecture **9:***1178, 1184*, 1219
  Auckland **9:**1229
  British settlers **9:**1182–1185
  ceremonies **9:**1221
  diseases **9:**1181, 1183
  family and society **9:**1224
  food **9:**1222
  legal and social status **9:**1185, 1189, 1216
  literature **9:**1218
  music **9:**1220
  religion **9:**1123, 1179, 1182, 1189, 1223
Maroons **2:**174, 273, 278
Mbenga (people) **5:**609, *673*
M'Bochi (people) **5:**684, 692
Mbum (people) **5:**656
Mbundu (people) **5:**599, 608, 622
Mbuti (people) **5:**609
Mecca **4:**455

Melanesians **8:**1012, 1014, 1026–1028, 1036, 1038, 1042, 1112, 1130, 1138, 1142, 1144; **9:**1174, 1190, 1268
Mende (people) **2:**178, 273, 275, 278
Merina (people) **6:**767, 769
Meru (people) **4:**530
Methodism
  Australia **10:**1384, 1385
  Benin **3:**332
  Fiji **8:**1040, 1043, 1047
  Ghana **3:**380, 384, *385*
  Ivory Coast **3:***392*, 401
  New Zealand **9:**1182, 1223
  Papua New Guinea **8:**1103, 1104
  Samoa **9:**1242, 1249
  Solomon Islands **8:**1132
  Tonga **9:**1186, 1190, 1260, 1263, 1267, 1268
Micronesians (people) **8:**1012, 1014, 1036–1038, 1074, 1130, 1132; **9:**1189, 1190, 1206, 1284
missionaries **1:**38, 43, 46; **8:**1104, 1124
  Angola **5:**622
  Belgian Congo **5:**667, 671
  Central African Republic **5:**651
  central West Africa **3:**319, 324, 325, 360, 377, 380, 401
  eastern Africa **4:**455, 458, 464, 466, 489, 492, *507*, 529, 554, 559
  Kongo **5:**598, 600, 603, 674
  Madagascar **6:**766, 769
  Malawi **6:**745, 779, 782
  Rwanda **5:**707–708, 709–711
  Western Pacific **8:**1032, 1033, 1034, 1038, 1042, 1071, *1081*, 1095, 1103
  Zambia **6:**849, 851
  Zimbabwe **7:**897, 926, 956, 997
monasteries **4:**455, 492, 506
Mongo ((people) **5:**607, 674
Monophysite Christians **4:**455
Mormons **9:**1223, 1237, 1242, 1246
mosques **3:**358, *359*, 363, 399, 404; **4:**527, 529, *535*, 548, *549*
Mossi (people) **3:**311, 350, 355, 357, 359, 360, 363
Mouridist brotherhood **2:**261
Mthethwa (people) **7:**889, 895
Muslims *see* Islam
Mwiri (indigenous faith) **1:**8

N

Nakomse (people) **3:**311
Nama (people) **7:**901, 926, 932, 934, 935
National Church of Nigeria and the Cameroons **1:**112, 113
Nauruan Independent Church **8:**1081
Ndebele (people) **7:**888, 893, 896, 900, 951, 957, 988, 994, 995, *996*, 997
  uprising **7:**991
  ZAPU supporters **7:**992, 993, 1000
Ndwandwe (people) **7:**889, 895, 896
Ngati Tumatakokiri (people) **9:**1180
Ngoni (people) **6:**739, 744, 746, 747, 782, 852
Nguni (people) **7:**887, 888, 892, 893, 896, 900, 980, 986, 995
Ngwane (people) *see* Swazi
Nilotic (people)s **6:**739, 748
Njembe (indigenous faith) **1:**88
Nuna (people) **3:**311, *358*
Nyamwezi (people) **6:**739, 744, 746, 748, 835, 837
Nzebi (people) **1:**48

O

Oceanic peoples **8:**1029, 1036
Oduduwa (god) **1:**31, 32, 33
Ogiso (rulers of the sky) **1:**33
Ogoni (people) **1:**104
Ogun (god) **1:**42
Olurun (god) **1:**31
Ombwiri (indigenous faith) **1:**8
Oromo (people) **4:**464, 467, 509
Orthodox Christians **10:**1384, 1385
  see also Ethiopian Orthodox Church
Osun (spirit goddess) **1:**42
Ottamari (people) **3:**341
Ouatchi (people) **3:**420
Ovambo (people) **7:**889, 901, 926, 928, 932, 934
Ovimbundu (people) **5:**608, 612, 622
Owu (people) **1:**317
Oyoko clan **3:**314

P

Pacific Islanders **8:**1036; **9:**1224, 1225, 1226, 1228, 1268
Pallotine Order **1:**46
Papel (people) **2:**173, 226

Pentecostal churches **3:**370, 380, 401; **4:**556, 565; **7:**905, 910, 942, 956, 982, 997; **8:**1071, 1111
Peuhl (people) **2:**211, 231
Polynesians (people) **8:**1030, 1036, 1037, 1074, 1130, 1132; **9:**1189–1192, 1229, 1280, 1284, 1291; **10:**1416
  European contacts **9:**1181, 1186
  migration **9:**1174–1176, 1177, 1180, 1189, 1196, 1198, 1240, 1256
Poro (animists) **2:**243, 277
Presbyterianism **6:**776, 782; **8:**1138, 1143; **9:**1123, 1223; **10:**1384, 1385
Protestantism
  Angola **5:**612, 616, 622
  Benin **3:**332, 341
  Burkina Faso **3:**352, 360
  Burundi **5:**639
  Cameroon **1:**60
  Cape Verde **2:**182, 188
  Central African Republic **5:**648, 656
  Congo, DR **5:**664, 674
  Congo, Rep. **5:**684, 692
  Equatorial Guinea **1:**75
  Ethiopia **4:**498, 508
  Gabon **1:**80, 88
  Gambia **2:**194, 201
  Ghana **3:**370, 380
  Guinea **2:**213
  Ivory Coast **3:**392, 401–403
  Kenya **4:**520, 529
  Liberia **2:**232, 243
  Madagascar **6:**742, 763, 769
  Mozambique **6:**810
  Nigeria **1:**97, 112
  Rwanda **5:**700, 709, 710
  Senegal **2:**261
  Tanzania **6:**830, 837
  Togo **3:**412, 420
  Uganda **4:**565
  West African coast **2:**174, 179
  Zambia **6:**846, 853
Pulaar (people) **2:**161, 260
pygmies **5:**609
  see also Twa

Q

Quakers **2:**235

R

Rastafarianism **4:**502, 513
Ratana Church **9:**1189, 1223
razana (ancestor spirits) **6:**769–770

razana (*continued*)
  Polynesia **9:**1186, 1189, 1190, 1191
  Roman Catholicism **1:**49; **3:**319, 324
    Angola **5:**612, 620, 621, 622, 623, 624
    Australia **10:**1350, 1362, 1384, 1385, 1401
    Benin **3:**332, 335, 338, 339, 341, 344
    Botswana **7:**905, 910
    Burkina Faso **3:**352, 360, 363
    Burundi **5:**630, 634, 638, 639, 642
    Cameroon **1:**52, 60, 62, 63
    Cape Verde **2:**179, 182, 188
    Central African Republic **5:**648, 651, 654, 656
    Congo, DR **5:**664, 667, 674
    Congo, Rep. **5:**684, 692, 694
    Djibouti **4:**478
    Equatorial Guinea **1:**70, 73, 75
    Eritrea **4:**491, 492
    Fiji **8:**1040, *1044,* 1047
    Gabon **1:**80, 88, 90
    Gambia **2:**194, 200, 201
    Ghana **3:**370, 380, 384
    Guam **8:**1053
    Guinea **2:**206, 213
    Guinea-Bissau **2:**226
    Ivory Coast **3:**392, 396, 398–399, 401, 402, 403, *404*
    Kenya **4:**520, 529
    Kiribati **9:**1200, 1206, 1207
    Kongo **5:**598, 599, 600, 674
    Lesotho **7:**916, 921, 922, 923
    Liberia **2:**232, 243
    Madagascar **6:**763, 769, 771
    Malawi **6:**779, 782
    Marshall Islands **8:**1056, 1061
    Mauritius **6:**790, 793, 795, 796
    Micronesia **8:**1066, 1071
    Mozambique **6:**802, *808,* 809, 810
    Namibia **7:**928
    Nauru **8:**1081
    New Caledonia **8:**1085
    New Zealand **9:**1182, 1186, 1189, 1212, 1223
    Nigeria **1:**97, 112
    Northern Mariana Islands **8:**1086, 1087
    Palau **8:**1090, 1093, 1095
    Papua New Guinea **8:**1100, 1103, 1104, 1111
    Portugal **4:**459, 464
    Reunion **6:**748, 817
    Rwanda **5:**700, 704, 709, 710, 711, 712

Samoa **9:**1242, 1249
São Tomé and Príncipe **1:**132, 137, 138
Senegal **2:**252, 257, 261, *263*
Seychelles **6:747,** 748, 820, 824, 825, 826
Solomon Islands **8:**1126, 1132
South Africa **7:**943, 956
Swaziland **7:**976, 982
Tanzania **6:**830, 837
Togo **3:**412, 419, 420, 423
Tonga **9:**1260, 1268
Uganda **4:**469, 556, 565
Vanuatu **8:**1138, 1143
Wallis and Futuna **9:**1291
Zambia **6:**846, 851, 853
Zimbabwe **7:**988, 997
Roman Uniate Catholics **4:**484

S

Samo (people) **3:**318
San (people) **7:**901
  musical bow **7:**952
  rock art **7:***889, 904,* 921, 933, *933,* 951, 995
Sande (animists) **2:**243, 277
Sao (people) **1:**27, 29, 50
Sawa (people) **1:**57, 59
Seke (people) **1:**46
Senhaja Berbers **2:**164
Senufo (people) **3:**323, 328, 360, 398
Seventh-Day Adventists **8:**1040, 1047, 1138, 1143
Sharia (Islamic law) **1:**36, 40, 41, 104, 112, 114, 121; **4:**545, 547
Shiva (Hindu god) **6:**794, *795*
Shona (people) **7:**886, 900–901, 988, 992, 994, 995, 996, 997
Somali (people) **4:**464, 465, 467, 470, 474, 475, 476, 529, 540, 542, 546
  clans **4:**550
  see also Issa
Somba (people) **3:**338–339
Soninke (people) **2:**164, 178, 258
Sotho (people) *see* Basotho
Sousou (Susu) (people) **2:**178, 204, 211, 212, 213, 214
South Asians **6:**748, 783, 816
  Malawi **6:**783
  Mauritius **6:**788, 794–796
  Reunion. **6:**816
  South Africa **7:**892, 901, 947, 952, 956–958, 964, 967
  Tanzania **6:**833, 834
  see also Indo-Fijians

Sufism **2:**167, 177, 257, 260, *262;* **4:**477, 508, 548, 550
  Somalian music **4:**549
Sukuma (people) **6:**739, 746, 747, 748, 837
Sunni Muslims *see* Islam
Susu *see* Sousou
Swahili (people) **4:**457–458, 459, *460,* 466, 469; **6:**739, 740–743, 746, 747, 748, 750, 756, 760, 835, 837
  art and architecture **4:**526, 527
Swazi (people) **7:**889, 895, 900, 974, 976, 980, 982
syncretic religions **7:**988, 997

T

Téké (people) **5:**599, 689–690, 692, 694
Tem (people) **3:**419
Temne (people) **2:**172, 173, 174, 177–178, 273, 275, 278
Tigré (people) **4:**468, 490, 491
Tigrinya (people) **4:**492, 493
Tonga (people) **6:**746–747, 853
Torres Strait Islanders **10:**1355–1356, 1362, 1387, 1388, 1390
traditional beliefs
  Benin **3:**333, 341
  Botswana **7:**905, 910
  Burkina Faso **3:**352, 360, 361
  central West Africa **3:***310,* 311
  Ghana **3:**370, 380
  Ivory Coast **3:**392, 401
  Lesotho **7:**916, 921, 922
  Mossi states **3:**312
  Namibia **7:**928, *933,* 934
  Papua New Guinea **8:**1100, 1111, 1114
  South Africa **7:**956, 959
  Swaziland **7:**982
  Togo **3:**412, 419, 420
  Vanuatu **8:**1143
  Zimbabwe **7:**988, 997
Tsonga (people) **6:**746, 747, 810
Tswana (people) **7:**872–873, 888–889, 896, 900, 902, 906, 908, 909, 910, 911, 957
Tuareg (people) **2:**164, 168; **3:**317
Tumbuka (people) **6:**781, 782
Tutsi (people) **5:**599, 628, 630, 632, 711, 713, 714
  Burundi violence **5:**634–635, 638, 639, 642, 643, 644
  colonial policies **5:**609, 633, 642, 703, 709, 711
  Congo Wars **5:**670

cultural expression **5:**636, 637, 706
Ruanda kingdom **5:**698, 703, 711
Rwandan genocide **5:**670, 698, 704–705, 709, 712
Rwandan government **5:**702, 708, 712
Tuvaluans (people) **8:**1047, 1081
Twa (people) **5:***608,* 609, 630, 639, 674, 692, 705, 709

U

Umbundu (people) **5:**607, 608
Uniting Church in Australia **10:**1384

V

Vai (people) **2:**178, 240, 241
Venda (people) **7:**889, 947
Voortrekkers *see* Afrikaaners
Voudoun **3:**339, 341, 418–420

W

Wesleyan Methodist Missionary Society **8:**1103
White Fathers **5:**709, 710; **6:**851
Wolayta (people) **4:**468
Wolof (people) **2:**176, 177, *178,* 198, 200, 201, 252, 256, 257, 258, 259, 261

X

Xhosa (people) **7:**888, *889,* 891, 894, 900, 920, 922, 957, 982

Y

Yakoma (people) **5:**651, 652, 656
Yao (people) **6:**746, 747, 782, 807
Yoruba (people) **1:**12, 13, 47, 48, 100, 101, 102, 103, 104, 114, 117; **3:**335, 341
  art and architecture **1:**31, *31, 32,* 48
  cultural expression **1:**105, 106, 108, 110
  dress **1:**115
  Ibadan **1:**120
  Lagos **1:**123
  religion **1:**112

Z

Zion Christian churches **7:**900, 956, 976, 982
Zulu (people) **6:**739, 747; **7:**888, 892, 893, 900, 920, 922, 951, 957, 962, 982

Landscape and Climate Index

Numbers in **boldface** refer to
volume numbers; those in *italic*
refer to illustrations:

A

Adamawa Plateau **1:**11, 14, 24
Afar Depression **4:**438, 445
Albert Rift Valley **5:**585
Anambra River Basin **1:**12
Arabian-Nubian Shield **4:**442
Aso Rock **1:**119
Aurora Australis **10:***1429*
Ayers Rock, **10:**1307, 1413, 1418

B

bamboo forest **5:**595
Banfora Escarpment **3:**297–298
Bani River 8
Banto Faros (grasslands) **2:**150
baobab trees **1:***23;* **4:***488;* **7:***987*
Barkly Tableland **10:**1304–1306
Batéké Plateau **5:**584, 604
Benguela Current **5:***582,* 588,
    589, 624, 627
Benue Trough **1:**16, 17
Bié Plateau **5:**582, 583, 626
biodiversity **2:**160–163
Bongo Massif **5:**584
Burdekin Falls **10:**1410
bushfires (Australia) **10:**1324,
    1325, 1408
Bushveld (southern Africa)
    7:870, 872

C

Campbell Plateau **9:**1164
carbon sink **5:**591
Central African Plateau **5:**594
Central Lowlands (Australia)
    10:1309
Central Uplands (Australia)
    10:1307
Chad Basin **1:**11, 16
Chaillu Massif **1:**15, 16
Chappal Waddi 11
climate change **6:**731, 734;
    7:881; **8:**1022
    Antarctica **10:**1328, 1418,
        1425, 1430
    Congo Basin **5:**591, 593
    eastern Africa **4:**447
    Fiji **8:**1047
    Guam **8:**1059
    Gulf of Guinea **1:**21

Namibia **7:**936
Somalia **4:**553
Vanuatu **9:**1162, 1169, 1203,
    1274, *1276,* 1279, 1284
collision zones **8:**1018
Congo Basin **1:**46, 57
continental plates **4:**442
coral atolls **8:**1014, 1029–1031,
    1054, 1062; **9:**1158, 1160,
    1161, 1162, 1163, 1165, 1198
coral reefs **4:**449–450; **6:**729
    Australia **10:**1308, 1310,
        1329, 1335
    New Zealand and Polynesia
        9:1160, 1162, 1163, *1165*
    Western Pacific **8:**1012, 1014,
        1015, 1016, 1018, 1021,
        1024, 1025, 1031
    see also Great Barrier Reef
crater lakes **1:**17
Cross River Basin **1:**12
cyclones
    Australia **10:**1321, 1323–1324
    Indian Ocean islands **6:**732,
        734
    tropical Pacific **9:**1166, 1168,
        1169, *1169,* 1236, 1271
    Western Pacific islands
        8:*1019,* 1022, 1145

D

deforestation
    Burkina Faso **3:**365, *367*
    Burundi **5:**644
    Central African Republic **5:**660
    Ethiopia **4:**516
    Ivory Coast **3:**408
    Republic of the Congo **5:**696
    Rwanda **5:**714
desert
    Australia **10:**1304, 1306–1307,
        1321–1322, 1323, 1330
    Eastern Africa **4:**438, *440,*
        444, 445, 446, 480
    West African coast **2:**163
    see also karoo
desertification **7:**881
Drakensberg Escarpment
    5:582–583; **7:**870–871,
    873, 879, 882, 895, 896
drought
    Angola **5:***588,* 589
    Australia **10:**1329, 1350,
        1358, *1406,* 1408, 1410

Cape Verde **2:**180, 188–190
eastern Africa **4:**444, 445,
    446, 447, 448, 504, 514,
    515, 516, 525, 531, 537, 547
Fiji **8:**1021–1022
Lesotho **7:**924
Namibia **7:**936
South Africa **7:**971
southern Africa **7:**880–881,
    892, 895, 924, 936, 985
Swaziland **7:**985
dust storms **10:**1323, 1324

E

earthquakes
    New Zealand **9:**1128, 1164
    Western Pacific **8:**1014, 1145
East African Craton, East
    Africa **4:**442
East African Rift System **4:**438,
    439, 443, 448; **6:**727, 731
East Antarctic Ice Sheet
    10:1312, 1313
ENSO (El Niño–Southern
    Oscillation) **1:**18; **7:**881;
    8:1020, 1134
environmental damage
    Nigeria **1:**104
    Western Pacific **8:**1014, 1074,
        1134
environmental protection,
    Antarctica **10:**1431,
    1432–1433
Ethiopian Highlands
    4:439–440, 452, 454
Ethiopian Rift **4:**438
Etosha Pan **7:**883, 936, 937
eucalyptus **10:**1311, 1330, *1333*

F

faults **8:**1018
Ferlo Plateau and Valley **2:**151
ferns **9:**1170–1171
flooding **2:**150; **6:**734, 746
    Botswana **7:***904*
    Brisbane **10:**1398
    Burundi **5:**590
    Central African Republic **5:**590
    Congo, DR **5:**591
    Mozambique **6:**806, 813
    Senegal River **2:**148, 150
    Zambia **6:**858
forests
    Australia **10:**1329, 1406, 1411

bamboo **5:**595
Benin **3:**348
eastern Africa **4:**449, 451
Ghana **3:**388
New Zealand **9:**1170, 1171,
    1172, 1185
West African coast **2:**161–162
Fouta Djallon Massif **2:**148,
    150, 151, 152, 156, 158
Funtua Plateau **1:**10
fynbos **7:**885

G

geothermal hotspots **9:**1165
geysers **9:**1165
Gippsland Basin **10:**1301, 1311
glaciers **9:**1159, 1165; **10:**1313,
    1314, *1315, 1320,* 1328
global warming *see* climate
    change
grasslands *see* savanna
Great Artesian Basin **10:**1309,
    1318, 1410
Great Australian Bight
    10:1307, 1318
Great Barrier Reef **8:**1012;
    9:1181; **10:***1308,* 1310,
    1318, 1329, 1346, *1415*
Great Dividing Range **10:**1304,
    1309, 1310, 1311, 1318,
    1321, 1329, 1350, 1411
Great Escarpment *see*
    Drakensberg Escarpment
Great Lakes of Africa **4:**438, 439
Great Rift Valley **4:**438–439,
    440, 442, 443, *443,* 449,
    468, 469; **6:**724, 727, 731,
    748
    Eritrea **4:**493
    hominid fossils **4:**518
    Kenya **4:**523, 525, 533, 537
    lakes **4:**451
Great Sandy Desert **10:**1304,
    1306
Gregory Rift **4:**438, 439
Guinea Current **1:**19
Guinea Highlands **2:**152–153
Guinea savanna **1:**23–24
Gurara Falls **1:***13*

H

Harer Massif **4:**440
harmattan wind **1:**20; **3:**302,
    305

Haud (pasture) **4:**440, 546
Huila Plateau **5:**583
hurricanes **9:**1274

I

icebergs **10:**1312, 1431
ice sheets **10:**1312, 1313, 1319, 1320, 1326, 1336, 1432
  melting **10:**1328, 1418, 1425
ice shelves **10:**1313, 1328, 1353
Indo-Australian Plate **9:**1164, 1165
Intertropical Convergence Zone (ITCZ) **1:**18; **3:**302–303; **4:**444; **5:**588
irrigation
  Australia **1:***1411*; **10:**1410
  Ethiopia **4:**453
Ivory Coast Plateau **3:**295–296

J

Jos Plateau **1:**10, 20, 26, 47, 127

K

Kalahari Basin **5:**583
Karoo **7:**870, 872, 877, 885, 891
karst landscape **6:**728, *729*; **10:**1307
Katanga Plateau **5:**583, 590
Kingman Reef **9:***1161*, 1163, 1285, 1288
Kyushu-Palau Ridge **8:**1018

L

lagoons **1:**23; **3:**294, 309, 349, 405
Larsen Ice Shelf **10:***1312*, 1314
limestone **6:**728, *729*, 857; **8:**1015, 1016, *1074*; **9:**1160, *1165*; **10:***1305*, 1307, 1318, 1320
limnic eruption **1:**14, 17
Livingstone Falls **5:**694

M

Malebo Pool **5:**580, 583, 677, *682*, 694
Maletsunyane Falls **7:***916*
Mambilla Plateau **1:**11, 24, 25
mangroves **1:**23, 57; **4:**449–450; **8:**1015; **9:**1159, 1173
  Central West Africa **3:**308–309
  Tonga **9:**1173
  West African coast **2:**150, 151, 152, 160–161
  Western Pacific **8:**1024, *1025*
Mariana Trench **8:**1018
Marungu Plains **5:**583
McMurdo Dry Valleys **10:**1313–1314

miombo woodlands **5:**595
monsoon, West Africa **2:**156
Mount Nimba Highlands **3:**296
Murchison Falls **4:***438*
Murray-Darling Basin **10:**1304, *1307*, 1308, 1309, 1311, 1348

N

Namib Sand Sea **7:**874
New Hebrides Trench **8:**1012
Ngorongoro Crater **6:**727, 843
Niari Valley **5:**584, 696
Niger-Benue Trough **1:**10, 19
Niger Delta Basin **1:**13, 16, 17
Niger Plains **2:**152
nor'wester (wind) **9:**1168–1169

O

Obudu Plateau **1:**12, 24
oceanic faults **1:**17
Okavango Delta **7:**883, *904*, *910*
ozone layer hole **10:**1339, 1418, 1425, 1430

P

Pacific Plate **8:**1014; **9:**1164, 1165
Pacific Ring **8:**1017
Pan-African orogeny **2:**154; **3:**300, 300–301
pandanus leaves **9:**1204, *1205*
Pongsona **8:***1021*, 1022

R

rainfall
  Australia **10:**1321–1322, 1324, 1325
  Congo Basin **5:**588, 589, 590–591
  eastern Africa **4:**444–445, 446, 447, 449
rain forest
  Burundi **5:**644
  central West Africa **3:**294, *302*, 306, 307–308, 310, 322
  Congo Basin **5:**583, *584*, *590*, 591, 592–595, *594*, 596, 660, 678, 679, 695, 696
  Liberia **2:**248
  Nigeria and Gulf of Guinea **1:**13, 14, 17, 22, 23, 26, 57, *64*, 77
  Polynesia **9:**1173
  West Africa **2:**150
  Western Pacific **8:**1014, 1015, 1023, 1024
rapids **5:**583
rias (flooded river valleys) **2:**150
rift system **1:**16; **4:**438, 439, 443, 448

Rift Valley **6:**724, 726, 727, 731, 738
Ronne-Filchner Ice Shelf **10:**1313
Ross Ice Shelf **10:**1313, 1353

S

salt lakes **10:**1306, 1309
salt mines **1:**28; **2:***151*; **5:**597
sand dunes **3:**298–299, *303*
  Hadejia-Nguru **1:**11
sandstone **10:**1310, 1318, 1319, 1320, *1342*
  rock formation **10:**1413
savanna
  Central African Republic **5:***646*, 660
  coastal **3:**308
  Congo Basin and Angola **5:**583, 584, 585, 592, *594*, 595
  eastern Africa **4:**448–449, 451
  eastern Central Africa **6:**726, *730*, 735, *736*, 738
  eastern South Africa **7:**870, 874, *875*, *987*
  Ghana **3:**380
  Guinea **1:**23–24
  Nigeria **1:**10, 11, 22, 23–24
  Republic of the Congo **5:***684*
  Sahel **1:**24
  southern Africa **7:**870, 874, *875*
  sub-Sahara **3:**294, *295*, 297–298, 306–307, 310
  Sudan **1:**24
  termite mounds **2:**218
  West Africa coast **2:**150, 151, *161*, 162–163
  Western Pacific **8:**1024
  Zimbabwe **7:***987*
sea level rise *see* climate change
sea mounts **1:**17
Solomon Basin **8:**1012
Solomon Trench **8:**1012
South Sandwich Trench **10:**1302
Stanley Pool *see* Malebo Pool
Stellenbosch Valley **7:***967*
subtropical forest **10:**1399

T

Tanzanian Craton **4:**442
Tasman Glacier **9:**1159, 1165
tropical cyclones *see* cyclones
tropical forest *see* rain forest
tsunami **6:**826; **9:***1166*, 1245, 1253
typhoons **8:**1021, 1022; **9:**1236

U

Ubangi Plateau **5:**583

V

Victoria Falls **6:**724, *726*, 727, 744, 855, 859; **7:**875
volcanic activity
  Antarctica **10:**1320
  Cameroon **1:**50
  Comoros **6:***751*
  East Africa **4:**439, *440*, 443
  eastern Central Africa **6:**729, 731, 736
  Gulf of Guinea **1:**15, 17, *17*, 19
  Mauritius **6:***790*
  New Zealand and Polynesia **9:**1158, 1159, *1159*, 1160, 1162, 1163, 1164, 1165; **10:**1320
  Saint Helena **7:**872, 877, 938
  São Tomé and Príncipe **1:***131*, *132*
  southern Africa **7:**872, 877, 938
  West African coastal islands **2:**153, 155, 190
  Western Pacific **8:**1014, 1015, 1016, 1017, *1018*, *1123*, *1137*
Voltaian Basin **3:**294–295, 300, 328

W

Waterberg Plateau **7:**872
water scarcity
  southern Africa **7:**878, 912, 936
  Tuvalu **9:**1284–1285
  see also drought
West African craton **1:**16
West African Shield **2:**154; **3:**300, 301
West Antarctic Ice Sheet **10:**1312, 1313, 1425
Western Australian Shield **10:**1316–1317
Western Plateau **10:**1304, 1305, 1306
Western Rift Valley **5:**585, *586*
wetlands **1:**24; **3:**307
wildlife reserves **6:**726, *729*; **7:**883, 885; **9:**1163, 1172, 1286, *1288*; **10:**1335, 1413
  Zambia **6:**843, 859
  Zimbabwe **7:***984*, *986*
winds **9:**1168–1169
  Antarctica **10:***1326*, 1327, 1336
  see also harmattan wind

Z

Zimbabwe craton **7:**876
Zuma Rock **1:***14*

Historical and Biographical Index

Numbers in **boldface** refer to volume numbers; those in *italic* refer to illustrations:

A

Abacha, Sani **1**:104
Aba women's riot (1929) **1**:100
Abessole, Paul Mba **1**:84
abolitionism **2**:172, 173, 174, 175, 180, 235, 273, 280
Aboriginal Land Rights Act (1976) **10**:1355, 1358
Abreha, king of Himyar **4**:455
Abubakar, Abdulsalam **1**:104
Abushiri revolt (1888) **6**:833
Acheampong, Ignatius **3**:375–376
Adadura movement **1**:112
Ade, King Sunny **1**:108, *109*
Adelaide, queen of Great Britain **10**:1397
Adoboli, Eugene Koffi **3**:416
Adoula, Cyrille **5**:669
Adowa (Adwa), Battle of (1896) **4**:465, 502, 514
Aedisius **4**:455
Afghanistan war (2001) **6**:749
Afonso I, king of Kongo **5**:598, 674
African Americans
  Liberia colonization **2**:230, 235–236, 246, 247
  Roots Festival **2**:198, 199, 203
  Sierra Leone settlement **2**:174–175, 179, 268, 273, 275, 280
African Democratic Rally **2**:209
African Forum for Reconstruction (Gabon) **1**:82
African independence movement **1**:55
African National Congress **6**:806, 844; **7**:919, 944, 945, 992
  anti-apartheid campaign **7**:940, 946, 947, 954
  economic recovery programs **7**:969–970
  election win **7**:948–949, 969

African Party for the Independence of Guinea and Cape Verde **2**:184, 185, 218, 222, 223, 227
African traditional religions **2**:178, 194, 200, 206, 213, 226, 232, 243, 261, 270, 278
African Union **4**:502, 506, 512, 517, 547; **6**:755, 834
Agadjah, king of Abomey **3**:322
Aguiyi-Ironsi, Johnson **1**:103
Ahidjo, Ahmadou **1**:55–56, 60
Ahmad ibn Ibrihim al-Ghazi **4**:462, 464
Ahmed, Sharif **4**:547
Ahmed ibn Ali **1**:30
Ahomadégbé, Justin **3**:335
Aidid, Mohammed Farah **4**:547
AIDS *see* HIV/AIDS
Aimata Pomare IV, queen of Tahiti **9**:1186
Akan states **3**:310, 319, 322
  art and architecture **3**:312–313
  Ashanti Confederation **3**:314–315, 321
Akis, Timothy **8**:1107
Akofa, Henriette **3**:417
Aksum kingdom **4**:439, 453–456, 463, 470, 482, 489, 491, 496, 506
Akuffo, Fred **3**:376
Akufo-Addo, Nana **3**:376
Akwamu state **3**:313, 321
al- *for Arabic names containing al-, see under the following part of the name.*
Alesana, Tofilau Eti **9**:1253
Ali Ghadjideni ibn Dunama **1**:29
Ali Kwame, king of Bono **3**:313
Allada kingdom **3**:322
Alliance for Democracy (Nigeria) **1**:99
Alliance for Patriotic Reorientation and Construction (Gambia) **2**:196, 197
Alliance for Peace and Democracy (Liberia) **2**:234

All Nigeria People's Party **1**:99
All People's Congress (Sierra Leone) **2**:272, *273*, 274
Almeida, Manuel de **1**:135
Almoravid dynasty **2**:164–165
Alula, Ras **4**:465, 487
Alvaro I, king of Kongo **5**:598
Amadou Tall, sultan of Ségou **2**:168
Amari Ngoene Sobel **2**:166
"Amazons" **3**:322
Amda Seyon, emperor of Ethiopia **4**:464
American Colonization Society **2**:175, 226, 235–236, 246, 247
Amin, Idi **4**:554, 559, 560, 565, 568; **6**:834
Amundsen, Roald **10**:1353
Amundsen-Scott Station **10**:*1429*
Ana de Sousa (Nazinga Mbande) **5**:599
ANC *see* African National Congress
Andesite Line **8**:1017
Andrianampoinimerina, king of Madagascar **6**:742, 768, 770
Anglo-Boer Wars **7**:891; **9**:1185, 1215; **10**:1366
  First (1880–1881) **7**:893
  Second (1899–1902) **7**:894, 898–899, 940, 945, 962, 965, 967, 979
Anglo-Portuguese Treaty (1891) **6**:745
Anglo-Zulu War (1879) **7**:894
Angolan civil war **5**:582, 593, 610, 614, 617–618, 619, 625
  land mines **5**:618, 626
  public holiday **5**:621
  reconstruction **5**:620, 622, 627
Ankole kingdom **4**:457, 562
Annan, Kofi **3**:*375*; **4**:525
Ansa Sasraku, king of Akwamu **3**:313
Antarctic Service, U.S. **10**:1424
Antarctic Treaty (1959) **10**:1418, 1423, 1425,

1426, 1430, 1431, 1432, 1434
Antonio I, king of Kongo **5**:598
ANZAC forces **10**:1366
ANZUS Pact (1951) **9**:1216; **10**:1369
apartheid **7**:902, 907, 911, 919, 926, 931, 963, 965, 974, 979
  end **7**:940, 947, 948, 960, 969
  establishment **7**:946
  ideology **7**:967–968
  international boycotts **7**:968–969, 984
  musical forms **7**:952, 953
  protests **7**:946, 947, 948, 950, 953, 966
  societal effects **7**:957, 958, 959–960, 961, 967–968, 969, 970
  Truth and Reconciliation Commission **7**:949
Apithy, Sourou-Migan **3**:335
Aptidon, Hassan Gouled **4**:475
Aquamboes kingdom **3**:328
Arden-Clarke, Charles **3**:374
Armed Forces Provisional Ruling Council (Gambia) **2**:197
Armed Forces Revolutionary Council (Sierra Leone) **2**:274
Arusha Agreement (Burundi, 2003) **5**:635, 643
Arusha Declaration (Tanzania, 1967) **6**:840
Arusha peace accord (Rwanda, 1993) **5**:702, 705
Asaman, king of Bono **3**:313
Asfa Wossen **4**:503
Ashanti (Asante) confederation **3**:313, 314–315, 321, 324, 325, 328–329, 376
  decorative arts **3**:378
  Kumasi **3**:385
  social structure **3**:380
  territory **3**:368
Ashanti Wars **3**:315, 324, 326, 368, 373, 385
Ashmun, Jehudi **2**:174

ASODEGUE (Association for Democratic Solidarity in Equatorial Guinea) **1**:72
Aubame, Jean-Hilaire **1**:83
Australasian Antarctic Expedition **10**:1354
Awandji revolt (1920s) **1**:83
Azikiwe, Nnamdi **1**:112

B

Babangida, Ibrahim **1**:104
Bachwezi kingdom **6**:739
Bagaza, Jean-Baptiste **5**:634
Bah, Chernor **2**:276
Bainimarama, Mahendra **8**:1044
Bainimarana, Vorege **8**:1042
Balewa, Abubakar Tafawa **1**:101
Ballance, John **9**:1215
Bamako Initiative (1987) **2**:213
Bamana Empire **2**:168, 171
Banana, Canaan **7**:992
Banda, Hastings Kazumu **6**:774, 778, 779, 780, 784, 785, 786
Banda, Rupiah **6**:848, 850
Bantustans (homelands) **7**:940, 946, 947, 948–949, 957, 960, 963
Baol kingdom **2**:166, 172
Barclay, Edwin J. **2**:237
Barghash, sultan of Zanzibar **6**:743, 745
Barotse kingdom **7**:896
Barre, Muhammad Siad *see* Siad Barre, Muhammad
Barton, Edmund **10**:1365
Basotho kingdom **7**:894, 914, 919, 923
Bass, George **10**:1301
Batepá Massacre **1**:130, 135
Bathurst, Henry **2**:201
Batman, John **10**:1400
Bau kingdom **8**:1038
Bavadra, Timoci **8**:1044
Bayol, Jean-Marie **2**:172
Beavogui, Louis Lansana **2**:210
Bédié, Henri Konan **3**:396, 406
Behanzin, king of Danhome **3**:323, 325–326
Bellingshausen, Fabian Gottfried von **10**:1352
Bello, Ahmadu **1**:103, 120
Benguela Railroad **5**:582, 583
Benin Kingdom **1**:33–35, 38; **3**:322, 330, 335
Bérandjoko, ruler of Lobaye **5**:651
Bérenger, Paul **6**:793

Berlin, Treaty of (1889) **9**:1187
Berlin Conference (1884–1885) **2**:172; **3**:325; **5**:604, 605; **6**:805
Berlin Convention (1899) **9**:1187
Bicentennial, Australian (1988) **10**:1373, 1380
Biko, Steve **7**:947
Bilsen, A. A. van **5**:667
Binger, Louis-Gustave **3**:325
Bio, Julius Maada **2**:274
Biram state (Hausa) **1**:36
Bisho Massacre (1992) **7**:948
Biya, Paul **1**:54, 56, 60
Bizimungu, Pasteur **5**:705
"black-birding" **8**:1034
black townships *see* Bantustans
Bligh, William **10**:1348
Bloemfontein Convention (1854) **7**:893
Blood River, Battle of (1838) **7**:892, 896, 962
Boer Wars *see* Anglo-Boer Wars
Bokassa, Jean-Bédel **5**:646, 652, 658, 659
Bolger, Jim **9**:1216, 1217, 1233
Bondu imamate **2**:168, 172
Bongo, Ali **1**:82, 84
Bongo, Omar **1**:78, 82, 83, 84, 88
Boni, Yayi **3**:*334*, 336, 347
Bono state **3**:312, 313
Borchgrevink, Carsten Egeberg **10**:1353
Borgu kingdom **1**:32
Borno State **1**:10, 20
Bornu Empire **1**:29–30, 36
Botha, Louis **7**:899, 945, *947*
Botha, P. W. **7**:947
Bougainville, Louis-Antoine de **8**:1033; **9**:1181; **10**:1346
Bounty, HMS (ship) **9**:1188, 1191, 1238; **10**:1416
Bouvet de Lozier, Jean Baptiste Charles **10**:1426
Bozizé, François **5**:650, 652
Branco, Joaquim Rafael **1**:135
Bransfield, Edward **10**:1352
Brash, Nora Vagi **8**:1106
Brazza, Giacomo de **5**:604
Brazza, Pierre Savorgnan de **1**:46; **5**:603, 604, 682, 687, 694
Brazzaville Conference (1944) **1**:55
Brisbane, Thomas Macdougall **10**:1398
British Commonwealth **7**:945–946

British East Africa Company **4**:466, 523, 535, 567
British East Africa Protectorate **4**:466, 469, 518, 523–525, 527, 533, 535, 536, 546
British East India Company **7**:938
British First Fleet landing (1788) **10**:1344, 1346, 1347, 1358, 1372, 1380, 1383, 1385, 1387, 1404
British Military Administration **4**:488
British Phosphate Commission **9**:1203
British Royal Adventurers **1**:39
British South Africa Company **6**:745, 844, 849; **7**:896, 986, 991, 999
British West African Anti-Slave Trade Squadron **2**:273
Bruce, Stanley **10**:1367
Buganda kingdom **4**:457, 466, 469, 554, 558, 559, 561, 562–563, 567
Buhari, Mohammedu **1**:104
Bunyoro kingdom **4**:457, 554, 558, 559, 561, 562
Burke, Robert O'Hara **10**:1350
Burton, Charles **5**:603
Burton, Richard **6**:744
Burundi civil war **5**:593, 607, 609, 628, 632, 633, 634, 635, 643
  economic and social effects **5**:639, 640, 641, 645
  literature **5**:636
Busby, James **9**:*1182*, 1183
Busia, Kofi **3**:375
Buyoya, Pierre **5**:634, 635
Byrd, Richard E. **10**:1424
Byron, John **9**:1181; **10**:1346

C

Cabral, Amilcar **2**:185, 223, 225, 227
Cabral, Luis **2**:223, 228
Cabral, Vasco **2**:224
Cadamosto, Advise **2**:169
Cakobau, Seru Epenisa **8**:1043
caliphate **1**:37, 40, 47
Camara, Moussa Dadis **2**:210
Cameron, Verney L. **5**:603
Cameroon National Union **1**:55, 56
Cameroon People's Democratic Movement *see* MDPC
Canterbury Association **9**:1184, 1230

Cão, Diogo **5**:600; **7**:890
Cape Floral Kingdom **7**:885
Caprivi, Leo von **7**:897
Caramansa (Akan chief) **3**:313
Carpentier, Pieter de **10**:1300
Carstenszoon, Jan **10**:1300
Carteret, Philip **8**:1033; **9**:1181; **10**:1346
Carthaginians **2**:148
Cartwright, Silvia **9**:1224
Casely-Hayford, J. E. **3**:374, 377
Casement, Roger **5**:606
Cassard, Jacques **2**:169
Castle Hill Rising (1804) **10**:1348
Castro, Fidel **7**:931
CCM (Chama Cha Mapinduzi) **6**:832, 834, 836
Cetshwayo kaMpande, king of the Zulus **7**:895–896
Chan, Julius **8**:1105
Chapel of the Tablet (Aksum) **4**:452, 508
Chaudhry, Mahendra **8**:1044
Chelmsford, Lord **7**:896
Chifley, Joseph Benedict ("Ben") **10**:1368
child soldiers **4**:561, 565
Chilembwe, John **6**:779
Chilibula Mission **6**:851
Chiluba, Frederick **6**:850, 853
Chimurenga resistance **7**:992
Chissano, Joaquim **6**:806
cholera epidemic **7**:1000
Chuuk state **8**:*1068*, 1069, 1070, 1072, 1079, 1080
Civil Union Act (2004, New Zealand) **9**:1224
civil wars
  Congo, DR **5**:593, *607*, 661, 662, 698
  Congo, Rep. **5**:682, 687, 688, 690, 694, 697
  flora and fauna effects **5**:593, 607, 609
  Guinea-Bissau **2**:223, 226, 227, 228, 229
  Ivory Coast **3**:397, 400, 401, 406, 407
  Sierra Leone **2**:239, 268, 273, 274, 278, 279, 280, 281, 282, 283
  see also Angolan civil war; Liberian civil war; Mozambique civil war
Clark, Helen **9**:1217, 1224, 1233
Clay, Henry **2**:235
Clifford, Hugh **1**:101
Cocoa Marketing Board **3**:373, 374

coins, Aksumite **4:**454–455, 456
Cold War **6:**749
   Angola **5:**617, 625
   Australia **10:**368–369
   Congo, DR **5:**669
   Guinea **2:**204, 209–210
   Malawi **6:**779
   Namibia **7:**931
   South Africa **7:**946
Communism
   Eritrea **4:**488, 495
   Ethiopia **4:**496, 500,
      503–504, 505–506, 508,
      509, 511, 512, 514, 515
   Guinea **2:**209
   see also Cold War; Marxism
Compagnie Camerounaise
   d'Aluminium **1:**66
Compaoré, Blaise **3:**350, 354,
   356, 359, 364
Condé, Alpha **2:**210
Condominium of the New
   Hebrides **8:**1141, 1145
Congo-Ocean Railroad **5:**687
Congo Wars (1996–1997,
   1998–2003) **5:**593, 607,
   618, 661, 662, 666, 668,
   670, 673, 677, 698
   Angola **5:**618, 670, 678, 705
   deaths and devastation **5:**609,
      662, 670, 678, 681, 705
   economic effects **5:**678, 680,
      681
Congress for Democracy and
   Justice (Gabon) **1:**82
Congress for Democratic
   Change (Liberia) **2:**234
Conté, Lansana **2:**208, 210, 215
contract labor **8:**1034
Convention on the Conservation
   of Antarctic Marine Living
   Resources (1982) **10:**1339,
   1430–1431
convict settlements
   Australia **10:**1372, 1378, 1387,
      1398, 1402, 1404, 1406
   Norfolk Island **10:**1416
Cook, James
   Antarctica **10:**1416
   Australia **10:***1344*, 1346,
      1346, 1352, 1404
   New Zealand and Polynesia
      9.*1180*, 1181, 1182, 1186,
      1188, 1194, 1209, 1236,
      1263, 1266
   Western Pacific **8:**1033,
      1084, 1136
Coral Sea, Battle of the (1942)
   8:1104; **10:**1367
Costa, Manuel Pinto da **1:**135

Country Party (Australia)
   10:1367, 1368, 1369,
   1370, 1371
Cuffee, Paul **2:**175
Curtin, John **10:**1368

D

Da'amat kingdom **4:**453, 454
Daar, Aden Abdullah Ousman
   4:547
Dacko, David **5:**652
Dampier, William **8:**1033
dan Fodio *see* Usman dan Fodio
Darboc, Ousainou **2:**197
Daura State **1:**36
David, Tannatt Edgeworth
   10:1353, *1354*
Dawit, emperor of Ethiopia
   4:464
Dawson, Anderson **10:**1351
Deakin, Alfred **10:**1365
De Beers Company **2:**282; **7:**896,
   912, 913, 936, 967, 971
Debre Damo **4:***454*, *456*
de Klerk, F. W. **7:**947, 948, *949*,
   969
Democratic Action (São Tomé
   and Príncipe) **1:**134
Democratic Party of Equatorial
   Guinea **1:**72
Democratic Union of
   Cameroon **1:**48
Denkyera state **3:**312, 313, 314,
   321
de Wet, Christiaan **7:**899
Dhanis, Francis **5:**606
Dhu Nuwas, king of Himyar
   4:455
Dia, Mamadou **2:**255
Dileita, Dileita Mohamed **4:**474
Dingane kaSenzangakhona,
   Zulu king **7:**895
Dingiswayo, Mthethwa chief
   7:895
dinosaurs **10:**1320, 1425
Diouf, Abdou **2:**256, 264
Discovery (ship) **10:**1424
Diwan Salatin Barnu **1:**28
Djolof kingdom **2:**165, 172
Dodds, Alfred-Amédée **3:**326
Doe, Samuel **2:**234, 238–239,
   247; **3:**396
Dogbé, Yves Emmanuel **3:**417
Doré, Jean-Marie **2:**210
Dowlyogo, Bernard **8:**1078
Drake, Francis **2:**169; **10:**1352
Duarte, Cristina **2:***184*
Duarte, Fausto **2:**224
Dufresne, Marc-Joseph Marion
   10:1346

Duguwa dynasty **1:**28
Dumont d'Urville, Jules
   Sébastien-César **10:**1352
Dunama, caliph of Sokoto **1:**30
Dunama Dibalami Selmami,
   Sawfawa ruler **1:**28, 29
d'Urban, Benjamin **7:**964
"Dutch Disease" **8:**1120
Dutch East India Company
   7:890, 940, 956, 963, 967;
   9:1180–1181; **10:**1344–1345
Dutch West India Company
   1:39; **2:**170
Dzeliwe, Swazi queen mother
   7:979

E

East Asian fiscal crisis (1997)
   10:1408
Ebola virus **1:**89; **5:**676, 693
ECOMOG (multinational force)
   2:239, 274
ECOWAS (East Africa Economic
   and Security Organization)
   2:239, 274, 280
Eguguojo, Yoruba ruler **1:**32
Elias, Sian **9:**1224
Elizabeth II, queen of Great
   Britain **10:**1369
Ella Amida, king of Aksum **4:**455
emirate system **1:**40, 40–41
Endugis, king of Aksum
   4:454–455
Eri, Vincent Serei **8:**1106
Eritrean People's Liberation
   Front **4:**488, 492, 493,
   503, 504
Esigie, ruler of Benin **1:**34
European Union **9:**1231;
   10:1369
Ewedo, ruler of Benin **1:**33
Eweka, ruler of Benin **1:**33
Ewuare the Great, ruler of
   Benin **1:**33, 34
Eyadéma, Étienne (later
   Gnassingbé Eyadéma)
   3:410, 414, 415, 416, 419,
   424, 425, 426
Eyre, Edward John **10:**1350
Ezana, king of Aksum **4:**455

F

fa'a matai system **9:**1249–1250
Faidherbe, Louis **2:**172
Family Code of 1972 (Senegal)
   2:261
famines **4:**447
   Ethiopia **4:**496, 502, 503,
      504, 514, 515
   Somalia **4:**540, 547

Fante confederacy **3:**312, 313,
   315, 321, 324, 328
Fasilides, emperor of Ethiopia
   4:*463*, 464
Fatafehi Tu'ipelehake, prince
   of Tonga **9:**1264
Felipe I, king of Ndongo **5:**599
Ferguson, George Ekem **3:**326
Figiel, Sia **9:**1246
Finlay, Robert **2:**175
Finsch, Otto **8:**1103
Firestone Tire and Rubber
   Company **2:**237
First Anglo-Boer War **7:**893
First Liberian Civil War **2:**239
Fisher, Andrew **10:***1365*, 1366
FLNKS (Front de Libération
   Nationale Kanak
   Socialiste) **8:**1084, 1085
Forbes, George William **9:**1216,
   1231
forced labor **5:**604, 606, 615,
   616, 626, 635, 667, 679,
   687; **6:**805; **8:**1034
   see also slavery
Force for Change/Democratic
   Movement (São Tomé and
   Príncipe) **1:**134, 135
Forrest, John **10:**1350
fossils **4:**452, 518; **6:**738, 750
   oldest hominid **4:**452, 453
Franco-Danhomean Wars
   3:323, 324–326, 330, 335
Franco-Hova Wars **6:**742, 745
François, Curt von **7:**897
Fraser, Malcolm **10:**1370
Fraser, Peter **9:**1216
freed slave settlements
   2:174–175, 176, 179, 240
   Liberia **2:**226, 230, 234,
      235–236, 247
   Sierra Leone **2:**174–175, 179,
      268, 273, 275, 280
Free French Forces **1:**83, 90;
   4:475, 479; **5:**687, 694;
   9:1186
Free Traders Party (Australia)
   10:1365
Frelimo (Mozambique
   Liberation Front) **6:**800,
   804, 805–806, 809, 810,
   812, 813
French Communist Party **2:**209
French Company of Senegal
   1:39; **2:**170, 171
French East India Company
   6:745
Frere, Bartle **7:**896
Friendship, Treaty of (1970)
   9:1258

frigate bird cult **8:**1080
Frontier Wars (1781–1852) **7:**891, 894
Frumentius, Saint **4:**455
Fuchs, Vivian **10:**1425
Fugitive Slave Act (1850, U.S.) **2:**235
Fulani Empire **1:**40–42, 45
Fulani jihad (1804) **1:**40, 42, 45, 47, 49, 112, 122
Fulbe imamate **3:**311, 323
Fulbe kingdom **2:**166–167, 168, 172, 176
Furneaux, Tobias **10:**1346

G
Gabonese Democratic Party **1:**82, 83.1.84
Gadarat, king of Aksum **4:**454
Gajemasu, Hausa ruler **1:**122
Galawdewos, emperor of Ethiopia **4:**464
Gallipoli Campaign (1915) **9:**1210, 1215, 1221; **10:**1366, 1380
Gama, Vasco da **7:**890
Gan kingdom **3:**311
Gao Empire **3:**310, 317
Garcia II, king of Kongo **5:**598
Garcia IV, king of Kongo **5:**599
Gaza kingdom **6:**739, 747, 805
Gbagbo, Laurent **3:**396, 397, 406
Gelele, king of Danhome **3:**323
genocide *see* Herero genocide; Rwandan genocide
George (Siaosi) Tupou I, king of Tonga **9:**1186–1187, 1262, 1263, 1268, 1270
George Tupou II, king of Tonga **9:**1186, 1263
Gerlache, Adrien de **10:**1353
Gezo (Danhome king) **3:**322–323
Ghana Empire **2:**164, 166; **3:**368, 374
Gillard, Julia **10:**1371
Gizenga, Antoine **5:**669
global financial crisis (2008–2009) **10:**1400, 1413
Gnassingbé, Faure **3:**414, *414*, 416, 425
Gnassingbé Eyadéma *see* Eyadéma, Étienne
Gobir (Hausa state) **1:**36, 37, 42
Goering, Heinrich **7:**897
Goering, Hermann **7:**897
Goldie, George **1:**43
Gondwana (supercontinent) **2:**154; **4:**442–443; **9:**1164,

1170; **10:**1317, 1319, 1320, 1329, 1330, 1334
Gonzal, Jean Étienne **10:**1345
Gore-Brown, Stewart **6:**850
Gorton, John **10:**1369
Gowon, Yakubu **1:**103
Graaf-Reinet uprising (1795) **7:**891
Grant, James **4:**466
Great Trek (Afrikaaners) **7:**892, 893, 901, 940, 946, 962
Great Zimbabwe **7:**886–887, 896, 951, *994*, 995
Griffin, Marion Mahony **10:**1396
Griffin, Walter Burley **10:**1396
Grunitzky, Nicolas **3:**415
Guadalcanal, Battle of (1942–1943) **8:***1034*, 1035, 1124, 1129, 1133
Guam Organic Act **8:**1052
Guebuza, Armando **6:**806
Guél, Robert **3:**396
Guelleh, Ismail Omar **4:**474, 475
Guggisberg, Frederick Gordon **3:**373
Guinean Democratic Party **2:**209, 210
Gulf War (1991) **6:**749
Gunjur pilgrimage **2:**199
Gun War **7:**919, 923
Gurmantche kingdom **3:**311
Gyaaman kingdom **3:**390

H
Habyarimana, Juvénal **5:**635, 704–705
Hadar **4:**453
Hagos, Bahta **4:**487
Hahl, Albert **8:**1103–1104
Haidara Kontofilli (Muslim uprising) **2:**273
Haile Selassie I, emperor of Ethiopia **4:**468, 496, 502, 503, 512, 513, 514
Hajj Malick Sy, al- **2:**260
Hamilton-Gordon, Arthur **8:**1043
Hanno (Carthaginian navigator) **2:**148
Hanseman, Adolf von **8:**1103
Hanson, Pauline **10:**1371
Harris, William Wade **3:**401
Hartog, Dirk **10:**1344
Harvester Judgment (1907) **10:**1365
Hassan, Muhammad Abdullah **4:**465, 546, 548
Hatubou, Salim **6:**756

Hausa city-states **1:**27, 30, 36–37, 47
Fulani jihad (1804) **1:**40, 42
Hawke, Bob **10:**1370, 1371
Heavily Indebted Poor Countries (HIPC) program **1:**64; **3:**387; **5:**643, 695, 713; **6:**785, 813, 841, 857
Henry the Navigator, prince of Portugal **1:**38; **2:**169
Herero genocide **7:**897, 901, 926, 933
Hertzog, J. B. M. **7:**945, 946
Higgins, Henry Bourne **10:**1365
Himyarite kingdom **4:**454, 455
HIV/AIDS
Angolan low rate **5:**623
Botswana **7:**910, 912
Burundi low rate **5:**641
Cameroon **1:**60–61
control programs **3:**382, 403
Eritrea **4:**492
Gabon. 189
Gambia **2:**200
Kenya **4:**531
Lesotho **7:**922, 924
Liberia **2:**244
Malawi **6:**782–783, 785
Mozambique **6:**810, 811, 813
Namibia **7:**934, 936
Nigeria **1:**116
South Africa **7:**949, 958, 959–960, 970
Swaziland **7:**974, 979, 982, 984
Tanzania **6:**837, 840
Uganda **4:**554, 566, 569
Zambia **6:***853*, 854, 857
Zimbabwe **7:**995, 998, 1002
Hobson, William **9:**1183
Hodgson, Frederick **3:**315
Hogan, P. J. **10:**1379
Holland, Sidney **9:**1216
Holmes, William **8:**1104
Holt, Harold **10:**1369, *1370*
Holyoake, Keith **9:**1216–1217
homelands *see* Bantustans
hominid fossils **4:**452, 453, 518
Hongi Hika (Maori chief) **9:**1179
Houngbo, Gilbert **3:**414, 416
Houphouët-Boigny, Félix **3:**390, 395–396, 404, 406
House of Slaves (Gorée) **2:***171*, 263
Howard, Daniel Edward **2:**236
Howard, John **10:**1371
Hughes, William Morris ("Billy") **10:**1367
Hughes doctrine (1924) **10:**1425

human rights abuses
Central African Republic **5:**652
Congo Free State **5:**606, 667, 677
Eritrea **4:**492
Gambia **2:**200
Guinea **2:**210
Liberia **2:**238, 239
Malawi **6:**779
Sierra Leone **2:**274, 278
Somalia **4:**554
South Africa **7:**946, 947, 949
Uganda **4:**561
Hummay (Sayfawa ruler) **1:**28
Hut Tax War **2:**273

I
Ialá, Lumba **2:**228
Ibn Battuta **6:**740
Ibrahim Nikale, Kanem ruler **1:**29, 30
Ibrahim Njoya, Bamum ruler **1:**57
Idris Katakarmabi, Bornu ruler **1:**29
Idros Alooma, Bornu ruler **1:**29–30
Igbo Ukwu **1:**27
Igodo, Ogiso ruler **1:**33
Iloilo, Josefa **8:**1044
Imbokodvo National Movement **7:**979
Inácio, Luiz **3:**334
Indénié kingdom **3:**390
influenza **9:**1181, 1182, 1245
International Court of Justice **1:**56; **2:**239
International Criminal Tribunal **5:**707
International Geophysical Year (1947–1958) **10:**1425, 1430
International Labor Organization **1:**60
International Monetary Fund
Benin **3:**336, 346–347
Burkina Faso **3:**364–365
Burundi **5:**643
Cameroon **1:**56, 64
Cape Verde **2:**185
Congo, Rep. **5:**695
Ghana **3:**386, 387
Guinea **2:**216
Ivory Coast **3:**403
Madagascar **6:**772
Mozambique **6:**813
Nigeria **1:**125, 126
Rwanda **5:**713
São Tomé and Príncipe **1:**135
Senegal **2:**264
Seychelles **6:**827

Sierra Leone **2:**281
Tanzania **6:**834, 840
Zambia **6:**855
International Whaling Commission **10:**1432
Iraq invasion (1993) **6:**749
Isandiwana, Battle of (1879) **7:**894, 896
Iyasu V, emperor of Ethiopia **4:**502

J
Jameson, Leander **7:**898
Jammeh, Yahya **2:**196, 197
Janszoon, Willem **10:**1300, 1344
Jawara, Dawda Karaiba **2:**196, 197
Jeannot, Koudou **3:**401
Jefferson, Thomas **2:**175
Jentsch, Adolph **7:**933
João I, king of Kongo **5:**598, 600, 602
John II, king of Portugal **5:**600
John IV, emperor of Ethiopia **4:**501
John Frum Movement **8:**1141, 1143
John Paul II, Pope **3:**396, 404
Johnson-Sirleaf, Ellen **2:***234*, 239
Jonathan, Leabua **7:**914, 919
Jos State **1:**42, 113
Joubert, Piet **7:**893
Jugnauth, Anerood **6:**793

K
Kaabu kingdom **2:**164, 166, 172, 179
   slave trade **2:**171
Kabbah, Ahmad Tejan **2:**274
Kabila, Joseph **5:**666, 670
Kabila, Laurent-Désiré **4:**561; **5:**618, 662, *669*, 670, 673, 705
Kabua, Amata **8:**1058
Kabua, Imata **8:**1058
Kaduna riots **1:**121
Kagame, Paul **5:***702*, 705
Kalep, king of Aksum **4:**455
Kalonji, Albert **5:**669
Kanem-Bornu empire **1:**27, 28–30, 36
Kanemi, Mohammed el Amin al- **1:**30
Kanem kingdom **1:**28, 29, 30, 36
Kano (Hausa state) **1:**36, 37, 42, 47
KANU (Kenyan African National Union) **4:**522, 524, 525

Kanuri dynasty **1:**29, 30
Kapsiki Peak **1:**11, *12*
Karamoko (Muslim leader) **2:**167
Karnu (religious leader) **5:**651
Karume, Abeid Amani **6:**834
Karume, Amani Abeid **6:***834*
Kasavubu, Joseph **5:**667, 668, 669
Kassa Mercha *see* John IV
Kauage, Mathias **8:**1107
Kaunda, Kenneth **6:**844, 849, 850, 853
Kayibanda, Grégoire **5:**704
Kayor kingdom **2:**166, 172
Kazembe I, king of Kazembe **6:**739
Kazembe IV, king of Kazembe **6:**739
Kazembe kingdom **6:**739, 844
Keating, Paul **10:**1370–1371
Kebbi **1:**42, 47
Keïta, Modibo **2:**255
Kemakeza, Allan **8:**1134
Kenemiyin dynasty **1:**30
Kenilorea, Peter **8:**1129, 1130
Kenyan African National Union *see* KANU
Kenyatta, Jomo **4:**469, 518, 524–525, 528, 534
Kérékou, Mathieu **3:**330, 334, 336, 346–347
Kerr, John **10:**1370
Key, John **9:**1217
Khalid bin Barghash **6:**743
Khama, Ian **7:***906*, 907
Khama, Seretse **7:**907, 909
Khama III, Tswama **7:**902
Kibaki, Mwai **4:**525, 532, *558*
Kigeli V, king of Ruanda-Burundi **5:**704
Kimbangu, Simon **5:**674, 692
Kimberley, siege of **7:**898
King, Charles D. B. **2:**237
Kinigi, Sylvie **5:**635
Kirk, Norman **9:**1217
Kitchener, Lord **7:**899
Kiwanuka, Benedicto **4:**560
Klusubi Royal Tombs **4:**562
Kodjo, Agbéyomé **3:**416
Kodjo, Edem **3:**416
Koffigoh, Joseph Kokou **3:**416
Kolelas, Bernard **5:**692
Kolingba, André **5:**652
Kolone, Va'ai **9:**1253
Kong empire **3:**311, 390
Kongo kingdom **5:**580, 597–599, 600–602, 603, 608, 610, 615, 656, 662, 671, 674, 682

Kony, Joseph **4:**561
Korean War **10:**1369, 1380
Koroma, Ernest Bai **2:***272*, 274
Koroma, Johnny-Paul **2:**274
Kouyaté, Lansana **2:**210
Kruger, Paul **7:***892*, 893, 898, 962
Kuba kingdom **5:**597
Kufuor, John Agyekum **3:***372*, 376
Kutusi Royal Tombs **4:**457
Kwaku Dua III Asamu, king of Ashanti **3:**326

L
Ladysmith, siege of **7:**898
Laird, Macgregor **1:**43
Lalibela, emperor of Ethiopia **4:**456
Lamb, William, Viscount Melbourne **10:**1400
Lamizana, Sangoulé **3:**355
Lancaster House Agreement (1979) **7:**992
land mines **5:**618, 626; **6:**806, 810
Lange, David **9:**1217, 1233
Lapita culture **8:**1026–1027, *1028*, 1029; **9:**1174; **10:**1026–1027
Latte period **8:**1030
League of Nations **3:**415, 424; **9:**1216
   Australia **10:**1367
   Liberia **2:**237
   mandates **9:**1187, 1240, 1245
   trusteeships **1:**50, 55; **5:**628, 633, 698, 703, 712; **6:**828, 833, 838, 839; **8:**1035, 1054, 1059, 1064, 1069, 1074, 1079, 1086, 1093, 1098, 1104, 1105
Leahy, Michael James **8:**1104
Lealofi, Tupua Tamasese **9:**1253
Lebna Dengel, emperor of Ethiopia **4:**464
Leichhardt, Ludwig **10:**1350
Lekhanya, Justin **7:**919
Leluh site **8:**1031
Leo Africanus **1:**37
Leopold II, king of the Belgians **3:**325; **5:**599, 603, 604, 605–606, *606*, 662, 677
Letsie III, ruler of Lesotho **7:**914, 919, 921
Liberal-Country Party (Australia) **10:**1407
Liberal Party (Australia) **10:**1364, 1368, 1369, 1370, 1371, 1407

Liberian civil war **2:**215, 230, 237, 239, 240, 246, 247, 248, 249
   social upheaval **2:**243, 245, *247*
Liberians United for Reconciliation and Democracy **2:**239
Liberty Party (Liberia) **2:**234
Light, William **10:**1397
Lij Kasa *see* Theodore II
Limann, Hilla **3:**376
Lindblad, Lars-Eric **10:**1433
Lini, Walter **8:**1141, 1143
Lissouba, Pascal **5:**688
Little America headquarters station **10:**1424, 1429
Livingstone, David **4:**464; **5:**603; **6:**744, 745, 782, 849
Loango kingdom **5:**682, *684*
Lobengula, king of Matabele **7:**896
Lomé Convention **3:**423
Long Chronology Model **8:**1029
Lord's Resistance Army **4:**554, 561, 565, 566, 569
Lozi kingdom **6:**739, 747, 849
Luba kingdom **5:**597, 662
Lubosi I, Lozi ruler **6:**739, 849
"Lucy" (hominid fossil) **4:**453
Lüderitz, Adolf **7:**897
Lugard, Frederick **1:**43–44, 100, 101; **4:**567
Lumumba, Patrice **5:**668, 670
Lunda empire **5:**597, 598, 599, 662
Lusaka Accord (1999) **5:**618, 670
Lutangu Sipopa, Lozi ruler **6:**739
Lutse, Kwassi **3:**416
Luvum, Janani **4:**560
Lyons, Enid **10:**1389
Lyons, Joseph **10:**1367

M
Maasina Rule **8:**1129
Mabo Judgment (1992) **10:**1371
Macauley, Herbert **1:**101, 112
MacCarthy, Charles **2:**174; **3:**315, 324
Machel, Josina **6:**809
Machel, Samora **6:**806, 809, 812
Mackay, Alistair Forbes **10:**1353, *1354*
Maclean, George **3:**324
Macquarie, Lachlan **10:**1348
Mafeking, siege of (1899–1900) **7:**898, *899*
Maga, Hubert **3:**335

Magal pilgrimage **2:**260
Magellan, Ferdinand **8:**1031, 1086
Magomi family **1:**28
Magyar, László **5:**603
Maharero, Samuel **7:**897
Mahdi **4:**487, 501
Mahmadu Lamine **2:**168, 172
Maire, Jacob le **9:**1180
Majid, sultan of Zanzibar **6:**743
Maji Maji revolt (1906) **6:**833
Majuba Hill, Battle of **7:**891
Maka, Julian **8:**1130
Malak Sagad III *see* Susenyos
malaria **1:**60, 89, 137; **2:**262, 279; **3:**381, 402–403, 421–422; **5:**623, 641, 657, 676, 693, 711; **8:**1114, 1132, 1143
Mali Empire **2:**164, 165, 166, 169, 176, 178, 204, 250; **3:**312, 328, 350
Malietoa Laupepa, king of Samoa **9:**1187
Malietoa Tanumafili II, Samoan chief of state **9:**1244, 1245
Mali Federation **2:**255, 263
Malletoa Vai'inupo Tavita, Samoan chief of state **9:**1245, 1249
Malvatumaori **8:***1140*, 1142
Mamae, Ghuty **1:**75
Mamaloni, Solomon **8:**1129
Mancham, James **6:**822, 823
Mandela, Nelson **5:**635; **7:**940, 947, 963
   South African presidency **7:**948–949, 969
Mandingo Empire **2:**250
Mané, Ansumane **2:**223
Manuel II, king of Kongo **5:**599
Mara, Kamisese **8:**1044
Marara, emperor of Zagwé **4:**455
Maravi Confederacy **6:**739, 746, 774, 779
Margai, Albert **2:**274
Margai, Milton **2:**273, 274
Marques, Lorenço **6:**812
Marsden, Samuel **9:**1223
Marshall, John (explorer) **8:**1054
Marxism
   Angola **5:**614, 617, 622, 626
   Benin **3:**330, 334, 336, 338, 341, 343, 346
   Burkina Faso **3:**355, 356, 364
   Congo, Rep. **5:**682, 686, 687, 688, 689, 690, 693, 695
   Guinea **2:**209, 215

Mozambique **6:**804, 806, 812, 813
   Seychelles **6:**822
   see also Communism
Maryland-in-Africa **2:**235, 236
Maryland State Colonization Society **2:**235
Masire, Quett **7:**907
Massamba-Débat, Alphonse **5:**688
Massari, Alfono Maria **5:**604
Massey, William Ferguson **9:**1216
Massina Empire **3:**323
Matabele kingdom **7:**896
Mataio Tuitonga, king of Niue **9:**1188
Matamba kingdom **5:**601, 602
Matane, Paulias **8:**1106
Matswa, André **5:**687, 692
Matswanism **5:**692
Mau Mau uprising **4:**469, 518, 523, 524–525, 536
Mawahib, Abu al- **6:**740
Mawson, Douglas **10:**1353, 1354
Mazrui sultans **4:**460
M'ba, Léon **1:**78, 83, *84*
M'Backé, Amadou Bamba **2:**260
Mbari Mbayo club (Nigeria) **1:**109
Mbeki, Thabo **7:***948*, 949, 959–960
Mbida, André-Marie **1:**55
Mboya, Tom **4:**525
Mbwila, Battle of (1665) **5:**598
McFarlane, Samuel **8:**1104
McGregor, William **8:**1104
McMahon, William **10:**1369
Mdadaye, Melchior **5:**635
MDC (Movement for Democratic Change) (Zimbabwe) **7:**990, 993, 998, 1000, 1001, 1003
MDPC (Cameroon People's Democratic Movement) **1:**54, 56
Melbourne, Viscount (William Lamb) **10:**1400
Menalamba guerrillas **6:**765
Mendaña de Neira, Alvaro **8:**1033; **9:**1180
Menelik I, legendary king of Ethiopia **4:**452, 468, 505
Menelik II, emperor of Ethiopia **4:**465, 496, 501–502, 512, 513, 514
Menezes, Fradique Melo da **1:***134*, 135
Mengistu Haile Mariam **4:**496, 503, 504, 505, 514
Menzies, Robert **10:**1368, 1369

Mercer, Charles F. **2:**175
Merina dynasty **6:**742, 760, 766, 771
Meroe kingdom **4:**455
Merrick, Joseph **1:**46
Mfecane (migration) **7:**892, 893, 895, 896
Michel, James **6:**823
Micombero, Michel **5:**632, 634
Mills, John Atta **3:**376
Milner, Alfred **7:**898
Minol, Bernard **8:**1106
Mitterrand, François **3:**395
Mkwawa (Hehe leader) **6:**833
Mobutu Sese Seko **4:**561; **5:**618, 662, 669–670, 671, 673, 677, 678, 681, 705
Modekngei movement **8:**1095
Mogae, Festus **7:**907
Mohammed, Murtala **1:**103
Mohammed Korau **1:**36
Moi, Daniel arap **4:**525, 527, 528, 536
Mokhele, Ntsu **7:**919
Moll, Herman **1:**29
Momoh, Joseph **2:**274
Mondlane, Eduardo **6:**805, 806, 809
Monroe, James **2:**175, 235, 246
Monteiro, Antonio Mascarenhas **2:**185
Montreal Protocol **10:**1430
Moore, Mike **9:**1217
Morel, E. D. **5:**606
Morris Carter Commission **7:**991
Moshoeshoe I, king of Basotho **7:**914, 919, 921, 923
Moshoeshoe II, king of Basotho **7:**919
Mosisili, Pakalitha **7:**919
Mossi Empire **3:**310–312, 316–318, 323, 350, 355, 357, 359, 363
   French protectorate **3:**312, 318, 326, 350
   language group **3:**311, 328
   military might **3:**312, 318
Motlanthe, Kgalema **7:**949
Movement for Democracy (Cape Verde) **2:**184, 185
Movement for Democracy in Liberia **2:**239
Movement for Democratic Change (Zimbabwe) *see* MDC
Movement for the Emancipation of the Niger Delta **1:**104
Movement for the Liberation of São Tomé and Príncipe **1:***134*, 135

Mozambican National Resistance *see* Renamo
Mozambique civil war **6:**785, 800, 804, 805
   economic and social effects **6:**806, 810, 812, 813
   peace commemoration **6:**809
Mozambique Liberation Front *see* Frelimo
Mpande kaSenzangakhona, king of Zululand **7:**895
MPLA (Popular Movement for the Liberation of Angola) **5:**610, 614, 616, 617, 618, 619, 625, 687
Mswati II, king of Swazi **7:**974, 979
Mswati III, king of Swazi **7:**978, 981
Mugabe, Robert **7:**949, 986, 990, 992, 993, 996, 997, 1000–1001, 1003
Muhammad, Prophet **1:**42; **2:**212, 259, 260, 277; **4:**455, 477, 508
Muhammad Bello, sultan-caliph of Sokoto **1:**42
Muhammad Muntaga Tall **2:**168
Muldoon, Robert **9:***1216*, 1217
Mulinu'u, Mata'afa **9:**1245, 1253
Mulungushi Reforms (1968) **6:**850, 855
Muluzi, Bakili **6:**779
Murray, Hubert **8:**1104, 1105
Museveni, Yoweri **4:**558, 560–561, 568
Musket Wars **9:**1182–1183
Muslim Students Society **1:**113
Mussolini, Benito **4:**546
Mutapa kingdom **7:**887
Mutare III, king of Ruanda-Burundi **5:**704
Mutesa I, king of Buganda **4:**466, *563*, 567
Mutesa, Edward **4:**559
Mutharika, Bingu wa **6:**778, 779
Muzorewa, Abel **7:**992
Mvemba *see* Afonso I
Mwambutsa IV, king of Burundi **5:**634
Mwanawasa, Levy **6:**848, 850
Mwanga II, king of Buganda **4:**466
Mwenemutapa kingdom **6:**741
Mwinyi, Ali Hassan **6:**834, 840
Mzilikazl, king of Zulu **7:**896

N

Naaba Dulugu, king of Mossi **3**:318, 360, 363

Naaba Kango, king of Mossi **3**:318

Naaba Kugri, king of Burkina Faso **3**:318

Naaba Siguiri, king of Mossi **3**:318, 326

Nabahani dynasty **6**:741

Nachtigal, Gustav **1**:46; **3**:325

Nakayama, Tosiwo **8**:1069

Nan Madol site **8**:1031, *1039*

Nash, Walter **9**:1216

Natalia republic **7**:892, 895

National Alliance for Democracy and Development (Gambia) **2**:196, 197

National Council for Democracy and Development (Guinea) **2**:208, 210

National Council of Chiefs **8**:*1140*, 1142

National Council of Nigeria and the Cameroons **1**:112

National Diamond Mining Company **2**:282

Nationalist Party (Australia) **10**:1367

National Movement for the Liberation of Equatorial Guinea **1**:73

National Party (Australia) **10**:1364

National Party (South Africa) **7**:907, 911, 931, 940, 945–946, 947, 948, 958, 974 *see also* apartheid

National Provisional Ruling Council (Sierra Leone) **2**:274

National Union for Democracy and Progress (Cameroon) **1**:54

National Union for the Total Independence of Angola *see* UNITA

National Woodcutter's Rally-Democratic (Gabon) **1**:82, 84

National Youth Movement (Nigeria) **1**:101

Native Land Trust Board (Fiji) **8**:1043

Nauru Phosphate Corporation **8**:1079, 1083

Ndizeyeto, Charles *see* Ntare V

Ndongo kingdom **5**:597, 599, 601, 602, 610

Neto, Agostinho **5**:617, 619, 621

Neves, José Maria Peira **2**:185

New Guinea Company **8**:1103

New Zealand Association **9**:1183

New Zealand Company **9**:1184, 1228

New Zealand Wars **9**:1179, *1183*, 1184, 1185, 1209

Ngazargamo (Birni Gazargamo) **1**:29, 30

Ngendandumwe, Pierre **5**:634

Ngola a Hari *see* Felipe I

Ngola Mbandi, king of Ndongo **5**:599

Ngouabi, Marien **5**:688, 695

Nguema, Francisco Macias **1**:72, 73, 74, 76

Nguema, Teodoro Obiang **1**:68, 72, 73, 74

Ngwane III, king of Swazi **7**:974

Nigerian Civil War **1**:48, *102*, 113, 119, 121, 124, 126

Nigerian National Democratic Party **1**:101

Nimba rebellion (1989) **2**:239

Nimrod Expedition (1907) **10**:1353, *1354*

Nkomo, Joshua **7**:992, 995

Nkrumah, Kwame **3**:368, 372, 374, 375, 386, 388, 396 memorial and tomb **3**:*374*

Nkumbula, Harry **6**:844

Noli, António da **2**:169

Northern War **9**:1185

Note, Kessai Hesa **8**:*1058*, 1059

Ntaryamira, Cyprien **5**:635, 705

Ntombi, queen mother of Swazi **7**:979

Nubia **4**:454, 455

nuclear testing **8**:1059, 1060, 1063

Nuclear Victims Remembrance Day **8**:1060

Nuñez de Balboa, Vasco **8**:1031, *1033*

Nupe kingdom **1**:32, 112

Nyasaland African Congress **6**:778, 779

Nyerere, Julius **4**:560; **6**:828, 833, 834, 840, 843

Nyobé, Ruben Um **1**:55

Nzinga a Nkuwu *see* João I

O

Oba dynasty **1**:31

Obasanjo, Olusegen **1**:56, 103, 128

Obey, Commander Ebenezer **1**:108

Obote, Milton **4**:554, 558, 559, 560, 561, 568

Obunumankoma, king of Bono **3**:313

Odinga, Oginga **4**:468, 525

Odinga, Raila **4**:468, 525

Ogaden War **4**:503, 504, 513, 514, 547, 552

Ojukwu, Chukwuemeka **1**:103; **3**:396

Okello, Tito **4**:560, 561

Olympio, Gilchrist **3**:414, 416, 424

Olympio, Sylvanus **3**:414, 415, 416

Omani Empire **4**:460–461

Ondongo, Nicolas **5**:689

Ondo State **1**:12

OPEC (Organization of the Petroleum Exporting Countries) **5**:625

Operation Hijump Expedition **10**:1424

Ophir **4**:452

Opobo city-state **1**:43

Opoku Ware I, king of Ashanti **3**:314

Oranmiyan, ruler of Benin **1**:33

Organization for the Victory of Islam **1**:113

Organization of African Unity *see* African Union

Orompoto, ruler of Yoruba **1**:32

Osei Bonsu, king of Ashanti **3**:313, 314

Osei Kwadwo, king of Ashanti **3**:314

Osei Tutu I, king Ashanti **3**:314, 385

Oshoffa, Samuel Bilehou **3**:341

Ottoman Turks **4**:459, 462, 464, 482, 491, 540

Ouattara, Alassane **3**:396, 397

Oubangui-Shari **1**:46

Ouedraogo (Mossi legendary founder) **3**:311, 316

Ouidah kingdom **3**:322, 330

Ovonramwen, ruler of Benin **1**:35

Oyo kingdom **3**:322, 345

Ozolua the Conqueror, ruler of Benin **1**:34

P

Pacific Community **8**:1084

Pacific Forum **8**:1133; **9**:1264

Páez, Pedro **4**:464

Palmer, Geoffrey **9**:1217

Palmer, Nathaniel **10**:1352

Pangaea **10**:1320

Papunya-Tulu movement **10**:1375

Paris Club **1**:56

Party for Social Renewal (Guinea-Bissau) **2**:223

Pass Laws (South Africa) **7**:960

Patassé, Ange-Félix **5**:650, 652

Pearl Harbor attack **8**:1035

Pedro IV, king of Kongo **5**:598–599

Pedro VI, king of Kongo **5**:599

Peleliu, Battle of (1944) **8**:1093

Pellew, Sir Edward **10**:1300

penal colonies *see* convict settlements

People's Democratic Party (Nigeria) **1**:99

People's Movement for Democratic Change (Sierra Leone) **2**:272

People's Progressive Party (Gambia) **2**:196, 197

People's Redemption Council (Liberia) **2**:238, 247

Pereira, Aristides **2**:185

Pereira, Fernando **1**:135

Phillip, Arthur **10**:1346, 1347

Pidjiguiti massacre **2**:223, 225

piracy **2**:169
Somalia **4**:475, 547, 553

Pires, Pedro **2**:185

Plymouth Company **9**:1184

Pohamba, Hifikepunye **7**:931

Pomare II, king of Tahiti **9**:1186

Pomare V, king of Tahiti **9**:1186, 1196

Popo kingdom **3**:345

Popular Movement for the Liberation of Angola *see* MPLA

Pore-Daka, Battle of (1896) **2**:167, 172

Potatau, king of Maori **9**:1185

prehistory *see* fossils

Pre-Latte period **8**:1030

Prempeh I, king of Ashanti **3**:326; **6**:823

Prester John **1**:38; **4**:456

Pretoria Agreement **3**:397

Pretoria Minute (1990) **7**:948

Pretorius, Andries **7**:892, 962

Pretorius, Marthinus **7**:893, 962

Progressive Alliance of Liberia **2**:238

Q

Qaeda, al- **4**:547

Quirós, Pedro Fernández de **8**:1033; **9**:1180

R

Rabemananjara, Charles **6:**_764_

Rabih az-Zubayr **1:**30

Rabuka, Sitiveni **8:**1044

racial segregation *see* apartheid

Radama I, king of Madagascar **6:**742, 745, 771

Radama II, king of Madagascar **6:**742

Rafohy, queen of Merina **6:**742

Rajoelina, André **6:**765

Ralaimongo, Jean **6:**765

Ramaema, Elias Phisoana **7:**919

Ramanantsoa, Gabriel **6:**765

Ramaphosa, Cyril **7:**948

Ramgoolam, Navim **6:**793

Ramgoolam, Seewoosagur **6:**793

Rampontchombo, Antochouwé Kowe (Denis) **1:**45–46

RAMSI (Regional Assistance Mission to the Solomon Islands) **8:**1129, 1134

Ranavalona I, queen of Madagascar **6:**742, 745, 765, 769, 771

Ranavalona III, queen of Madagascar **6:**742

Rand Revolt (1922) **7:**965, 967

Rano (Hausa state) **1:**36

rape, military **2:**243, 278; **5:**640, 656, _670_

Ras Tafari Makkonen *see* Haile Selassie I

Ratana, Tahupotiki Wiremu **9:**1189, 1223

Ratsimandrava, Richard **6:**765

Ratsiraka, Didier **6:**764, 765

Ravalomanana, Marc **6:**764, 765

Rawlings, Jerry **3:**368, 372, 376, 386

Read, Gabriel **9:**_1185_

Rebmann, Johannes **6:**744

Red Terror (Ethiopia) **4:**512

Reeves, William Pember **9:**1215, 1218

Reid, George **10:**1365

Remeliik, Haruo I. **8:**1093

Remengesau, Thomas Esang, Jr. **8:**_1093_

Renamo **6:**800, 804, 806, 810, 812, 813

René, France-Albert **6:**822, 823

Reunification Monument (Yaoundé) **1:**_58_, 63

Revolutionary United Front (Sierra Leone) **2:**274, 278, 281

Rey, Jacobus de la **7:**899

Rhodes, Cecil **6:**745, 844, 849; **7:**893, 896, 898, 907, 967

Riale (Mandé hunter) **3:**311

Riebeeck, Jan van **7:**890

Rivonia trial (1963–1964) **7:**947

Roberto, Holden **5:**617

Roberts, Joseph Jenkins **2:**236, _236_

Roberts, Lord **7:**898–899

Rocha de Serpa Pinto, Alexandre Alberto da **5:**603

Roggeveen, Jacob **9:**1180–1181, 1186; **10:**1346

Roman Empire **4:**454, 455

Roosevelt, Theodore **2:**236

Ross, James Clark **10:**1352

Royal Niger Company **1:**35, 43

Ruanda kingdom **5:**698, 703, 706, 711, 712, 713

Rudd, Kevin **10:**1371

Rugyendo, Mukotani **4:**562

Rwagasore, Louis **5:**634, 638

Rwandan genocide **5:**607, 609, 670, 698, 703–707

deaths **5:**709, 712

economic effects **5:**713

memorials **5:**_704_, 708, 712

Rwandan Patriotic Front **5:**698, 702, 704, 705, 708, 709, 712, 715

S

Sa'id, Al Bu **6:**741, 743

Saint Allouam, François-Alesno **10:**1346

Sakassou kingdom **3:**390

Saker, Alfred **1:**46

Salazar, António de Oliveira **2:**185; **5:**615

Salii, Lazarus E. **8:**1093

Salim, Aboucar Said **6:**756

Salisbury, Lord (Robert Cecil) **7:**999

Salote Topou III, queen of Tonga **9:**1263

Sambi, Ahmed Abdallah Mohamed **6:**754

Samori Ture (Samoury Touré) **2:**209, 168, 172, 173; **3:**326

Sand River Convention **7:**893

Sanha, Malam Bacai **2:**223

Sankara, Thomas **3:**355–356, 357, 359, 364

Sankoh, Foday **2:**274

Santos, Arnaldo **5:**619

Santos, José Eduardo dos **5:**614, 617, 618

Sanwi kingdom **3:**390

Sarki Babari, Gobir ruler **1:**37

Sassou-Nguesso, Denis **5:**_686_, 688

Saudeleur dynasty **8:**1031

Savage, Michael **9:**1216, 1231

Savimbi, Jonas **5:**617, 618

Sayfawa dynasty **1:**28, 29, 30, 36

Sayf ibn Dhi Yazan, ruler of Yemen **1:**28

Sayyid Sa'id ibn Sultan **6:**741, 743

Schouten, Willem **8:**1033; **9:**1180

Schweitzer, Albert **1:**87

scientific exploration, Western Pacific **8:**1033

Scott, Robert **10:**1314, 1353, _1354_, 1424

"scramble for Africa" **2:**172, 173; **3:**325–326; **4:**465, 501; **5:**602, 603, 604, 605, 615; **6:**743

Scullin, James **10:**1367

scurvy **9:**1181

SEATO (South East Asian Treaty Organization) **9:**1216

Seck, Idrissa **2:**256

Second Anglo-Boer War **7:**894, 898–899, 940, 945, 962, 965, 967, 979

Second Angolan Civil War **7:**931

Second Congo War **5:**618, 662, 666, 671, 673; **7:**931

deaths **5:**670, 678, 705

economic effects **5:**678, 680, 681

Second Liberian Civil War **2:**239

Seddon, Richard John **9:**1215

Ségou kingdom **2:**168

Sékou Touré, Ahmed **2:**204, 209, 210, 211, 212, 215, 255; **3:**396

Seku Amadu **3:**323

Senegalese Democratic Bloc **2:**255

Senegalese Democratic Party **2:**256

Senegambia Confederation **2:**192, 197, 250, 256

Senghor, Léopold Sédar **2:**250, 255–256, _255_, 257, 264, 275; **3:**395, 417; **5:**653

Sese Seko *see* Mobutu Sese Seko

Sewell, Henry **9:**1185

Shabaab, al (Somali militant organization) **4:**545

Shackleton, Ernest **10:**1314, 1353, 1354, 1428

Shaka, king of Zulu **6:**744

Shaka kaSenzangakhona, king of Zulu **7:**892, 895, 896, 900, 920, 964

Sharp, Granville **2:**174, 280

Sharpeville massacre (1960) **7:**946, 954

Sheba, queen of **4:**452, 463, 464, 468, 502, 505

Shepstone, Theophilus **7:**896

Shermarke, Abdirashid Ali **4:**547

Shimbra Kure, Battle of (1529) **4:**462, 464

Shipley, Jenny **9:**1217

Shirazi dynasties **6:**740–741

Shoa kingdom **4:**456, 501

Short Chronology Model **8:**1029

Siad Barre, Muhammad **4:**540, 544, 545, 547, 548, 550

Siaosi Tupou V, king of Tonga **9:**1264–1265, 1268, 1272

Sierra Leone Company **2:**173, 174–175, 268, 280

Sierra Leone People's Party **2:**272, 273, 274

Sierra Leone Selection Trust **2:**282

Sierra Leone Truth and Reconciliation Commission **2:**274

Silva, João Carlos **1:**136

Simango, Daviz **6:**804

Simina, Wesley **8:**_1068_

Sine kingdom **2:**172

Singh, Vijay **8:**1048

Sithole, Ndabaningi **7:**992

Skate, Bill **8:**1119

Slater, Ransford **3:**373

Slave Coast **3:**321, 322, 325

slavery **2:**186, 237; **7:**890–891, 901, 963

Liberia **2:**237

São Tomé and Príncipe **1:**38, 130, 135, 137, 138

slave trade

abolition **2:**172, 180; **3:**322–323, 324, 325; **5:**602, 603, 604, 615

Benin **1:**34, 35

British ban **1:**35, 42, 45, 46, 68, 76; **2:**172, 173, 192, 197, 268, 273; **3:**322,–323, 324, 325; **6:**744

Cape Verde **2:**179, 180, 185, 186

Central African Republic **5:**646

central West Africa **3:**313, 314, 315, 318, 319, 320, 345, 383

Congo **5:**605, 675, _684_; **6:**682

Danhome kingdom **3:**321, 322, 324, 328, 330
Douala **1:**63
Dutch Republic **2:**171, 250, 268, 280
eastern Central Africa **6:**739, 740, 741, 743, 744–745, 748, 821
embarkation sites **2:**198, 250, 263
Gabon **1:**45, 46
Gambia **2:**192, 197, 198
Gorée **2:**171, 250, 263
Guinea **2:**204
Guinea-Bissau **2:**218, 227
Gulf of Guinea **1:**39, 42
Hausa states **1:**36
Kongo **5:**590, 597, 598, 599, *600,* 601
Lagos **1:**38, 123
Mali Empire **2:**166
Mauritius **6:**788, 796
Nigeria **1:**38–39, *39,* 45, 46
Niger River Delta **1:**43
peak years **3:**321
Portugal **5:**598, 599, 601, 602, 615, 624
Seychelles **6:**921
Sierra Leone **2:**268, 280
Togo **3:**410
West Africa **2:**169, 170, 171, 204
Yoruba **1:**32
Slave Trade Act of 1807 (British) **1:**45, 46
Smith, Ian **7:**992, 995
Smith, William **10:**1352
Smuts, Jan **7:**945, 946
Snowy River Project **10:**1368, 1410
Sobhuza II, Swazi king **7:**974, 978, 979, 981, 984
Social Democratic Convergence (Equatorial Guinea) **1:**72
Social Democratic Front (Cameroon) **1:**54, 56
Socialist Party (Senegal) **2:**254, 255, 256
Soglo, Nicéphore **3:**336, 346–347
Soilihi, Ali **6:**756
Sokoto emirate **3:**329
Solomon, King (biblical) **4:**452, 463, 464, 468, 502, 505
Solomonic dynasty, founding legend **4:**505
Somare, Michael **8:***1102,* 1105
Songhai empire **1:**27, 29, 36; **2:**166; **3:**312, *327*
Sonni Ali (Songhai king) **3:**312

Sopi Coalition (Senegal) **2:**256
Soro, Guillaume **3:**394, 397, 406
Soshangane (Ngoni leader) **6:**739, 747
Souaré, Ahmed Tidiane **2:**210
Southern African Customs Union **7:**936, 985
Southern African Development Community **6:**859
South Pacific Forum **9:**1264
South Sea Evangelical Mission **8:**1132
South West Africa People's Organization *see* SWAPO
Soweto uprising (1976) **7:**947, 954, 966
Spanish-American War **8:**1034–1035, 1052, 1093
Speight, George **8:**1044
Speke, John Hanning **4:**466; **5:**603; **6:**744
spice trade **8:**1033
Spinola, António de **2:**223
Stairs, William Grant **5:**605–606
Stanley, Henry Morton **5:**603–604, 605, 677
Stellaland republic **7:**896
Stevens, Jimmy **8:**1141
Stevens, Siaka **2:**272, 274
Steyn, Marthinus Theunis **7:**898
Stirling, James **10:**1347
"Stolen Generation" (Aboriginal children) **10:**1356, 1371, 1373, 1388
Strasser, Valentine **2:**274
Strijdom, Johannes G. **7:**946
Strzelecki, Paul **10:**1311
Stuart, John McDouall **10:**1350
Sturt, Charles **10:**1348
Sukuna, Lala **8:**1043
Suleyman, mansa of Mali **2:**165
Susenyos, emperor of Ethiopia **4:**464
Suso, Foday Musa **2:**199
Swan River colony **10:**1347, 1358, 1403
SWAPO (South West Africa People's Organization) **7:**926, 930, 931, 947
Sydney, Viscount (Thomas Townshend) **10:**1404

T
Tabai, Jeremia **9:**1203
Tadjoura sultanate **4:**465, 470, 475, 479
Takrur (early state) **2:**164–165
Talansan, Battle of **2:**167
Tange, Kenzo **1:**119

TANU (Tanganyika African National Union) **6:**832, 833, 834, 836
Taranaki War **9:**1185
Tarawa, Battle of (1943) **9:**1198, 1203
Tasman, Abel Janszoon **8:**1033; **9:**1180, 1209; **10:**1300, 1345
Taufa'ahau Tupou IV, king of Tonga **9:**1264, *1269*
Tawhiao, king of Maori **9:**1185
Taylor, Charles **2:**239; **3:**396
Taytu, empress of Ethiopia **4:**512
Tekle, Afework **4:**506
Tenkodogo kingdom **3:**311, 316, 350
Te Rauparaha (Maori chief) **9:**1179
Terra Nova Expedition **10:**1353, *1354*
terra nullius concept **10:**1348
terrorism
    Kenya **4:**537, 538
    Uganda **4:**560, 561, 565
Te Wherowhero, Maori king **9:**1185
Thatcher, Margaret **7:**992
Theodore II, emperor of Ethiopia **4:**496, 501, 505
Thias, Limamu Laye **2:**260
Thuwayn, sultan **6:**743
Tidjani Tall, caliph **2:**168
Tieba Traore **2:**168
Tigrayan People's Liberation Front **4:**503, 504, 509
Tio (Tyo) kingdom **5:**599, 602, 682, 694
Tippu Tib (Arab trader) **5:**599, 605
Tito, Teburoro **9:**1203
Toihiri, Mohamed **6:**756
Tolbert, William R., Jr. **2:**230, 238, 247; **3:**396
Tomeing, Litokwa **8:**1058
Tordesillas, Treaty of (1494) **1:**38; **2:**170; **3:**320
Toribiong, Johnson **8:***1092*
Toro kingdom **4:**558, 562
Torres, Luís Vaz de **8:**1033; **10:**1344
Torwa kingdom **7:**887
Toucouleur Empire **2:**167–168, 172; **3:**323
Touré, Ahmed Sékou *see* Sékou Touré, Ahmed
Touré, Samoury *see* Samori Ture
Townshend, Thomas, Viscount Sydney **10:**1404

Trans-Antarctic Expedition **10:**1425
transatlantic slave trade *see* slave trade
Traoré, Diarra **2:**210
Treich-Lapène, Marcel **3:**325
Triangular Trade **1:**39; **2:**171
Trotha, Lothar von **7:**897
Trovoada, Miguel **1:**135
Trovoada, Patrice **1:**135
True Whig Party (Liberia) **2:**237
Truth and Reconciliation Commission (South Africa) **7:**949
Tshombe, Moïse **5:**668, 669
Tsirana, Philibert **6:**765
Tsvangirai, Morgan **7:**990, 993, 1001
Tubman, William **2:**238, 240, 241, 247
Tu'i Kanokupolu dynasty **9:**1263
Tu'i Tonga dynasty **9:**1258, 1263, *1266*
Tupou dynasty **9:**1186–1187, 1258, 1262, 1270
Tupua Tamasese Meaole, Samoan chief of state **9:**1245
Ture, Samori *see* Samori Ture
Tuvalu Trust Fund **9:**1284
Tyo kingdom *see* Tio (Tyo)

U
Uganda Railroad **4:**523, 533, 535, 536, 539, 559, 562, 568, 571
UGTAN (Guinea) **2:**209
Ujamaa villages policy **6:**834, 840
Umar, sultan of Kanemiyin **1:**30
Umar ibn Idris, ruler of Kanuri **1:**29
Umar Tall, caliph **2:**167–168, 172, 260; **3:**323
Union of Gabonese People **1:**82, 84
Union of the Peoples of Cameroon **1:**55, 56
UNITA (National Union for the Total Independence of Angola) **5:**610, 614, 616, 617, 618, 625, 670
United Africa Company **1:**43; **3:**415, 424
United Nations **3:***375,* 415
    Angola **5:**617, 618
    Australia **10:**1368, 1389
    Benin **3:**342
    Burundi **5:**628, 633

United Nations (*continued*)
Cameroon **1:**50, 55
Congo, DR **5:**670
Eritrea **4:**482, 488, 493, 495, 502, 504
Ethiopia **4:**513
Human Development Index **5:**656
Ivory Coast peacekeeping **3:**397, 406
Katanga secession **5:**668, 669
Liberia **2:**237, 239, 247
Namibia **7:**926, 931
New Zealand **9:**1216
Rwanda **5:**698, 712
Samoa **9:**1240, 1253–1254
Sierra Leone **2:**268, 274, 278, 281
Somalia **4:**533, 546, 547, 551
South Africa **7:**947
Western Pacific **8:**1035, 1059, 1064, 1069, 1073, 1079, 1093, 1097, 1105, 1118
Zimbabwe **7:**986
United States Exploring Expedition **10:**1352
Unity and Progress Party (Guinea) **2:**210
Unity Party (Liberia) **2:**234
Upper Senegal-Niger (French colony) **3:**350, 355, 363
Usman dan Fodio, caliph of Sokoto **1:**30, 37, 40, 41–42, 45, 47, 112
Uwilinglyamana, Agathe **5:**705

V
Veiga, Carlos **2:**185
Versailles, Treaty of **2:**237
Verwoerd, Hendrik **7:**946, 947
Vichy France **1:**83, 90; **4:**475, 479
Vieira, João Bernardo **2:**222, 223, 228
Vieyra, Paulin Soumanou **2:**258
Vlamingh, Willem de **10:**1344, 1403
Vogelsang, Heinrich **7:**897
Vohou-Vohou movement **3:**398
Voltaic Republic **3:**355
Vorster, John **7:**947
voting rights
Australia **10:**1388, 1389
New Zealand **9:**1185, 1215, 1224, 1245

W
Wade, Abdoulaye **2:***254*, 256

Wagadougou (Wagadugu) kingdom **3:**311, 316, 318, 326, 350, 360, 363
Wairau Affray (1841) **9:**1184
Waitangi, Treaty of **9:**1179, 1183, 1184, 1209, 1217
Wakefield, Edward Gibbon **9:**1184; **10:**1348
Wakefield System **9:**1184
Wallis, Samuel **9:**1181, *1181*, 1186; **10:**1346
war crimes
Liberia **2:**239, 248
Sierra Leone **2:**274, 278
Ward, Joseph **9:**1216
Wassoulou Empire **2:**168, 172; **3:**326
Waterberg, Battle of **7:**897
Watson, John Christian ("Chris") **10:**1365
Weah, George **2:**234, 239
Weddell, John **10:**1352
Wegbaja, king of Abomey **3:**322
Welleseley, Arthur, duke of Wellington **9:**1228
Wendt, Albert **9:**1246
West African Frontier Force **1:**44
Westminster, Statute of **9:**1210, 1216, 1231; **10:**1358
"White Australia" policy **10:**1350, 1357, 1368, 1370, 1385, 1388
Whitlam, Gough **10:**1369, 1370
Whydah *see* Ouidah kingdom
Wichale, Treaty of **4:**465, 501–502
Wilkes, Charles **10:**1352
Willaumez, Bouet **1:**45–46
Willis, William John **10:**1350
Wilson, Edward **10:**1353, *1354*
Winton, Francis de **5:**605
Wiriyamu Massacre **6:**806
Wissmann, Herman von **5:**604
Wolof kingdoms **2:**164, 165–166, 169, 171, 172
Wolseley, Garnet **3:**315, 324
World Bank
Benin **3:**336
Burkina Faso **3:**364–365
Burundi **5:**643
Cameroon **1:**50, 64
Central African Republic **5:**659–660
Congo, DR **5:**679
Congo, Rep. **5:**695
Ghana **3:**386, 388
Guinea **2:**216
Kenya **4:**536, 537
Nigeria **1:**125
Rwanda **5:**713

São Tomé and Príncipé **1:**135
Senegal **2:**264
Sierra Leone **2:**281, 282
Uganda **4:**561
World Conservation Society **1:**84
World Food Programme **2:***247*; **4:**531
World Health Organization **1:**89
World War I
Australia **10:**1358, 1366–1367, 1380, 1396
Cameroon **1:**44, 46, 55, 60, 62, 63, 83
Fiji **8:**1035, 1038, 1043
Gabon **1:**83
Ghana **3:**373
Liberia **2:**237
Marshall Islands **8:**1054, 1059
Micronesia **8:**1064, 1069
Nauru **8:**1074, 1079
New Zealand **9:**1210, 1215–1216, 1221
Nigeria **1:**44
Northern Mariana Islands **8:**1086
Papua New Guinea **8:**1098, 1104, 1117
Polynesia **9:**1187
Samoa **9:**1240, 1245, 1252
Togo **3:**410, 415, 423
World War II **9:**1186, *1288*, *1289*
Australia **10:**1358, 1367, 1368, 1380, 1396, 1398, 1402, 1406
Cameroon **1:**50, 55
Coral Sea battle **8:**1104; **10:**1367
Eritrea **4:**482, 487, 488, 489, 494
Ethiopia **4:**496
Fiji **8:**1043, 1049
Freetown **2:**280
French Somaliland **4:**475, 479
Gabon civil war **1:**83, 90
Gambia **2:**197
Guadalcanal battle **8:***1034*, 1035, 1124, 1129, 1133
Guam **8:**1052
Ivory Coast **3:**374
Kiribati **9:**1198, 1203, 1208, 1209
Liberia **2:**237
Marshall Islands **8:**1054, 1059
Micronesia **8:**1064, 1069, 1073
Nauru **8:**1074, 1079
New Guinea **8:**1098, *1105*, 1117, 1118

New Zealand **9:**1191, 1210, 1216, 1231
Nigeria **1:**101
Norfolk Island **10:**1416
Northern Mariana Islands **8:**1086
Pearl Harbor attack **8:**1035
Peleliu battle **8:**1093
Samoa **9:**1245, 1252
Solomon Islands **8:**1124, 1129, 1131, 1133, 1134
Somalia **4:**540, 546, 551
Tarawa battle **9:**1198, 1203
Tonga **9:**1263, 1270
Tuvalu **9:**1274, 1279
Vanuatu **8:**1141, 1143, 1145

Y
Yapese Empire **8:**1031
Yatenga kingdom **3:**311, 316, 318, 350
Yekuno Amlak, Solomonic emperor **4:**456
Yennenga, Dagomba princess **3:**311
Yitbarek, Zagwé emperor **4:**456
Yoruba city-states **1:**27, 31–32
Yoruba kingdom **3:**322, 324, 338, 345
Youlou, Fulbert **5:**687–688
Youssouf, Sitti Saïd **6:**756
Yusuf, Abdullahi **4:**547

Z
Zafy, Albert **6:**765
Zaghawa Duguwa dynasty **1:**28
Zagwé dynasty **4:**455, 456, 463
ZANU (Zimbabwe African National Union) **7:**992
ZANU–PF (Zimbabwe African National Union–Patriotic Front) **7:**990, 992, 993, 998, 1000, 1001, 1002, 1003
ZAPU (Zimbabwe African People's Union) **7:**992, 993, 995, 1000
Zara Yacob, emperor of Ethiopia **4:**464
Zauditu, empress of Ethiopia **4:**502
Zenawi, Meles **4:***500*, 514
Zisco Corporation **7:**1003
Zongo, Norbert **3:**356
Zoskales, king of Aksum **4:**454
Zoungrara (Mossi legendary king) **3:**316
Zulu kingdom **7:**883, 892, 894, 895–896, 900, 940
Zuma, Jacob **7:***944*, 949

Cultural and Artistic Index

Numbers in **boldface** refer to volume numbers; those in *italic* refer to illustrations:

A

Abdallah, Ahmed **6:**755
Abdallah, Yohanna Barnaba **6:**807
Abega, Severin Cecile **1:**58
Abranches, Henrique **5:**619
Abrantes, José Mena **5:**619
Absa, Moussa Sene **2:**258
accordion players **7:**921
AC/DC (rock band) **10:***1377,* 1378
Achebe, Chinua **1:**105
Adangme language **3:**329
Addis Ababa University **4:**511
Adichie, Ngozi **1:**105
Adja language **3:**338
adobe architecture **3:**358, 378, 399, 419
Afrikaans language **7:**895, 932, 940, 950, 954, 957
    education **7:**961, 968
Afro, Lily **1:**74
Afro-A-Kom (sculpture) **1:**59
Afro-beat music **1:**108
Afro-Cuban rumba **5:**672–673
Afropop music **2:**277; **5:**655, 672–673, 690, 707
Agbetiafa, Komlan **3:**417
Agostinho Neto University **5:**623
Agualusa, Eduardo **5:**619
Agüe, María Nsue **1:**74
Ahmadiyya **2:**226
Ahyi, Paul **3:**418
Aido, Anna **3:**377
Akanji, Adebisi **1:**106
Akan language **3:**328
Akendengué, Pierre-Claver **1:**86
Akplodjegou, Kuevi Kangui **3:**418
Aksum Obelisk **4:**454, *455,* 506
Aladji, Victor **3:**417
Alarinjo (Yoruba traveling theater) **1:**105
Alasia, Sam Lidimani **8:**1130
Albert Schweitzer Hospital **1:**88
Alemayehu, Haddis **4:**505

Allaleh, Abdi Nuur **4:**476–477
Amakhosi Township Square Cultural Center **7:**996
Ambasse Bey music **1:**59
Amharic language **4:**468, 505, 512
Amon d'Aby, François Joseph **3:**398
Amu, Ephraim **3:**378–379
Amukoto, David **7:**933
Ana Clara Guerra Marques Contemporary Dance Company **5:**621
Analla, Gnoussira **3:**417
Ananou, David **3:**417
Andreas, Neshani **7:**932
ANZAC Day **9:**1221, 1247–1248; **10:**1380, *1381,* 1396
Arch 22 (Banjul) **2:***197,* 198, 201
archaeology **7:**886, 889
Armah, Ayi Kwei **3:**377
Armstrong, Gillian **10:**1379
Arthur Rimbaud French Cultural Center **4:**476
Ashanti language **3:**377
Asheri, Jedida **1:**58
Ashton, Julian **10:**1375
Atepa, Pierre Goudiaby **2:***257,* 258
Australia Day **10:**1300
Australia National University **10:**1393
Australian Rules Football **8:**1080, *1113;* **10:**1382
Australian War Memorial **10:**1396
Austronesian languages **8:**1026–1027, 1036
Avila Laurel, Juan Tomás **1:**74
Azande language **5:**661, 671

B

Bacar, Mohamed **6:**755
Bah, Chernor **2:**276
Baines, Thomas **7:**908
Baker, Herbert **7:**951
Baldeh, Fodeh **2:**198
Bambino, Sekouba **2:**212
Bamboté, Pierre Makombo **5:**654
Banda language **5:**653
Bangura, Hassan **2:**276

Bantu languages **1:**26, 45, 47–48, 57, 63, 78; **3:**327; **4:**457–458, 462, 468, 469; **5:**596, 597, 607, 633; **6:**735, 738, 739, 742, 746, 747, 748, 756, 760, 774, 828, 844; **7:**888, 892, 900–901, 908
    see also Swahili language
Barbosa, Jorge **2:**186
Baria, Yemane **4:**490
bark cloth *see tapa*
basketry
    Botswana **7:**908, *909*
    Lesotho **7:**920
    Tutsi **5:***707*
Bastos, Waldemar **5:**620
batiks **2:**258
Batuque (dance) **2:**187
Bayajidda (founding hero) **1:**36
beehive dwelling **7:**951, 980
Beier, Ulli **1:**106, 109
Bekalé, Eric-Joël **1:**85
Bekele, Kenenisa **4:***505,* 507
Bela (Congolese artist) **5:**672
Bemba, Sylvain **5:**689, 690
Bemba language **3:**311; **6:**746, 846, 851, 853
Bennett, Gordon **10:**1375
Benue-Kongo languages **1:**47, 48–49
Beresford, Bruce **10:**1379
Besong, Bate **1:**58
Bessora (Gabonese author) **1:**85, *87*
Beti, Mongo **1:**57–58
Beyala, Calixthe **1:**58
Bezuidenhout, Evita **7:**953
Bhély-Quénum, Olympe **3:**338
Bhoipuri language **6:**794, 795
Biazin, Clément-Marie **5:**654
Bible **4:**452, 455, 502, 529
    translations **4:**492, 505
"big man" status (Papua New Guinea) **8:**1112, 1113
Bikindi, Simon **5:**707
Biklia, Abebe **4:**507
Bikutsi music **1:**59
Binns, Vivienne **10:**1375
Biramah, Fatou **3:**417
Bisa language **3:**357
Bislama (Creole language) **8:**1142

Bissau Cathedral **2:***224*
Black Arcade **10:***1388*
Blackman, Charles **10:**1375
blanket garment, Lesotho **7:**921
Blixen, Karen **4:**526
Blondy, Alpha **3:**399
Blouin, Andrée **5:**653
Blyden, Edward W. **2:**240
body art **10:**1374
Boganda, Barthélemy **5:**652, 655
Boleká, Justo Bolekia **1:**74
Bonapriso Center for Arts **1:**59
Bonga (singer-songwriter) **5:**620
Boni, Nazi **3:**357
boomerang **10:**1343, 1387
Boturu, Recardo Silebo **1:**74
Bouyain, Sarah **3:**357
Bow Project **7:**953
Boyd, Arthur **10:**1375
Boys, Bhundu **7:**995
Bradman, Donald **10:**1382
brass **1:**33–34
brass bands, Ghana **3:**379
breadfruit **8:***1027*
Breytenbach, Breyten **7:**950
Brink, André **7:**950
bronze casting **1:**31, 33–34, *34, 35,* 48, 59, 106, 124
Brown, Andy **7:**996
Brown, Vernon **9:**1219
Buika, Concha **1:**74
Bulletin (Australian weekly magazine) **10:**1372, 1373
Bulu Festival **8:**1046
Bundu mask **2:**276
Bunny, Rupert **10:**1374
Burney-Nicol, Miranda **2:**276
bush taxis **2:**215
bush tucker (traditional Aboriginal food) **10:**1383
Butake, Bole **1:**58

C

Camara, Fodé **2:**258
Cambridge, Ada **10:**1372
Campbell, John Logan **9:**1218
canoes **8:**1045, 1060; **9:**1204, *1205,* 1219, 1246, 1247, *1249,* 1266, 1280
Canterbury University **9:**1230
Carey, Peter **10:**1373

cargo cult **8:**1141, 1143
Carlos, Jérôme **3:**338
carving
   Angola **5:**619
   Maori **9:***1178, 1184, 1219*
   Pitcairn **9:**1238
   Samoa **9:**1246–1247
   Tonga **9:**1266
   Wallis and Futuna **9:***1319*
   Zimbabwe **7:**995
   see also masks; wood carving
Casely-Hayford, Adelaide
   2:275
Casely-Hayford, Gladys May
   2:275
Casset, Mama **2:**258
Castle, Len **9:**1219
cave art *see* rock art
Cawley, Evonne Goolagong
   10:1382
Cazneaux, Harold **10:**1375
ceramics *see* pottery
Chadic languages **1:**47
Chakela, Mosotho **7:**921
Chamorro language **8:**1037
Chandia, Flinto **6:**851
chants **8:**1060, 1070
Chaold, Pyabelo Kouly **3:**417
Chapel of the Tablet (Aksum)
   4:452, *452*, 508
Charley, Dele **2:**275
Chauvel, Charles **10:**1379
Cheikh Anta Diop University
   2:*256*, 262
Cheyney-Coker, Syl **2:**275
Chichewa language **6:**746, 780
Chikwava, Brian **7:**994
children
   Aboriginal Australian
      10:1356, 1371, 1373, 1388
   Cameroon **1:**60
   Congo, Democratic Republic
      of **5:**675
   Liberian civil wars **2:**243,
      244, 245, 246
   Sierra Leone civil war **2:**274,
      279
Chimbetu, Simon **7:**995–996
Chimombo, Steve **6:**780
chimurenga (musical style)
   7:995
Chingono, Julius **7:**994
Chinodya, Shimmer **7:**994
Chirikure, Chirikure **7:**994
Chiweshe, Stella **7:**995
Chiyao language **6:**747, 780
Chiziane, Paulina **6:**807
cholera epidemic **7:**1000
Christ Church Cathedral
   10:1402, *1402*

Chuukese language **8:**1037,
   1070, 1071
Cisse, Soly **2:**258
Clarke, Marcus **10:**1372
Clegg, Johnny **7:**953
Clock Tower (Victoria) **6:**826
Coetzee, Basil **7:**952
Coetzee, J. M. **7:**950; **10:**1373
coffee ceremony, Eritrea **4:**492
coins, Aksumite **4:**454–455, 456
Cole, Robert Wellesley **2:**275
Commonwealth Avenue Bridge
   10:*1395*
Commonwealth Games **7:**496
Cooper, Charles **2:**240
copper working **5:**596
Cotton Tree (Freetown) **2:**280
Couchoro, Félix **3:**338, 417
Counihan, Noel **10:**1375
coupé-décalé (musical style) **3:**399
Court, Margaret **10:**1382
cowrie shells **5:**597, 600
Creole language **6:**794, 795,
   823, 824
cricket (sport) **4:**528; **9:**1221;
   10:1382, *1400*, 1401
Cruz, Viriato da **5:**619
Cry, The Beloved Country (Paton)
   7:950
Cuca (Angolan beer) **5:**621
Cuoto, Mia **6:**807
Cushitic languages **4:**457, 548
cycling **4:**491

D

Dabani language **3:**328
Dadié, Bernard **3:**398
Dagara language **3:**357
Dairo, J. K. **1:**108
dance
   Aboriginal Australians
      10:1377, *1378*
   Botswana **7:**909
   Burundi **5:***637, 638*
   Congo, Republic of **5:**690
   Fiji **8:***1046*
   Kiribati **9:**1204–1205
   Lesotho **7:**921, *922*
   Namibia **7:**933
   Palau **8:**1094
   Papua New Guinea **8:**1109
   Rwanda **5:**707, *708*
   Samoa **9:***1246*, 1247
   Senegal **2:**258
   Sierra Leone **2:**276
   Solomon Island **8:**1131
   Swaziland **7:***978*, 981
   Tonga **9:***1259*, 1266
   Tuvalu **9:**1281
   Uganda **4:**562–563, *564*

Dangarembga, Tsitsi **7:**994
Danquah, J. B. **3:**377
Dao, Bernadette Sanou **3:**357
Dark, Eleanor **10:**1373
Davies, Jacob Stanley **2:**275
Davis, Jack **10:**1379
Dawson, Smoky **10:**1378
Debre Damo Church **4:***456*
Debtera Alaka Zenab **4:**505
de Graft-Johnson, J. C. **3:**377
Dembo, Leonard **7:**996
Denard, Robert **6:**755
Dennis, C. J. **10:**1373
Desta, Gebrekirstos **4:**506
Devi, Ananda **6:**794
Dias, Jorge **6:**808
Diba, Viyé **2:**258
Dibango, Manu **1:**59
Dibba, Ebou **2:**198
Diescho, Joseph **7:**932
Dimé, Moustapha **2:**258
Diome, Fatou **2:**257
Diop, Birago **2:**257
Diop, Boubacar Boris **2:**257
Diop, Cheikh Anta **2:**257
Diouf, Ibou **2:**258
Dioula language **3:**328, 357,
   398
Dipoko, Mbella Sonne **1:**58
Djédjé, Ernesto **3:**399
Djohar, Said Mohamed **6:**755
Dogon language **3:**328
Doguicimi (Hazoumé) **3:**338
Dôlé (film) **1:**87
Dome Argus (Dome A) **10:**1312
Dongala, Emmanuel **5:**689
Dorley, Morris **2:**241
"dot art" **10:**1374, 1375, *1375*
Dow, Unity **7:**908
drumming
   Benin **3:**339
   Botswana **7:**909
   Burkina Faso **3:**358
   Burundi **5:***636*, 637–638,
      645
   Central African Republic
      5:654, *655*
   Congo, Democratic Republic
      of **5:**672
   Ghana **3:***378*
   Namibia **7:**933
   Samoa **9:**1247
   Tonga **9:***1265*, 1266
   Uganda **4:**562–563
Duarte, Fausto **2:**224
Duff, Alan **9:**1218
Duggan, Maurice **9:**1218
Duiker, K. Sello **7:**950
Dusty, Slim **10:**1378
Dywill, Nofinishí **7:**953

E

Ebalé, Ramón Esono **1:**74
Ebola virus **5:**676, 693
ecotourism **1:**84
Église Évangélique du Gabon
   1:88
Ekosso, Rosemary **1:**58
Ekué, Lauren **3:**417
Ekwensi, Cyprian **1:**105
elder respect **3:**402
Elebe, Lisembé **5:**672
Elliott, Stephan **10:**1379
Ely, Bonnie **10:**1375
Emecheta, Buchi **1:**105
Engida, Agegehu **4:**506
Espírito Santo, Alda Graça do
   1:136
Évora, Cesária **2:**187, *187*
Ewe language **3:**328, 377
Exhibition Building **10:**1376

F

faatele performance **9:**1281
fado singers **6:**808–809
Fairweather, Ian **10:**1375
Fakoly, Tiken Jah **3:**399
fale (house) **9:**1246, 1266
Fall, Khadi **2:**257
famo music **7:**921
Fante language **3:**377
Farah, Nuruddin **4:**548
Faye, Safi **2:**258
Federation Square **10:***1401*
Félix Houphouét-Boigny
   Stadium **3:**405
Ferreira, António Baticã **2:**224
Fiat Tagliero Building **4:***490*,
   493
Field, Barron **10:**1372
Finn , Tim and Neil **9:**1220
fire dance, Samoa **9:**1247
First World Festival of Black
   Arts **2:**259
Fodio, Usman dan **1:**105
Flores, Paulo **5:**620
Foley, Fiona **10:**1375
Fonlon, Bernard **1:**58
Forna, Aminatta **2:**275
Fourah Bay College **2:**273,
   279, 280
Fourie, Johnny **7:**952
Frame, Janet **9:**1218
Franco (Frank Lesokwane)
   7:909
Franklin, Miles **10:**1373
Fraser, Dawn **10:**1382
French language **1:**57, 58, 60,
   61, 75, 80, 88; **2:**211, 257;
   5:571, 607, 636, 648, 653,
   689; **6:**766, 793, 794, 824

frigate bird cult **8**:1080
Frum, John **8**:1141, 1143
Frusoni, Sergio **2**:186
Fugard, Athol **7**:953
Fulani language **3**:328, 329, 358
Fuller, Alexandra **7**:994
funerary art **6**:767
Furphy, Joseph **10**:1373

G

Gadeau, Coffi **3**:398
Gahungu, Pierre Claver **5**:637
Gainsbourg, Serge **1**:87
Gebre-Mehdin, Tsegaye **4**:506, 507
Gebreselassie, Haile **4**:507
Gebreyesus, Afework **4**:505
Gebry-Medhin, Tesgary **4**:506
Ge'ez language **4**:453, 455, 468, 511
    alphabet **4**:505
Geoghegen, Edward **10**:1379
George, Crispin **2**:275
George, James **9**:1218
Gessesse, Tesfaye **4**:507
Gilbertese language **8**:1037
Ginibi, Ruby Langford **10**:1373
Girma, Bealu **4**:505, 506
glass painting **2**:258, 259
Glover, Denis **9**:*1218*
Glover, John **10**:1374
Gobarau Minaraet **1**:*37*
Godwin, Peter **7**:994
Golden Jubilee House (Accra) **3**:376, 383
golf **8**:1048
Gomes, Flora **2**:224
Gondarine style **4**:506
Gordimer, Nadine **7**:950
Goyémidé, Étienne **5**:653
Grace, Patricia **9**:1218
Graceland (album) **7**:953
graffiti (as art form) **1**:86
Grahamstown National Arts Festival **7**:954
Grande Mosque (Kankan) **2**:*206*
Great Faisal Mosque (Conakry) **2**:212, 214
Great Mosque (Touba) **2**:260, *262*
Great Stele (Aksum) **4**:454
Greenway, Francis **10**:1376
Grenville, Kate **10**:1373
Grey-Johnson, Nana **2**:198
griot (traveling storyteller)
    Benin **3**:338
    Burkina Faso **3**:358
    Gambia **2**:199

Guinea **2**:211, 212
Guinea-Bissau **2**:225
Ivory Coast **3**:398, 399
Liberia **2**:241
Senegal **2**:257, 258
Togo **3**:419
Group Architects movement **9**:1219
Gubegna, Abe **4**:505
Guedes, Amancio d'Apoim (Pancho) **6**:808
Guerard, Eugene von **10**:1374
gumbe music **2**:225, 277
Gur language **3**:311, 328, 398
Gurunsi language **3**:357

H

Hadrawi (Muhammad Ibrahim Warsame) **4**:548
Haley, Alex **2**:198
Hall, Roger **9**:1220
Hankinson, Michael **7**:953
Harare University **7**:998, 999
Harpur, Charles **10**:1372
Harris, Max **10**:1373
Harris, René **8**:1078
hats, grass-woven **7**:920, *921*
Hau'ofa, Epeli **9**:1265
haus tambaran (men's meeting house) **8**:1107
Hazoumé, Paul **3**:338
Head, Bessie **7**:908
Heidelberg School (Australian art movement) **10**:1374
Hellala Festival **9**:1267
Henson, Bill **10**:1375
Hereniko, Vilsoni **8**:1045
Hewett, Dorothy **10**:1379
Hibiscus Festival **8**:1046
highlife (musical style) **1**:108; **2**:241; **3**:379
Hindi language **8**:1045
HIP-CO (musical style) **2**:241
Hiruy, Emealf **4**:506
Hodgkins, Frances **9**:1219
Hoffmann, Giselher **7**:932
Honwana, Luis Bernardo **6**:807
Hope, A. D. **10**:1373
horse racing **10**:1401
Hotel Rwanda (film) **5**:712
Hove, Chenjerai **7**:994
Hulme, Keri **9**:1218
Hunter, Lucilda **2**:275
Hussein, Ebrahim **6**:835
Hyde, Robin **9**:1218

I

Ibrahim, Abdullah **7**:952
Ihimaera, Witi **9**:1218

Ilboudo, Monique **3**:357
"imaginary voyages" literature **10**:1372
Instituto Cardenal Cisneros **1**:75
International Art and Craft Fair *see* SAIO
Intore Dance Troupe **5**:707
INXS (rock band) **10**:1378
Ipeko-Etomane, Faustin-Albert **5**:653
Ireland, Kevin **9**:1218
Isegawa, Moses **4**:562
Ivanga, Imunga **1**:87
ivory carving **5**:619

J

Jacinto, António **5**:619
Jamieson, Trevor **10**:1379
jazz **2**:277; **7**:952, 995
Johnson, Colin **10**:1373
Johnson, Lemuel **2**:275
Jones, Lloyd **9**:1218
juju (musical style) **1**:108
Juluka (duo) **7**:953
Jumbam, Kenjo wan **1**:58
Júnior, António Assis **5**:619

K

Kaboré, Gaston **3**:358
Kaburahe, Antoine **5**:636
Kabuto, Daniel **5**:636
Kachamba, Daniel **6**:781
Kadavu pottery **8**:1045
Kagame, Alexis **5**:706
Kakala, Sofele **9**:*1267*
Kamanda, Kama **5**:672
Kamatari, Esther **5**:636
Kane, Cheikh Hamidou **2**:257
Kano Market Literature **1**:105
Kanté, Mory **2**:212
Kaoze, Stefano **5**:671
Kappata, Stephen **6**:851
Kariuki, J. M. **4**:525
Kebra negast (Ethiopian myth collection) **4**:463–464, 505
Keita, Souleymane **2**:258
Keneally, Thomas **10**:1373, 1379
Kennedy, Peter **10**:1375
Kente, Gibson **7**:953
kente cloth **3**:378, 385, 389
Kentridge, William **7**:951
kewela music **6**:781
Kezilahabi, Euphrase **6**:835
Khalam (music group) **2**:258
Kidjo, Angélique **3**:*338*, 339
Kidude, Bi **6**:836
Kifle, Yonas **4**:489
Kikongo language **5**:619, 684, 689

Kimbundu languages **5**:608, 619
Kinaxixi Market **5**:620
King Ezana's Stele **4**:454
King Toffa's Palace **3**:339, 345
Kinyarwanda language **5**:609, 661, 671, 700, 703, 706
Kippel, Robert **10**:1375
Kirundi *see* Rundi language
Ki-Zerbo, Joseph **3**:357
Kngwarreye, Emily **10**:1375
Kodjo, Michel **3**:398
Kombuis, Koos **7**:953
Koné, Tanella **3**:398
Kong Mosque **3**:399
Kongo language **5**:607, 664, 671
Koobi Fora site **4**:453
Kosraean language **8**:1037, 1070, 1071
Kossi, Agbagli **3**:418
Koteba Ensemble **3**:400
Koulibaly, Isaïe Biton **3**:398
Koumba, Henri **1**:87
Kourouma, Ahmadou **3**:398
Kramer, Daniel **7**:953
krar (musical instrument) **4**:506
Kreol language **6**:824
Kru linguistic group **3**:328, 398
Kubandwa festival **5**:638
Kumalo, Mzilikazi **7**:953
Kunama language **4**:489, 491
Kunta Kinte **2**:198
Kuoh-Moukoury, Thérèse **1**:58
Kuti, Fela Anikulapo **1**:108
Kuti, Femi **1**:*109*
Kwa linguistic group **3**:328, 398
Kwame Nkrumah University **3**:*379*, 382, 385
kwasa-kwasa (rhumba form) **7**:909

L

Ladysmith Black Mambazo (group) **7**:953
Laluah, Auqah (G. M. Casely-Hayford) **2**:275
language groups **1**:26, 45, 47–49, 52, 57; **3**:327–329, 398; **5**:607, 619
    see also Bantu languages; Swahili language
Lattier, Christian **3**:398
Laver, Rod **10**:1382
Lawler, Ray **10**:1379
Lawson, Henry **10**:1372–1373
Laye, Camara **2**:211

Layen (Islamic brotherhood) 2:260
Leakey, Richard 4:453
Le Clézio, Jean-Marie Gustave 6:794
Le Guma, Alex 7:950
Leh, Abdallah 4:476–477
Lemma, Mengistu 4:506, 507
Leshoal, B. L. 7:920
Liking, Werewere 1:58; 3:400
Lilanga, George 6:835
Lilburn, Douglas 9:1220
Lima, Kiki 2:186
Lindsay, Lionel 10:1375
Lindsay, Norman 10:1375
Lingala language 5:607, 664, 671, 684
lingua franca 5:607; 6:748, 794
Lô, Ismaël 2:258
Loboch, Francisco Zamora 1:74
Lomani-Tshibamba, Paul 5:671
London Whitechapel Exhibition, Australian Contemporary Art 10:1374–1375
Lopès, Henri 1:85; 5:689
Lopes, Manuel 2:186
Lopes da Silva, Baltasar 2:186
Lorenz, Bente 6:851
Loueke, Lionel 3:339
Lubaki, Albert 5:672
Luba language 5:607, 661, 671
Luhrmann, Baz 10:1379
Lumu, Henry 4:562
Luzira Head (sculpture) 4:562

M
Macheso, Aleck 7:996
Mackennal, Bertram 10:1375
Madabbar, Johannes 4:505
Maddy, Yulisa Amadu 2:275
Magagula, Salayedvwa Modison 7:980
Maimo, Sankie 1:58
Makeba, Miriam 7:952, 953
Makerere University 4:562, 566, 567
Makouta-Mboukou, Jean-Pierre 5:689
Makua language 6:746, 747, 807, 810
Malagasy language 6:748, 766, 767, 768, 769
Malangan Festival 8:1109
malaria 3:381, 402–403, 421–422; 5:623, 641, 657, 676, 693, 711

Malembe, Timothée 5:672
Malley, Erin (fictional poet) 10:1373
Malonga, Jean 5:689, 690
Malouf, David 10:1373
Malunga, Benedicto 6:780
Mambèti, Djibril Diop 2:258
Mande language 3:313, 328
Maning, Frederick 9:1218
Manirampa, Antoine 5:636–637
Manjia language 5:653
Manresa Bodipo, Desiderio 1:74
Mansfield, Katherine 9:1218
Mapanje, Jack 6:780
Mapfumo, Thomas 7:995, 996
Maran, René 5:653
marathons 4:489, 507, 528
Marechera, Dambudzo 7:994
Mariam Dearit festival 4:488
maringa (music) 2:277
Marques, Marcelino 2:224
Marshallese language 8:1037, 1059
Masekela, Hugh 7:952
Mashakada, Cephus 7:995
Mask Festival 8:1109
masks 1:31; 3:318; 5:596; 6:748
  Benin 3:338
  Burkina Faso 3:357, 358
  Cameroon 1:59
  Central African Republic 5:654
  Congo, Democratic Republic of 5:672, 673
  Equatorial Guinea 1:74
  Fiji 8:1046
  Gabon 1:85, 86
  Ghana 3:378
  Guinea 2:212
  Ivory Coast 3:399, 401
  Liberia 2:240–241
  Malawi 6:780
  Micronesia 8:1070
  Mozambique 6:807
  Nigeria 1:107
  Papua New Guinea 8:1106
  Sierra Leone 2:276
  Tanzania 6:835
  Zimbabwe 7:996
Mason, Bruce 9:1220
matriarchal society 5:692
Matriki festival 9:1221
matrilineal society 8:1071, 1081, 1112, 1143
mats, woven 5:654
Matsebula, Shadrack Mkhulunyelwa 7:980

Mbande, Venancio 6:808
Mbanga, Lapiro de 1:59
McAuley, James 10:1373
McCahon, Colin 9:1219
McCall-Smith, Alexander 7:908
McGregor, Chris 7:952
Mchunu, Sipho 7:953
Mda, Zakes 7:920, 950
Meadmore, Clement 10:1375, 1376
megaliths 5:646
Meke dancers 8:1046, 1109
Melanesian Pidgin (language) 8:1130
Melba, Nellie 10:1378
Melbourne Cricket Ground 10:1400, 1401
Melbourne Cup 10:1381, 1401
Memorial to the Martyrs (Burkina Faso) 3:356
Menga, Guy 5:689, 690
Merey-Apinda, Edna 1:85
Merkato market 4:513
mermaid myths 2:163
Merritt, Robert 10:1379
metalwork 2:240; 3:312–313; 5:690
Metzger, Louise Isabella ("Gaga") 2:276
Mhlanga, Cont 7:996
Miano, Léonora 1:58
Michael, Kebede 4:506
Milles Collines (Kigali hotel) 5:712
milo-jazz 2:277
Minogue, Kylie 10:1378
Mintsa, Justine 1:85
Mkhonta, Elias Adam Bateng 7:980
Mkhonza, Sarah 7:980
Mnyampaia, Mathias 6:835
Modisane, William Bloke 7:950
Moffatt, Tracy 10:1375
Mofolo, Thomas 7:920, 950
Molisa, Grace 8:1142
Momple, Lília 6:807
Monash University 10:1393, 1401
Mongita, Albert 5:671–672
Mongo language 5:607, 661, 671
Monokutuba language 5:607, 684, 689
Moore, Bal T. 2:240
Mopeli-Paulus, A. S. 7:920
Moresby, John 8:1117
Morgan, Sally 10:1373
Morija Festival 7:921

Morija Press 7:920
morna (musical form) 2:187
Mortlockese language 8:1037, 1070
Mount Hagen Show 8:1109
Mouridist (Islamic brotherhood) 2:261
Mpando, Gédéon (artist) 1:58
Mphahlele, Eskia 7:950
Mtukudzi, Oliver (Tuku) 7:995, 996
mud-brick buildings see adobe architecture
Muianga, Carmene 6:808
Mulaisho, Dominic 6:851
Mungoshi, Charles 7:994
mural art, Lesotho 7:920
Murcutt, Glenn 10:1376
Murray, Les 10:1373
Mustapha, Mukhtarr 2:275
Muthewuye, Marcos 6:808
mvet (musical instrument) 1:74
My Brilliant Career (Franklin) 10:1373

N
Nagbe, K. Moses 2:240
Namatjira, Albert 10:1375
Nandan, Satendra 8:1045
Nang'undu, Nyakenya 6:807–808
National Carillon (Australia) 10:1396, 1396
National Dance Troupe (Sierra Leone) 2:276
National Museum of Liberia 2:240
National Theater (Ghana) 3:378
National University of Benin 3:343, 344
Nauruan language 8:1037, 1080
Ndadaye, Melchior 5:638
N'Debeka, Maxime 5:689
Ndereba, Catherine 4:528
Ndiaye, Iba 2:258
Ndimurukundo-Kururu, Barbara 5:636
Ndongo-Bidyogo, Donato 1:74
N'Dour, Youssou 2:258
Negash, Ghirmai 4:489
negritude movement 2:257; 3:417
New Australian Poetry movement 10:1373
New Yam Festival (Nigeria) 1:110
Nfah-Abbenyi, Juliana 1:58
Ngale, Ilongo Fritz 1:58

Nganang, Patrice **1**:58

Ngando (Lomami-Tshibamba) **5**:671

Ngondo festival **1**:59

Ngozi, Chimamanda **1**:105

Ngubane, Jordan **7**:950

Nguema Madja, Fernando **1**:74

Ngugi wa Thiong'o **4**:526, 527

Ngunga troupe **5**:69

N'Hada, Sana Na **2**:224

Nichol, Abioseh **2**:275

Niger-Bantu languages **5**:607

Niger-Congo languages **3**:327–329; **5**:607, 609

Nigerian National Mosque (Abuja) **1**:*113*, 119

Nigussie, Yoftahe **4**:507

Nikashama, Ngandu **5**:672

Nilotic language **4**:457, 468–469

N'Kodia, Alain **5**:690

Nkurunziza, Innocent **5**:706

No. 1 Ladies' Detective Agency (McCall-Smith) **7**:908

Nok culture **1**:26, 31, 106

Nolan, Sidney **10**:1375

Nollywood **1**:106, 129

Noronha, Rui de **6**:807

Notre Dame de Apotres Cathedral (Cotonou) **3**:*344*

Nsukka School (Nigerian arts) **1**:106

Nthunya, Mpho' M'atsepo **7**:920

Nukuleka site **9**:1174

Nyama, Jean Divassa **1**:85

Nyamwezi language **6**:739, 744, 746, 748, 835, 837

Nyangoma, Nadine **2**:224

Nyeko, Monica Arac de **4**:562

Nyonda, Vincent de Paul **1**:85

Nzinga, Raymond Lema A'nsi **5**:672

N'Zongo Soul **5**:690

O

Oduduwa (god) **1**:31, 32, 33

Ofori, Dominic **2**:275

Ogiso (rulers of the sky) **1**:33

Ogonga, Jimmy **4**:526–527

Ogot, Grace **4**:526

Ogunde, Hubert **1**:105

Okri, Ben **1**:105

Olaniyi, Taiwo **1**:106

Olumuyiwa, Oluwole **1**:107

Olurun (god) **1**:31

Olympic Games **4**:507; **7**:946; **10**:1382, 1401, 1405

Omar Bongo University **1**:90

Omotic languages **4**:467, 468

Onabolu, Aina **1**:106

Onitsha Market Literature **1**:105

Onka, Destin **5**:*691*

On Trial for My Country (Samkange) **7**:994

Orisha (god) **1**:*32*

Osogbo School (Nigerian arts) **1**:106

O'Sullivan, Vincent **9**:1218

Ouedraogo, Dimdolobsom **3**:357

Ouedraogo, Idrissa **3**:358

Our Lady of Peace of Yamoussoukro Basilica **3**:396, 399, 404, *404*

Owondo, Laurent **1**:85

Owusu, Martin **3**:377

Oyono, Ferdinand **1**:57, 58

P

Pacific Arts Festivals **8**:1080

Palais des Sports de Treichville **3**:*403*

Pan-African Event **3**:300–301

Panafrican Film and Television Festival **3**:363, 367

Panafrican Music Festival **3**:358, 363

Parr, Mike **10**:1375

Paterson, A. B. ("Banjo") **10**:1373

Pathé 'O (fashion designer) **3**:398

Paton, Alan **7**:950

Paul and Clara Gebauer Collection **1**:59

Peace Pole (Kumasi) **3**:*379*

Pene, Omar **2**:258

Peters, Lenrie **2**:198

Petersen, Taliep **7**:953

petroglyphs **8**:1130

photography **10**:1375–1376

Pidgin English **8**:1106, 1116

Pliya, Jean **3**:338

Pohnpeian language **8**:1037, 1070, 1071

polygamy **1**:60, 89, 114, 137; **2**:177, 200, 213, 226, 243, 261, 278; **3**:341, 361, 381, 402, 420; **4**:464, 530, 550, 565, 566; **6**:746, 756, 782

Porquet, Niangoran **3**:399

Portuguese language **2**:186, 224; **5**:607, 612, 619

Poto-Poto School (painting) **5**:689

pottery **5**:*599*; **9**:1174

Angola **5**:619

Cape Verde **2**:186

Choiseul **8**:1130

Fiji **8**:1045

Gambia **2**:199

Lapita **9**:1174

Maori **9**:1219

Melanesia **8**:1026–1027, 1028, 1029

Micronesia **8**:1029, 1031

Namibia **7**:933

New Zealand **9**:1219

Rwanda **5**:706

Samoa **9**:1174

Pouka, Louis-Maraie **1**:57

Praed, Mrs. Campbell (Rosa) **10**:1372

praise poetry **7**:952

Preston, Margaret **10**:1375

Prichard, Katherine Susannah **10**:1373

Proença, Helder **2**:224

Puttkamer, Jesko von **1**:59

Q

Qadiriyyah (Islamic brotherhood) **2**:260

Qarshe, Abdillah **4**:549

qat (khat) **4**:*476*, 478, 553

R

Rabearivelo, Jean-Joseph **6**:766

Rabemananjara, Jacques **6**:766

raffia cloth **5**:597, 600

Rakotoson, Michèle **6**:766

Ranaivo, Flavien **6**:766

rape

civil wars **5**:640, *670*

spousal **5**:656

Raponda Walker, André **1**:85

Rashidi-Kabamba, Maguy **5**:672

Rawiri, George **1**:85

Redda, Tewelde **4**:490

Reed Dance Day (Swaziland) **7**:981, 983

Rhodes Memorial **7**:951

rhumba style **7**:995–996

Richardson, Henry Handel **10**:1373

Rimbaud, Arthur **4**:476

Roba, Fatuma **4**:507

Robert, Shabaan **6**:835

Roberts, Tom **10**:1374

Rocado Zulu Théâtre **5**:690

rock art **4**:526; **7**:*889*, 976

Aboriginal Australians **10**:1318, 1374, 1413

Botswana **7**:*904*, 908, *908*

Lesotho **7**:920, 921

Namibia **7**:933, *933*

South Afric **7**:951

Zimbabwe **7**:995

rock-hewn churches **4**:456, *456*, 506, 517

Roos, Nico **7**:933

Roots (Haley book and TV series) **2**:198

Roots Festival (Gambia) **2**:198, 199, 203

Rossini, Carlo Conti **4**:489

Rotini, Ola **1**:105

Rousseau, Jean-Jacques **9**:1181

Rova palace complex **6**:771

Royal Drummers of Burundi **5**:*636*, 637

Royal Palace of Bassar **3**:*420*

Rugamba, Cyprien **5**:706, 707

rugby **7**:954; **8**:1048; **9**:1220, 1221, 1229, *1246*; **10**:1382

Rui, Manuel **5**:619

Rundi language **5**:609, 630, 636

running, long-distance **4**:489, *505*, 507, 528

Russell, John Peter **10**:1374

Rwanda language *see* Kinyarwanda language

S

Sadji, Abdoulaye **2**:257

Said, Abdulkadir Ahmed **4**:549

Saint Anne Basilica **5**:690, 694

Saint Charles's Church Regent **2**:276

Saint George's Cathedral **2**:276, 280; **4**:513, *513*

Saint Joseph's Cathedral **4**:*491*

Saint Mary of Zion Church **4**:452, 508

Saint Mary's Catholic Cathedral **10**:*1384*

Sakyi, Kwabena **3**:377

Salama, Abba **4**:505

Salik of Debre **4**:505

Samkange, Stanlake **7**:994

Sammy-Mackfoy, Pierre **5**:654

Samputu, Jean-Paul **5**:707

Samy, Domingas **2**:224

sand drawings **8**:1142; **10**:1374

sand painting **2**:*259*

Sangho language **5**:607, 608, 648, 651, 653

Sanjane, Eusébio **6**:807

Sankawulo, Wilson **2**:240

Sargeson, Frank **9**:1218

Saro-Wiwa, Ken **1**:105

Sassine, Williams **2**:211

Saunana, John **8**:1130

Schools of the Air **10:**1393
sculpture **6:**748
  Australia **10:**1375, *1376*
  Ivory Coast **3:**398
  Mozambique **6:**807–808
  Tanzania **6:**835
  Togo **3:**418
  Zambia **6:**851
  see also carving; wood
    carving
segaba tradition **7:**909
Seifu, Debebe **4:**506
Selassie, Hiruy Wolde **4:**505
semba (Angolan music genre)
  5:620
Sembène, Ousmane **2:**257,
  258
Semedo, Odete **2:**224
Semitic languages **4:**453, 467,
  468
Senufo language **3:**357, 398
Sepamia, Sipho **7:**950
Sepik art **8:**1106, 1107, *1111*
Setlhako, Ratsie **7:**909
Seydou, Chris **3:**398
Seydou Nourou Tall mosque
  2:*257*
Shadbolt, Maurice **9:**1218
shantytowns
  Angola **5:**620, 622, 624
  Burundi **5:**642
  Congo, Democratic Republic
    of **5:**677
  Mozambique **6:**810, 812
  Rwanda **5:**706
  South Africa **7:***957*
  Zambia **6:**855
  Zimbabwe **7:**999
shell necklace **8:***1028*
Shityuwete, Helao **7:**932
SIAO (International Art and
  Craft Fair) **3:**357, 359,
  363, 367
Siegu, Pierre Monsard **1:**85
Sila, Abdulai **2:**224
Simon, Paul **7:**953
Sinyangwe, Binwell **6:**851
Sipolo, Jully **8:**1130
Sithole, Lucas **7:**951
Slave, The (Couchoro) **3:**338
soapstone carved birds **7:**995
soccer **1:**62, *74*, *110*; **3:***342*,
  360, *381*, 384, *419*; **4:**491,
  507; **5:***619*, *691*; **10:**1382
  see also World Cup
Socialist Realist style **5:**690
Somali language **4:**472, 476,
  542, 548
Sosseh, Laba **2:**199
Soul Makossa (song) **1:**59

South Pacific Arts Society
  9:1246
Sow, Ousmane **2:**258
Soyinka, Wole **1:**105
Spanish language **1:**70, 75
sports
  Angola **5:***619*
  Australia **10:**1382, *1400*,
    1401
  Benin **3:***342*
  Burkina Faso **3:***360*
  Cameroon **1:**62
  Equatorial Guinea **1:***74*
  Eritrea **4:**489, 491
  Ethiopia **4:***505*, 507
  Fiji **8:**1048
  Ghana **3:***381*, 384
  Kenya **4:**528
  New Zealand **9:**1221, 1229
  Nigeria **1:***110*
  Samoa **9:***1246*
  South Africa **7:**954
  Togo **3:***419*
  see also Olympic Games;
    World Cup
Stead, Christina, (Australian
  writer) **10:**1373
Stead, C. K. (New Zealand
  writer) **9:**1218
stelae **4:**454, 455, 506
Stele of Aksum **4:***455*
Stellenbosch University **7:**961
Stern, Irma **7:**951
Stewart, Harold **10:**1373
stone carving **7:**995
stone complexes, Great
  Zimbabwe **7:***886*, 887,
    986, *994*, 995
story-boards (Palau) **8:**1094
Streeton, Arthur **10:**1374
sulu (Fijian garment) **8:**1045
Sunset Boys (music group)
  2:241
Sutherland, Afua **3:**377
Sutherland, Joan **10:**1378
Swahili languages **4:**458, 467,
  526, 556, 562; **5:**607, 664,
  671; **6:**739, 740, 741, 742,
  743, 746, 747, 748, 750,
  756, 760, 835, 837
Sydney Harbour Bridge
  10:*1404*, 1405
Sydney Opera House **10:**1376,
  1376, 1378, 1379, *1404*,
  1405

T

Taal, Omar Foutiyou **2:**199
Tadjo, Véronique **3:**398
Tansi, Sony Labou **5:**689, 690

Tanyi-Tang, Anne **1:**58
tapa (bark cloth) **8:**1107, 1130;
  9:1247, 1265–1266, *1280*
tapu (taboos), Maori **9:**1179,
  1182, 1223
tattoos **4:**526; **8:**1130; **9:**1247,
  1266
Tavares, Eugénio **2:**186, 187
Tayali, Henry **6:**851
Tchicaya, Gérald Félix **5:**653
Tchicaya U Tam'si **5:**689
Tchichellé Tchivela **5:**689
Teixeira de Sousa, Henrique
  2:186
Te Kanawa, Kiri **9:**1220
Tench, Watkin **10:**1372
tennis **10:**1382
Tenreiro, José Francisco **1:**136
Tesfai, Alemseged **4:**489
Teso language **4:**562
Têtes Brûlées, Les (music
  group) **1:**59
Teuila festival **9:**1248
textile dyes **2:**199, 212, 258,
  276
Thaman, Konai Helu **9:**1265
theater
  Australia **10:**1378, 1379
  Burkina Faso **3:**358
  Ethiopia **4:**507
  Ivory Coast **3:**399–400
  Kenya **4:**527
  Nigeria **1:**108–109
  São Tomé and Príncipe **1:**136
  South Africa **7:**953
  Uganda **4:**563
  Zimbabwe **7:**996
Théâtre d l'Éclair **5:**690
Thomas, Rover **10:**1375
Thorpe, Ian **10:**1382
Thukela River **7:**895, 896
Tiendrébéogo, Marie
  Bernadette **2:**211
Tigré language **4:**468, 489,
  491, 492
Tigrinya language **4:**468, 489
Tijaniyya (Islamic
  brotherhood) **2:**260
Tingatinga, Edward Saidi **6:**835
Tjapaltjarri, Clifford Possum
  10:1375
Todd, Judith **7:**995
Tok Pisin (Pidgin English)
  8:1106, 1116
Tol'Ande, Mweya **5:**672
totem, clan **8:**1071
Toure Kunda (music group)
  2:258
traditional medicine **5:**692,
  693

Traoré, Mahama Johnson **2:**258
Tsiolkas, Christos **10:**1373
Tucker, Albert **10:**1375
Tutuola, Amos **1:**105, 106
Tuvalu Maritime Training
  Institute **9:**1282, 1285
Tuwhare, Hone **9:**1218

U

Uhuru Park **4:***533*, 534
Ulithian language **8:**1037
Uluru (Ayers Rock) **10:**1307,
  1413, 1418
Umbundu language **5:**608,
  612, 619
Union Buildings (Pretoria)
  7:951, *962*
Universidade Católica de
  Angola **5:**623
Universidade Lusiada de São
  Tomé and Príncipe **1:**137
Universidad Nacional de
  Educación **1:**75
Universidad Nacional de
  Guinea Ecuatorial **1:**75,
  76
Université Omar Bongo **1:**88
University Collage (Ibadan)
  1:107
University of Bangui **5:**657, 658
University of Burundi **5:**641,
  642
University of Ibadan **1:**120
University of Otago **9:***1227*
University of Papua New
  Guinea **8:**1106, 1116, 1117
University of the South Pacific
  8:1045, 1048, 1049, 1130,
  1132, 1144; **9:**1204, 1246,
  1265, 1282
Unnuth, Abhimanyu **6:**794
Urban, Keith **10:**1378
Urban Grooves (popular
  music) **7:**996
Uys, Pieter-Dirk **7:**953

V

Vailele site **9:**1174
Vali, Justin **6:**768
Vasco da Gama Church **4:***458*
Vaughan-Richards, Alan **1:**107
Vera, Yvonne **7:**994
Veramo, Joseph **8:**1045
vidomegon practice **3:**341–342
Villa Ki-Yi (arts training
  center) **3:**400
Volans, Kevin **7:**953
Voltaic languages **3:**328
Voortrekker Monument **7:***893*,
  962

W

Waberi, Abdourahman A. **4**:476
Wainaina, Binyavanga **4**:526
Waitangi Day **9**:*1217*, 1221
Wallabies (rugby team) **10**:1382
Wallas Players **5**:690
Wall of Names (Rwanda) **5**:*704*
wall paintings **4**:506
Walter Lini Day **8**:1143
"Waltzing Matilda" (song) **10**:1373
Walukumbu-Bene, Withankenge **5**:672
Wangboje, Solomon **1**:106
Wassu stone circle **2**:*199*
Watt, Emmanuel **8**:1142
weaving
　Central African Republic **5**:*654*
　Ghana **3**:378, 389
　Lesotho **7**:920, *921*
　Madagascar **6**:767
　Samoa **9**:1246
　Tonga **9**:1265
　Tuvalu **9**:1280
　see also basketry
Weir, Peter **10**:1379
Wemba, Papa **5**:673
Werrason (singer-songwriter) **5**:673
Wertenbaker, Timberlake **10**:1379
West Atlantic languages **1**:47; **2**:176, 177
Western Desert Language **10**:1356
White, Eduardo **6**:807
White, Patrick **10**:1373, 1379

Whiteley, Brett **10**:1375
Williamson, David **10**:1379
Williamson, James Cassius **10**:1379
Winton, Tim **10**:1373
Witwatersrand University **7**:961, 966
Woide, Mamo **4**:507
women's status **1**:60, 114; **10**:1370, 1389
　agricultural labor **5**:602, 608, 692, 710
　Benin **3**:341, 342, 343
　Burkina Faso **3**:356, 361, 366
　Burundi **5**:632, 635, 640
　Cape Verde **2**:188
　Central African Republic **5**:656–657
　Comoros **6**:756
　Congo, Democratic Republic of **5**:675
　Congo, Republic **5**:692, 693
　Danhome **3**:322
　Djibouti **4**:478
　Eritrea **4**:492
　Ethiopia **4**:509
　Fiji **8**:1048
　Gambia **2**:200, 202
　Ghana **3**:381
　Guinea **2**:213
　Guinea-Bissau **2**:226
　Ivory Coast **3**:402
　Kenya **4**:532
　Kiribati **9**:1206
　Lesotho **7**:922
　Liberia **2**:243–244
　Malawi **6**:782
　Maori **9**:1224
　Marshall Islands **8**:1061
　Mauritius **6**:795
　Micronesia **8**:1071

　Mozambique **6**:810
　Namibia **7**:934, 937
　Nauru **8**:1081
　New Zealand **9**:1185, 1215, 1224–1225
　Palau **8**:1095
　Papua New Guinea **8**:1112, 1116
　Rwanda **5**:711
　Samoa **9**:1250–1251
　Senegal **2**:261, 265
　Seychelles **6**:825
　Sierra Leone **2**:276, 278, 279
　Somalia **4**:550
　South Africa **7**:957–958
　Swaziland **7**:978, 979, 981, 983
　Togo **3**:417, 420–421
　Tonga **9**:1268
　Uganda **4**:*565*, 566
　Wolof kingdoms **2**:165
　Zambia **6**:853
　Zimbabwe **7**:998
wood carving **1**:*31*, 33; **6**:748
　Angola **5**:619
　Benin **3**:338
　Burkina Faso **3**:357
　Burundi **5**:637
　Cameroon **1**:59
　Congo, Democratic Republic of **5**:672
　Equatorial Guinea **1**:74
　Fiji **8**:1045, *1046*
　Madagascar **5**:757; **6**:771
　Malawi **6**:*781*
　Mozambique **6**:808
　Nauru **8**:1080
　Palau **8**:1094
　Papua New Guinea **8**:1106, 1107, *1111*
　Rwanda **5**:706

　Solomon Islands **8**:1130, *1131*
　Tanzania **6**:835
　Vanuatu **8**:1142
　Yap **8**:*1070*
　see also carving; masks
Worku, Dagnachew **4**:505
World Cup **7**:949, 954, 970, 972, *973*; **10**:1382
world music **2**:199; **5**:707; **7**:953
Wright, Judith **10**:1373

X

X-ray art **10**:1374
xylophone orchestras **6**:808

Y

Yapese language **8**:1037, 1070, 1071
yaqona (Fiji national beverage) **8**:1045, 1046
Yavoucko, Cyriaque Robert **5**:654
Yeha ruined temple **4**:*53*, 453
Yirenkyi, Asiedu **3**:377
Yoruba language **3**:338

Z

Zaourou, Bernard Zadi **3**:399
Zaria School (Nigerian arts) **1**:106
Zawiya (Islamic community) **2**:167
Zé Carlos **2**:224, 225
Zerihun, Birhanu **4**:505
Zhakata, Leonard **7**:996
Zimunya, Musaemura **7**:994
Zongo, Norbert **3**:357
zouglou (musical style) **3**:399

Economic Index

Numbers in **boldface** refer to volume numbers; those in *italic* refer to illustrations:

A
aluminum **6:**815
auto industry **3:**344; **7:**972

B
bananas **5:**638, 643, 708

C
cassava *see* manioc
coal **5:**679; **7:**912, 971, 985, 1002; **10:**1432
  Australia **10:**1310, 1402, *1408*, 1409, 1410, 1414, 1415
cobalt **5:**633, 643, 662, 668, 679, 681; **6:**731; **10:**1409
cocoa **1:**77, 83, 139; **3:**415, 424
  Cameroon **1:**64, 65, 67, 73
  Ghana **3:**373, 374, 375, 383, 385, 386, 387, 388, 389
  Ivory Coast **3:**395, 396, 406, 407, 408
coconut products **6:**749; **8:**1034, 1093, 1118; **9:**1204, 1205, 1208, 1209, *1254*, 1281, 1284, 1285
coffee **1:**77; **4:**536; **5:**660, 661, 679
  Angola **5:**602, 616, 621, 626
  Burundi **5:**633, 642, 643, 644, 645
  Cameroon **1:**64, 65–66, 67
  Ethiopia **4:**515, 516, 517
  Ivory Coast **3:**396, 406, 407, 408
  Rwanda **5:***591*, 714, 715
copper **7:**936, 937; **8:**1012
  Botswana **7:**912, 913, 936
  Bougainville **8:**1015, 1105, 1118, 1119, 1120
  Congo Basin **5:**582, 583, 596, 626, 633, 643, 662, 668, 679, 696
  eastern Central Africa **6:**727, 731, 739, 745, 844, 849, 850, 856–857, *857*, 858, 859
corn **2:**187; **5:**602, 638, 643, 660, 679; **6:**726, 786, 858; **7:**889, 895

cotton **3:**347, 348; **5:**602, 616, 651, 661; **8:**1043
  Burkina Faso **3:**355, 365, 366, 367
  Burundi **5:**633, 644, 645

D
diamonds **2:**216; **5:**668, 681, 696, 713; **6:***841*; **7:**1002; **10:**1305, 1409
  Angola **5:**625–626, 627
  Botswana **7:**902, 907, 912, 913
  Central African Republic **5:**652, 659, 661
  Liberia **2:**247, 248, 249
  Namibia **7:**873, 874, 877, 897, 936, 937
  Sierra Leone **2:**273, 274, 281, 282, 283
  South Africa **7:**893, 896, 898, 962, 965–966, 967, 971

E
employment
  Angola **5:**627
  Australia **10:**1407, 1408
  Benin **3:**347
  Botswana **7:**912
  Burkina Faso **3:**364, 365
  Burundi **5:**645
  Cameroon **1:**67
  Cape Verde **2:**191
  Central African Republic **5:**661
  Comoros **6:**759
  Congo, Democratic Republic of **5:**681
  Congo, Republic **5:**696
  Djibouti **4:**471, 480, 481
  Eritrea **4:**483, 495
  Ethiopia **4:**515
  Fiji **8:**1050
  Gambia **2:**203
  Ghana **3:**388
  Guinea **2:**217
  Guinea-Bissau **2:**229
  Ivory Coast **3:**402, 407, 409
  Kiribati **9:**1208
  Lesotho **7:**925
  Liberia **2:**245, 249
  Madagascar **6:**773
  Malawi **6:**786

Marshall Islands **8:**1063
Mauritius **6:**797
Micronesia **8:**1073
Mozambique **6:**815
Namibia **7:**936
New Zealand **9:**1234
Nigeria **1:**129
Palau **8:**1097
Rwanda **5:**715
Samoa **9:**1254
São Tomé and Príncipe **1:**132, 139
Senegal **2:**267
Seychelles **6:**827
Sierra Leone **2:**283
South Africa **7:**969, 970
Swaziland **7:**984
Tanzania **6:**841
Togo **3:**425
Tonga **9:**1271
Tuvalu **9:**1285
Zambia **6:**857
Zimbabwe **7:**1002

F
film industry
  Australia **10:**1379
  Burkina Faso **3:**358, 367
  Congo-Brazzaville **5:**690
  Gabon **1:**87
  Nigeria **1:**106, 109, 129
  Senegal **2:**258, 259
fishing
  Angola **5:**627
  Annobón **1:**15
  Antarctica **10:**1302, 1337, 1339, 1430, 1431, 1432–1433
  Australia **10:***1329*, 1334, 1411
  Burundi **5:***628*, 638, 644
  Cameroon **1:**63
  Cape Verde **2:**190–191
  Central African Republic **5:**660
  Comoros **6:**750, 759
  Congo Basin **5:***580*, *582*, 594
  Congo, Republic **5:**696
  Djibouti **4:**481
  Eastern Africa **4:**436, 439, 451, 481, 516, 528, 537–538, 553, 564, 570
  Fiji **8:**1051
  French Southern Territories **10:**1434

Gabon **1:**87, 92
Gambia **2:***192*, *202*, 203
Ghana **3:**309, 388
Guinea-Bissau **2:**229
Ivory Coast **3:**408
Kenya **4:**528, 537–538
Kiribati **9:**1205, 1208, 1209
Liberia **2:**249
Madagascar **6:**776
Malawi **6:**786
Mauritius **6:**788, 797
Micronesia **8:**1073
Mozambique **6:**815
Nauru **8:**1083
New Zealand **9:**1172, 1173, 1176, 1177, 1185, 1234
Nigeria **1:**12, *125*, 128
Palau **8:**1097
Rwanda **5:**714
Saint Helena **7:**938
Samoa **9:**1248, 1253, 1255
São Tomé and Príncipe **1:***137*
Senegal **2:**266
Seychelles **6:**824, 826, 827
Sierra Leon **2:***282*, 283
Solomon Islands **8:**1134
South Africa **7:**955, *971*, 972
southern Africa **7:***885*, 937
Tanzania **6:**842–843
Togo **3:***427*
Tonga **9:**1270, 1273
Tuvalu **9:**1274, 1280, 1281, 1284, 1285
Vanuatu **8:**1146
West African coast **2:**160, *178*, 190
Zambia **6:**858
"flag of convenience" (Liberia) **2:**246, 249

G
GDP (gross domestic product)
  Angola **5:**612, 625, 627
  Australia **10:**1360, 1405, 1406, 1407, 1408, 1410, 1412, 1413, 1415
  Benin **3:**331, 347, 348
  Botswana **7:**903, 912
  Burkina Faso **3:**364, 365
  Burundi **5:**630, 645
  Cameroon **1:**52, 67
  Cape Verde **2:**181, 190, 191
  Central African Republic **5:**647, 661

Comoros **6:**751, 759
Congo, Democratic Republic of **5:**664, 670, 681
Congo, Republic **5:**684, 696
Djibouti **4:**471, 480, 481
Equatorial Guinea **1:**70, 77
Eritrea **4:**483, 495
Ethiopia **4:**498, 515, 516, 517
Fiji **8:**1039, 1050
Gabon **1:**79, 91, 92, 93
Gambia **2:**193, 202, 203
Ghana **3:**371, 386, 388
Guam **8:**1053
Guinea **2:**206, 216, 217
Guinea-Bissau **2:**219, 228, 229
Ivory Coast **3:**392, 406, 407, 409
Kiribati **9:**1199, 1208, 1209
Lesotho **7:**924, 925
Liberia **2:**231, 249
Madagascar **6:**761, 773
Malawi **6:**775, 786
Marshall Islands **8:**1056, 1063
Mauritius **6:**790, 797
Mayotte **6:**799
Micronesia **8:**1065, 1073
Mozambique **6:**802, 815
Namibia **7:**928, 936
Nauru **8:**1075, 1083
New Caledonia **8:**1085
New Zealand **9:1212,** 1234, 1235
Nigeria **1:**97, 127, 129
Northern Mariana Islands **8:**1087
Palau **8:**1097
Reunion **6:**817
Rwanda **5:**715
Samoa **9:**1241, 1254, 1255
São Tomé and Príncipe **1:**132, 139
Senegal **2:**252, 264, 267
Seychelles **6:**819, 827
Sierra Leone **2:**270, 283
South Africa **7:**969, 970, 971
Swaziland **7:**975, 984, 985
Tanzania **6:**830, 841
Togo **3:**411, 426
Tonga **9:**1259, 1271, 1272, 1273
Tuvalu **9:**1275, 1284
Zambia **6:**846, 857
Zimbabwe **7:**988, 1002, 1003
gold **1:**38; **4:**459, 469; **6:**810, 841
    Australia **10:**1305, 1306, 1311, 1349, 1358, 1385, 1400, 1405, 1406, 1409
    Bismarck seabed **8:**1012

Central African Republic **5:**659
central West Africa **3:**311, 312, 313, 319, 365, 367, 407
Congo, Democratic Republic of **5:**679, 681
Ghana **3:**372, 388, 389
migrant labor **7:**958
New Zealand **9:**1184, 1185, 1191, 1215
Papua New Guinea **8:**1104, 1118, 1120
Republic of the Congo **5:**696
Rwanda **5:**713
Solomon Islands **8:**1134
South Africa **7:**871, 876, 893, 898, 958, 962, 965–966, 967, *969,* 971
West African coast **2:**164, 166, 169, 216, 228, 247, 248, 265, 281
Zimbabwe **7:**887
grain **9:**1184; **10:**1406, 1411
groundnuts (peanuts) **2:**197, 202–203, 217, 229, 248; **3:**325; **5:**660
Senegal **2:**255, 263, 264, 266, 267
Sierra Leone **2:**277

I

ilmenite **6:**773, 815
Internet suffix sale **9:**1274, 1284
iron ore
    Australia **10:**1305, 1409, 1414
    Benin **3:**347
    Congo, Democratic Republic of **5:**679
    Guinea **2:**216
    Ivory Coast **3:**407
    Liberia **2:**238, 240, 247, 248, 249
    Sierra Leone **2:**273, 281
    West Africa **2:**154, 164
ivory **4:**454; **5:**599, 600, 606, 619, 651, 687; **7:**887, 889

K

kava **8:**1046, 1146–1147

L

lamb **9:**1184, 1231, *1233,* 1234
liquefied natural gas **8:**1120–1121

M

manganese **3:**365; **5:**679
manioc (cassava) **3:**319; **5:**602, 638, 655, 660, 673, 679, *690,* 691, 696, 714

millet **3:**311, 359, 365
minerals and mining
    Angola **5:**622, 625–626
    Antarctica **10:**1431, 1432
    Australia **10:**1300, 1304, 1305, 1306, 1311, 1350, 1371, 1406, 1409, 1411–1412
    Belgian Congo **5:**633
    Botsana **7:**912
    Burundi **5:**643
    Cameroon **1:**64, 65
    Central African Republic **5:**659
    Congo Basin **5:**583, 605, 606
    Congo, Democratic Republic of 681; **5:**670, 678, 679, 680
    Equatorial Guinea **1:**77
    Gabon **1:**83, 84, 91–92, 93
    Katanga province **5:**668
    Kimberley mine **7:**893, 898, 971
    Mozambique **6:**810, 814
    Namibia **7:**936–937
    Nigeria **1:**127
    Papua New Guinea **8:**1118, 1120
    Solomon Islands **8:**1134
    South Africa **7:**965–966, 967, 968, 969, 970, 971, 972
    Tanzania **6:**841, 843
    Togo **3:**424
    Zimbabwe **7:**1002
    see also specific ores
money laundering **8:**1079, 1083

N

natural gas *see* oil and natural gas
nickel **5:**643; **7:**912, 1002; **8:**1084

O

offshore banking **8:**1079, 1083
oil and natural gas
    Angola **5:**582, 618, 622, 623, 625, 627
    Antarctica **10:**1431, 1432
    Australia **10:**1301, 1311, 1407, 1409, 1409–1410, 1410, 1414
    Benin **3:**347–348
    Botswana **7:**912
    Cameroon **1:**14, 17, 50, 56, 64–65, 65, 66, 67
    Congo, Republic of **5:**687, 688, 695, 696

Equatorial Guinea **1:**15, 68, 73, 76, 77, 92
Gabon **1:**15, 17, 78, 83, *85,* 90, 91, 92, 93
Ghana **3:**388
Gulf of Papua **8:**1012
Ivory Coast **3:**407
Namibia **7:**936
New Zealand **9:**1233
Niger Delta Basin **1:**13
Nigeria **1:**13, 17, 103, 104, 107, 121, 125, 126, 127, 129, 135
Papua New Guinea **8:**1118, 1120
Rwanda **5:**713
São Tomé and Príncipe **1:**130, 135, 137
Western Pacific **8:**1012

P

palm products **1:**43, 73; **2:**273, 280; **3:**323, 325, 344, 388, *408*
peanuts *see* groundnuts
phosphate
    Nauru **8:**1014, 1074, *1078,* 1079, 1080, 1081, 1083
    New Zealand **9:**1203, 1208, 1209
    Palau **8:**1093
    Solomon Islands **8:**1134
    Togo **3:**424, 427
    Tuvalu **9:**1279, 1284
plantain **5:**638, 643, 660
postage stamp sales **10:**1416

R

recording industry **8:**1108–1109, 1131, 1143
rice **2:**148, 150, 277, 282; **6:**726, *772,* 776
rubber **5:**606, 651, 687
    Liberia **2:***160,* 237, 247–249
rutile **2:**281, 283

S

salt **1:**28; **2:***151;* **5:**597
sandalwood **8:**1034, 1038, 1084, 1136, 1146
sheep **9:**1160, 1231, *1233,* 1234; **10:**1348, 1406, 1410–1411, 1411
smuggling **5:**681; **7:**1002
spices **6:**726, 743, 756, 842; **8:**1032
stamps, Tuvalu **9:**1279
standard of living
    Angola **5:**627
    Australia **10:**1407, 1408

standard of living (*continued*)
  Benin **3:**347
  Botswana **7:**912
  Burkina Faso **3:**365
  Burundi **5:**645
  Cameroon **1:**67
  Cape Verde **2:**190, 191
  Central African Republic
    5:661
  Comoros **6:**759
  Congo, Democratic Republic
    of **5:**681
  Congo, Republic **5:**696
  Djibouti **4:**481
  Equatorial Guinea **1:**77
  Eritrea **4:**495
  Ethiopia **4:**515
  Fiji **8:**1050
  Gabon **1:**88, 91, 93
  Gambia **2:**203
  Ghana **3:**388
  Guinea **2:**217
  Guinea-Bissau **2:**229
  Ivory Coast **3:**407
  Kiribati **9:**1208
  Lesotho **7:**925
  Liberia **2:**249
  Madagascar **6:**773
  Malawi **6:**786
  Marshall Islands **8:**1063
  Mauritius **6:**797
  Micronesia **8:**1073
  Mozambique **6:**815
  Namibia **7:**936
  Nauru **8:**1083
  New Zealand **9:**1234
  Nigeria **1:**129
  Palau **8:**1097
  Rwanda **5:**715
  Samoa **9:**1254
  São Tomé and Príncipe **1:**139
  Senegal **2:**267
  Seychelles **6:**827
  Sierra Leone **2:**283
  South Africa **7:**969
  Swaziland **7:**984
  Tanzania **6:**841
  Togo **3:**424, 426
  Tonga **9:**1271–1272
  Tuvalu **9:**1285
  Zambia **6:**857
  Zimbabwe **7:**1002
sugar **1:**130, 138; **7:**985; **8:**1086
  Australia **10:**1388, 1411
  eastern Central Africa **6:**729,
    748, 793, 797, 816
  Fiji **8:**1037, 1038, *1042,*
    1043, 1047, 1050
  slave labor **5:**598, 601, 602

T

taro **8:***1031,* 1110
tax havens **8:**1145, 1147
textile dyes
  Gambia **2:**199
  Guinea **2:**212
  Senegal **2:**258
  Sierra Leone **2:**276
textiles
  Burkina Faso **3:**363, 367
  Congo Basin **5:**597
  Ghana **3:**378, 385, 389
  Ivory Coast **3:**398
  Northern Mariana Islands
    8:1086
timber **9:***1231,* 1254
  Angola **5:**582, 591, 626
  Cameroon **1:**66, 67
  Central African Republic
    5:659, 660, 661
  Congo, Democratic Republic
    of **5:**680
  Congo, Republic **5:**696
  Equatorial Guinea **1:**77
  Gabon **1:**83, 92–93
  Liberia **2:**247, 249
  Samoa **9:**1254
  Sierra Leone **2:**273, 283
tin **5:**583, 633, 643, 662, 679,
    713; **7:**936

tobacco **6:**785, 786
tourism
  Antarctica **10:**1314, 1418,
    1430, 1431, 1432, 1433
  Australia **10:**1310–1311,
    1396, 1399, 1401, 1413,
    1415
  Benin **3:**345
  Botswana **7:**913
  Burkina Faso **3:**367
  Cameroon **1:**67
  Cape Verde **2:**191
  Cook Island **9:**1194
  Ethiopia **4:**513, 517
  Fiji **8:**1038, 1044, 1049,
    1050, 1051
  French Polynesia **9:**1163
  Gambia **2:**150, 192, 198, 201,
    202, 203
  Ghana **3:**309, 385
  Guam **8:**1052
  Ivory Coast **3:**405, 409
  Kenya **4:**533, 535, *537,* 538
  Kiribati **9:**1209
  Madagascar **6:**773
  Malawi **6:***776,* 787
  Mauritius **6:**729, 796, 797
  Micronesia **8:**1073
  Mozambique **6:**812, 815
  Namibia **7:**937
  New Zealand **9:**1160, 1235
  Norfolk Island **10:**1416
  Palau **8:**1018, 1097
  Papua New Guinea **8:**1107,
    1109
  Pitcairn **9:**1238
  Reunion **6:**729
  Samoa **9:**1247, 1255
  Senegal **2:***250, 251, 261,*
    263, 265, 266–267
  Seychelles **6:**729, 818, 826,
    827
  Solomon Islands **8:**1135
  South Africa **7:**871, 872, 963,
    964, 972, 973

  Swaziland **7:**983, 984
  Tanzania **6:**726, 839, 843
  Togo **3:**423
  Tonga **9:**1258, *1272,* 1273
  Uganda **4:**441, 571
  Vanuatu **8:***1138,* 1142, 1145,
    1146, 1147
  Zambia **6:**727, 851, 855, 859
tungsten **7:**936

U

uranium **5:**583, 626, 643
  Central African Republic
    5:652, 659
  Congo, Democratic Republic
    of **5:**662, 668, 679
  Congo, Republic **5:**696
  Namibia **7:**936

V

vanilla **6:**776, 798
vineyards **7:**872; **10:**1308,
    1410, 1411

W

whaling **8:**1033; **10:**1302,
    1339, 1348, 1352, 1430,
    1432, *1433*
wheat *see* grain
wine
  Australia **10:**1411
  New Zealand **9:**1222, *1235*
  South Africa **7:**872, 955,
    967, 971
wool **9:**1184, 1231; **10:**1406,
    1410, 1411

Y

yams **3:**310, 379, 400

Z

zinc **5:**583, 633, 679, 696
  Namibia **7:**936

Comprehensive Index

Numbers in **boldface** refer to volume numbers; those in *italic* refer to illustrations:

A

aardvarks **5**:595
Abacha, Sani **1**:104
Aba women's riot (1929) **1**:100
Abdallah, Ahmed **6**:755
Abdallah, Yohanna Barnaba **6**:807
Abega, Severin Cecile **1**:58
Abemama Atoll **9**:1203, *1207*
Abessole, Paul Mba **1**:84
Abidjan **3**:294, 329, 363, 394, *394*, 400, *403*, 405, *407*, 409
  architecture **3**:398–399, 405
  climate **3**:304
  history **3**:395, 396, 405
  as "Paris of Africa" **3**:398, 405
  population **3**:405
  university **3**:403
abolitionism **2**:172, 173, 174, 175, 180, 235, 273, 280
Abomey *see* Danhome
Aboriginal Australians **10**:1307, 1355–1357, 1358, 1413
  contemporary life **10**:1388, 1390, 1392
  cultural expression **10**:1318, 1342, 1372, 1373, 1374, 1375, 1377, *1378*, 1379, 1381, 1413
  discrimination **10**:1356, 1369–1370, 1371, 1373, 1388, 1406, 1455
  "Stolen Generation" **10**:1371, 1373, 1388
  early history **10**:1340–1343, 1344, 1346, 1348, 1355, 1387–1388, 1398, 1399, 1402–1405
  food and drink **10**:1383
  kinship system **10**:1343
  population **10**:1355, 1362
  sacred places **10**:1307, 1318, *1341*, *1343*
  spirituality **10**:1342, 1384, 1385, 1386, 1413
Aboriginal Land Rights Act (1976) **10**:1355, 1358

Abranches, Henrique **5**:619
Abrantes, José Mena **5**:619
Abreha, king of Himyar **4**:455
Absa, Moussa Sene **2**:258
Abubakar, Abdulsalam **1**:104
Abuja **1**:103, 104, 119, 123
  architecture **1**:107, *113*
  population **1**:10, 119
  slum demolition **1**:118
Abushiri revolt (1888) **6**:833
accordion players **7**:921
Accra **3**:308, 381, 383–384, 423
  climate **3**:304, 305
  history **3**:313, 319, *320*, 329, 373, 374, 383
  Nkrumah memorial **3**:*374*
  population **3**:294, 383
AC/DC (rock band) **10**:*1377*, 1378
Acheampong, Ignatius **3**:375–376
Achebe, Chinua **1**:105
Achuago site **8**:1029
Adadura movement **1**:112
Adal (Adel) **4**:462, 464, 467, 540
Adamawa (people) **1**:47, 48–49, 50
Adamawa Plateau **1**:11, 14, 24
Adamawa State **1**:11, 42, 47, 57
Adamstown **9**:1163, *1239*
Adangme language **3**:329
Addis Ababa **4**:438, 439, 445, 475, 479, 480, 512, 512–513, 517
  climate **4**:447
  cultural activity **4**:506, 507
  history **4**:502, 512, 514
Addis Ababa University **4**:511
Ade, King Sunny **1**:108, *109*
Adelaide **10**:1381, 1393, 1397, 1415
  history **10**:1348, 1350, 1357, 1358
Adelaide, queen of Great Britain **10**:1397
Adichie, Ngozi **1**:105
Adja (people) **3**:322, 328, 330, 340
Adja language **3**:338
Admiralty Islands **8**:1015, 1027
adobe architecture **3**:358, 378, 399, 419

Adoboli, Eugene Koffi **3**:416
Adoula, Cyrille **5**:669
Adowa (Adwa), Battle of (1896) **4**:465, 502, 514
Adventure Network International/Antarctic Logistics and Expeditions **10**:1433
Aedisius **4**:455
Afadjato, Mount **3**:295, *296*
Afar (people) **4**:467, 470, 474, 475, 476–477, 478, 480, 491
Afar Depression **4**:438, 445
Afars and Issas, French Territory of **4**:470, 475, 479, 480
Afghanistan War (2001) **6**:749
Afonso I, king of Kongo **5**:598, 674
African Americans **2**:174, 175, 179
  Liberia colonization **2**:230, 235–236, 246, 247
  Roots festival **2**:198, 199, 203
  Sierra Leone settlement **2**:174–175, 179, 268, 273, 275, 280
African churches **3**:341, 342, *343*, 401; **6**:802, 810, 853; **7**:900, 905, 910, 916, 922, 928, 934, 942, 956, 997, 998
African Democratic Rally **2**:209
African Forum for Reconstruction (Gabon) **1**:82
African independence movement **1**:55
African National Congress **6**:806, 844; **7**:919, 944, 945, 992
  anti-apartheid campaign **7**:940, 946, 947, 954
  economic recovery programs **7**:969–970
  election win **7**:948–949, 969
African Party for the Independence of Guinea and Cape Verde **2**:184, 185, 218, 222, 223, 227
African Union **4**:502, 506, 512, 517, 547; **6**:755, 834
African wild dog **7**:*882*

Afrikaaners (Boers) **7**:890–891, 892, 893, 894, 895, 901, 940, 958, 962, 964
  Basotho conflict **7**:919
  Great Trek **7**:892, 893, 901, 940, 946, 962
  Namibia **7**:926, 945
  nationalism **7**:894, 899, 945–946, 956
  Zulu conflicts **7**:895, 896, 962
Afrikaans language **7**:895, 932, 940, 950, 954, 957
  education **7**:961, 968
Afro, Lily **1**:74
Afro-A-Kom (sculpture) **1**:59
Afro-beat music **1**:108
Afro-Brazilians **3**:329, 335, 338, 345
Afro-Cuban rumba **5**:672–673
Afro-European Creoles **2**:179, 183, 185, 186
Afropop music **2**:277; **5**:655, 672–673, 690, 707
Agadjah, king of Abomey **3**:322
Agbetiafa, Komlan **3**:417
Agostinho Neto University **5**:623
agriculture
  Angola **5**:582, 602, 625, 626
  Australia **10**:1406, 1410–1411
  Benin **3**:337, 347, 348
  Botswana **7**:912
  Burkina Faso **3**:364, 365–366
  Burundi **5**:638, 643–644
  Cameroon **1**:14, 64, 65–66
  Cape Verde **2**:190
  Central African Republic **5**:655, 659, 660
  colonial policies **5**:633; **7**:890–891, 892, 991
  Comoros **6**:759
  Congo, Democratic Republic of **5**:679
  Congo, Republic **5**:584, 696
  Djibouti **4**:480
  early and precolonial **1**:26; **3**:310, 311, 319; **5**:596, 602, 608; **6**:738; **7**:888–889; **8**:1026, 1027, 1028; **10**:1305, 1306, 1309, 1325
  Equatorial Guinea **1**:77

agriculture (*continued*)
Eritrea **4:**439, 494, 495
Ethiopia **4:**440, 452, 453, 514–515, 516
European crops **9:**1181, 1182
Fiji **8:**1050–1051
Gabon **1:**92–93
Gambia **2:**197, 202–203
Ghana **3:**388
Gold Coast **3:**373
Guinea **2:**215, 216–217
Guinea-Bissau **2:***220*, 228–229
Ivory Coast **3:**396, 408
Kenya **4:**441, 536, 537, 537–538, 539
Kiribati **9:**1208, 1209
Lesotho **7:**924
Liberia **2:**248
Madagascar **6:**772, 773
Malawi **6:**727, 785, 786
Maori **9:**1177–1178, 1179
Marshall Islands **8:**1063
Mauritius **6:**729, 797
Micronesia **8:**1073
Mozambique **6:**814–815
Namibia **7:**874, 937
New Zealand **9:**1159, 1184, 1185, 1215, 1231, 1234, 1235
Nigeria **1:**12, 13, 125, 127–128, 129
Palau **8:**1097
Papua New Guinea **8:**1110, *1118*, 1119, 1121
precolonial *see subhead early and precolonial*
Rwanda **5:***591*, 710, 713, 714, *715*
Samoa **9:**1253, 1254
São Tomé and Príncipe **1:**130, 135, 139
Senegal **2:**255, 264, 265–266
Senegal River Valley **2:**148, 150, *175*
Sierra Leone **2:**281, 282–283
Solomon Islands **8:**1134
Somalia **4:**440, 552, 553
South Africa **7:**871, 872, 971–972
Swaziland **7:**985
Tanzania **6:**726, 841–843
Togo **3:***424, 425,* 426
Tokelau **9:**1256
Tonga **9:**1258, 1264, 1271, 1272–1273
Tuvalu **9:**1274
Uganda **4:**441, 568, 569–570, *571*

Vanuatu **8:**1146
Zambia **6:**857–858
Zimbabwe **7:**100, 1000, *1001*, 10032
see also specific crops
Agualusa, Eduardo **5:**619
Agüe, María Nsue **1:**74
Aguiyi-Ironsi, Johnson **1:**103
Ahidjo, Ahmadou **1:**55–56, 60
Ahmad ibn Ibrihim al-Ghazi **4:**462, 464
Ahmadiyya (revivalist movement) **2:**226
Ahmed, Sharif **4:**547
Ahmed ibn Ali **1:**30
Ahomadégbé, Justin **3:**335
Ahyi, Paul **3:**418
Aidid, Mohammed Farah **4:**547
Aido, Anna **3:**377
AIDS *see* HIV/AIDS
Aimata Pomare IV, queen of Tahiti **9:**1186
Ajache *see* Porto-Novo
Akagera National Park **5:***594, 700*
Akan (people) **3:**312–313, 314, 328, *377*, 378, 379, 380, 381, 401, 402
Akanji, Adebisi **1:**106
Akan language **3:**328
Akan states **3:**310, 319, 322
art and architecture **3:**312–313
Ashanti Confederation **3:**314–315, 321
Akendengué, Pierre-Claver **1:**86
Akis, Timothy **8:**1107
Akofa, Henriette **3:**417
Akosombo Dam **3:**292, 294, 295, 305, 375, *376*, 388
Akplodjegou, Kuevi Kangui **3:**418
Aksum (city) **4:**452, 454, 459, 508, 517
Aksum kingdom **4:**439, 453–456, 463, 470, 482, 489, 491, 496, 506
Aksum Obelisk **4:**454, *455*, 506
Akuffo, Fred **3:**376
Akufo-Addo, Nana **3:**376
Akwamu state **3:**313, 321
al- *for Arabic names containing al-, see under the following part of the name.*
Aladji, Victor **3:**417
Alarinjo (Yoruba traveling theater) **1:**105
Alasia, Sam Lidimani **8:**1130
Albert, Lake **6:**739
Albert Rift Valley **5:**585

Albert Schweitzer Hospital **1:**88
Aldabra Island **6:**649, 729
giant tortoise **6:**736, *818*
Alemayehu, Haddis **4:**505
Alesana, Tofilau Eti **9:**1253
Alice Springs **10:**1307, *1343, 1362*
climate **10:**1321, 1322
Ali Ghadjideni ibn Dunama **1:**29
Ali Kwame, king of Bono **3:**313
Allada kingdom **3:**322
Allaleh, Abdi Nuur **4:**476–477
Alliance for Democracy (Nigeria) **1:**99
Alliance for Patriotic Reorientation and Construction (Gambia) **2:**196, 197
Alliance for Peace and Democracy (Liberia) **2:**234
All Nigeria People's Party **1:**99
All People's Congress (Sierra Leone) **2:**272, *273*, 274
Almeida, Manuel de **1:**135
Almoravid dynasty **2:**164–165
Alo **9:**1162, 1186, 1290
Alofi **9:**1160, 1162, 1290
cyclone damage **9:**1168, 1236
Alula, Ras **4:**465, 487
aluminum **6:**815
Alvaro I, king of Kongo **5:**598
Amadou Tall, sultan of Ségou **2:**168
Amakhosi Township Square Cultural Center **7:**996
Amari Ngoene Sobel **2:**166
"Amazons" **3:**322
Ambasse Bey music **1:**59
Ambo (people) *see* Ovambo
Amda Seyon, emperor of Ethiopia **4:**464
American Colonization Society **2:**175, 226, 235–236, 246, 247
American Revolution, freed slaves **2:**174, 175, 235, 280
American Samoa **9:**1192–1193
cyclone hazard **9:**1168
geography **9:**1158, 1163, 1192
history **9:**1174, 1187, 1192, 1245, 1252
peoples **9:**1189–1190, 1191, 1193
Americo-Liberians **2:**179, 230, 234, 235–236, 237, 238–239, 241, 243, 246
as political elite **2:**240, 247
Amhara (people) **4:**464, 467–468, 509

Amharic language **4:**468, 505, 512
Amin, Idi **4:**554, 559, 560, 565, 568; **6:**834
Amon d'Aby, François Joseph **3:**398
Amu, Ephraim **3:**378–379
Amukoto, David **7:**933
Amundsen, Roald **10:**1353
Amundsen-Scott South Pole Station **10:**1326, 1328, *1429*
Ana Clara Guerra Marques Contemporary Dance Company **5:**621
Ana de Sousa (Nazinga Mbande) **5:**599
Analla, Gnoussira **3:**417
Anambra River Basin **1:**12
Ananou, David **3:**417
ANC *see* African National Congress
ancestor veneration
Madagascar **6:**767, 768, 769–770
Papua New Guinea **8:**1111
Samoa **9:**1249
Solomon Islands **8:**1132
Vanuatu **8:**1143
Andesite Line **8:**1017
Andreas, Neshani **7:**932
Andrianampoinimerina, king of Madagascar **6:**742, 768, 770
Anglicanism
Australia **10:**1350, 1362, 1384, 1385, 1401, 1402
Botswana **7:**905, 910
Burundi **5:**639
Congo, Democratic Republic of **5:**674
Ethiopia **5:**508
Kenya **4:**520, 529
Lesotho **7:**922
Malawi **6:**782
Namibia **7:**92, 9348
New Zealand **9:**1182, 1184, 1212, 1219, 1223, 1230
Nigeria **1:**112
Papua New Guinea **8:**1104, 1111
Rwanda **5:**700, 709
Saint Helena **7:**939
Seychelles **6:**820, 825, 826
Solomon Islands **8:**1126, 1132
South Africa **7:**939, 943, 956
Swaziland **7:**976, 982
Tanzania **6:**830, 837
Uganda **4:**556, 559, 560, 565, *567*

Vanuatu **8:**1138, 1143;
9:1182
Zambia **6:**846, 853
Zimbabwe **7:**988, 997
Anglo-Boer Wars **7:**891;
9:1185, 1215; **10:**1366
First (1880–1881) **7:**893
Second (1899–1902) **7:**894,
898–899, 940, 945, 962,
965, 967, 979
Anglo-Portuguese Treaty
(1891) **6:**745
Anglo-Zulu War (1879) **7:**894
Angola **5:**610–627
art and architecture
5:619–620, 622, 624
climate **5:**582, 588–589,
591, 610, 624
cultural expression
5:619–621
daily life **5:**622–623
economy **5:**611–612,
625–627
education **5:**623, 625
family and society **5:**623
festivals and ceremonies
5:621
flag **5:**612
flora and fauna **5:**592–595
food and drink **5:***620*, 621
geography **5:**580–584, 610
geology **5:**586–587, 625
government and political
parties **5:**612, 614
health and welfare **5:**623
history
chronology **5:**613
Congo Wars **5:**618, 670,
678, 705
modern **5:**610, 615–618,
669
precolonial **5:**597–599,
600–604, 608
independence **5:**614, 616,
624, 625
languages **5:**607, 619
literature **5:**619
music **5:**620–621
peoples **5:**607, 608, 612, 619,
622
population **5:**610–611
religion **5:**612, 622
resources **5:**610, 622,
625–626
transportation and
communication **5:**612,
624, 627
Angolan civil war **5:**582, 593,
610, 614, 617–618, 619, 625
land mines **5:**618, 626

public holiday **5:**621
reconstruction **5:**620, 622,
627
animism **1:**57, 80, 132; **2:**200,
226, 243, 261, 277, 278;
5:622, 639, 656, 692, 709
Anjouan Island **6:**728, 736, 750,
753, 754, 755, 758, 798
Ankole kingdom **4:**457, 562
Annan, Kofi **3:***375*; **4:**525
Annobón **1:**10, 15, 17, 21, 68,
76, 138
local government **1:**72
Annobones (people) **1:**75
Ansa Sasraku, king of Akwamu
3:313
Antananarivo **6:**728, 742, *765*,
769, 771
architecture **6:**767, 771
Antarctica **10:**1329, 1418–1433
chronology **10:**1422
climate **10:**1314, 1326–1328,
1336, 1337, 1418, 1425
climate change **10:**1328,
1339, 1418, 1425, 1428,
1430
daily life **10:**1428–1429
economy **10:**1430–1433
flora and fauna **10:**1336–
1339, 1418, 1432
geography **10:**1302–1303,
1312–1315, 1418, 1430
geology **1:**16; **10:**1319–1320
government **10:**1419, 1423
history **10:**1352–1354, 1418,
1424–1425
population **10:**1419
resources **10:**1302, 1419,
1430–1431, 1432
territorial claims **10:**1419,
1420–1421, 1423
transportation **10:**1419,
1428, 1433
Antarctic Ocean **10:**1411
Antarctic Peninsula **10:**1311,
1314, 1319, 1320, 1418,
1424, 1433
Antarctic Service, U.S. **10:**1424
Antarctic Treaty (1959)
10:1418, 1423, 1425,
1426, 1430, 1431, 1432,
1434
anteater **5:**595
antelope **4:**448, 449, 450;
5:592, 593, 594, 595, *595*;
7:*984*
Antisirabé **6:***769, 770*
Antonio I, king of Kongo **5:**598
Antsiranana (formerly Diego
Suaraz) **6:**728, 742

ANZAC Day **9:**1221, 1247–1248;
10:1380, *1381*, 1396
ANZAC forces **10:**1366
ANZUS Pact (1951) **9:**1216;
10:1369
Apapa **1:**124
apartheid **7:**902, 907, 911, 919,
926, 931, 963, 965, 974,
979
end **7:**940, 947, 948, 960, 969
establishment **7:**946
ideology **7:**967–968
international boycotts
7:968–969, 984
musical forms **7:**952, 953
protests **7:**946, 947, 948,
950, 953, 966
societal effects **7:**957, 958,
959–960, 961, 967–968,
969, 970
Apia **9:**1163, 1167, 1251, 1252,
1254
history **9:**1174, 1187, 1245,
1252
Apithy, Sourou-Migan **3:**335
Apolima Strait **9:**1162–1163
Aptidon, Hassan Gouled **4:**475
Aquamboes kingdom **3:**328
Arabia **4:**452–453, 454, 459,
462, 551
Arabian-Nubian Shield **4:**442
Arabs **6:**739, 740–741, 742,
744, 748, 750, 758, 800,
818, 828, 834
Arch 22 (Banjul) **2:***197*, 198, 201
archaeology **7:**886, 889
Arden-Clarke, Charles **3:**374
Argentina **10:**1426, 1433
Ark of the Covenant **4:**452,
464, 508
Armah, Ayi Kwei **3:**377
Armed Forces Provisional
Ruling Council (Gambia)
2:197
Armed Forces Revolutionary
Council (Sierra Leone)
2:274
Armstrong, Gillian **10:**1379
Arnhem Land **10:**1300, 1304,
1305, 1343, 1344, 1356
Arthur Rimbaud French
Cultural Center **4:**476
Arusha **6:**837, 838, 839, 841
Arusha Agreement (Burundi,
2003) **5:**635, 643
Arusha Declaration (Tanzania,
1967) **6:**840
Arusha peace accord (Rwanda,
1993) **5:**702, 705
Asaman, king of Bono **3:**313

Ascension **7:**872, 880, 938
Asfa Wossen **4:**503
Ashanti (Asante)
confederation **3:**313,
314–315, 321, 324, 325,
328–329, 376
decorative arts **3:**378
Kumasi **3:**385
social structure **3:**380
territory **3:**368
Ashanti language **3:**377
Ashanti Wars **3:**315, 324, 326,
368, 373, 385
Asheri, Jedida **1:**58
Ashmun, Jehudi **2:**174
Ashton, Julian **10:**1375
Asian immigrants **10:**1350,
1357, 1384, 1386, 1389,
1401, 1405
see also Chinese, ethnic;
South Asians
Asmara **4:**439, 445, *490*, 491,
493
Italian influences **4:**487, 490,
493
ASODEGUE (Association for
Democratic Solidarity in
Equatorial Guinea) **1:**72
Aso Rock **1:**119
Assab **4:**439, 465, 487, 495
Assal, Lake **4:**436, 438, *472*
Assembly of God **8:**1040, 1047,
1056, 1061
Atafu Atoll **9:**1161, 1256
Atakora Mountains (Massif)
3:295, 304, 339, 347
Atepa, Pierre Goudiaby **2:***257*,
258
Atherton Plateau **10:**1309,
1310
Atlantic humpback dolphin
3:309
Aubame, Jean-Hilaire **1:**83
Auckland **9:**1159, 1229, 1235
cathedrals **9:**1123
festivals **9:**1221
history **9:**1185, 1229
Aurora Australis **10:***1429*
Australasia **10:**1300
Australasian Antarctic
Expedition **10:**1354
Australia **8:**1034, 1035, 1133,
1134; **9:**1183, 1185, 1279,
1284; **10:**1358–1415
art and architecture **10:**1318,
1374–1376, 1381, 1396,
1401, 1405
climate **10:**1305, 1321–1325,
1329, *1406*, 1408, 1410,
1411

Australia (*continued*)
climate change **10:**1325, 1371
climatic hazards
10:1323–1324
cultural expression
10:1372–1383
daily life **10:**1384–1394
economy **10:**1358, 1360,
1369, 1371, 1406–1416
education **10:**1370,
1392–1393, 1397, 1398,
1401, 1405, 1406
family and society
10:1387–1393
federation **10:**1350–1351,
1358, 1365, 1368, 1388,
1395, 1401, 1406
festivals and ceremonies
10:*1356, 1357,*
1380–1381, 1397
flag **10:**1359
flora and fauna
10:1329–1335, 1374
food and drink **10:**1383
geography **10:**1300–1301,
1304–1311
geology **10:**1316–1318
government and political
parties **10:**1360, 1364,
1368, 1371, 1407
health and welfare **10:**1370,
1390–1391, 1406, 1407,
1408
history
British First Fleet landing
10:1344, 1346, 1347,
1358, 1372, 1380, 1383,
1385, 1387, 1404
chronology **10:**1363
colonial **10:**1347–1351,
1358
European explorers
10:1344–1346
modern **10:**1365–1371,
1388–1389, 1398,
1400–1401, 1402,
1404–1405, 1406
languages **10:**1356, 1362,
1372
literature **10:**1372–1373,
1379
music **10:**1377–1378, 1381
Nauru **8:**1074, 1079, 1080,
1081, 1083
Papua New Guinea **8:**1098,
1104, 1105, 1117, 1118,
1122
peoples **10:**1340–1343,
1355–1357, 1362, 1368,
1370, 1371, 1378, 1384,

1387, 1388–1389, 1397,
1403, 1405
population **10:**1359–1360,
1387
religion **10:**1350, 1362,
1384–1386
resources **10:**1306, 1358,
1409–1410
Solomon Islands **8:**1133, 1134
states and territories
10:1362, 1388
transportation and
communication **10:**1360,
1398, 1399, 1401, 1405,
1413, 1415
Australia Day **10:**1300
Australian Alps **10:**1311, 1323,
1325
Australia National University
10:1393
Australian Capital Territory
10:1356, 1396
see also Canberra
Australian Methodist Society
8:1104
Australian Rules Football
8:1080, *1113;* **10:**1382
Australian War Memorial
10:1396
Austral Islands **9:**1163
Austronesian languages
8:1026–1027, 1036
automobile industry **3:**344;
7:972
Avila Laurel, Juan Tomás **1:**74
Awandji (people) **1:**46
Awandji revolt (1920s) **1:**83
Awasa **4:***496,* 515
Ayers Rock **10:**1307, 1413,
1418
Azande language **5:**661, 671
Azikiwe, Nnamdi **1:**112

B

Babangida, Ibrahim **1:**104
Babelthuap Island **8:**1015,
1032, 1093, 1096
baboons **4:***449,* 450
Bacar, Mohamed **6:**755
Bachwezi kingdom **6:**739
Bafing River **2:**148
Bafoulabé **2:**148
Baganda (people) **4:**469, 559,
562, 565
Bagaza, Jean-Baptiste **5:**634
Baghirmi (people) 30
Bah, Chernor **2:**276
Baines, Thomas **7:**908
Bainimarama, Mahendra
8:1044

Bainimarana, Vorege **8:**1042
Bairiki **9:**1161, 1207
Baka Pygmies **1:**57
Bakassi Peninsula **1:**56, 65
Bakau **2:***192,* 201
Baker, Herbert **7:**951
Baker Island **9:**1263, 1286
Bakoye River **2:**148
Bakrlavento Islands **2:**153
Bakweri (people) **1:**45, 46
Balante (people) **2:**166, 173,
178–179, 218, 224, 226,
261
Baldeh, Fodeh **2:**198
Balewa, Abubakar Tafawa **1:**101
Balkan immigrants **10:**1357,
1388, 1389, 1401, 1403
Ballance, John **9:**1215
Bamako **3:**350, 395
Bamako Initiative (1987) **2:**213
Bamana Empire **2:**168, 171
Bambino, Sekouba **2:**212
bamboo forest **5:**595
Bamboté, Pierre Makombo
5:654
Bamenda **1:***50,* 60
Banaba Island **9:**1198, 1202,
1203, 1284
Banana (port) **5:**605, 681
Banana, Canaan **7:**992
bananas **5:**638, 643, 708
Banda (people) **5:**609, 648,
656
Banda, Hastings Kazumu
6:774, 778, 779, 780, 784,
785, 786
Banda, Rupiah **6:**848, 850
Banda language **5:**653
Banfora **3:***352,* 367
Banfora Escarpment
3:297–298
Bangui **5:**583, 652, 654, 657,
661
architecture **5:**654
climate **5:***591*
history **5:**604
Bangura, Hassan **2:**276
Bani River 8; **1:**8
Banjul **2:**150, 173, 192, 197,
201, 203
architecture **2:***197,* 198, *200*
history **2:**150, 173, 192, 197,
201
banking **9:**1235, 1255, 1279
offshore **8:**1079, 1083
Banto Faros (grasslands) **2:**150
Bantu (people) **5:**607, 609,
674; **6:**738–739, 740, 746,
747, 748, 800; **7:**914, 940,
986

Bantu languages **1:**26, 45,
47–48, 57, 63, 78; **3:**327;
4:457–458, 462, 468, 469;
5:596, 597, 607, 633;
6:735, 738, 739, 742, 746,
747, 748, 756, 760, 774,
828, 844; **7:**888, 892,
900–901, 908
see also Swahili language
Bantustans (homelands)
7:940, 946, 947, 948–949,
957, 960, 963
Banyangs (people) 46
baobab trees **1:***23;* **4:***488;* **7:***987*
Baol kingdom **2:**166, 172
Baptist churches **1:**60, 112;
5:648, 651, 656, 674–675,
692
Barbosa, Jorge **2:**186
Barclay, Edwin J. **2:**237
Barghash, sultan of Zanzibar
6:743, 745
Baria, Yemane **4:**490
bark cloth *see tapa*
Barkly Tableland **10:**1304,
1305–1306
Barotse kingdom **7:**896
Barotseland **6:**739, 746, 844,
849
Barre, Muhammad Siad *see*
Siad Barre, Muhammad
Barton, Edmund **10:**1365
basketry
Botswana **7:**908, *909*
Lesotho **7:**920
Tutsi **5:***707*
Basotho (people) **7:**871,
888–889, 896, 900, 918,
919, 920, 921, 922, 923,
925, 957
Basotho kingdom **7:**894, 914,
919, 923
Bass, George **10:**1301
Bass Strait **10:**1301, 1311, 1342
Bastos, Waldemar **5:**620
Basutoland *see* Lesotho
Bata **1:**76, 77
Batéké Plateau **5:**584, 604
Batepá Massacre **1:**130, 135
Bathurst *see* Banjul
Bathurst, Henry **2:**201
batiks **2:**258
Batman, John **10:**1400
Batuque (performance dance)
2:187
Bau kingdom **8:**1038
Bavadra, Timoci **8:**1044
Baule (people) **3:**395, 402, 498
Baya (people) **5:**609, 648, 651,
653, 656

Bayajidda **1:**36
Bayol, Jean-Marie **2:**172
beach resorts *see* tourism
Beavogui, Louis Lansana **2:**210
Bechuanaland *see* Botswana
Bédié, Henri Konan **3:**396, 406
beehive dwelling **7:**951, 980
Behanzin, king of Danhome
    3:323, 325–326
Beier, Ulli **1:**106, 109
Beira **6:**726, 733, 785, 808,
    810, 815
    history **6:**740, 741, 745
Bekalé, Eric-Joël **1:**85
Bekele, Kenenisa **4:***505*, 507
Bela (Congolese artist) **5:**672
Belgian Congo **5:**606, 633,
    662, 667, 703, 712
    cultural expression **5:**671, 672
    independence **5:**668, 704
    see also Congo Free State;
        Congo, Democratic
        Republic of
Bellingshausen, Fabian
    Gottfried von **10:**1352
Bello, Ahmadu **1:**103, 120
Bemba (people) **3:**311; **6:**746,
    846, 851, 853
Bemba, Sylvain **5:**689, 690
Bemba language **3:**311; **6:**746,
    846, 851, 853
Benguela **5:**582, *611*, 615
Benguela Current **5:***582*, 588,
    589, 624, 627
Benguela Railroad **5:**582, 583
Benin **1:**27, 31, 49; **3:**330–349
    art and architecture **1:**33–34,
        35, 106; **3:**338–339, *344*
    climate **3:**302–305, 330
    cultural expression **3:**338–340
    daily life **3:**341–343
    economy **3:**336–337, 343,
        346–349
    education **3:**343, 347
    family and society **3:**341–342
    festivals and ceremonies
        3:339
    flag **3:**332
    flora and fauna **3:**306–309
    food and drink **3:**339–340
    geography **3:**292–299, 330
    geology **3:**300–301
    government and political
        parties **3:**330, 331, 334,
        335–337, 346, 347
    health and welfare **3:**342–343
    history
        chronology **3:**333
        colonial **3:**321–326, 328,
        335

early **1:**27, 31, 49; **3:**313,
    321, 322–323, 324, 328
modern **3:**330, 335–337
slave trade **3:**321
independence **3:**330, 335, 346
literature **3:**338
music **3:***338*, 339
peoples **3:**327–329, 332, 335,
    338, 339, 341, 345, 346
population **3:**331
religion **3:**332, 335, 339,
    341, *343*
resources **3:**330, 347–348
transportation and
    communication **3:**331,
    335, *346*, 349
Benin City **1:**33, 34, 35, 38
Benin Kingdom **1:**33–35, 38;
    3:322, 330, 335
Bennett, Gordon **10:**1375
Benue-Kongo languages **1:**47,
    48–49
Benue River **1:**8, 10, 11, 12, 13,
    14, 19, 65, 129
Benue Trough **1:**16, 17
Bérandjoko, Lobaye **5:**651
Berbera **4:**440, 446, 540, 544,
    553
Bérenger, Paul **6:**793
Beresford, Bruce **10:**1379
Berlin, Treaty of (1889) **9:**1187
Berlin Conference (1884–1885)
    2:172; **3:**325; **5:**604, 605;
    6:805
Berlin Convention (1899)
    9:1187
Besong, Bate **1:**58
Bessora (Gabonese author)
    1:85, *87*
Beti, Mongo **1:**57–58
Beti-Pahuin (people) **1:**45, 46,
    48, 57, 59
Betsileo (people) **6:**742, 769
Beyala, Calixthe **1:**58
Bezuidenhout, Evita **7:**953
Bhély-Quénum, Olympe **3:**338
Bhoipuri language **6:**794, 795
Biafra **1:**48, *102*, 103; **3:**324,
    396
Biazin, Clément-Marie **5:**654
Bible **4:**452, 455, 502, 529
    translations **4:**492, 505
Bicentennial, Australian
    (1988) **10:**1373, 1380
Bié Plateau **5:**582, 583, 626
"big man" status (Papua New
    Guinea) **8:**1112, 1113
Bijagós Archipelago **2:**151,
    160, 173, 223, 227
Bikindi, Simon **5:**707

Bikini Atoll **8:***1018*, 1059
Biklia, Abebe **4:**507
Biko, Steve **7:**947
Bikutsi music **1:**59
Bilsen, A. A. van **5:**667
Bimbia **1:**46
Binger, Louis-Gustave **3:**325
Bingerville **3:**395, 405
Binns, Vivienne **10:**1375
Bintimani Peak (Loma Mansa)
    2:152
Bio, Julius Maada **2:**274
biodiversity **2:**160–163
Bioko **1:**15, 17, 21, 25, 68, *70*,
    74, 75
    history **1:**26, 73, 138
    local government **1:**72
    Malabo **1:**76, 77
Biramah, Fatou **3:**417
Biram state (Hausa) **1:**36
bird species
    Angola **5:**595
    Australia **10:**1329,
        1333–1334, 1335
    eastern Africa **4:**449
    New Zealand and Polynesia
        9:1171, 1173, 1177, *1289*
Bisa (people) **3:**360
Bisa language **3:**357
Bisho Massacre (1992) **7:**948
Bislama (Creole language)
    8:1142
Bismarck Archipelago **8:**1012,
    1014, 1015
    charting **8:**1033
    early Melanesians **8:**1026
    German claims **8:**1103, *1105*
    World War II **8:**1105
Bismarck Sea **8:**1012
Bissau **2:**151, 169, 173, *220*,
    222, 223, *224*, 225, 227,
    228, *229*
Bissau Cathedral **2:***224*
Biu Plateau **1:**10–11
Biya, Paul **1:**54, 56, 60
Bizimungu, Pasteur **5:**705
Black Arcade **10:***1388*
"black-birding" **8:**1034
Blackman, Charles **10:**1375
Black Mountain **10:**1396
black rhinoceros **4:**448
black townships *see* Bantustans
Black Volta **3:**292, 294, 355
blanket garment, Lesotho
    7:921
Blantyre **6:**727, 781, 784, 786
Bligh, William **10:**1348
Blixen, Karen **4:**526
Bloemfontein Convention
    (1854) **7:**893

Blondy, Alpha **3:**399
Blood River, Battle of (1838)
    7:892, 896, 962
Blouin, Andrée **5:**653
Blue Mountains **10:**1310, 1311,
    1348
Blue Nile River **4:**439, 456, 515
Blyden, Edward W. **2:**240
Boa Vista island **2:**153, 191
Bobo (people) **3:**328, 360
Bobo-Dioulasso **3:**297–298,
    358, 359, 362, 367
body art **10:**1374
Boer republics *see* Orange Free
    State; Transvaal
Boers *see* Afrikaaners
Boer Wars *see* Anglo-Boer Wars
Boganda, Barthélemy **5:**652,
    655
Bokassa, Jean-Bédel **5:**646,
    652, 658, 659
Bolama **2:**173, 227
Boleká, Justo Bolekia **1:**74
Bolger, Jim **9:**1216, 1217, 1233
Boma **5:**580, 606
Bomi Lake **2:***232*
Bonapriso Center for Arts **1:**59
Bondi Beach **10:**1404, *1405*
Bondu imamate **2:**168, 172
Bonga (singer-songwriter) **5:**620
Bong Mountains **2:**154, 247
Bongo, Ali **1:**82, 84
Bongo, Omar **1:**78, 82, 83, 84,
    88
Bongo Massif **5:**584
Boni, Nazi **3:**357
Boni, Yayi **3:***334*, 336, 347
Bonny **1:**20, 27, 129
Bonny River **1:**8
bonobos **5:**593
Bono state **3:**312, 313
boomerang **10:**1343, 1387
Boosaaso **4:**440, 553
Bora Bora **9:***1159*, 1163, 1181,
    1186
Borchgrevink, Carsten Egeberg
    10:1353
Borgu kingdom **1:**32
Borno State **1:**10, 20
Bornu Empire **1:**29–30, 36
Bosumtwi, Lake **3:**295, *368*
Botany Bay **10:**1346, *1347*,
    1404, 1405
Botha, Louis **7:**899, 945, *947*
Botha, P. W. **7:**947
Botswana **7:**902–913
    art and architecture **7:***902*,
        908–909
    climate **7:**878–881, 884–885,
        902

health and welfare
5:640–641, 643
history
chronology **5:**631
colonial *see* German East
Africa; Ruanda-Urundi
Congo Wars **5:**678, 705
modern **5:**628, 633–635,
705
precolonial **5:**599, 628
independence **5:**628, 632,
633, 634, 638, 645
languages **5:**630, 636
literature **5:**636
music **5:***636*, 637–638
peoples **5:**599, 609, 628,
630, 632, 634–635, 636
see also Hutu; Tutsi
population **5:**629, 643, 644
religion **5:**630, 634, 638, 639
resources **5:**628, 643
transportation and
communication **5:**630,
642, *643*, 645
Burundi civil war **5:**593, 607,
609, 628, 632, 633, 634,
635, 643
economic and social effects
5:639, 640, 641, 645
literature **5:**636
Busby, James **9:***1182*, 1183
bushfires **10:**1324, *1325*, 1408
Australia **10:**1408
bush taxis **2:***215*
bush tucker (traditional
Aboriginal food) **10:**1383
Bushveld **7:**870, 872
Busia, Kofi **3:**375
Butake, Bole **1:**58
Butare **5:***700*, 703, 706, 711,
712, 713
Butaritari Atoll **9:**1203
Buyoya, Pierre **5:**634, 635
Bwiti (indigenous faith) **1:**88
Byrd, Richard E. **10:**1424
Byron, John **9:**1181; **10:**1346

C

Cabinda **5:**582, 619, 622, 626
history **5:**604, 610, 618
Cabo Blanco **1:**38
Cabral, Amilcar **2:**185, 223,
225, 227
Cabral, Luis **2:**223, 228
Cabral, Vasco **2:**224
Cacheu **2:**169, 173, 218, 223,
227
Cadamosto, Advise **2:**169
Caheu River **2:**151
Cakobau, Seru Epenisa **8:**1043

Calabar (city) **1:**27, 107, 129
Calabar (people) **1:**12, 49
Caledon River **7:***868*, 870, 871,
923
caliphate **1:**37, 40, 47
Camara, Fodé **2:**258
Camara, Moussa Dadis **2:**210
Cambridge, Ada **10:**1372
Cameron, Verney L. **5:**603
Cameroon **1:**50–67
art and architecture **1:**59, *62*,
63
climate **1:**18–21, 50
cultural expression **1:**57–59
daily life 60–61
economy **1:**52, 56, 64–67
education **1:**61
family and society **1:**60
festivals and ceremonies **1:**59
flag **1:**51
flora and fauna **1:**22–25
food and drink **1:**59
geography **1:**10, 11, 12,
13–15, *16*, 18, 50
geology **1:**16
government and political
parties **1:**52, 54
health and welfare **1:**60–61
history
chronology **1:**53
colonial period *see* French
Cameroon; Kamerun
early **1:**27
modern **1:**50, 55–56
nineteenth-century
1:45–46
independence **1:**50, 55, *58*, 62
music **1:**59
peoples **1:**45, 47–49, 50, 52,
57
population **1:**10, 52
refugee camps **5:**657
religion **1:**52, 60
resources **1:**50, 64–65
transportation and
communication **1:**52, 62,
67
Cameroon Mountains **1:**25
Cameroon National Union
1:55, 56
Cameroon People's Democratic
Movement *see* MDPC
Cameroon, Mount **1:**14, 17, 18,
19, 21, 50, 59
Cameroon Mountains **1:**25
Campbell, John Logan **9:**1218
Campbell Islands **10:**1302
Campbell Plateau **9:**1164
Canary Islands **2:**256,
264–265

Canberra **10:**1311, 1376, 1393,
1395–1396
national capital **10:***1365*,
1366, 1367, 1369,
1395–1396, 1401
canoes **8:**1045, 1060; **9:**1204,
1205, 1219, 1246, 1247,
1249, 1266, 1280
Canterbury **9:**1165
Canterbury Association
9:1184, 1230
Canterbury Plains
9:1159–1160, 1168, 1230
Canterbury University **9:**1230
Cão, Diogo **5:**600; **7:**890
Cape Bojador **2:**169
Cape Coast **3:**321, 373, 381
Cape Colony **7:**890–893, 894,
896, 898, 902, 907, 911,
919, 923, 940, 945, 951,
962, 964, 967
Cape Floral Kingdom **7:**885
Cape Fold Mountains **7:**870,
872, *876*, 879
Cape Mesurado **2:**235
Cape of Good Hope **7:**890, 892
Cape Palmas **2:**150, 185
Cape Town **7:**872, 963, 972, 973
climate **7:**880, 881
cultural life **7:**952, 954
history **7:**890, 891, 940, 962,
963, 967
region **7:**868, 870, 872
university **7:**951
Cape Verde **2:**180–191
art and architecture
2:186–187
climate **2:**156, 159, 180, 188,
190
cultural expression **2:**186–187
daily life **2:**188
economy **2:**181, 188, 190–191
family and society **2:**188
flag **2:**182
flora and fauna **2:**160–163
food and drink **2:**187
geography **2:**148–153, 180,
186
geology **2:**155
government and political
parties **2:**182, 184
health and welfare **2:**188
history
chronology **2:**182
modern **2:**180, 185, 223
Portuguese rule **2:**166,
169, 172, 173, 179, 180,
185, 186, 189, 190, 223
independence **2:**180, 184,
185, 222, 223

literature **2:**186
music **2:**187
peoples **2:**179, 180, 182, 185,
186, 188
population **2:**181
religion **2:**179, 182, 188
resources **2:**180, 190–191
transportation and
communication **2:**182,
191
Cape Verde Archipelago **2:**153,
155, 156–159, 172, 173,
180
Cape Verde Islands **1:**38; **2:**153
Cape York Peninsula **10:**1300,
1309, 1310
Caprivi, Leo von **7:**897
Cap-Vert Peninsula **2:**150, 260,
263
Caramansa (Akan chief) **3:**313
carbon sink **5:**591
Carey, Peter **10:**1373
cargo cult **8:**1141, 1143
Carlos, Jérôme **3:**338
Caroline Islands **8:**1029, 1031,
1032, 1033, 1034, 1035,
1054, 1059, 1064, 1069,
1086, 1093, 1094, 1098
see also Micronesia
Carpentaria, Gulf of **10:**1300,
1305, *1307*, 1309, 1310,
1345, 1350
Carpentier, Pieter de **10:**1300
Carstenszoon, Jan **10:**1300
Carteret, Philip **8:**1033; **9:**1181;
10:1346
Carthaginians **2:**148
Cartwright, Silvia **9:**1224
carving
Angola **5:**619
Maori **9:***1178*, *1184*, *1219*
Pitcairn **9:**1238
Samoa **9:**1246–1247
Tonga **9:**1266
Wallis and Futuna **9:***1319*
Zimbabwe **7:**995
see also masks; wood carving
Casamance region **2:**150, 172,
173, 258, 260, 261
separatist movement **2:**150,
172, 173, 256, 265
Casamance River **2:**150, 169
Casely-Hayford, Adelaide
2:275
Casely-Hayford, Gladys May
2:275
Casely-Hayford, J. E. **3:**374,
377
Casement, Roger **5:**606
cashews **6:**815

Cassard, Jacques **2**:169
cassava *see* manioc
Casset, Mama **2**:258
Castle, Len **9**:1219
Castle Hill Rising (1804) **10**:1348
Castro, Fidel **7**:931
Catholicism *see* Roman Catholicism
cave art *see* rock art
Cawley, Evonne Goolagong **10**:1382
Cazneaux, Harold **10**:1375
CCM (Chama Cha Mapinduzi) **6**:832, 834, 836
Central African Plateau **5**:594
Central African Republic **1**:67; **5**:646–661
  art and architecture **5**:654
  climate **5**:589, 590, *591*, 646
  cultural expression **5**:653–655
  daily life **5**:656–657
  economy **5**:647, 659–661
  education **5**:657, 658, 659
  family and society **5**:656–657
  festivals and ceremonies **5**:655
  flag **5**:648
  flora and fauna **5**:592, 593
  food and drink **5**:655
  geography **5**:580–585, 646
  geology **5**:586–587
  government and political parties **5**:648, 650, 659
  health and welfare **5**:657
  history
    chronology **5**:648
    colonial *see* Ubangi-Shari
    modern **5**:646, 651–652, 658
  independence **5**:646, 650, 651, 652, 655
  languages **5**:648, 653
  lingua franca **5**:607, 651, 653
  literature **5**:653–654
  peoples **5**:608–609, 648, *653*, 656
  population **5**:647
  religion **5**:648, 655, 656
  resources **5**:646, 652, 659
  transportation and communication **5**:648, 658, 659, 661
Central Deserts **10**:1304, 1306–1307
Central Kalahari Game Reserve **7**:885
Central Lowlands (Australia) **10**:1309

Central Uplands (Australia) **10**:1307
ceramics *see* pottery
Cetshwayo kaMpande, king of the Zulus **7**:895–896
CFCs (chlorinated fluorocarbons) **10**:1425
Chad **1**:30, 46, 56, 66, 67; **5**:652, 657, 670, 678, 694, 705
Chad, Lake **1**:11, 24, 29, 50, 128
  desertification **1**:8
  Kanem kingdom **1**:28, 36
Chad Basin **1**:11, 16
Chad Basin National Park **1**:24
Chadic languages **1**:47
Chagos Islands **6**:729, 749
Chaillu Massif **1**:15, 16
Chakela, Mosotho **7**:921
Chalbi Desert **4**:441, 445
Chamorro (people) **8**:1032, 1052, 1086
Chamorro language **8**:1037
Chan, Julius **8**:1105
Chandia, Flinto **6**:851
chants **8**:1060, 1070
Chaold, Pyabelo Kouly **3**:417
Chapel of the Tablet (Aksum) **4**:452, *452*, 508
Chappal Waddi **1**:11
Charley, Dele **2**:275
Chatham Islands **9**:1160
Chaudhry, Mahendra **8**:1044
Chauvel, Charles **10**:1379
Chavuma Falls **6**:724
Cheikh Anta Diop University **2**:*256*, 262
Chelmsford, Lord **7**:896
Chewa (people) **6**:746, 778, 780, 781, 782, 852, 853
Cheyney-Coker, Syl **2**:275
Chichewa language **6**:746, 780
Chifley, Joseph Benedict ("Ben") **10**:1368
Chikwava, Brian **7**:994
children
  Aboriginal Australian "Stolen Generation" **10**:1356, 1371, 1373, 1388
  Cameroon **1**:60
  Congo, Democratic Republic of **5**:675
  Liberian civil wars **2**:243, *244*, 245, 246
  Sierra Leone civil war **2**:274, 279
child soldiers, Somalian **4**:561, 565
Chilembwe, John **6**:779

Chilibula Mission **6**:851
Chiluba, Frederick **6**:850, 853
Chimbetu, Simon **7**:995–996
Chimombo, Steve **6**:780
chimpanzees **5**:593; **6**:736
chimurenga (musical style) **7**:995
Chimurenga resistance **7**:992
China
  Angola **5**:625, 627
  Central African Republic **5**:659
  Congo, Democratic Republic of **5**:681
  Congo, Republic of **5**:688, 690, 695, 696, 697
  Gabon **1**:84, 91, 92, 93
  Gambia **2**:203
  Guinea **2**:209, 214, 217
  Guinea-Bissau **2**:222
Chinese, ethnic **1**:75, 88, 91; **8**:1037, *1079*, 1080, 1081, 1134
Chingono, Julius **7**:994
Chinodya, Shimmer **7**:994
Chiounda Mosque **6**:758
Chirikure, Chirikure **7**:994
Chissano, Joaquim **6**:806
Chiweshe, Stella **7**:995
Chiyao language **6**:747, 780
Chiziane, Paulina **6**:807
Choiseul Island **8**:1016, 1130
Chokwe (people) **5**:619, 622, 672
cholera epidemic **7**:1000
Christchurch **9**:1160, 1210, 1223, 1230
  architecture **9**:1219, 1230
  Arts Festival **9**:1221
  climate **9**:1168
  history **9**:1184, 1185, 1230
Christ Church Cathedral **10**:1402, *1402*
Christianity *see* missionaries; Protestantism; Roman Catholicism; *specific churches, denominations, and sects*
Christmas Island **9**:1161; **10**:1411
Church Missionary Society **2**:273
Church of England *see* Anglicanism
Chuukese language **8**:1037, 1070, 1071
Chuuk lagoon **8**:*1066*, 1068, *1069*
Chuuk state **8**:*1068*, 1069, 1070, 1072, 1079, 1080
cichlid fish **4**:451

Cidade Velha **2**:169, 186, 189
cinema *see* film industry
Ciskei **7**:947, 948
Cisse, Soly **2**:258
Civil Union Act (2004, New Zealand) **9**:1224
civil wars
  Congo, Democratic Republic of **5**:593, *607*, 661, 662, 698
  Congo, Republic of **5**:682, 687, 688, 690, 694, 697
  flora and fauna effects **5**:593, 607, 609
  Guinea-Bissau **2**:223, 226, 227, 228, 229
  Ivory Coast **3**:397, 400, 401, 406, 407
  Sierra Leone **2**:239, 268, 273, 274, 278, 279, 280, 281, 282, 283
  see also Angolan civil war; Liberian civil war; Mozambique civil war
Claretian order **1**:75
Clark, Helen **9**:1217, 1224, 1233
Clarke, Marcus **10**:1372
Clay, Henry **2**:235
Clegg, Johnny **7**:953
Clifford, Hugh **1**:101
climate change
  Antarctica **10**:13/28, 1418, 1425, 1430
  Congo Basin **5**:591, 593
  eastern Africa **4**:447
  eastern Central Africa **6**:731, 734
  Fiji **8**:1047
  Guam **8**:1059
  Gulf of Guinea **1**:21
  Namibia **7**:936
  Somalia **4**:553
  southern Africa **7**:881; **8**:1022
  Vanuatu **9**:1162, 1169, 1203, 1274, *1276*, 1279, 1284
Clock Tower (Victoria) **6**:826
cloves **6**:743, 842
coal
  Antarctica **10**:1432
  Australia **10**:1310, 1402, *1408*, 1409, 1410, 1414, 1415
  Botswana **7**:912
  South Africa **7**:971
  Swaziland **7**:985
  Zimbabwe **7**:1002
cobalt **5**:633, 643, 662, 668, 679, 681; **6**:731; **10**:1409

cocoa
  Cameroon **1:**64, 65, 67, 73
  Equatorial Guinea **1:**73, 77
  Gabon **1:**83
  Ghana **3:**373, 374, 375, 383, 385, 386, 387, 388, 389
  Ivory Coast **3:**395, 396, 406, 407, 408
  Nigeria **1:**139
  Togo **3:**415, 424
Cocoa Marketing Board **3:**373
coconut crabs **9:***1170,* 1173
coconut products **6:**749; **8:**1034, 1093, 1118; **9:**1204, 1205, 1208, 1209, *1254,* 1281, 1284, 1285
coelacanth ("living fossil") 750
Coetzee, Basil **7:**952
Coetzee, J. M. **7:**950; **10:**1373
coffee
  Angola **5:**602, 616, 621, 626
  Burundi **5:**633, 642, 643, 644, 645
  Cameroon **1:**64, 65–66, 67
  Central African Republic **5:**660, 661
  Congo, Democratic Republic of **5:**679
  Equatorial Guinea **1:**77
  Ethiopia **4:**515, 516, 517
  Ivory Coast **3:**396, 406, 407, 408
  Kenya **4:**536
  Rwanda **5:***591,* 714, 715
coffee ceremony, Eritrea **4:**492
coins, Aksumite **4:**454–455, 456
Cold War
  Angola **5:**617, 625
  Australia **10:**368–369
  Congo, Democratic Republic of **5:**669
  Guinea **2:**204, 209–210
  Malawi **6:**779
  Namibia **7:**931
  South Africa **7:**946
  see also Soviet Union
Cole, Robert Wellesley **2:**275
collision zones **8:**1018
Commonwealth Avenue Bridge **10:***1395*
Commonwealth Games **7:**496
Communauté Financière Africaine franc **1:**91
Communism
  Eritrea **4:**488, 495
  Ethiopia **4:**496, 500, 503–504, 505–506, 508, 509, 511, 512, 514, 515
  Guinea **2:**209
  see also Cold War; Marxism

Comoros **6:**750–759
  art and architecture **6:**756
  climate **6:**732–733, 750
  cultural expression **6:**755
  daily life **6:**756
  economy **6:**751, 759
  education **6:**756
  flag **6:**752
  flora and fauna **6:**736, *757*
  geography **6:**728–729, 750
  geology **6:**731
  government and political parties **6:**752, 754, 755
  history
    chronology **6:**753
    modern **6:**745, 750, 754, 759
    precolonial **6:**740, 750
  independence **6:**750, 755
  islands of union **6:**753, 754
  literature **6:**756
  music **6:**756
  peoples **6:**748, 750, 752
  population **6:**751, 759
  religion **6:**752, 756, 757, 758
  resources **6:**750, 759
  transportation and communication **6:**752, 759
  see also Mayotte
Compagnie Camerounaise d'Aluminium **1:**66
Compaoré, Blaise **3:**350, 354, 356, 359, 364
Conakry **2:***152,* 158, *204, 208, 209,* 212, 214, 217
  history **2:**209, 214
Condé, Alpha **2:**210
Condominium of the New Hebrides **8:**1141, 1145
Congo *see* Congo, Democratic Republic of; Congo, Republic of
Congo (people) **2:**179, 243
Congo, Democratic Republic of **1:**46; **5:**662–681
  art and architecture **5:**672
  Burundi **5:**642, 643, 645
  climate **5:**589–591, 662
  cultural expression **5:**671–673, 689, 690, 706
  daily life **5:**674–676
  economy **5:**664, 678–681
  education **5:**676
  family and society **5:**675
  festivals and ceremonies **5:**673
  flag **5:**664
  flora and fauna **5:**592–593, 595

food and drink **5:**673
geography **5:**580–585, 662
geology **5:**586–587
government and political parties **5:**661, 664, 670
health and welfare **5:**657, 675–676
history
  chronology **5:**661
  colonial *see* Belgian Congo; Congo Free State
  Congo Wars **5:**618, 670, 678, 705
  modern **5:**617, 618, 652, 662, 667–670, 698
  precolonial **5:**597–599, 600, 608, 662
  as Zaire **5:**662, 669–670
Hutu refugees **5:**670, 705, 709, 713
independence **5:**662, 668, 673, 678
languages **5:**664, 671
lingua franca **5:**607, 671
literature **5:**671–672
music **5:**655, 672–673, 689, 690, 706
peoples **5:**607, 608, 664, 667, 671, 673
population **5:**663, 664
religion **5:**664, 674–675
resources **5:**583, 596, 662, 668, 679
transportation and communication **5:**664, 677, 679, 681
Congo Free State **5:**604, 605–606, 662, 667, 677, 694
  see also Belgian Congo, Congo, Democratic Republic of
Congo-Ocean Railroad **5:**687
Congo, Republic of **1:**90; **5:**682–697
  art and architecture **5:**689
  climate **5:**589, 590, 682
  cultural expression **5:**689–691
  daily life **5:**692–693
  economy **5:**684, 695–697
  education **5:**693, 694
  family and society **5:**692
  festivals and ceremonies **5:**690–691
  flag **5:**683
  food and drink **5:***690,* 691
  geography **5:**580, 582, 583, 584, 682
  geology **5:**586–587
  government and political parties **5:**684, 686

health and welfare **5:**657, 692–693
history
  chronology **5:**685
  colonial *see* Middle Congo
  modern **5:**682, 687–688, 695
  precolonial **5:**600, 608
independence **5:**682, 687, 691, 694
languages **5:**684, 689
lingua franca **5:**607, 684, 689
literature **5:**689
music **5:**689, 690
peoples **5:**607, 608, 609, 684, 692
population **5:**683, 692
religion **5:**684, 692
resources **5:**682, 695, 696
transportation and communication **5:**684, 694, 695, 697
Congo Basin **1:**46, 57
  European intervention **5:**600–602, 603
Congo-Brazzaville *see* Congo, Republic of
Congo River **5:**580, 582, 583, 584, 585, 589, 592, 593, 594, 597, 599, 660, 661, 677, *682,* 694
  exploration **5:**600, 603, 604, 605
  navigation **5:**604, 606, 677, 681
Congo Wars (1996–1997, 1998–2003) **5:**593, 607, 618, 661, 662, 666, 668, 670, 673, 677, 698
  Angola **5:**618, 670, 678, 705
  deaths and devastation **5:**609, 662, 670, 678, 681, 705
  economic effects **5:**678, 680, 681
Congregationalism
  Australia **10:**1384, 1385
  Kiribati **9:**1200, 1206, 1207
  Marshall Islands **8:**1056, 1061
  Micronesia **8:**1071
  Nauru **8:**1081
  Polynesia **9:**1187, 1189, 1190, 1237, 1257
  Samoa **9:**1242, 1249
  Tuvalu **9:**1276, 1282
Congress for Democracy and Justice (Gabon) **1:**82
Congress for Democratic Change (Liberia) **2:**234

Conté, Lansana **2:**208, 210, 215
continental plates **4:**442
contract labor **8:**1034
Convention on the Conservation of Antarctic Marine Living Resources (1982) **10:**1339, 1430–1431
convict settlements
  Australia **10:**1372, 1378, 1387, 1398, 1402, 1404, 1406
  Norfolk Island **10:**1416
Cook, James
  Antarctica **10:**1416
  Australia **10:***1344,* 1346, *1346,* 1352, 1404
  New Zealand and Polynesia **9:***1180,* 1181, 1182, 1186, 1188, 1194, 1209, 1236, 1263, 1266
  Western Pacific **8:**1033, 1084, 1136
Cook, Mount **9:**1158, 1159, 1165
Cook Islands **9:**1194–1195
  climate change threat **9:**1169
  climate hazards **9:**1168, 1169
  geography **9:**1160, 1194
  history **9:**1175, 1180, 1181, 1188, 1194, 1215
  independence **9:**1217
  migrants to New Zealand **9:**1225, 1229
  peoples **9:**1189, 1191, 1195
  religion **9:**1189, 1195
Cook Strait **9:**1158, 1159, 1228
Cooper, Charles **2:**240
copper
  Angola **5:**626
  Botswana **7:**912, 913, 936
  Bougainville **8:**1012, 1015, 1105, 1118, 1119, 1120
  Congo Basin **5:**582, 583, 596, 626, 633, 643, 662, 668, 679, 696
  eastern Central Africa **6:**727, 731, 739, 745, 844, 849, 850, 856–857, 857, 858, 859
  Namibia **7:**936, 937
copper working **5:**596
copra *see* coconut products
Coptic Christians **4:**459, 484, 490, 508
coral atolls **8:**1014, 1029–1031, 1054, 1062; **9:**1158, 1160, 1161, 1162, 1163, 1165, 1198
coral reefs **4:**449–450; **6:**729, *820*

Australia **10:**1308, 1310, 1329, 1335
New Zealand and Polynesia **9:**1160, 1162, 1163, *1165*
Western Pacific **8:**1012, 1014, 1015, 1016, 1018, 1021, *1024,* 1025, 1031
see also Great Barrier Reef
Coral Sea **8:**1012
Coral Sea, Battle of the (1942) **8:**1104; **10:**1367
Coral Sea Island Territory **10:**1310
corn **2:**187; **5:**602, 638, 643, 660, 679; **6:**726, 786, 858; **7:**889, 895
Corubal River **2:**151
Costa, Manuel Pinto da **1:**135
Costa da Pimenta **2:**169
Côte d'Ivoire *see* Ivory Coast
Cotonou **3:**304, 337, 341, 344, 345, 349
  architecture **3:**338, *344*
  history **3:**323, 325, 329, 330, 335, 344
  population **3:**294, 344
cotton
  Angola **5:**602, 616
  Benin **3:**347, 348
  Burkina Faso **3:**355, 365, 366, 367, *367*
  Burundi **5:**633, 644, 645
  Central African Republic **5:**651, 661
  Fiji **8:**1043
Cotton Tree (Freetown) **2:**280
Couchoro, Félix **3:**338, 417
Counihan, Noel **10:**1375
Country Party (Australia) **10:**1367, 1368, 1369, 1370, 1371
coupé-décalé (musical style) **3:**399
Courland (Latvia) **2:**171, 192
Court, Margaret **10:**1382
cowrie shells **5:**597, 600
crater lakes **1:**17
creation legends **1:**31, 36, 48
Creole language **6:**794, 795, 823, 824
Creoles **6:**748, 793, 795, 817, 821, 825
  see also Afro-European Creoles; Krio
cricket (sport) **4:**528; **9:**1221; **10:**1382, *1400,* 1401
crime
  Solomon Islands **8:**1132, 1133, 1134
  South Africa **7:**958, 959, 970
Cristal Mountains **1:**15

crocodiles **3:**307, *307,* 308; **10:**1333
Cross River Basin **1:**12
Crozet Islands **10:**1315, 1337, 1434
cruise ships **10:***1432,* 1433
Cruz, Viriato da **5:**619
Cry, The Beloved Country (Paton) **7:**950
Cuba **5:**610, 617, 625; **7:**931
Cuca (Angolan beer) **5:**621
Cuffee, Paul **2:**175
Cunene River **5:**582, 583; **7:**874, 883, *928*
Cuoto, Mia **6:**807
curandeiros (healers) **6:**810
Curtin, John **10:**1368
Cushitic languages **4:**457, 548
cycling **4:**491
cyclones
  Australia **10:**1321, 1323–1324
  Indian Ocean islands **6:**732, 734
  tropical Pacific **9:**1166, 1168, 1169, *1169,* 1236, 1271
  Western Pacific **8:***1019,* 1022, 1145
Cypriot immigrants **10:**1357, 1389

D
Da'amat kingdom **4:**453, 454
Daar, Aden Abdullah Ousman **4:**547
Dabani language **3:**328
Dacko, David **5:**652
Dadié, Bernard **3:**398
Dagara language **3:**357
Dagbon (people) **3:**314
Dahomey *see* Benin
Dairo, J. K. **1:**108
Dakar **2:**150, 159, 179, 261, 263, 267; **3:**335, 395
  architecture **2:***257,* 258, *265*
  festivals **2:**259
  history **2:**169, *173,* 209, 250, 255, 263
  universities **2:***256,* 262
Dallol Salt Flats **4:**439
Daloa **3:**297, 403
Dampier, William **8:**1033
dams **1:**8, 10
Dan (people) **3:**398
Danakil Desert **4:**438, *440,* 445, 467
dance
  Aboriginal Australians **10:**1377, *1378*
  Botswana **7:**909
  Burundi **5:**637, *638*

Congo, Republic of **5:**690
Fiji **8:***1046*
Kiribati **9:**1204–1205
Lesotho **7:**921, *922*
Namibia **7:**933
Palau **8:**1094
Papua New Guinea **8:**1109
Rwanda **5:**707, *708*
Samoa **9:***1246,* 1247
Senegal **2:**258
Sierra Leone **2:**276
Solomon Island **8:**1131
Swaziland **7:***978,* 981, 983
Tonga **9:***1259,* 1266
Tuvalu **9:**1281
Uganda **4:**562–563, *564*
dan Fodio *see* Usman dan Fodio
Dangarembga, Tsitsi **7:**994
Danhome **3:**321, 322–323, 324, 328
  cities **3:**344, 345
  cultural expression **3:**338, 339
  French rule **3:**323, 325–326, 330, 335, 338, 344, 346, 415
  name change **3:**330
  see also Benin
Danhome, Republic of **3:**335–336
Danquah, J. B. **3:**377
Dao, Bernadette Sanou **3:**357
Darboc, Ousainou **2:**197
Dar es Salaam **6:**726, 837, 838, 839, 843, 859
Dark, Eleanor **10:**1373
Darling River *see* Murray-Darling Basin
Darwin **10:**1305, 1350, 1367, 1394
  climate **10:**1323, 1324
Daura State **1:**36
David, Tannatt Edgeworth **10:**1353, *1354*
Davies, Jacob Stanley **2:**275
Davis, Jack **10:**1379
Dawit, emperor of Ethiopia **4:**464
Dawson, Anderson **10:**1351
Dawson, Smoky **10:**1378
Deakin, Alfred **10:**1365
De Beers company **2:**282; **7:**896, 912, 913, 936, 967, 971
Debre Damo **4:***454, 456*
Debre Damo Church **4:***456*
Debtera Alaka Zenab **4:**505
Deception Island **10:**1424
deforestation
  Burkina Faso **3:**365, *367*
  Burundi **5:**644

Central African Republic
5:660
Congo, Republic of 5:696
Ethiopia 4:516
Ivory Coast 3:408
Rwanda 5:714
de Graft-Johnson, J. C. 3:377
de Klerk, F. W. 7:947, 948, *949*, 969
Dembo, Leonard 7:996
Democratic Action (São Tomé and Príncipe) 1:134
Democratic Party of Equatorial Guinea 1:72
Democratic Union of Cameroon 1:48
Denard, Robert 6:755
Denkyera state 3:312, 313, 314, 321
Denmark, Gold Coast 3:314, 320, 321, 324, *329*, 368, 377, 383
Dennis, C. J. 10:1373
D'Entrecasteaux Islands 8:1015, 1104
desert
  Australia 10:1304, 1306–1307, 1321–1322, 1323, 1330
  Eastern Africa 4:438, *440*, *444*, 445, 446, 480
  karoo (semidesert) 7:870, 872, 877, 885, 891
  West African coast 2:163
  see also names of specific deserts
desertification 1:8; 7:881
Desta, Gebrekirstos 4:506
Devi, Ananda 6:794
de Wet, Christiaan 7:899
Dhanis, Francis 5:606
Dhu Nuwas, king of Himyar 4:455
Dia, Mamadou 2:255
diamonds
  Angola 5:625–626, 627
  Australia 10:1305, 1409
  Botswana 7:902, 907, 912, 913
  Central African Republic 5:652, 659, 661
  Congo, Democratic Republic of 5:668, 681
  Congo, Republic of 5:696
  Guinea 2:216
  Liberia 2:247, 248, 249
  Namibia 7:873, 874, 877, 897, 936, 937
  Rwanda 5:713
  Sierra Leone 2:273, 274, 281, 282, 283

South Africa 7:893, 896, 898, 962, 965–966, 967, 971
  Tanzania 6:*841*
  Zimbabwe 7:1002
Dias, Jorge 6:808
Diba, Viyé 2:258
Dibango, Manu 1:59
Dibba, Ebou 2:198
Diego Garcia 6:*728*, 729, 749
Diégo-Suarez *see* Antsiranana
Diescho, Joseph 7:932
Difaqane *see* Mfecane
Dileita, Dileita Mohamed 4:474
Dimé, Moustapha 2:258
Dimlang, Mount 1:11
Dingane kaSenzangakhona, Zulu king 7:895
Dingiswayo, Mthethwa chief 7:895
dinosaurs 10:1320, 1425
Diome, Fatou 2:257
Diop, Birago 2:257
Diop, Boubacar Boris 2:257
Diop, Cheikh Anta 2:257
Diouf, Abdou 2:256, 264
Diouf, Ibou 2:258
Dioula (peoplo) 3:313, 317
Dioula language 3:328, 357, 398
Dipoko, Mbella Sonne 1:58
Discovery (ship) 10:1424
disease 9:1181, 1182, 1188, 1245; 10:1344, 1347, 1391, 1405
  see also specific diseases
Diwan Salatin Barnu 1:28
Djédjé, Ernesto 3:399
Djibouti 4:470–481
  art and architecture 4:476
  climate 4:438, 444, 446, 447, 470, 480
  cultural expression 4:476–477
  daily life 4:478
  economy 4:471, 480–481
  flag 4:472
  flora and fauna 4:448–451
  geography 4:436, 438, 470
  geology 4:442–443
  government and political parties 4:470, 471, 474
  history
    chronology 4:473
    colonial *see* French Somaliland
  history, modern 4:475, 480, 545
  independence 4:470, 475, 477, 480
  literature 4:476
  music 4:476–477

peoples 4:467, 472, 474, 476, 478, 480, 546
  population 4:470
  religion 4:470, 472
  resources 4:470, 480
  transportation and communication 4:471, 481
Djibouti (city) 4:475, 476, 477, 478, 479, 481
  history 4:438, 465, 470, 479, 502
  population 4:479
Djohar, Said Mohamed 6:755
Djolof kingdom 2:165, 172
Dodds, Alfred-Amédée 3:326
Dodoma 6:726, 733, 838
Doe, Samuel 2:234, 238–239, 247; 3:396
Dogbé, Yves Emmanuel 3:417
Dogoli 4:465, 487
Dogon language 3:328
Doguicimi (Hazoumé) 3:338
Dôlé (film) 1:87
dolphins 3:309; 7:885
Dome Argus 10:1312
Dongala, Emmanuel 5:689
Doré, Jean-Marie 2:210
Dorley, Morris 2:241
"dot art" 10:1374, 1375, *1375*
Douala (city) 1:59, 60, 63, 67
  history 1:45, 46, 62, 63
  population 1:14, 63
Douala (people) 1:45, 46, 59
Dow, Unity 7:908
Dowlyogo, Bernard 8:1078
Drake, Francis 2:169; 10:1352
Drakensberg Escarpment 5:582–583; 7:870–871, *873*, 879, 882, 895, 896
Drake Passage 10:1320
DRC *see* Congo, Democratic Republic of
Dreamtime (Aboriginal Australians) 10:1372, 1377, 1386
drought
  Angola 5:588, 589
  Australia 10:1329, 1350, 1358, *1406*, 1408, 1410
  Cape Verde 2:180, 188, 189, 190
  eastern Africa 4:444, 445, 446, 447, 448, 504, 514, 515, 516, 525, 531, 537, 547
  Fiji 8:1021–1022
  Lesotho 7:924
  Namibia 7:936
  South Africa 7:971

southern Africa 7:880–881, 892, 895, 924, 936, 985
  Swaziland 7:985
drug traffic, Guinea-Bissau 2:228
drumming
  Benin 3:339
  Botswana 7:909
  Burkina Faso 3:358
  Burundi 5:*636*, 637–638, 645
  Central African Republic 5:654, *655*
  Congo, Democratic Republic of t5:672
  Ghana 3:*378*
  Namibia 7:933
  Samoa 9:1247
  Tonga 9:*1265*, 1266
  Uganda 4:562–563
Duarte, Cristina 2:*184*
Duarte, Fausto 2:224
Ducie Island 9:1163, 1238
duck-billed platypus 10:1331
Duff, Alan 9:1218
Dufresne, Marc-Joseph Marion 10:1346
Duggan, Maurice 9:1218
Duguwa dynasty 1:28
Duiker, K. Sello 7:950
duikers (skulking antelope) 5:593, 595
Dumont d'Urville, Jules Sébastien-César 10:1352
Dunama, caliph of Sokoto 1:30
Dunama Dibalami Selmami, Sawfawa ruler 1:28, 29
Dunedin 9:1160, 1168, 1184, 1185, *1223*
  Octagon 9:*1212*
Durban 7:870, 880, 895, *951*, 964, 973
d'Urban, Benjamin 7:964
dust storms 10:1323, 1324
Dusty, Slim 10:1378
"Dutch Disease" 8:1120
Dutch East India Company 7:890, 940, 956, 963, 967; 9:1180–1181; 10:1344–1345
Dutch East Indies *see* Indonesia
Dutch Reformed Church 7:943, 956, 997
Dutch Republic *see* Netherlands
Dutch West India Company 1:39; 2:170
Dywill, Nofinishí 7:953
Dzeliwe, Swazi queen mother 7:979

E

earthquakes
New Zealand **9:**1128, 1164, 1165
Western Pacific **8:**1014, 1145
East African Craton **4:**442
East African Rift System **4:**438, 439, 443, 448; **6:**727, 731
East Antarctic Ice Sheet **10:**1312, 1313
East Antarctic Mountains **10:**1314
East Asian fiscal crisis (1997) **10:**1408
East Cameroon *see* French Cameroon
Easter Island **9:**1181
Eastern Cape Province **7:**870, 871, 883, 892, 900, 957, 958
Ebalé, Ramón Esono **1:**74
Ebeye **8:**1059, 1061
Ebola virus **1:**89; **5:**676, 693
ebony **4:**448
echidnas **10:***1330,* 1331
ECOMOG (multinational force) **2:**239, 274
ecotourism **1:**84; **3:**367
ECOWAS (East Africa Economic and Security Organization) **2:**239, 274, 280
Edie Creek **8:**1104
Edo (people) **1:**33, 35; **3:**322
Efaté Island **8:**1145
Egbeda **1:**120
Église Évangélique du Gabon **1:**88
Eguguojo, Yoruba ruler **1:**32
Egypt **4:**452, 453, 459, 465, 466, 487, 508
Eighty Mile Beach (Australia) **10:**1306
Ekosso, Rosemary **1:**58
Ekué, Lauren **3:**417
Ekwensi, Cyprian **1:**105
elder respect **3:**402
see also ancestor veneration
Elebe, Lisembé **5:**672
Elem 27
elephants
Burkina Faso **3:**306
Congo Basin **5:**594, 595
East Africa **4:***447,* 448, *448,* 453
southern Africa **7:***880,* 883
West African coast **2:**161–162
Elgon, Mount **4:**439, 440–441, 443, 446

Elias, Sian **9:**1224
Elisabethville *see* Lubumbashi
Elizabeth II, queen of Great Britain **10:**1369
Ella Amida, king of Aksum **4:**455
Ellice Islands *see* Tuvalu
Elliott, Stephan **10:**1379
Elmina **3:**313, 315, 319, 320, 321, 324
Elobey Islands **1:**75
Ely, Bonnie **10:**1375
Emecheta, Buchi **1:**105
emeralds **6:**857
emirate system **1:**40, 40–41
employment
Angola **5:**627
Australia **10:**1407, 1408
Benin **3:**347
Botswana **7:**912
Burkina Faso **3:**364, 365
Burundi **5:**645
Cameroon **1:**67
Cape Verde **2:**191
Central African Republic **5:**661
Comoros **6:**759
Congo, Democratic Republic of **5:**681
Congo, Republic **5:**696
Djibouti **4:**471, 480, 481
Equatorial Guinea **1:**77
Eritrea **4:**483, 495
Ethiopia **4:**515
Fiji **8:**1050
Gabon **1:**93
Gambia **2:**203
Ghana **3:**388
Guinea **2:**217
Guinea-Bissau **2:**229
Ivory Coast **3:**402, 407, 409
Kiribati **9:**1208
Lesotho **7:**925
Liberia **2:**245, 249
Madagascar **6:**773
Malawi **6:**786
Marshall Islands **8:**1063
Mauritius **6:**797
Micronesia **8:**1073
Mozambique **6:**815
Namibia **7:**936
New Zealand **9:**1234
Nigeria **1:**129
Palau **8:**1097
Rwanda **5:**715
Samoa **9:**1254
São Tomé and Príncipe **1:**132, 139
Senegal **2:**267
Seychelles **6:**827

Sierra Leone **2:**283
South Africa **7:**969, 970
Swaziland **7:**984
Tanzania **6:**841
Togo **3:**425
Tonga **9:**1271
Tuvalu **9:**1285
Zambia **6:**857
Zimbabwe **7:**1002
endangered species **10:**1335, 1339, 1430–1431
Endugis, king of Aksum **4:**454–455
Enewetak atoll **8:**1059
Engida, Agegehu **4:**506
England *see* Great Britain
English Company of Royal Adventurers **2:**170
English immigrants **10:**1357, 1358, 1387, 1389, 1406
ENSO (El Niño–Southern Oscillation) **1:**18; **7:**881; **8:**1020, 1134
Entebbe **4:**436, 447, *561,* 567, 571
Israeli airport rescue (1976) **4:**560
Enugu **1:**20
environmental damage
Nigeria **1:**104
Western Pacific **8:**1014, 1074, 1134
see also climate change; deforestation
environmental protection, Antarctica **10:**1431, 1432–1433
Epupa Falls **7:***928*
Equatorial Guinea **1:**68–77
art and architecture **1:**74
climate **1:**18, 21, 68
cultural expression **1:**74
daily life **1:**75
economy **1:**70, 73, 77
education **1:**75
festivals and food **1:**74
flag **1:**69
flora and fauna **1:**22–25
geography **1:**10, 15, 17, 68
government and political parties **1:**68, 70, 72
health and welfare **1:**75
history
chronology **1:**71
modern **1:**73
independence **1:**73, 76
literature **1:**74
music **1:**74
peoples **1:**47–49, 70, 73, 74, 75

population **1:**70
religion **1:**70, 75
resources **1:**68, 77, 92
transportation and communication **1:**70
see also Bioko
Erebus, Mount **10:**1314, *1319,* 1433
Eri, Vincent Serei **8:**1106
Eritrea **4:**482–495
art and architecture **4:**487, 489–490, 493
climate **4:**444, 445, 447, 482
cultural expression **4:**489–490
daily life **4:**491–492
economy **4:**483, 494–495
flag **4:**484
flora and fauna **4:**448–451
geography **4:**436, 439, 482
geology **4:**442–443
government and political parties **4:**483–484, 486, 488
history
chronology **4:**485
modern **4:**465, 482, 487–488, 489, 492, 493, 494, 501–502, 503, 504, 514, 546
independence **4:**482, 486, 487, 488, 493, 495, 496, 504
literature **4:**489
music **4:**490
peoples **4:**467–468, 484, 491
population **4:**483
religion **4:**484, 490, 491
resources **4:**482, *494,* 495
transportation and communication **4:**484, 495
Eritrean People's Liberation Front **4:**488, 492, 493, 503, 504
Escravos River **1:**8
Esigie, ruler of Benin **1:**34
Espírito Santo, Alda Graça do **1:**136
Espiritu Santo **8:**1136, 1141
Ethiopia **4:**496–517
art and architecture **4:**454, 456, 506, 513
climate **4:**444–445, 447, 496
cultural expression **4:**505–507
daily life **4:**508–511
economy **4:**498, 514–517
education **4:**511, 513
family and society **4:**509

festivals and ceremonies **4:**507, 508

flag **4:**497

flora and fauna **4:**448–451

food and drink **4:**507

geography **4:**436–440, *442,* 496

geology **4:**442–443

government and political parties **4:**498, 500, 502, 503, 509

health and welfare **4:**510

history

  chronology **4:**499

  colonial *see* Eritrea; Italian Somaliland

  early **4:**452–456, 459–460, 463–464

  modern **4:**465, 496, 501–504, 512, 513, 514

literature **4:**505–506

music **4:**506–507

peoples **4:**467–468, 498, 509, 546

population **4:**498

religion **4:**498, 505, 508, 512

resources **4:**496, 515

transportation and communication **4:**481, 498, 513, 517

Ethiopian Highlands **4:**439–440, 452, 454

Ethiopian Orthodox Church **4:**455, 459, 464, 467, 468, 484, 490, 498, 502, 505, 506, 507, 512, 513

  Communist regime **4:**503, 508

  Eritrea **4:**491, 492

  liturgical text **4:**468, 511

Ethiopian Rift **4:**438

Ethiopian wolf **4:**450–451

Etosha National Park **7:**883, *883*

Etosha Pan **7:**883, 936, 937

eucalyptus **10:**1311, 1330, *1333*

European Union **9:**1231; **10:**1369

Evangelical Christians **3:**401, 420; **8:**1047, 1111, 1126, 1132

Evangelical Church of Polynesia **9:**1191

Évora, Cesária **2:**187, *187*

Ewe (people) **1:**47, 49; **3:**324, 328, 379, 380, 410, 417, 419, 420, 421, 423

Ewedo, ruler of Benin **1:**33

Eweka, ruler of Benin **1:**33

Ewe language **3:**328, 377

Ewuare the Great, ruler of Benin **1:**33, 34

Exhibition Building **10:**1376

Eyadéma, Étienne (later Gnassingbé Eyadéma) **3:**410, 414, 415, 416, 419, 424, 425, 426

Eyre, Edward John **10:**1350

Eyre, Lake **10:**1309, *1321,* 1322, 1343

Eyre Peninsula **10:**1304, 1308

Ezana, king of Aksum **4:**455

F

fa'a matai system **9:**1249–1250

faatele performance **9:**1281

fado singers **6:**808–809

Faidherbe, Louis **2:**172

Fairweather, Ian **10:**1375

Fakaofo Atoll **9:**1161, 1256, *1257*

Fakoly, Tiken Jah **3:**399

Fako Peak **1:**14, 17, 50

Falashas (Jewish sect) **4:**508

fale (house) **9:**1246, 1266

Falkland Islands **10:**1315, 1423, 1426

Fall, Khadi **2:**257

Family Code of 1972 (Senegal) **2:**261

famines **4:**447

  Ethiopia **4:**496, 502, 503, 504, 514, 515

  Somalia **4:**540, 547

famo music **7:**921

Fang (people) **1:**45, 46, 47–48, 68, 70, 73, 74, 75, 76, 85, 86, 88

Fante confederacy **3:**312, 313, 315, 321, 324, 328

Fante language **3:**377

Farah, Nuruddin **4:**548

farming *see* agriculture

Fasilides, emperor of Ethiopia **4:***463,* 464

Fatafehi Tu'ipelehake, prince of Tonga **9:**1264

faults **1:**17; **8:**1018

Faye, Safi **2:**258

Federation Square **10:***1401*

Felipe I, king of Ndongo **5:**599

Félix Houphouét-Boigny Stadium **3:***405*

female genital mutilation **2:**200, 213, 226, 244; **3:**342, 361, 381, 420; **4:**478, 492, 532, 550; **5:**656–657, 675

Ferguson, George Ekem **3:**326

Ferlo Plateau and Valley **2:**151

Fernando Poo *see* Bioko

ferns **9:**1170–1171

Ferreira, António Baticã **2:**224

Fiat Tagliero Building **4:***490,* 493

Field, Barron **10:**1372

Figiel, Sia **9:**1246

Fiji 9; **8:**1038–1051; **9:**1123, 1162, 1169, 1180, 1225, 1265, 1274

  art and architecture **8:**1045–1046

  chronology **8:**1041

  climate **8:**1019–1022, 1038

  cultural expression **8:**1045–1046

  daily life **8:**1047–1048

  economy **8:**1038, 1039, 1049, 1050–1051

  education **8:**1048

  family and society **8:**1045, 1047–1048

  festivals, food, and drink **8:**1045, 1046

  flag **8:**1040

  flora and fauna **8:**1023–1025

  geography **8:**1014, 1016, 1038

  geology **8:**1017–1018

  government and political parties **8:**1039, 1042, 1050

  health and welfare **8:**1048

  history

    colonial **8:**1034–1035

    early **8:**1026–1027, 1033

    modern **8:**1034, 1038, 1042, 1043–1044, 1045

    independence **8:**1038, 1043, 1044, 1046, 1049

  languages **8:**1040, 1045

  literature **8:**1045

  music **8:**1046

  New Zealand **9:**1180, 1225

  peoples **8:**1036, 1037, 1040, 1042, 1043, 1044, 1045, 1047

  population **8:**1039

  religion **8:**1040, 1043, 1046, 1047

  resources **8:**1038, 1050–1051

  Tonga **9:**1265

  transportation and communication **8:**1039–1040, 1048, 1051

  Tuvalu **9:**1274

Fijians (people) **8:**1036, 1038, 1042, 1043, 1044, 1046, 1047–1048, 1051

Filipinos, ethnic **8:**1037, 1094, 1095

film industry

  Australia **10:**1379

  Burkina Faso **3:**358, 367

  Congo-Brazzaville **5:**690

  Gabon **1:**87

  Nigeria **1:**106, 109, 129

  Senegal **2:**258, 259

financial services **6:**797, 827, 843, 859

  see also banking

Finlay, Robert **2:**175

Finn, Tim and Neil **9:**1220

Finsch, Otto **8:**1103

Fiordland **9:**1166

Fiordland National Park **9:**1172

fire dance, Samoa **9:**1247

Firestone Tire and Rubber Company **2:**237

First Anglo-Boer War **7:**893

First Congo War **5:**593, 670, 673, 678, 705

First Fleet *see* British First Fleet landing

First Liberian Civil War **2:**239

First World Festival of Black Arts **2:**259

fish and fishing

  Angola **5:**627

  Annobón **1:**15

  Antarctica **10:**1302, 1337, 1339, 1430, 1431, 1432–1433

  Australia **10:***1329,* 1334, 1411

  Benin **3:**348

  Burundi **5:***628,* 638, 644

  Cameroon **1:**63

  Cape Verde **2:**190–191

  Central African Republic **5:**660

  Comoros **6:**750, 759

  Congo, Republic **5:**696

  Congo Basin **5:***580, 582,* 594

  Djibouti **4:**481

  eastern Africa **4:**436, 439, 451, 481, 516, 528, 537–538, 553, 564, 570

  Fiji **8:**1051

  French Southern Territories **10:**1434

  Gabon **1:**87, 92

  Gambia **2:***192, 202,* 203

  Ghana **3:**309, 388

  Guinea-Bissau **2:**229

  Ivory Coast **3:**408

  Kenya **4:**528, 537–538

  Kiribati **9:**1205, 1208, 1209

  Lake Malawi **6:**786, 842

  Liberia **2:**249

fish and fishing (*continued*)
  Madagascar **6:**776
  Mauritius **6:**788, 797
  Micronesia **8:**1073
  Mozambique **6:**815
  Nauru **8:**1083
  New Zealand **9:**1172, 1173, 1176, 1177, 1185, 1234
  Nigeria **1:**12, *125*, 128
  Palau **8:**1097
  Rwanda **5:**714
  Saint Helena **7:**938
  Samoa **9:**1248, 1253, 1255
  São Tomé and Príncipe **1:***137*
  Senegal **2:**266
  Seychelles **6:**824, 826, 827
  Sierra Leon **2:***282*, 283
  Solomon Islands **8:**1134
  South Africa **7:**955, *971*, 972
  southern Africa **7:***885*, 937
  Tanzania **6:**842–843
  Togo **3:***427*
  Tonga **9:**1270, 1273
  Tuvalu **9:**1274, 1280, 1281, 1284, 1285
  Vanuatu **8:**1146
  West African coast **2:**160, *178, 190*
  Zambia **6:**858
Fisher, Andrew **10:***1365*, 1366
"flag of convenience" (Liberia) **2:**246, 249
flamingos **6:**736, *737*; **7:**883
Flinders Island **10:**1301
Flinders Mountains **10:**1304, 1308, 1309
FLNKS (Front de Libération Nationale Kanak Socialiste) **8:**1084, 1085
flooding **6:**734, 746
  Botswana **7:***904*
  Brisbane **10:**1398
  Burundi **5:**590
  Central African Republic **5:**590
  Congo, Democratic Republic of **5:**591
  Mozambique **6:**806, 813
  Senegal River **2:**148, 150
  West African coast **2:**150
  Zambia **6:**858
Flores, Paulo **5:**620
flying fox **6:**736, *757*
Fogo island **1:**24; **2:**153, 190
Foley, Fiona **10:**1375
Fon (people) **3:**322, 328, 335, 338, 339, 340, 341, 417, 419
Fongafale **9:**1279, 1280, 1283
Fonlon, Bernard **1:**58

Forbes, George William **9:**1216, 1231
forced labor **5:**604, 606, 615, 616, 626, 633, 635, 667, 679, 687; **6:**805; **8:**1034
  see also slavery
Force for Change/Democratic Movement (São Tomé and Príncipe) **1:**134, 135
forest elephants **2:**161–162
forests
  Australia **10:**1329, 1406, 1411
  bamboo **5:**595
  Benin **3:**348
  eastern Africa **4:**449, 451
  Ghana **3:**388
  New Zealand **9:**1170, 1171, 1172, 1185
  West African coast **2:**161–162
  see also deforestation; rain forest; timber
Forna, Aminatta **2:**275
Forrest, John **10:**1350
fossils **4:**452, 518; **6:**738, 750
  oldest hominid **4:**452, 453
Fourah Bay College **2:**273, 279, 280
Fourie, Johnny **7:**952
Fouta Djallon **2:**164, 166, 167–168, 209
  French control **2:**172–173, 209
  peoples **2:**176
  slave trade **2:**171
Fouta Djallon Massif **2:**148, 150, 151, 152, 156, 158
Frame, Janet **9:**1218
France **1:**30, 39, 83; **3:**312, 314, 320, 329, 373, 383; **4:**465, 487, 501, 502, 546; **5:**603, 604, 659, 682
  Afars and Issas **4:**470, 475, 479, 480
  cultural influence **5:**689, 690
  Gabon **1:**46, 78, 83, 90, 91
  Mossi system **3:**318, 350
  New Caledonia **8:**1084–1085
  Pacific exploration **9:**1181
  Polynesia **9:**1186, 1196, 1290
  semi-independent colonies **3:**395
  southern Africa **7:**890
  West African coast **2:**167, 168, 169, 170–171, 204, 263, 268, 280
  Western Pacific **8:**1032, 1033, 1034, 1037, 1084–1085, 1136, 1141, 1145, 1147
  see also Danhome; French *headings*; Ivory Coast;

Middle Congo; Senegal; Togoland; Upper Volta
Franceville **1:**88
Franco (Frank Lesokwane) **7:**909
Franco-Danhomean Wars **3:**323, 324–326, 330, 335
Franco-Hova Wars **6:**742, 745
François, Curt von **7:**897
Franklin, Miles **10:**1373
Fraser, Dawn **10:**1382
Fraser, Malcolm **10:**1370
Fraser, Peter **9:**1216
freed slave settlements **2:**174–175, 176, 179, 240
  Liberia **2:**226, 230, 234, 235–236, 247
  Sierra Leone **2:**174–175, 179, 268, 273, 275, 280
Free French Forces **1:**83, 90; **4:**475, 479; **5:**687, 694; **9:**1186
Free State **7:**868, 871, 889, 893, 971
  people **7:**900
Freetown **2:**276, *278*, 280, 283
  history **2:**169, 173, 174–175, 268, 273, 274, 275, 279, 280
Free Traders Party (Australia) **10:**1365
Frelimo (Mozambique Liberation Front) **6:**800, 804, 805–806, 809, 810, 812, 813
Fremantle **10:**1305, 1403
French Cameroon **1:**50, 55, 56, 60, 63
  economy **1:**64
  literature **1:**57–58
  Yaoundé **1:**62
French Communist Party **2:**209
French Community **3:**355, 395, 415
French Company of Senegal **1:**39; **2:**170, 171
French Congo *see* Middle Congo
French East India Company **6:**745
French Equatorial Africa **1:**46; **5:**694, 695
  Gabon **1:**78, 83, 90, 91
  see also Middle Congo; Ubangi-Shari
French Guinea **2:**172, 173, 184, 204, 209, 211, 214
French Huguenots **7:**890, 901, 957, 963
French Indian Ocean islands **6:**724, 741, 742, 745, 816, 825, 826

French language **1:**57, 58, 60, 61, 75, 80, 88; **2:**211, 257; **5:**571, 607, 636, 648, 653, 689; **6:**766, 793, 794, 824
French Polynesia **9:**1158, 1196–1197
  climate **9:**1166, 1167
  flora and fauna **9:**1170, 1173
  geography **9:**1163, 1196
  history **9:**1175, 1180, 1181, 1186, 1196
  peoples **9:**1189, 1190–1191, 1196
  religion **9:**1191, 1196
French Somaliland **4:**465, 470, 479
  see also Djibouti
French Southern Territories **6:**762; **10:**1315, 1423, 1426, 1434–1435
French Sudan **2:**173, 250, 255, 263; **3:**355
  see also Mali
French West Africa **2:**173, 209, 250, 255; **3:**350, 355, 415, 424
  Dakar **2:**263
  Ivory Coast **3:**390, 395, 406
  see also Guinea; Senegal
Frere, Bartle **7:**896
Friendship, Treaty of **9:**1258
frigate bird cult **8:**1080
FRODEBU (Front for Democracy in Burundi) **5:**632
Frontier Wars (1781–1852) **7:**891, 894
Frum, John **8:**1141, 1143
Frumentius, Saint **4:**455
Frusoni, Sergio **2:**186
Fuchs, Vivian **10:**1425
fufu (porridge) **5:**655
Fugard, Athol **7:**953
Fugitive Slave Act (1850, U.S.) **2:**235
Fugumba (holy city) **2:**167
Fula (people) *see* Fulani
Fulani (Fula) (people) **1:**10, 37, 40, 47, 50, 57, 101, 102, 103, 112, 128, 192; **2:**176–177, 198, 200, 204, 211, 212, 213, 218, 224, 226, 258; **3:**310, 318, 322, 323, 329, 341, 355, 360; **5:**608, *653*
Fulani Empire **1:**40–42, 45
Fulani jihad (1804) **1:**40, 42, 45, 47, 49, 112, 122
Fulani language **3:**328, 329, 358

Fulbe imamate **3**:311, 323
Fulbe kingdom **2**:166–167, 168, 172, 176
Fuller, Alexandra **7**:994
Funafuti Atoll **9**:*1262, 1274, 1276*, 1278, 1279, 1283
funerary art **6**:767
Funtua Plateau **1**:10
Furneaux, Tobias **10**:1346
Furphy, Joseph **10**:1373
Futa Tooro **2**:164, 166, 167, 168, 171, 172, 176
Futuna *see* Wallis and Futuna
fynbos (scrubland fine bush) **7**:885

G
Gä (people) **3**:328, 329, 379, 380, 383
Gabon **1**:78–93; **2**:173
    art and architecture **1**:85–86
    climate **1**:18, 21, 78
    cultural expression **1**:85–87
    daily life **1**:88–89
    economy **1**:78, 79, 83–84, 88, 90, 91–93
    education **1**:88, 90
    family life **1**:89
    flag **1**:79
    flora and fauna **1**:22–25
    food and drink **1**:87
    geography **1**:10, 15, 17, 78
    government and political parties **1**:80, 82, 83, 84
    health and welfare **1**:88–89
    history
        chronology **1**:81
        French rule **1**:46, 78, 83, 90, 91
        modern **1**:83–84
        nineteenth-century **1**:45–46
    independence **1**:78, 83, 90
    literature **1**:85
    music **1**:86–87
    peoples **1**:45–46, 47–49, 80, 85
    population **1**:79
    religion **1**:80, 85, 88
    resources **1**:78, 91–92
    transportation and communication **1**:80, 90, 91, 93
Gabonese Democratic Party **1**:82, 83.1.84
Gabon River **1**:90
Gaborone **7**:873, 911, 913
Gabriel's Gully **9**:*1185*
Gadarat, king of Aksum **4**:454
Gadeau, Coffi **3**:398

Gagnoa **3**:297, *392*
Gahungu, Pierre Claver **5**:637
Gainsbourg, Serge **1**:87
Gajemasu, Hausa ruler **1**:122
Galawdewos, emperor of Ethiopia **4**:464
Gallipoli Campaign (1915) **9**:1210, 1215, 1221; **10**:1366, 1380
Galmudug **4**:545, 547, 552
Gama, Vasco da **7**:890
Gambia **2**:192–203
    art and architecture **2**:*197*, 198–199, 201
    climate **2**:156–157, 192
    cultural expression **2**:198–199
    daily life **2**:200
    economy **2**:192, 193, 200, 201, 202–203
    family and society **2**:199, 200
    festivals and ceremonies **2**:198, 199, 203
    flag **2**:193
    flora and fauna **2**:160–163
    food and drink **2**:199
    geography **2**:148–153, 192
    geology **2**:154
    government and political parties **2**:194, 196, 197, 201
    health and welfare **2**:200
    history
        British rule **2**:173, 192, 197, 198, 201, 203
        chronology **2**:195
        early **2**:164–168, 171, 192
        modern **2**:197, 201, 250, 256
    independence **2**:192, 197
    literature **2**:198
    music **2**:199
    peoples **2**:176, 178, 194, 198, 200, 201
    population **2**:193, 202
    religion **2**:194, 198, 199, 200, 201
    resources **2**:192, 202
    Senegal **2**:192, 197, 250, 256
    transportation and communication **2**:194, 203
Gambia River **2**:150, 169, 170, 171, 172, 192, *194*, 197, 201, 202, 203
    slave trade **2**:192, 197, 198
Gambier Islands **9**:1163, 1186
Gamburtsev Mountains **10**:1312, 1314

game preserves *see* wildlife reserves
Gamji Gate (Kaduna) **1**:121
Ganda (people) *see* Baganda
Gan kingdom **3**:311
Gao Empire **3**:310, 317
Garcia II, king of Kongo **5**:598
Garcia IV, king of Kongo **5**:599
Garlep Dam and Reservoir **7**:868
Gauteng Province **7**:882, 888, 900, 973
    gold mine **7**:969, 971
Gaza kingdom **6**:739, 747, 805
Gbagbo, Laurent **3**:396, 397, 406
GDP (gross domestic product)
    Angola **5**:612, 625, 627
    Australia **10**:1360, 1405, 1406, 1407, 1408, 1410, 1412, 1413, 1415
    Benin **3**:331, 347, 348
    Botswana **7**:903, 912
    Burkina Faso **3**:364, 365
    Burundi **5**:630, 645
    Cameroon **1**:52, 67
    Cape Verde **2**:181, 190, 191
    Central African Republic **5**:647, 661
    Comoros **6**:751, 759
    Congo, Democratic Republic of **5**:664, 670, 681
    Congo, Republic of **5**:684, 696
    Djibouti **4**:471, 480, 481
    Equatorial Guinea **1**:70, 77
    Eritrea **4**:483, 495
    Ethiopia **4**:498, 515, 516, 517
    Fiji **8**:1039, 1050
    Gabon **1**:79, 91, 92, 93
    Gambia **2**:193, 202, 203
    Ghana **3**:371, 386, 388
    Guam **8**:1053
    Guinea **2**:206, 216, 217
    Guinea-Bissau **2**:219, 228, 229
    Ivory Coast **3**:392, 406, 407, 409
    Kiribati **9**:1199, 1208, 1209
    Lesotho **7**:924, 925
    Liberia **2**:231, 249
    Madagascar **6**:761, 773
    Malawi **6**:775, 786
    Marshall Islands **8**:1056, 1063
    Mauritius **6**:790, 797
    Mayotte **6**:799
    Micronesia **8**:1065, 1073
    Mozambique **6**:802, 815
    Namibia **7**:928, 936

    Nauru **8**:1075, 1083
    New Caledonia **8**:1085
    New Zealand **9**:1234, 1235
    Nigeria **1**:97, 127, 129
    Northern Mariana Islands **8**:1087
    Palau **8**:1097
    Reunion **6**:817
    Rwanda **5**:715
    Samoa **9**:1241, 1254, 1255
    São Tomé and Príncipe **1**:132, 139
    Senegal **2**:252, 264, 267
    Seychelles **6**:819, 827
    Sierra Leone **2**:270, 283
    South Africa **7**:969, 970, 971
    Swaziland **7**:975, 984, 985
    Tanzania **6**:830, 841
    Togo **3**:411, 426
    Tonga **9**:1259, 1271, 1272, 1273
    Tuvalu **9**:1275, 1284
    Zambia **6**:846, 857
    Zimbabwe **7**:988, 1002, 1003
Geba **2**:169, 173
Geba River **2**:151, 227
Gebre-Mehdin, Tsegaye **4**:506, 507
Gebreselassie, Haile **4**:507
Gebreyesus, Afework **4**:505
Gebry-Medhin, Tesgary **4**:506
Gedi (settlement) **4**:457, *460*
Ge'ez language **4**:453, 455, 468, 511
    alphabet **4**:505
Gelele, king of Danhome **3**:323
General Electric **8**:1079, 1083
genocide *see* Herero genocide; Rwandan genocide
Geoghegen, Edward **10**:1379
George (Siaosi) Tupou I, king of Tonga **9**:1186–1187, 1262, 1263, 1268, 1270
George, Crispin **2**:275
George, James **9**:1218
George Tupou II, king of Tonga **9**:1186, 1263
geothermal hotspots **9**:1165
Gerlache, Adrien de **10**:1353
German Cameroon *see* Kamerun
German East Africa **4**:465, 466, 523; **5**:604, 609, 628, 633, 642, 651, 698, 703, 706, 709, 712; **6**:743, 744, 745, 828, 833, 838, 839, 849
    see also Burundi; Tanzania
German immigrants **10**:1388, 1397

German New Guinea **8**:1103–1104, *1105*, 1111, 1117, 1118

German Samoa **9**:*1186*, 1187, 1192, 1216, 1240, 1245, 1249, 1252, 1254
see also Western Samoa

German South-West Africa **7**:896, 897, 901, 903, 926, 931, 932, 934, 945
Windhoek **7**:935
see also Namibia

Germany **3**:324
Nauru **8**:1074, 1079, 1080
Polynesia **9**:1186, 1187
Solomon Islands **8**:1124, 1129
see also Caroline Islands; Kamerun; Togoland

Gessesse, Tesfaye **4**:507

geysers **9**:1165

Gezo (Danhome king) **3**:322–323

Ghana **1**:38, 39, 49; **2**:164, 171, 172, 241; **3**:368–389
art and architecture **3**:377–378, 383–384, 385
climate **3**:302–305, 368
cultural expression **3**:377–379, 383–384
daily life **3**:380–382
economy **3**:370, 375, 386–389
education **3**:382
family and society **3**:380–381
festivals and ceremonies **3**:379
flag **3**:369
flora and fauna **3**:306–309
food and drink **3**:379
geography **3**:292–299, 368
geology **3**:300–301
government and political parties **3**:370, 372
health and welfare **3**:342, 381–382
history
chronology **3**:371
colonial *see* Gold Coast
early **3**:310, 311, 312, 313, 314
modern **3**:373–376, 386–387
independence **3**:368, 373, 374, 375, 385, 386
Ivory Coast **3**:396
literature **3**:374, 377
music **3**:378–379
peoples **3**:311, 327–329, 370, 377, 380, 381
population **3**:370
religion **3**:370, 377, 379, 380, 384
resources **3**:348, 368, 388
Togo **3**:417
transportation and communication **3**:367, 370, 373, 383, 385, 389

Ghana Empire **2**:164, 166; **3**:368, 374

Gibson Desert **10**:1304, 1306

Gilbertese language **8**:1037

Gilbert Islands *see* Kiribati

Gillard, Julia **10**:1371

Ginibi, Ruby Langford **10**:1373

Gio (people) **2**:239, 243

Gippsland Basin **10**:1301, 1311

giraffes **4**:448; **5**:*594*, 595

Girma, Bealu **4**:505, 506

Gitega **5**:642, 645

Gizenga, Antoine **5**:669

glaciers **9**:1159, 1165; **10**:1313, 1314, *1315*, *1320*, 1328

glass painting **2**:258, 259

global financial crisis (2008–2009) **10**:1400, 1413

global warming *see* climate change

Glorioso Islands **6**:762; **10**:1434

Glover, Denis **9**:*1218*

Glover, John **10**:1374

Gnassingbé, Faure **3**:414, *414*, 416, 425

Gnassingbé Eyadéma *see* Eyadéma, Étienne

Gobarau Minaraet **1**:*37*

Gobir (Hausa state) **1**:36, 37, 42

Godwin, Peter **7**:994

Goering, Heinrich (father) **7**:897

Goering, Hermann (son) **7**:897

gold **1**:38
Australia **10**:1305, 1306, 1311, 1349, 1358, 1385, 1400, 1405, 1406, 1409
Bismarck seabed **8**:1012
Central African Republic **5**:659
central West Africa **3**:311, 312, 313, 319, 365, 367, 407
Congo, Democratic Republic of **5**:679, 681
Congo, Republic of **5**:696
eastern Africa **4**:459, 469
Ghana **3**:372, 388, 389
migrant labor **7**:958
Mozambique **6**:810

New Zealand **9**:1184, 1185, 1191, 1215
Papua New Guinea **8**:1104, 1118, 1120
Rwanda **5**:713
Solomon Islands **8**:1134
South Africa **7**:871, 876, 893, 898, 958, 962, 965–966, 967, *969*, 971
Tanzania **6**:841
West African coast **2**:164, 166, 169, 216, 228, 247, 248, 265, 281
Zimbabwe **7**:887

Gold Coast (Australia) **10**:1310, 1398, 1399, 1413
architecture **10**:1376

Gold Coast (West Africa) **2**:171, 172, 174, 176; **3**:312, 315, 319, 322
British rule **3**:320, 321, 324–325, 326, 330, 355, 368, 373, 374, 375, 377, 383, 385, 386, 410, 415, 424
European forts **3**:313, 320, 321, 324, 325, 326, 368, 377, 383
see also Ghana

Golden Jubilee House (Accra) **3**:376, 383

Golden Stool (Ashanti symbol) **3**:314, 315, 378, 385

Goldie, George **1**:43

golf **8**:1048

Gombe **1**:42, 47

Gomes, Flora **2**:224

Gondarine style **4**:506

Gonder **4**:*463*, 464, 517

Gondwana (supercontinent) **2**:154; **4**:442–443; **9**:1164, 1170; **10**:1317, 1319, 1320, 1329, 1330, 1334

Gonzal, Jean Étienne **10**:1345

Gordimer, Nadine **7**:950

Gore-Brown, Stewart **6**:850

Gorée Island **2**:170, 171, 172, 250, 258, 262, 263
festival **2**:259

gorillas **4**:441, 451; **5**:*591*, *593*, 595
Rwanda **5**:712, 715
Uganda **4**:571

Gorton, John **10**:1369

Gouro (people) **3**:398

Gowon, Yakubu **1**:103

Goyémidé, Étienne **5**:653

Graaf-Reinet uprising (1795) **7**:891

Grace, Patricia **9**:1218

Graceland (album) **7**:953

graffiti (as art form) **1**:86

Grahamstown National Arts Festival **7**:954

grain **9**:1184; **10**:1406, 1411

Grand-Bassam **3**:398, 405

Grande Comore **6**:*751*, *752*, 753, 754, 755, 758

Grande Mosque (Kankan) **2**:*206*

Grant, James **4**:466

Granville Town *see* Freetown

Grassfields (Cameroon) **1**:57, 59

grasslands *see* savanna

Great Artesian Basin **10**:1309, 1318, 1410

Great Australian Bight **10**:1307, 1318

Great Barrier Reef **8**:1012; **9**:1181; **10**:*1308*, 1310, 1318, 1329, 1346, *1415*

Great Britain **1**:33, 39; **2**:180, 263, 273; **4**:458, 465, 501, 512
Ashanti conflict **3**:314–315, 321, 324, 326, 368, 373, 385
Basutoland **7**:914, 919, 923, 924
Bechuanaland **7**:902, 907, 911
Cape Verde **2**:180
Eritrea **4**:482, 487, 488, 489, 493, 494, 502
Fiji **8**:1043–1044, 1045, 1046, 1047, 1050
Gambia **2**:173, 192, 197, 198, 201, 203
Gilbert and Ellice Islands **9**:1161–1162, 1203, 1204, 1208, 1278, 1279
Kenya *see* British East Africa Protectorate
New Guinea **8**:1098, 1102, 1103, 1104, 1117, 1118
New Zealand and Polynesia **9**:1179, 1181, 1182–1185, 1186, 1187, 1188, 1191, 1194, 1198, 1209, 1212, 1216, 1217, 1221, 1224, 1229, 1230, 1236, 1238, 1256, 1258, 1262, 1263, 1290
Northern Rhodesia **6**:849–850, 856
Pacific exploration **9**:1181, 1194
Polynesia **9**:1186, 1187, 1188, 1198, 1236, 1238, 1256, 1258, 1262, 1263, 1290

Gun War **7**:919, 923
Gur (people) **3**:311, 320, 401
Gurara Falls **1**:*13*
Gur language **3**:311, 328, 398
Gurma (people) **3**:323
Gurmantche kingdom **3**:311
Gurunsi (people) **3**:360
Gurunsi language **3**:357
Gyaaman kingdom **3**:390

H

Habyarimana, Juvénal **5**:635, 704–705
Hadar **4**:453
Hadrawi (Muhammad Ibrahim Warsame) **4**:548
Hagos, Bahta **4**:487
Hahl, Albert **8**:1103–1104
Haidara Kontofilli (Muslim uprising) **2**:273
Haile Selassie I, emperor of Ethiopia **4**:468, 496, 502, 503, 512, 513, 514
Hajj Malick Sy, al- **2**:260
Haley, Alex **2**:198
Hall, Roger **9**:1220
Hamersley Mountains **10**:1304, 1305, 1306, 1409
Hamilton-Gordon, Arthur **8**:1043
Hankinson, Micahel **7**:953
Hanno (Carthaginian navigator) **2**:148
Hanseman, Adolf von **8**:1103
Hanson, Pauline **10**:1371
Harare **7**:875, 990, 995, 999, 1000
    climate **7**:811, 880, 999
    cultural life **7**:994, 996
    university **7**:998, 999
Harare University **7**:998, 999
Harer **4**:462, 508
Harer Massif **4**:440
harmattan wind **1**:20; **3**:302, 305
Harpur, Charles **10**:1372
Harris, Max **10**:1373
Harris, René **8**:1078
Harris, William Wade **3**:401
Hartog, Dirk **10**:1344
Harvester Judgment **10**:1365
Hassan, Muhammad Abdullah **4**:465, 546, 548
hats, grass-woven **7**:920, *921*
Hatubou, Salim **6**:756
Haud (pasture) **4**:440, 546
Hau'ofa, Epeli **9**:1265
Hausa (people) **1**:10, 40, 47, 101, 102, 103, 112, 114, 117; **3**:317

cultural expression **1**:106, 108
Kano **1**:122
Hausa city-states **1**:27, 30, 36–37, 47
Fulani jihad (1804) **1**:40, 42
haus tambaran (men's meeting house) **8**:1107
Havannah Harbour **8**:1141, 1145
Hawke, Bob **10**:1370, 1371
Haya (people) **6**:746, 747–748, 837
Hazoumé, Paul **3**:338
Head, Bessie **7**:908
Heard Island **10**:1315, 1328, 1337, 1411, 1423, 1426
Heavily Indebted Poor Countries (HIPC) program
    Burundi **5**:643
    Cameroon **1**:64
    Congo, Republic of **5**:695
    Ghana **3**:387
    Malawi **6**:785
    Mozambique **6**:813
    Rwanda **5**:713
    Tanzania **6**:841
    Zambia **6**:857
Hehe (people) **6**:739, 833
Heidelberg School (Australian art movement) **10**:1374
Heke (people) **9**:1185
Hellala Festival **9**:1267
Henderson Island **9**:1163, 1176, 1238
Henry the Navigator, prince of Portugal **1**:38; **2**:169
Henson, Bill **10**:1375
Herbertshöhe *see* Kokopo
Hereniko, Vilsoni **8**:1045
Herero (people) **7**:889, 932, 934, 935
Herero genocide **7**:897, 901, 926, 933
Hertzog, J. B. M. **7**:945, 946
Hewett, Dorothy **10**:1379
Hibiscus Festival **8**:1046
Higgins, Henry Bourne **10**:1365
highlife (musical style) **1**:108; **2**:241; **3**:379
Hima (people) **6**:747–748
Himyarite kingdom **4**:454, 455
Hindi language **8**:1045
Hinduism
    Fiji **8**:1040, 1043, 1046, 1047, 1048
    Mauritius **6**:790, 793, 794, 795, 796
    Reunion **6**:817

Seychelles **6**:820
South africa **7**:956
Tanzania **6**:837
HIP-CO (musical style) **2**:241
Hiruy, Emealf **4**:506
Hisbi Islam **4**:545
HIV/AIDS
    Angolan low rate **5**:623
    Botswana **7**:910, 912
    Burundi low rate **5**:641
    Cameroon **1**:60–61
    control programs **3**:382, 403
    Eritrea **4**:492
    Gabon **2**:189
    Gambia **2**:200
    Kenya **4**:531
    Lesotho **7**:922, 924
    Liberia **2**:244
    Malawi **6**:782–783, 785
    Mozambique **6**:810, 811, 813
    Namibia **7**:934, 936
    Nigeria **1**:116
    South Africa **7**:949, 958, 959–960, 970
    Swaziland **7**:974, 979, 982, 984
    Tanzania **6**:837, 840
    Uganda **4**:554, 566, 569
    Zambia **6**:*853*, 854, 857
    Zimbabwe **7**:995, 998, 1002
Hlane Royal National Park **7**:*974*
Hluhluwe-Umfolozi game preserve **7**:883
Hobart **10**:*1359*, 1394
Hobson, William **9**:1183
Hodgkins, Frances **9**:1219
Hodgson, Frederick **3**:315
Hoffmann, Giselher **7**:932
Hogan, P. J. **10**:1379
Holland, Sidney **9**:1216
Holmes, William **8**:1104
Holt, Harold **10**:1369, *1370*
Holyoake, Keith **9**:1216–1217
homelands *see* Bantustans
hominid fossils **4**:452, 453, 518
Hongi Hika (Maori chief) **9**:1179
Honiara **8**:1016, 1128, 1129, 1130, 1133
    crime and riots **8**:1132, 1133, 1134
Honwana, Luis Bernardo **6**:807
Hoorn Islands **9**:1162, 1290
Hope, A. D. **10**:1373
Horn of Africa **4**:436, 438, 448, 452, 462, 487, 546, 551

horse racing **10**:1401
horticulture *see* agriculture
Hotel Rwanda (film) **5**:712
Houngbo, Gilbert **3**:414, 416
Houphouët-Boigny, Félix **3**:390, 395–396, 404, 406
House of Slaves (Gorée) **2**:*171*, 263
Hova (people) **6**:742, 766, 771
Hove, Chenjerai **7**:994
Howard, Daniel Edward **2**:236
Howard, John **10**:1371
Howland Island **9**:*1288*
    geography **9**:1163, 1286
Huambo **5**:583, 589, 615, 617, 623
    reconstruction **5**:620
Hughes, William Morris ("Billy") **10**:1367
Hughes doctrine (1924) **10**:1425
Huila Plateau **5**:583
Hulme, Keri **9**:1218
human rights abuses
    Burundi **5**:640
    Central African Republic **5**:652, 656
    Congo, Democratic Republic of **5**:*670*
    Congo Free State **5**:606, 667, 677
    Eritrea **4**:492
    Gambia **2**:200
    Guinea **2**:210
    Liberia **2**:238, 239, 243
    Malawi **6**:779
    Sierra Leone **2**:274, 278
    Somalia **4**:554
    South Africa **7**:946, 947, 949
    Uganda **4**:561
    see also apartheid; Herero genocide; Rwandan genocide; war crimes
Hummay (Sayfawa ruler) **1**:28
Hunter, Lucilda **2**:275
Hunter River and Valley **10**:1310, 1402
Huon Peninsula **8**:1015, 1026, 1103
hurricanes **9**:1274
Hussein, Ebrahim **6**:835
Hut Tax War **2**:273
Hutu (people) **5**:599, 628, 630, 632, 713
    Burundi violence **5**:634–635, 638, 639, 642, 643, 644
    colonial policies **5**:609, 633, 642, 703, 704, 709, 711
    Congo Wars **5**:670
    language **5**:636

percentage in Rwanda **5:**706,
709
Rwandan genocide **5:**670,
698, 704–705, 709, 712
Rwandan government **5:**702
Hwange National Park **7:***875*
Hyde, Robin **9:**1218
hydroelectric power
Australia **10:**1368, 1401,
1406
eastern Africa **4:**440, 441,
512, 515, 537, 569, 570;
6:724
Malawi **6:**785–786
Mozambique **6:**813–814
southern Africa **7:**871, *925,*
1003
Zambia **6:**857

I
Ialá, Lumba **2:**228
Ibadan **1:**13, 20, 120
Ibibio (people) **1:**12, 49
Ibn Battuta **6:**740
Ibo (people) **1:**12, 47, *48,* 101,
102, 103, 112, 114, 115,
117
Ibrahim, Abdullah **7:**952
Ibrahim Nikale, Kanem ruler
1:29, 30
Ibrahim Njoya, Bamum ruler
1:57
icebergs **10:**1312, 1431
ice sheets **10:**1312, 1313, 1319,
1320, 1326, 1336, 1432
melting **10:**1328, 1418, 1425
ice shelves **10:**1313, 1328,
1353
Idris Katakarmabi, Bornu ruler
1:29
Idros Alooma, Bornu ruler
1:29–30
Ifat **4:**462, 464
Ife (Ile-Ife) **1:**27, 31, 32, 106
Igbo (people) *see* Ibo
Igbo Ukwu **1:**27
Igodo, Ogiso ruler **1:**33
Ihimaera, Witi **9:**1218
I-Kiribati (people) **9:**1204,
1205, 1206
Ilboudo, Monique **3:**357
Ile-Ife *see* Ife
ilmenite **6:**773, 815
Iloilo, Josefa **8:**1044
"imaginary voyages" literature
10:1372
Imbangala (people) **5:**599
Imbokodvo National
Movement **7:**979
Inácio, Luiz **3:**334

Indénié kingdom **3:**390
indentured labor **6:**788, 793,
823; **8:**1037, 1038, 1043,
1047
Indian immigrants *see* South
Asians
Indian Ocean **6:**724, 732–734;
7:870
Antarctica **10:**1411, 1423,
1426
East Africa **4:**438, 443, 449,
457, 459, 469, 475, 481,
535, 547
Portuguese-Dutch rivalry
7:890
southern Africa **7:**870, 883,
890
trade routes **6:**740, 741, 748
tsunami **6:**826
Indian Ocean islands **6:**724,
726, 729, 741, 745, 816,
825, 826
climate **6:**732–733, 734
endemic species **6:**735,
736–737
European annexation **6:**745
French colonies **6:**741, 742,
788
peoples **6:**746, 748
slave trade **6:**744
volcanism **6:**731
see also British Indian Ocean
Territory; Comoros;
Madagascar; Mauritius;
Reunion; Seychelles
Indo-Australian Plate **9:**1164,
1165
Indo-Fijians **8:**1037, 1038,
1042, 1043, 1044, 1045,
1046, 1047, 1048, 1050
Indonesia (formerly Dutch East
Indies) **8:**1033, 1034,
1103; **9:**1180; **10:**1300,
1308, 1344, 1345
Indonesians **6:**748, 750, 760,
766, 769, 816
industry and services
Angola **5:**624, 627
Australia **10:**1305, 1310, 1396,
1397, 1398, 1401, 1402,
1405, 1406, 1411–1413
Benin **3:**348
Botswana **7:**912–913
Burkina Faso **3:**363,
366–367
Burundi **5:**644
Cameroon **1:**66
Cape Verde **2:**189, 191
Central African Republic
5:660

Comoros **6:**758, 759
Congo, Democratic Republic
of **5:**677, 680
Congo, Republic of **5:**694,
696
Djibouti **4:**480, 481
Eritrea **4:**493, *494,* 495
Ethiopia **4:**512–513, 517
Gabon **1:**90, 93
Gambia **2:**203
Ghana **3:**383, 385, 389
Guinea **2:**217
Guinea-Bissau **2:**229
Ivory Coast **3:**405, 409
Kenya **4:**525, 533, 535, 536,
537, 538
Kiribati **9:**1209
Lesotho **7:**923, 924–925
Liberia **2:**246, 249
Madagascar **6:**773
Malawi **6:**786
Mauritius **6:**796, 797
Mozambique **6:**812, 815
Namibia **7:**935, 937
New Zealand **9:**1225, 1229,
1230, 1231, *1232,* 1233,
1234–1235, 1235
Nigeria **1:**120, 121, 123, 124,
126, 128–129
Rwanda **5:**712, 714–715
Samoa **9:**1254, 1255
São Tomé and Príncipe **1:**139
Senegal **2:**263, 264, 265,
266
Sierra Leone **2:**283
Somalia **4:***552,* 553
South Africa **7:**871, 962, 963,
964, 965–966, 972
Swaziland **7:**983, 985
Tanzania **6:**839, 843
Togo **3:**423, 426–427
Tonga **9:**1273
Tuvalu **9:**1284
Uganda **4:**567, 570–571
Zambia **6:**855, 859
Zimbabwe **7:**999, 1003
influenza **9:**1181, 1182, 1245
Instituto Cardenal Cisneros
1:75
Interahamwe **5:**698, 705, 712
International Art and Craft Fair
see SIAO
International Court of Justice
1:56; **2:**239
International Criminal
Tribunal **5:**707
International Geophysical Year
(1947–1958) **10:**1425, 1430
International Labor
Organization **1:**60

International Monetary Fund
Benin **3:**336, 346–347
Burkina Faso **3:**364–365
Burundi **5:**643
Cameroon **1:**56, 64
Cape Verde **2:**185
Congo, Republic of **5:**695
Ghana **3:**386, 387
Guinea **2:**216
Ivory Coast **3:**403
Kenya **4:**536, 537
Madagascar **6:**772
Mozambique **6:**813
Nigeria **1:**125, 126
Rwanda **5:**713
São Tomé and Príncipe **1:**135
Senegal **2:**264
Seychelles **6:**827
Sierra Leone **2:**281
Tanzania **6:**834, 840
Uganda **4:**561, 568
Zambia **6:**855
International Whaling
Commission **10:**1432
Internet suffix sale **9:**1274,
1284
Intertropical Convergence
Zone (ITCZ) **1:**18;
3:302–303; **4:**444; **5:**588
Intore Dance Troupe **5:**707
INXS (rock band) **10:**1378
Inyanga Mountains **7:**870, 875
Ipeko-Etomane, Faustin-Albert
5:653
Iraq invasion (1993) **6:**749
Ireland, Kevin **9:**1218
Irish immigrants **10:**1349,
1357, 1387, 1405, 1406
iron ore
Australia **10:**1305, 1409,
1414
Benin **3:**347
Congo, Democratic Republic
of **5:**679
Guinea **2:**216
Ivory Coast **3:**407
Liberia **2:**238, 240, 247, 248,
249
Sierra Leone **2:**273, 281
West Africa **2:**154, 164
irrigation
Australia **1:***1411;* **10:**1305,
1309, 1311, 1410, *1411*
Ethiopia **4:**453
Iru (people) **6:**747, 748
Isandiwana, Battle of (1879)
7:894, 896
Isegawa, Moses **4:**562
Islam **1:**36, 48, 49; **5:**599
Australia **10:**1384, 1385

Islam (*continued*)
Benin **3:**332, 335, 339, 341, 342
Bono **3:**313
Burkina Faso **3:**352, 358, 359, 360, 361, 363
Burundi **5:**639
Cameroon **1:**52, 60, *61*
Central African Republic **5:**648, 656
Comoros **6:**752, 755, 756, 757, 758
Congo, Democratic Republic of **5:**664, 674, 675
Congo, Republic of **5:**684, 692
Djibouti **4:**470, 472, 476, 477, 478
eastern Africa **4:**455, 456, 467
eastern Central Africa **6:**740, 741, 742, 747, 748
Eritrea **4:**484, 490, 491, 493
Ethiopia **4:**463, 464, 496, 498, 502, *503*, 505, 508, 510, 512
Fiji **8:**1040, 1043, 1046, 1047, 1048
Fulani **1:**40–42, 45, 47
Fulani jihad **3:**310, 322, 323, 329
Gabon **1:**80, 88, *89*
Gambia **2:**194, 198, 199, 200
Ghana **3:**370, 379, 380
Guinea **2:**204, 206, 211, 212, 213
Guinea-Bissau **2:**225, 226
Hausa **1:**27, 36, 37, 40, 47
holidays **1:**59, 110; **3:**379, 400, 419
Ivory Coast **3:**390, 392, 397, 399, 401, 402, 406
Kanem-Bornu **1:**28, 29, 30
Kenya **4:**457, 460–461, 518, 520, 529
Liberia **2:**232, 243
Malawi **6:**782
Mauritius **6:**790, 795
Mayotte **6:**798, 799
Mossi Empire **3:**312, 318
Mozambique **6:**802, 810
Nigeria **1:**36, 97, 101, 102, 104, 112, 113, 114, 115, 119, 121, 122, 129
Rwanda **5:**700, 710, 712
Senegal **2:**250, 252, 257, 259, 260, 261, *262*
Sierra Leone **2:**270, 273, 277, 278
Sokoto **1:**10, 30

Somalia **4:**504, 529, 540, 542, 545, 547, 549, 550
Somalis **4:**440, 462, 464, 465, 467, 546, 548
South Africa **7:**956, 957
Swahilis **4:**459, *460*, 469
Swaziland **7:**976, 982
Tanzania **6:**830, 837
Togo **3:**412, 419, 420, 421
Uganda **4:**556, 560, 565
West African coast **2:**164–165, 166, 167–168, 172, 174, 177, 178
Zanzibar **6:**748
see also jihad; mosques; Sharia; Sufism
Islamic brotherhoods **2:**260–261
Israel (ancient) **4:**452
Israel (modern) **4:**560
Issa (people) **4:**470, 474, 475, 476–477, 478
Italian immigrants **10:**1357, 1388, 1401, 1403, 1405
Italian Somaliland **4:**482, 487, 488, 493, 502, 512, 540, 546, 548, 551, 552
Ivanga, Imunga **1:**87
ivory **4:**454; **5:**599, 600, 606, 651, 687; **7:**887, 889
carving **5:**619
Ivory Coast **2:**173, 178, 239; **3:**390–409
art and architecture **3:**398–399, 405
climate **3:**302–305, 390
cultural expression **3:**398–400
daily life **3:**401–403
economy **3:**386, 392, 402, 406–408
education **3:**403
family and society **3:**401–402
festivals and ceremonies **3:**400
flag **3:**391
flora and fauna **3:**306–309
food and drink **3:**400
geography **3:**292–299, 390
geology **3:**300–301
government and political parties **3:**392, 394, 404
health and welfare **3:**402–403, 407
history
chronology **3:**393
civil war **3:**397, 400, 401, 406, 407
early kingdoms **3:**310, 311, 312, 321, 390

French control **3:**324, 325, 326, 355, 364, 390, 395, 396, 397, 398, 400, 406
modern **3:**390, 395–397
independence **3:**395–396, 404, 406
Liberian rebels **2:**239
literature **3:**398
music **3:**399–400
peoples **3:**311, 323, 327–329, 392, 398, 401, 407
population **3:**391
religion **3:**392, 401, 402, 404
resources **3:**390, 407
transportation and communication **3:**367, 392, 404, 405, 409
Ivory Coast Plateau **3:**295–296
Iyasu V, emperor of Ethiopia **4:**502

J

Jacinto, António **5:**619
Jaja, Opobo ruler **1:**43
Jamaica **2:**268, 273; **4:**502
James Island **2:**171
Jameson, Leander **7:**898
Jamieson, Trevor **10:**1379
Jammeh, Yahya **2:**196, 197
Janszoon, Willem **10:**1300, 1344
Japan **8:**1034, 1035, 1052, 1054, 1059, 1064, 1069, 1073, 1074, 1079, 1080, 1086, 1093, 1094, 1098, 1105, 1117, 1118, 1124, 1129, 1133; **9:**1198, 1203, 1208
Jarvis Island **9:**1163, 1286
Jawara, Dawda Karaiba **2:**196, 197
jazz **2:**277; **7:**952, 995
Jeannot, Koudou **3:**401
Jefferson, Thomas **2:**175
Jentsch, Adolph **7:**933
Jesuits **4:**464
Jesus, Fort **4:***518*, 535
Jews **7:**956, 957; **9:**1191, 1223; **10:**1385
Ethiopia **4:**508
jihad **1:**30, 37
Fulani (1804) **1:**40, 42, 45, 47, 49, 112, 122
Somali **4:**465, 546, 548
Jinja **4:**441, 570, 571
João I, king of Kongo **5:**598, 600, 602
Johannesburg **7:**871, 882, 952, 964, 965–966, 972, 973
John II, king of Portugal **5:**600

John IV, emperor of Ethiopia **4:**501
John Frum Movement **8:**1141, 1143
John Paul II, Pope **3:**396, 404
Johnson, Colin **10:**1373
Johnson, Lemuel **2:**275
Johnson-Sirleaf, Ellen **2:***234*, 239
Johnston Atoll **9:**1163, 1286, 1288
Jola (people) **2:**258, 260, 261
Jolof (people) **2:**165–166, 250, 263
Jonathan, Leabua **7:**914, 919
Jones, Lloyd **9:**1218
Jos Plateau **1:**10, 20, 26, 47, 127
Jos State **1:**42, 113
Joubert, Piet **7:**893
Juan de Nova Island **6:**762
Jubba River **4:**440, 553
Jugnauth, Aneerood **6:**793
juju (musical style) **1:**108
Jukun (people) **1:**47, 48
Julio Escudero Station **10:**1429
Juluka (duo) **7:**953
Jumbam, Kenjo wan **1:**58
Júnior, António Assis **5:**619

K

Kaabu kingdom **2:**164, 166, 172, 179
slave trade **2:**171
Kaarpvaal craton **7:**876
Kaarta territory **2:**168
Kabbah, Ahmad Tejan **2:**274
Kabila, Joseph **5:**666, 670
Kabila, Laurent-Désiré **4:**561; **5:**618, 662, *669*, 670, 673, 705
Kaboré, Gaston **3:**358
Kabua, Amata **8:**1058
Kabua, Imata **8:**1058
Kaburahe, Antoine **5:**636
Kabuto, Daniel **5:**636
Kabye (Kabre) (people) **3:**328, 417, 420
Kachamba, Daniel **6:**781
Kadavu pottery **8:**1045
Kaduna riots **1:**121
Kaduna River **1:**8, 121
Kagame, Alexis **5:**706
Kagame, Paul **5:***702*, 705
Kainji Lake National Park **1:**24
Kainji Reservoir **1:**8, 10
Kakadu National Park **10:**1305, *1325*
Kakala, Sofele **9:***1267*
kakapo (parrot) **9:**1171, 1177

Kalabari **1**:27
Kalahari Basin **5**:583
Kalahari Desert **5**:583, 590;
    7:868, 870, 872–873, 874,
    878–879, 883, 884
Kalanga (people) **7**:908, 910
Kalenjin (people) **4**:468–469,
    528, 530
Kalep, king of Aksum **4**:455
Kalonji, Albert **5**:669
Kaloum Peninsula **2**:152, 214
Kamabalda **10**:1409
Kamanda, Kama **5**:672
Kamatari, Esther **5**:636
Kamerun (German Cameroon)
    1:46, 50, 55, 57, 59, 60,
    62, 63, 64, 83
Kampala **4**:441, 457, 535, 567,
    571
  architecture **4**:562
  climate **4**:447
  history **4**:560, 567
Kane, Cheikh Hamidou **2**:257
Kanem-Bornu empire **1**:27,
    28–30, 36
Kanemi, Mohammed el Amin
    al- **1**:30
Kanemiyin dynasty **1**:30
Kanem kingdom **1**:28, 29, 30,
    36
kangaroos **10**:*1330*, 1332, 1410
Kankan **2**:*206*, 217
Kano (city) **1**:10, 20, 21, 29,
    106, 122
Kano (Hausa state) **1**:36, 37,
    42, 47
Kano Market Literature **1**:105
Kansala (city) **2**:166
Kanté, Mory **2**:212
KANU (Kenyan African National
    Union) **4**:522, 524, 525
Kanuri dynasty **1**:29, 30
Kaoze, Stefano **5**:671
Kapingamarangi **8**:1030, 1037
Kappata, Stephen **6**:851
Kapsiki Peak **1**:11, *12*
Karamoko (Muslim leader)
    2:167
Kariba, Lake **6**:724, 727, 746,
    857, 858; **7**:883
Kariba Dam **6**:850, 857;
    7:1002, *1003*
Karisimbi, Mount **5**:585
Kariuki, J. M. **4**:525
Karnu (religious leader) **5**:651
karoo (semidesert) **7**:870, 872,
    877, 885, 891
Karre Mountains **5**:584
karst landscape **6**:728, *729*;
    10:1307

Karthala, Mount, eruption
    6:*751*
Karume, Abeid Amani (father)
    6:834
Karume, Amani Abeid (son)
    6:*834*
Kasai **5**:603, 604, 669
Kasai River **5**:583
Kasavubu, Joseph **5**:667, 668,
    669
Kassa Mercha *see* John IV
Kassena (people) **3**:311, 358
Katanga Plateau **5**:583, 590
Katanga provinces **5**:596, 599,
    605–606, 668, 669, 673,
    679; **6**:739
Katsina (city) **1**:10
Katsina (Hausa state) **1**:36, 37,
    42, 47
Kauage, Mathias **8**:1107
Kaunda, Kenneth **6**:844, 849,
    850, 853
kava **8**:1046, 1146–1147
Kavango River **7**:883
Kawa **1**:29
Kayibanda, Grégoire **5**:704
Kayor kingdom **2**:166, 172
Kazembe I, king of Kazembe
    6:739
Kazembe IV, king of Kazembe
    6:739
Kazembe kingdom **6**:739, 844
Keating, Paul **10**:1370–1371
Kebbi **1**:42, 47
Kebra negast (Ethiopian myth
    collection). **4**:463–464, 505
Keïta, Modibo **2**:255
Keita, Souleymane **2**:258
Kele (people) **1**:46
Kemakeza, Allan **8**:1134
Keneally, Thomas **10**:1373,
    1379
Kenemiyin dynasty **1**:30
Kenilorea, Peter **8**:1129, 1130
Kennedy, Peter **10**:1375
Kente, Gibson **7**:953
kente cloth **3**:378, 385, 389
Kentridge, William **7**:951
Kenya **4**:518–539; **5**:705
  art and architecture
    4:526–527
  climate **4**:444, 445–446,
    447, 518
  cultural expression
    4:526–528
  daily life **4**:529–532
  economy **4**:520, 536–539
  education **4**:532
  family and society **4**:530,
    531

  festivals and ceremonies
    4:528
  flag **4**:519
  flora and fauna **4**:448–451
  food and drink **4**:528
  geography **4**:436–441, *443*,
    518
  geology **4**:442–443
  government and political
    parties **4**:469, 518, 520,
    522, 536, 537
  health and welfare **4**:531
  history
    chronology **4**:521
    colonial *see* British East
      Africa Protectorate
    modern **4**:468, 469, 518,
      523–525
    precolonial **4**:453,
      457–458, 460, 518
  independence **4**:518, 523,
    525, 536
  literature **4**:526
  music **4**:527
  peoples **4**:457–458, 467,
    468–469, 520, 526, 528,
    530, 534, 546
  population **4**:520
  religion **4**:520, 529
  resources **4**:518, 537
  transportation and
    communication **4**:520,
    534, 539
Kenya, Mount **4**:439, 440,
    443, 446, 451, 469, 523
Kenyan African National
    Union *see* KANU
Kenyatta, Jomo **4**:469, 518,
    524–525, 528, 534
Kérékou, Mathieu **3**:330, 334,
    336, 346–347
Kerguelen Islands **10**:1315,
    1337, 1434
Kerr, John **10**:1370
Ketu (people) **1**:31
Keur Massar **2**:262
kewela music **6**:781
Key, John **9**:1217
Kezilahabi, Euphrase **6**:835
Kgalagadi Transfrontier Park
    7:885
Khalam (music group) **2**:258
Khalid bin Barghash **6**:743
Khama, Ian **7**:*906*, 907
Khama, Seretse **7**:907, 909
Khama III, Tswama **7**:902
khat (qat) **4**:*476*, 478, 553
Khoisan (people) **7**:888, 891,
    892, 901, 902, 908
Kibaki, Mwai **4**:525, 532, *558*

Kibara Mountains **5**:583
Kidjo, Angélique **3**:*338*, 339
Kidude, Bi **6**:836
Kifle, Yonas **4**:*489*
Kigali **5**:642, 705, 706, 708,
    709, 711, 712, 713, 715
Kigali Memorial Center **5**:*704*,
    712
Kigeli V, king of Ruanda-
    Burundi **5**:704
Kikongo language **5**:619, 684,
    689
Kikuyu (people) **4**:468, 469,
    524, 525, 526, 530, 534;
    6:746, 748
  churches **4**:529
  rain-making ceremony **4**:528
Kilimanjaro, Mount **6**:726,
    730, *731*, 733, 736, 843
  European explorers **6**:744
Kilimanjaro National Park
    6:*836*
Kilwa **6**:740–741, 743, 828
Kimbangu, Simon **5**:674, 692
Kimbanguist church
    5:674–675, 692
Kimberley, siege of
    (1899–1900) **7**:898
Kimberley mine **7**:893, 898,
    971
Kimberley Mountains **10**:1304,
    1305
Kimbundu (people) **5**:607,
    608, 612
Kimbundu languages **5**:608,
    619
Kinaxixi Market **5**:620
King, Charles D. B. **2**:237
King Ezana's Stele **4**:454
King Fahd Mosque **2**:198, *200*,
    201
King Jimmy's Watering Place
    2:280
Kingman Reef **9**:*1161*, 1163,
    1285, 1288
King movement (Maori)
    9:1185
king protea (South African
    national flower) **7**:885
King Toffa's Palace **3**:339, 345
Kinigi, Sylvie **5**:635
Kinshasa **5**:580, 583, *669*,
    675, 677, 681, 697
  architecture **5**:672
  climate **5**:590, 592
  cultural exchanges **5**:671
  history **5**:604, 606, 667, 670,
    677, 694
  music scene **5**:590, 673,
    689, 690

Kinyarwanda language **5**:609, 661, 671, 700, 703, 706
Kiowa Island **8**:1047
Kippel, Robert **10**:1375
Kirdi (people) **1**:45, 57
Kiribati **9**:1198–1209
　art and architecture **9**:*1202*, 1204
　climate **9**:1167
　climate change threat **9**:1169, 1203
　cultural expression **9**:1204–1205
　cyclones **9**:1166
　daily life **9**:1206
　economy **9**:1199, 1208–1209
　family and society **9**:1206
　festivals, food, and drink **9**:1205
　flag **9**:1199
　flora and fauna **9**:1173
　geography **9**:1161, 1163, 1198, 1204
　geology **9**:1165
　government and political parties **9**:1200, 1202
　history
　　chronology **9**:1201
　　modern **9**:1198, 1203, 1208
　independence **9**:1202, 1203
　languages **9**:1191, 1200, 1204
　literature **9**:1204
　music **9**:1204–1205
　peoples **9**:1189, 1190, 1198, 1200, 1204
　population **9**:1199
　religion **9**:1190, 1200, 1206, 1207
　resources **9**:1198, 1209
　transportation and communication **9**:1200, 1209
Kiritimati **9**:1161
Kirk, Norman **9**:1217
Kirundi *see* Rundi language
Kisangani **5**:580, 583, 669, 677, 681, 688
Kisumu **4**:436, 445
Kitchener, Lord **7**:899
Kivu, Lake **5**:585, *586*, *698*, 713, 714
Kiwanuka, Benedicto **4**:560
kiwi bird **9**:1171
Ki-Zerbo, Joseph **3**:357
Klira Dam **4**:569
Klusubi Royal Tombs **4**:562
Kngwarreye, Emily **10**:1375
koalas **10**:1332

Kodjo, Agbéyomé **3**:416
Kodjo, Edem **3**:416
Kodjo, Michel **3**:398
Koffigoh, Joseph Kokou **3**:416
Kokopo **8**:1103, 1116, 1117
Kolelas, Bernard **5**:692
Kolingba, André **5**:652
Kolone, Va'ai **9**:1253
Kolonia **8**:1019, 1072
Kombuis, Koos **7**:953
Koné, Tanella **3**:398
Kong (people) **3**:310
Kong empire **3**:311, 390
Kong Mosque **3**:399
Kongo (people) **5**:597, 607, 608, 667, 674, 687, 690, 692
　art and architecture **5**:*599*, 600
Kongo kingdom **5**:580, 597–599, 600–602, 603, 608, 610, 615, 656, 662, 671, 674, 682
Kongo language **5**:607, 664, 671
Konigstein Peak **7**:874, 926
Kono (people) **2**:178, 275, 278
Kony, Joseph **4**:561
Koobi Fora site **4**:453
kookaburras **10**:1334
Korean War **10**:1369, 1380
Koroma, Ernest Bai **2**:*272*, 274
Koroma, Johnny-Paul **2**:274
Koror **8**:1015, *1090*, 1093, 1096
Kosciuszko, Mount **10**:1311
Kosrae **8**:1031, 1064, 1069, 1070, 1071
Kosraean language **8**:1037, 1070, 1071
Kossi, Agbagli **3**:418
Koteba Ensemble **3**:400
Kotokoli (people) **3**:420
Koudougou **3**:362, 367
Koulibaly, Isaïe Biton **3**:398
Koumba, Henri **1**:87
Kourouma, Ahmadou **3**:398
Kouyaté, Lansana **2**:210
Kpelle (people) **2**:178, 213, 240, 243
Kramer, Daniel **7**:953
krar (musical instrument) **4**:506
Kreol language **6**:824
Kribi **1**:67
krill **10**:1302, 1337, 1338, 1339, 1430, 1432–1433
Krio (Creole) **2**:175, 179, 240, 273, 275, 278, 279, 280
Kru (people) **2**:178, 236, 237, 240, 243; **3**:401

Kruger, Paul **7**:*892*, 893, 898, 962
Kruger National Park **7**:871, *880*, *882*, 883, 889
Kru linguistic group **3**:328, 398
Kuba kingdom **5**:597
Kubandwa festival **5**:638
Kufuor, John Agyekum **3**:*372*, 376
Kukawa **1**:30
Kumalo, Mzilikazi **7**:953
Kumasi **3**:295, *370*, 381, 385, 389
　history **3**:314, 315, 324, 385
　Peace Pole **3**:*379*
Kumbi (city) **2**:164
Kunama language **4**:489, 491
Kunta Kinte **2**:198
Kuoh-Moukoury, Thérèse **1**:58
Kuti, Fela Anikulapo **1**:108
Kuti, Femi **1**:*109*
Kutusi Royal Tombs **4**:457
Kwajalein **8**:1059
Kwaku Dua III Asamu, king of Ashanti **3**:326
Kwa linguistic group **3**:328, 398
Kwame Nkrumah University **3**:*379*, 382, 385
Kwanyama *see* Ovambo
kwasa-kwasa (rhumba form) **7**:909
KwaZulu-Natal **7**:870–871, *873*, 879, 964
　climate **7**:881
　family life **7**:958
　flora and fauna **7**:883
　history **7**:895
　peoples **7**:888, 889, 900, 951, 957
　tourism **7**:972
Kwinana **10**:1305, 1403
Kyushu-Palau Ridge **8**:1018

L

La Digue Island **6**:729, *820*
Ladysmith, siege of (1899–1900) **7**:898
Ladysmith Black Mambazo (group) **7**:953
Lae **8**:1113, 1121
lagoons **1**:23; **3**:294, 309, 349, 405
Lagos **1**:13, 20, 21, 103–104, 119, 123–124, 129; **3**:294, 324
　architecture **1**:107
　history **1**:34, 38, 43, 100, 123–124
　population **1**:13, 123

Laird, Macgregor **1**:43
lakes *see key word*
Lalibela **4**:439, 456, 506, 517
Lalibela, emperor of Ethiopia **4**:456
Laluah, Auqah (G. M. Casely-Hayford) **2**:275
Lamb, William, Viscount Melbourne **10**:1400
Lambaréné **1**:88
lamb production **9**:1184, 1231, *1233*, 1234
Lami **8**:1049
Lamizana, Sangoulé **3**:355
Lamu **4**:441, 457, *527*, 538
Lancaster House Agreement (1979) **7**:992
land mines **5**:618, 626; **6**:806, 810
Lange, David **9**:1217, 1233
language groups **1**:26, 45, 47–49, 52, 57; **3**:327–329, 398; **5**:607, 609, 619
　see also Bantu languages; Swahili language
Langue de Barbarie National Park **2**:*165*, *168*
Lapita culture **8**:1026–1027, *1028*, 1029; **9**:1174; **10**:1026–1027
Larsen Ice Shelf **10**:*1312*, 1314
Latte period **8**:1030
Lattier, Christian **3**:398
Lau Islands **8**:1027
Laver, Rod **10**:1382
Lawler, Ray **10**:1379
Lawson, Henry **10**:1372–1373
Laye, Camara **2**:211
Layen (Islamic brotherhood) **2**:260
League of Nations **3**:415, 424; **9**:1216
　Australia **10**:1367
　Liberia **2**:237
　mandates **9**:1187, 1240, 1245
　trusteeships **1**:50, 55; **5**:628, 633, 698, 703, 712; **6**:828, 833, 838, 839; **8**:1035, 1054, 1059, 1064, 1069, 1074, 1079, 1086, 1093, 1098, 1104, 1105
Leahy, Michael James **8**:1104
Leakey, Richard **4**:453
Lealofi, Tupua Tamasese **9**:1253
Lebna Dengel, emperor of Ethiopia **4**:464
Lebombo Mountains **7**:870, 871
Lebou (people) **2**:260, 263

Le Clézio, Jean-Marie Gustave **6**:794
Le Guma, Alex **7**:950
Leh, Abdallah **4**:476–477
Leichhardt, Ludwig **10**:1350
Lekhanya, Justin **7**:919
Leluh site **8**:1031
Lemma, Mengistu **4**:506, 507
lemurs **6**:*735*, 737
Leo Africanus (Joannes Leo Africanus) **1**:37
Leopold II, king of the Belgians **3**:325; **5**:599, 603, 604, 605–606, *606*, 662, 677
Léopoldville *see* Kinshasa
Leshoal, B. L. **7**:920
Lesotho **7**:914–925
  art and architecture **7**:920–921, 923
  climate **7**:878, 879, 914, 923
  cultural expression **7**:920–921
  daily life **7**:922
  economy **7**:915, 924–925, 936
  family and society **7**:922
  festivals, food, and drink **7**:921
  flag **7**:915
  geography **7**:868–871, 914
  government and political parties **7**:915–916
  health, welfare, education **7**:922
  history
    chronology **7**:917
    modern **7**:907, 914, 918, 919, 923, 924
    precolonial **7**:896, 914
  independence **7**:914, 918, 919, 923
  languages **7**:916, 920
  literature **7**:920
  music **7**:921
  peoples **7**:900, 916, 920, 921, 922
  population **7**:915
  religion **7**:916, 922
  resources **7**:914, 924
  transportation and communication **7**:916, 923, 925
Letsie III, ruler of Lesotho **7**:914, 919, 921
Liberal-Country Party (Australia) **10**:1407
Liberal Party (Australia) **10**:1364, 1368, 1369, 1370, 1371, 1407
Liberia **2**:230–249; **3**:396
  art and architecture **2**:240–241

climate **2**:157–158, 159, 230
cultural expression **2**:240–241
daily life **2**:243–245
economy **2**:231, 237, 238, 247–249
education **2**:245, 246
family and society **2**:243–244
festivals and ceremonies **2**:241
flag **2**:231
flora and fauna **2**:160–163
food and drink **2**:241
geography **2**:148, 152–153, 230
geology **2**:154
government and political parties **2**:231, 234
health and welfare **2**:244–245, 246
history
  chronology **2**:233
  founding **2**:170, 172, 174, 175, 176, 179, 230–236, 240, 246
  modern **2**:237–239, 240, 247, 268
independence **2**:230, 236
literature **2**:240
music **2**:241
peoples **2**:178, 179, 232, 239, 243
population **2**:230
religion **2**:232, 243
resources **2**:230, 247–248
Sierra Leone **2**:239, 240, 268
transportation and communication **2**:232, 246, 249
Liberian civil war **2**:215, 230, 237, 239, 240, 246, 247, 248, 249
social upheaval **2**:243, 245, *247*
Liberians United for Reconciliation and Democracy **2**:239
Liberty Party (Liberia) **2**:234
Libreville **1**:15, 21, 46, 78, 84, 85, 86–87, *89*, 90
Light, William **10**:1397
Lij Kasa *see* Theodore II
Likiep Island **8**:1016
Liking, Werewere **1**:58; **3**:400
Likoma Island **6**:781, 782
Lilanga, George **6**:835
Lilburn, Douglas **9**:1220
Lilongwe **6**:727, 781, 784, 785
Lima, Kiki **2**:186
Limann, Hilla **3**:376
Limba (people) **2**:275, 278

limestone **6**:728, *729*, 857; **8**:1015, 1016, *1074*; **9**:1160, *1165*; **10**:*1305*, 1307, 1318, 1320
limnic eruption **1**:14, 17
Limpopo Province **7**:872, 888, 900
Limpopo River **7**:951
Limpopo Valley **7**:872, 886, 887
Lindblad, Lars-Eric **10**:1433
Lindsay, Lionel **10**:1375
Lindsay, Norman **10**:1375
Line Islands *see* Kiribati
Lingala language **5**:607, 664, 671, 684
lingua franca **5**:607; **6**:748, 794
Lini, Walter **8**:1141, 1143
liquefied natural gas **8**:1120–1121
Lissouba, Pascal **5**:688
Little America headquarters station **10**:1424, 1429
Liverpool (Australia) **10**:1404
Livingstone (city) **6**:849, 851, 859
Livingstone, David **4**:464; **5**:603; **6**:744, 745, 782, 849
Livingstone Falls **5**:694
Livingstone's fruit bat (flying fox) **6**:736, *757*
Lô, Ismaël **2**:258
Loango kingdom **5**:682, *684*
Lobamba **7**:974, 978, 981, 983
Lobengula, king of Matabele **7**:896
Lobito **5**:582, *609*
Loboch, Francisco Zamora **1**:74
Lofty Ranges, Mount **10**:1397
Lomani-Tshibamba, Paul **5**:671
Lomé **3**:304, *324*, 415, 420, 423
  architecture **3**:418
  history **3**:423, 424
Lomé Convention (1975) **3**:423
Lomwe (people) **6**:746, 747, 782, 810
London Missionary Society **6**:766, 769; **8**:1104; **9**:1186, 1188, 1206, 1245, 1249, 1279
London Whitechapel Exhibition, Australian Contemporary Art **10**:1374–1375

Long Chronology Model **8**:1029
Lopès, Henri **1**:85; **5**:689
Lopes, Manuel **2**:186
Lopes da Silva, Baltasar **2**:186
Lord's Resistance Army (Uganda) **4**:554, 561, 565, 566, 569
Lorenz, Bente **6**:851
Loueke, Lionel **3**:339
Louisiade Archipelago **8**:1015, *1099*, 1104
Lourenço Marques *see* Maputo
Loyalty Islands **8**:1016, 1084
Lozi (people) **6**:727, 746, 852, 853
Lozi kingdom **6**:739, 747, 849
Lualaba River **5**:580, 583, 681
Luanda **5**:582, 589, 623, 624, 625
  architecture **5**:620, 624
  climate **5**:*591*, 624
  Cuca sign **5**:621
  history **5**:598, 599, 602, 610, 615, 617, 624
  housing **5**:622
  population **5**:582, 624
  ruling elite **5**:623
Luangwa River **6**:734, 736
Luba (people) **5**:583, 607, 674
Lubaki, Albert **5**:672
Luba kingdom **5**:597, 662
Luba language **5**:607, 661, 671
Lubango **5**:582, *612*, *621*
Lubosi I, Lozi ruler **6**:739, 849
Lubumbashi **5**:583, 671, 672, *674*
"Lucy" (hominid fossil) **4**:453
Lüderitz, Adolf **7**:897
Lüderitz Bay **7**:897
Luganville **8**:*1136*, 1140, 1141, 1145, 1146
Lugard, Frederick **1**:43–44, 100, 101; **4**:567
Luhrmann, Baz **10**:1379
Luhya (people) **4**:468, 526, 530
Lulua River **5**:583
Lumu, Henry **4**:562
Lumumba, Patrice **5**:668, 670
Lunda empire **5**:597, 598, 599, 662
Luo (people) **4**:468, 469, 525, 526, 530
Lusaka **6**:727, 848, 849, 855, 859
  art scene **6**:851
Lusaka Accord (1999) **5**:618, 670
Lutangu Sipopa, Lozi ruler **6**:739

Lutheranism
　Australia **10**:1385, 1397
　Namibia **7**:928, 934
　Papua New Guinea **8**:1100, 1103, 1111
　Zimbabwe **7**:997
Lutse, Kwassi **3**:416
Luvum, Janani **4**:560
Luzira Head (sculpture) **4**:562
Lyell Range **9**:1160
Lyons, Enid **10**:1389
Lyons, Joseph **10**:1367
Lyttelton Harbor **9**:*1210*, 1230, 1235

M

Maasai (people) **4**:*467*, 468, 469, 523, 528, 534, *537*; **6**:739, 748, 837, 842
　decorative arts **4**:526, *527*
　social structure **4**:530
Maasina Rule **8**:1129
Mabo Judgment (1992) **10**:1371
Macauley, Herbert **1**:101, 112
MacCarthy, Charles **2**:174; **3**:315, 324
Macdonnell Mountains **10**:1307
mace **8**:1032
Machel, Josina **6**:809
Machel, Samora **6**:806, 809, 812
Macheso, Aleck **7**:996
Mackay, Alistair Forbes **10**:1353, *1354*
Mackennal, Bertram **10**:1375
Maclean, George **3**:324
Macquarie, Lachlan **10**:1348
Madabbar, Johannes **4**:505
Madagascar **6**:760–773
　art and architecture **6**:767
　climate **6**:732–734, 760
　cultural expression **6**:766–768
　daily life **6**:769–770
　economy **6**:761, 772–773
　education **6**:770
　festivals and food **6**:768
　flag **6**:762
　flora and fauna **6**:735–737
　geography **6**:724, 728, *729*, 760
　geology **6**:730–731
　government and political parties **6**:762, 764
　history
　　chronology **6**:763
　　modern **6**:745, 755, 760, 765, 772

precolonial **6**:740, 742, 745, 750, 760, 771
　independence **6**:760, 765
　literature **6**:766
　music **6**:766, *767*, 768
　peoples **6**:742, 748, 760, 762–763, 766, 769
　population **6**:760–761
　religion **6**:742, 763, 765, 769–770
　resources **6**:760, 773
　transportation and communication **6**:762, 773
Madang **8**:1103, 1113, 1116
Maddy, Yulisa Amadu **2**:275
Madina do Boé **2**:223, 227
Mafeking (now Mafikeng) **7**:902, 911
Mafeking, siege of (1899–1900) **7**:898, *899*
Mafia Island **6**:726, 740
Maga, Hubert **3**:335
Magagula, Salayedvwa Modison **7**:980
Magal pilgrimage **2**:260
Magellan, Ferdinand **8**:1031, 1086
magnetic South Pole *see* South Pole
Magomi family **1**:28
Magyar, László **5**:603
Maharero, Samuel **7**:897
Mahdi **4**:487, 501
Mahé Island **6**:729, 826
Mahmadu Lamine **2**:168, 172
Mailu **8**:1028
Maimo, Sankie **1**:58
Maire, Jacob le **9**:1180
Majid, sultan of Zanzibar **6**:743
Maji Maji revolt (1906) **6**:833
Majuba Hill, Battle of (1881) **7**:891
Majuro **8**:1059, 1061, 1062
Maka, Julian **8**:1130
Makeba, Miriam **7**:*952*, 953
Makerere University **4**:562, 566, 567
Makira **8**:1033, 1129
Makonde (people) **6**:746, 807
　sculpture **6**:748, 808, 835
Makouta-Mboukou, Jean-Pierre **5**:689
Makua (people) **6**:746, 747, 807, 810
Makua language **6**:746, 747, 807, 810
Malabo **1**:15, 75, 76, 77
Malagasy (people) **6**:748, 766, 767, 768, 769

Malagasy language **6**:748, 766, 767, 768, 769
Malaita Island **8**:1016, 1130, 1131, 1132
Malaitan (people) **8**:1124, 1129
Malak Sagad III *see* Susenyos
Malan, Daniel **7**:946
Malangan Festival **8**:1109
malaria **1**:60, 89, 137; **2**:262, 279; **3**:381, 402–403, 421–422; **5**:623, 641, 657, 676, 693, 711; **8**:1114, 1132, 1143
Malawi **6**:774–787
　art and architecture **6**:780–781
　climate **6**:732, 733, 734, 774
　cultural expression **6**:780–781
　daily life **6**:782–783
　economy **6**:775, 785–787
　family and society **6**:782, 785
　festivals and food **6**:781
　flag **6**:775
　geography **6**:724, 727, 736, 774
　geology **6**:731
　government and political parties **6**:776, 778
　health and education **6**:782–783, 785
　history
　　chronology **6**:777
　　modern **6**:745, 774, 779, 780, 784, 849
　　precolonial **6**:739, 747, 774
　independence **6**:774, 779, 784
　lingua franca **6**:748
　literature **6**:780
　music **6**:781
　peoples **6**:746, 747, 776, 778, 780, 782; **7**:896
　population **6**:774–775
　religion **6**:776, 782
　resources **6**:774, 785–786
　transportation and communication **6**:776, *785*, 787
Malawi (Nyasa), Lake **4**:438; **6**:724, 727, 731, 736, 739, 744–745, 746, 774, 781, 782
　ferry service **6**:*785*, 787
　fishing **6**:786, 842
　tourism **6**:*776*, 787
Malebo Pool **5**:580, 583, 677, *682*, 694
Malembe, Timothée **5**:672

Maletsunyane Falls **7**:*916*
Mali **1**:8, 27, 36; **2**:148, 154, 168, 192, 267; **3**:323, 395
　Burkina Faso war **3**:355
　early history **3**:310, 311, 312, 313
　formation **2**:250
　medieval Ghana Empire **3**:368, 374
　see also French Sudan
Mali Empire **2**:164, 165, 166, 169, 176, 178, 204, 250; **3**:312, 328, 350
Malietoa Laupepa, king of Samoa **9**:1187
Malietoa Tanumafili II, Samoan chief of state **9**:1244, 1245
Mali Federation **2**:255, 263
Malindi **4**:457, *458*, 535, 538; **6**:740
Malinke (Malinga) (people) **2**:178, 211, 212, 213
Malletoa Vai'inupo Tavita, Samoan chief of state **9**:1245, 1249
"Malley, Ern" (fictional poet) **10**:1373
Malolotja Nature Reserve **7**:*984*
Malonga, Jean **5**:689, 690
Maloti Mountains **7**:871, 923
Malouf, David **10**:1373
Maltese immigrants **10**:1357, 1401
Malunga, Benedicto **6**:780
Malvatumaori **8**:*1140*, 1142
Mamae, Ghuty **1**:75
Mamaloni, Solomon **8**:1129
Mambèti, Djibril Diop **2**:258
Mambilla Plateau **1**:11, 24, 25
manatee **2**:163
Mancham, James **6**:822, 823
Mandara Mountains **1**:11, 45
Mande (people) **3**:360, 398, 401
Mandela, Nelson **5**:635; **7**:940, 947, 963
　presidency **7**:948–949, 969
Mande language **3**:313, 328
Mandingo Empire **2**:250
Mandinka (Mandinga) (people) **2**:166, 176, 178, 198, 200, 201, 212, 226, 250, 260
Mané, Ansumane **2**:223
manganese **3**:365; **5**:679
mangroves **1**:23, 57; **9**:1159
　central West Africa **3**:308–309
　eastern Africa **4**:449–450

Tonga **9**:1173
West African coast **2**:150, 151, 152, 160–161
Western Pacific **8**:1015, 1024, *1025*
Maning, Frederick **9**:1218
manioc (cassava) **3**:319; **5**:602, 638, 714
Central African Republic **5**:655, 660
Congo, Democratic Republic of **5**:673, 679, *690*
Congo, Republic of **5**:*690*, 691, 696
Manirampa, Antoine **5**:636–637
Manjaca (people) **2**:115, 173, 226
Manjia language **5**:653
Mano (people) **2**:239, 240, 243
Manresa Bodipo, Desiderio **1**:74
Mansfield, Katherine **9**:1218
Manuel II, king of Kongo **5**:599
Manukau Harbour **9**:1229
Manzini **7**:980, 983
Maori (people) **9**:1170, 1177–1179, 1180, 1191, 1209, 1226, 1228, 1231
art and architecture **9**:*1178, 1184*, 1219
Auckland **9**:1229
British settlers **9**:1182–1185
ceremonies **9**:1221
disease decimation **9**:1181, 1183
family and society **9**:1224
food **9**:1222
legal and social status **9**:1185, 1189, 1216
literature **9**:1218
music **9**:1220
religion **9**:1123, 1179, 1182, 1189, 1223
Mapanje, Jack **6**:780
Mapfumo, Thomas **7**:995, 996
Mapungubwe **7**:886, 887, 889, 951
Maputo **6**:726, 733, *808*, 810, *811*, 812, 815
artists collective **6**:808
history **6**:805, 812, 813
Mara, Kamisese **8**:1044
Marampa **2**:273, 281
Maran, René **5**:653
Marara, emperor of Zagwé **4**:455
marathons **4**:489, 507, 528
Maravi Confederacy **6**:739, 746, 774, 779

Marechera, Dambudzo **7**:994
Margai, Albert **2**:274
Margai, Milton **2**:273, 274
Mariam Dearit festival **4**:488
Mariana Arc **8**:1018
Marianas **8**:1032, 1035
see also Northern Mariana Islands
Mariana Trench **8**:1018
marine turtles **3**:309; **4**:450
maringa (music) **2**:277
Marion Island **7**:868
Markala Dam **1**:8
Maroons **2**:174, 273, 278
Marques, Lorenço **6**:812
Marques, Marcelino **2**:224
Marquesas Islands **9**:1158, 1163, 1175, 1176, 1180, 1186, 1189, 1196
Marsden, Samuel **9**:1223
Marshall, John (explorer) **8**:1054
Marshallese language **8**:1037, 1059
Marshall Islands **8**:1054–1063
art and architecture **8**:1060
climate **8**:1019–1022, 1054
cultural expression **8**:1060
daily life **8**:1061
economy **8**:1056, 1063
family and society **8**:1061
festivals and food **8**:1060
flag **8**:1055
flora and fauna **8**:1023–1025
geography **8**:1014, 1016, 1054
geology **8**:1017–1018
government and political parties **8**:1056, 1058, 1061
history
chronology **8**:1057
colonial **8**:1034–1035
early **8**:1029, 1030–1031
modern **8**:1034, 1054, 1059, 1069
independence **8**:1054, 1058, 1059
languages **8**:1056, 1059
literature **8**:1060
music **8**:1059
nuclear bomb tests **8**:1059, 1060, 1063
peoples **8**:1036, 1056, 1061
population **8**:1054
religion **8**:1056, 1061
resources **8**:1054, 1063
transportation and communication **8**:1056, 1063
marsupials **10**:1330, 1332, 1334, 1335

Marungu Plains **5**:583
Marxism
Angola **5**:614, 617, 622, 626
Benin **3**:330, 334, 336, 338, 341, 343, 346
Burkina Faso **3**:355, 356, 364
Congo, Republic of **5**:682, 686, 687, 688, 689, 690, 693, 695
Guinea **2**:209, 215
Mozambique **6**:804, 806, 812, 813
Seychelles **6**:822
see also Communism
Maryland-in-Africa **2**:235, 236
Maryland State Colonization Society **2**:235
Mascarenes *see* Mauritius; Reunion
Mascarin Peak **7**:868
Masekela, Hugh **7**:952
Maseru **7**:871, 923, 925
Mashakada, Cephus **7**:995
Masina **2**:168
Masire, Quett **7**:907
Mask Festival **8**:1109
masks **1**:*31*; **3**:*318*; **5**:*596*; **6**:748
Benin **3**:338
Burkina Faso **3**:357, 358
Cameroon **1**:59
Central African Republic **5**:654
Congo, Democratic Republic of **5**:672, *673*
Equatorial Guinea **1**:74
Fiji **8**:*1046*
Gabon **1**:85, *86*
Ghana **3**:378
Guinea **2**:212
Ivory Coast **3**:*399*, 401
Liberia **2**:240–241
Malawi **6**:*780*
Micronesia **8**:1070
Mozambique **6**:807
Nigeria **1**:*107*
Papua New Guinea **8**:1106, 1109
Sierra Leone **2**:276
Tanzania **6**:*835*
Zimbabwe **7**:*996*
Mason, Bruce **9**:1220
Massamba-Débat, Alphonse **5**:688
Massangano **5**:599, 602
Massari, Alfono Maria **5**:604
Massawa **4**:439, 445, 465, 482, 493
architecture **4**:490
history **4**:487, 488, 501

Massey, William Ferguson **9**:1216
Massina Empire **3**:323
Matabele (people) *see* Ndebele
Matabele kingdom **7**:896
Matadi **5**:580, 590, 600, 677, 681
Mataio Tuitonga, king of Niue **9**:1188
Matamba kingdom **5**:601, 602
Matane, Paulias **8**:1106
Mata-Utu **9**:1162
Matavanu, Mount **9**:1163
matriarchal society **5**:692
Matriki festival **9**:1221
matrilineal society **8**:1071, 1081, 1112, 1143
mats, woven **5**:*654*
Matsebula, Shadrack Mkhulunyelwa **7**:980
Matswa, André **5**:687, 692
Matswanism **5**:692
Mau Mau uprising (1952–1960) **4**:469, 518, 523, 524–525, 536
Mauritania **2**:148, 164–168, 256; **3**:368, 374
geology **2**:154
Mauritius **6**:788–797
art and architecture **6**:794
climate **6**:732–733, 788
cultural expression **6**:794
daily life **6**:795
economy **6**:788, 790, 797
family and society **6**:795
festivals and food **6**:794
flag **6**:790
flora and fauna **6**:737
geography **6**:724, 729, 788
geology **6**:731
government and political parties **6**:788, 790, 792
history
chronology **6**:791
modern **6**:741, 745, 749, 788, 793, 796
independence **6**:788, 793, 796
lingua franca **6**:748, 794
literature **6**:794
music **6**:794
peoples **6**:*746*, 748, 749, 790, 793, 794, 795
population **6**:789
religion **6**:790, 795, 796
resources **6**:788, 797
Seychelles **6**:818, 823, 826
transportation and communication **6**:796, 797

Mawahib, Abu al- **6:**740

Mawson, Douglas **10:**1353, 1354

Mayotte **6:**729, 755, 758, 798–799

Mazrui sultans **4:**460

M'ba, Léon **1:**78, 83, *84*

Mbabane **7:**980, 983

M'Backé, Amadou Bamba **2:**260

Mbande, Venancio **6:**808

Mbanga, Lapiro de **1:**59

Mbari Mbayo club **1:**109

Mbeki, Thabo **7:***948*, 949, 959–960

Mbenga (people) **5:**609, *673*

Mbida, André-Marie **1:**55

Mbini **1:**15, 22, 68, 73, 75, 76, 77

M'Bochi (people) **5:**684, 692

Mboya, Tom **4:**525

Mbum (people) **5:**656

Mbundu (people) **5:**599, 608, 622

Mbuti (people) **5:**609

Mbwila, Battle of (1665) **5:**598

McAuley, James **10:**1373

McCahon, Colin **9:**1219

McCall-Smith, Alexander **7:**908

McDonald Islands **10:**1328, 1411, 1423, 1426

McFarlane, Samuel **8:**1104

McGregor, Chris **7:**952

McGregor, William **8:**1104

Mchunu, Sipho **7:**953

McMahon, William **10:**1369

McMurdo Dry Valleys **10:**1313–1314

McMurdo scientific station **10:**1314, 1327, 1428, 1429, 1433

Mda, Zakes **7:**920, 950

Mdadaye, Melchior **5:**635

MDC (Movement for Democratic Change) (Zimbabwe) **7:**990, 993, 998, 1000, 1001, 1003

MDPC (Cameroon People's Democratic Movement) **1:**54, 56

Meadmore, Clement **10:**1375, *1376*

measles **1:**89

Mecca **4:**455

meerkat **4:**448

megaliths **5:**646

Meke dancers **8:***1046*, 1109

Melanesia **8:**1014, 1026–1028, 1034

Melanesian Pidgin (language) **8:**1130

Melanesians (people) **8:**1012, 1014, 1026–1028, 1036, 1038, 1042, 1112, 1130, 1138, 1142, 1144; **9:**1174, 1190, 1268

Melba, Nellie **10:**1378

Melbourne **10:**1309, 1365, 1387, *1388*, 1395, 1400–1401, 1405, 1408, 1415

architecture **10:**1376, 1401

climate **10:**1324

cultural life **10:**1374, 1401

football club **10:**1382

geography **10:**1311

history **10:**1348, 1349, 1350, 1357, 1400–1401, 1405

holidays **10:**1381

housing **10:**1394, 1401

population **10:**1311, 1400, 1401

religion **10:**1384

universities **10:**1393, 1401

Melbourne, Viscount (William Lamb) **10:**1400

Melbourne Cricket Ground **10:***1400*, 1401

Melbourne Cup **10:**1381, 1401

Memorial to the Martyrs **3:***356*

Menalamba guerrillas **6:**765

Mendaña de Neira, Alvaro **8:**1033; **9:**1180

Mende (people) **2:**178, 273, 275, 278

Menelik I, legendary king of Ethiopia **4:**452, 468, 505

Menelik II, emperor of Ethiopia **4:**465, 496, 501–502, 512, 513, 514

Menezes, Fradique Melo da **1:***134*, 135

Menga, Guy **5:**689, 690

Mengistu Haile Mariam **4:**496, 503, 504, 505, 514

Menzies, Robert **10:**1368, 1369

Mercer, Charles F. **2:**175

Merey-Apinda, Edna **1:**85

Merina (people) **6:**767, 769

Merina dynasty **6:**742, 760, 766, 771

Merkato market **4:**513

mermaid myths **2:**163

Meroe kingdom **4:**455

Merrick, Joseph **1:**46

Merritt, Robert **10:**1379

Meru (people) **4:**530

metalwork **2:**240; **3:**312–313; **5:**690

see also bronze casting

Methodism

Australia **10:**1384, 1385

Benin **3:**332

Fiji **8:**1040, 1043, 1047

Ghana **3:**380, 384, *385*

Ivory Coast **3:***392*, 401

New Zealand **9:**1182, 1223

Papua New Guinea **8:**1103, 1104

Samoa **9:**1242, 1249

Solomon Islands **8:**1132

Tonga **9:**1186, 1190, 1260, 1263, 1267, 1268

Metzger, Louise Isabella ("Gaga") **2:**276

Meyer, Roelf **7:**948

Mfecane (migration) **7:**892, 893, 895, 896

Mhlanga, Cont **7:**996

Miano, Léonora **1:**58

Michael, Kebede **4:**506

Michel, James **6:**823

Micombero, Michel **5:**632, 634

Micronesia **8:**1064–1073

art and architecture **8:**1070

climate **8:**1019–1022, 1064

cultural expression **8:**1070

daily life **8:**1071

economy **8:**1065, 1073

family and society **8:**1071

festivals and food **8:**1070

flag **8:**1065

flora and fauna **8:**1023–1025

geography **8:**1014, 1016, 1064

geology **8:**1017–1018

government and political parties **8:**1065, 1068

health, welfare, education **8:**1071

history

chronology **8:**1067

colonial *see* Caroline Islands

early **8:**1029–1031, 1064

modern **8:**1069, 1073

independence **8:**1064, 1068, 1069, 1073

languages **8:**1066, 1070

music **8:**1070

peoples **8:**1029–1031, 1036, 1037, 1066, 1071

population **8:**1064, 1071

religion **8:**1066, 1071

resources **8:**1064, 1073

transportation and communication **8:**1066, 1073

Micronesians (people) **8:**1012, 1014, 1036–1038, 1074,

1130, 1132; **9:**1189, 1190, 1206, 1284

Middle Congo (French Congo) **1:**46, 90; **5:**580, 604, 651, 653, 658, 682, 687, 692, 694, 695

see also Congo, Republic of

Midway Islands **9:**1286, *1289*

geography **9:**1163, 1288

migrant labor **7:**922, 923, 924, 958, 960, 965, 966, 970, 985

Milles Collines (Kigali hotel) **5:**712

millet **3:**311, 359, 365

Mills, John Atta **3:**376

Milner, Alfred **7:**898

milo-jazz **2:**277

Milo River **2:***206*

Mindelo **2:***182*, 185, 189, 190, 191

minerals and mining

Angola **5:**622, 625–626

Antarctica **10:**1431, 1432

Australia **10:**1300, 1304, 1305, 1306, 1311, 1350, 1371, 1406, 1409, 1411–1412

Belgian Congo **5:**633

Botsana **7:**912

Burundi **5:**643

Cameroon **1:**64, 65

Central African Republic **5:**659

Congo Basin **5:**583, 605, 606

Congo, Democratic Republic of 681; **5:**670, 678, 679, 680

Equatorial Guinea **1:**77

Gabon **1:**83, 84, 91–92, 93

Katanga province **5:**668

Kimberley mine **7:**893, 898, 971

Mozambique **6:**810, 814

Namibia **7:**936–937

Nigeria **1:**127

Papua New Guine **8:**1118, 1120

Solomon Islands **8:**1134

South Africa **7:**965–966, 967, 968, 969, 970, 971, 972

Tanzania **6:**841, 843

Togo **3:**424

Zimbabwe **7:**1002

see also specific ores

Minogue, Kylie **10:**1378

Minol, Bernard **8:**1106

Mintsa, Justine **1:**85

miombo woodlands **5:**595

Missionaires du Sacré Coeur **9**:1206

missionaries **1**:38, 43, 46; **8**:1104, 1124
  Angola **5**:622
  Belgian Congo literacy **5**:667, 671
  Central African Republic **5**:651
  central West Africa **3**:319, 324, 325, 360, 377, 380, 401
  eastern Africa **4**:455, 458, 464, 466, 489, 492, *507*, 529, 554, 559
  Kongo **5**:598, 600, 603, 674
  Madagascar **6**:766, 769
  Malawi **6**:745, 779, 782
  Rwanda **5**:707–708, 709, 710, 711
  Western Pacific **8**:1032, 1033, 1034, 1038, 1042, 1071, *1081*, 1095, 1103
  Zamia **6**:849, 851
  Zimbabwe **7**:897, 926, 956, 997

Mitterrand, François **3**:395

Mkhonta, Elias Adam Bateng **7**:980

Mkhonza, Sarah **7**:980

Mkwawa (Hehe leader) **6**:833

Mnyampaia, Mathias **6**:835

Mobutu Sese Seko **4**:561; **5**:618, 662, 669–670, 671, 673, 677, 678, 681, 705

Moçambique **6**:741, 808, *809, 810*

Modekngei movement **8**:1095

Modisane, William Bloke **7**:950

Moffatt, Tracy **10**:1375

Mofolo, Thomas **7**:920, 950

Mogadishu **4**:440, *462*, 465, 504, 540, 545, 548, 551
  civil war damage **4**:547, 551

Mogae, Festus **7**:907

Mohammed, Murtala **1**:103

Mohammed Korau **1**:36

Mohéli Island **6**:729, 736, 750, 753, 754, 755, 758, 798

Moi, Daniel arap **4**:525, 527, 528, 536

Mokhele, Ntsu **7**:919

Mole-Dagbon (people) **3**:380

Molisa, Grace **8**:1142

Moll, Herman (cartographer) **1**:*29*

Mombasa **4**:441, *518*, 535, 536, 539
  climate **4**:447

history **4**:457, 459, 460, 467, 523, 533, 535

Momoh, Joseph **2**:274

Momple, Lília **6**:807

Monash University **10**:1393, 1401

monasteries **4**:455, 492, 506

Mondlane, Eduardo **6**:805, 806, 809

Monénembo, Tierno **2**:211

money laundering **8**:1079, 1083

Mongita, Albert **5**:671–672

Mongo (people) **5**:607, 674

Mongo language **5**:607, 661, 671

Monokutuba language **5**:607, 684, 689

Monophysite Christians **4**:455

Mono River **3**:348, 426

monotremes **10**:1330, 1331–1332

Monroe, James **2**:175, 235, 246

Monrovia **2**:152, 158, 159, 175, 235, 237, 239, 240, 246, 249

monsoon, West Africa **2**:156

Monteiro, Antonio Mascarenhas **2**:185

Montreal Protocol (1987) **10**:1430

Moore, Bal T. **2**:240

Moore, Mike **9**:1217

Moorea Island **9**:1163, 1176

Mopeli-Paulus, A. S. **7**:920

Morel, E. D. **5**:606

Moresby, John **8**:1117

Morgan, Sally **10**:1373

Morija Festival **7**:921

Morija Press **7**:920

Mormons **9**:1223, 1237, 1242, 1246

morna (musical form) **2**:187

Moroni (Comoros) **6**:728–729, 754, 758

Morris Carter Commission (1925) **7**:991

Mortlockese language **8**:1037, 1070

Mortlock Islands **8**:1070

Moshi **6**:837, 843

Moshoeshoe I, king of Basotho **7**:914, 919, 921, 923

Moshoeshoe II, king of Basotho **7**:919

Mosisili, Pakalitha **7**:919

mosques
  Burkina Faso **3**:358, *359*, 363

Kenya **4**:527, 529, *535*

Ivory Coast, **3**:399, 404

Nigeria **1**:*113*, 119

Senegal **2**:257

Somalia **4**:548, *549*

mosquitoes **3**:403; **4**:447; **5**:590

Mossi (people) **3**:311, 350, 355, 357, 359, 360, 363

Mossi Empire **3**:310–312, 316–318, 323, 350, 355, 357, 359, 363
  French protectorate **3**:312, 318, 326, 350
  language group **3**:311, 328
  military might **3**:312, 318

Motlanthe, Kgalema **7**:949

Mouhoun River **3**:292, 294

mountain gorillas **5**:*591, 593*, 595, 712, 715

mountain nyala herds **4**:450

mountains *see key word*

Mount Hagen Show **8**:1109

Mount Lofty Ranges **10**:1307, 1397

Mount Nimba Highlands **3**:296

Mouridist Islamic brotherhood **2**:261

Movement for Democracy (Cape Verde) **2**:184, 185

Movement for Democracy in Liberia **2**:239

Movement for Democratic Change (Zimbabwe) *see* MDC

Movement for the Emancipation of the Niger Delta **1**:104

Movement for the Liberation of São Tomé and Príncipe **1**:134, 135

movie industry *see* film industry

Mozambican National Resistance *see* Renamo

Mozambique **6**:800–815; **7**:999
  art and architecture **6**:807–808
  climate **6**:732–734, 800
  cultural expression **6**:807–809
  daily life **6**:810–811
  economy **6**:802, 806, 813–815
  family and society **6**:810–811
  festivals and food **6**:809
  flag **6**:802
  flora and fauna **6**:735
  geography **6**:724–728, 736, 800

geology **6**:730, 731
  government and political parties **6**:802, 804, 806
  health and education **6**:810, 811
  history
    chronology **6**:803
    colonial. **5**:599
    modern **6**:745, 800, 805–806, 812, 813
    precolonial **6**:739, 740, 741, 747, 800; **7**:886
    independence **6**:800, 804, 812, 813
  lingua franca **6**:748
  literature **6**:807
  music **6**:808–809
  peoples **6**:746, 747, 748, 802, 810; **7**:896
  population **6**:801–802
  religion **6**:802, 810
  resources **6**:800, 813–814
  transportation and communication **6**:785, 802, 815
  Zimbabwe guerrillas **7**:992

Mozambique Channel **6**:724, 728

Mozambique civil war **6**:785, 800, 804, 805
  economic and social effects **6**:806, 810, 812, 813
  peace commemoration **6**:809

Mozambique Liberation Front *see* Frelimo

Mpande kaSenzangakhona, king of Zululand **7**:895

Mpando, Gédéon (artist) **1**:*58*

Mphahlele, Eskia **7**:950

mpingo tree (African blackwood) **4**:448

MPLA (Popular Movement for the Liberation of Angola) **5**:610, 614, 616, 617, 618, 619, 625, 687

Mpumalanga Province **7**:888, 900, 971

Mswati II, king of Swazi **7**:974, 979

Mswati III, king of Swazi **7**:978, 981

Mthethwa (people) **7**:889, 895

Mtukudzi, Oliver (Tuku) **7**:995, 996

mud-brick buildings *see* adobe architecture

Mugabe, Robert **7**:949, 986, 990, 992, 993, 996, 997, 1000–1001, 1003

Muhammad, Prophet **1:**42; **2:**212, 259, 260, 277; **4:**455, 477, 508
Muhammad Bello, sultan-caliph of Sokoto **1:**42
Muhammad Muntaga Tall **2:**168
Muianga, Carmene **6:**808
Mulaisho, Dominic **6:**851
Muldoon, Robert **9:***1216*, 1217
Mulinu'u, Mata'afa **9:**1245, 1253
Mulungushi Reforms (1968) **6:**850, 855
Muluzi, Bakili **6:**779
Mungo, Lake **10:**1340–1341, 1342
Mungoshi, Charles **7:**994
mural art, Lesotho **7:**920
Murchison Falls **4:***438*
Murcutt, Glenn **10:**1376
Murray, Hubert **8:**1104, 1105
Murray, Les **10:**1373
Murray-Darling Basin **10:**1304, *1307*, 1308, 1309, 1311, 1348
Museveni, Yoweri **4:**558, 560–561, 568
Musket Wars **9:**1182–1183
Muslims *see* Islam
Muslim Students Society **1:**113
Mussolini, Benito **4:**546
Mustapha, Mukhtarr **2:**275
Mutapa kingdom **7:**887
Mutare III, king of Ruanda-Burundi **5:**704
Mutesa I, king of Buganda **4:**466, *563*, 567
Mutesa, Edward **4:**559
Mutharika, Bingu wa **6:**778, 779
Muthewuye, Marcos **6:**808
Mutsamudu **6:**754, 758
Muzorewa, Abel **7:**992
Mvemba *see* Afonso I
mvet (musical instrument) **1:**74
Mwambutsa IV, king of Burundi **5:**634
Mwanawasa, Levy **6:**848, 850
Mwanga II, king of Buganda **4:**466
Mwanza **6:**727, 838
Mwenemutapa kingdom **6:**741
Mweru, Lake **5:**585, 590
Mwinyi, Ali Hassan **6:**834, 840
Mwiri (indigenous faith) **1:**8
My Brilliant Career (Franklin) **10:**1373
Mzilikazl, king of Zulu **7:**896

N
Naaba Dulugu, king of Mossi **3:**318, 360, 363
Naaba Kango, king of Mossi **3:**318
Naaba Kugri, king of Burkina Faso **3:**318
Naaba Siguiri, king of Mossi **3:**318, 326
Nabahani dynasty **6:**741
Nacala **6:**726, 785
Nachtigal, Gustav **1:**46; **3:**325
Nagbe, K. Moses **2:**240
Nairobi **4:**469, 533–534, *534*, 538, 539
  architecture **4:**527
  history **4:**533
  population **4:**441, 533
  slums **4:***530*, 534
Nakambe River **3:**292, 294
Nakayama, Tosiwo **8:**1069
Nakomse (people) **3:**311
Nakoué, Lake **3:**294
Nakuru, Lake **4:**451
Nalubaale Dam **4:**436, 441, 569, 570
  power station **4:**562
Nama (people) **7:**901, 926, 932, 934, 935
Namatjira, Albert **10:**1375
Namib Desert **5:**588, 589, 594, 595; **7:**870, 874–875, 880, *881*, 884, 926, 931
Namibia **5:**583, 589, 595; **7:**926–937
  art and architecture **7:**932–933, 935
  climate **7:**878–881, 884, 926, 935
  cultural expression **7:**932–933
  daily life **7:**934
  economy **7:**928, 936–937
  festivals, food, and drink **7:**933
  flag **7:**927
  flora and fauna **5:**595; **7:**882–885, *926*
  geography **5:**583, 589; **7:**868, 870, 872–875, 926
  government and political parties **7:**928, 930
  health, welfare, and education **7:**934
  history
    chronology **7:**929
    colonial *see* German South-West Africa
    modern **7:**926, 931, 932, 935, 947

  precolonial **7:**889, 890, 891, 926
    Second Congo War **5:**670, 678, 705
  independence **7:**926, 930, 931, 932, 934, 935, 936
  languages **7:**928, 932
  literature **7:**932
  music **7:**933
  peoples **7:**901, 926, 928, 933, 934, 935
  population **7:**927–928
  religion **7:**928, 934
  resources **7:**926, 936
  transportation and communication **7:**928, 935, 937
Namib Sand Sea **7:**874
Nampula **6:**810, 815
Nandan, Satendra **8:**1045
Nang'undu, Nyakenya **6:**807–808
Nan Madol site **8:**1031, *1039*
Nanumea Atoll **9:**1279
Napier **9:**1159
Nash, Walter **9:**1216
Natal **7:**892, 893, 894, 896, 898, 940, 945, 956, 962, 964
Natalia republic **7:**892, 895
National Alliance for Democracy and Development (Gambia) **2:**196, 197
National Carillon (Australia) **10:**1396, *1396*
National Church of Nigeria and the Cameroons **1:**112, 113
National Council for Democracy and Development (Guinea) **2:**208, 210
National Council of Chiefs (Vanuatu) **8:***1140*, 1142
National Council of Nigeria and the Cameroons **1:**112
National Dance Troupe (Sierra Leone) **2:**276
National Diamond Mining Company **2:**282
Nationalist Party (Australia) **10:**1367
National Movement for the Liberation of Equatorial Guinea **1:**73
National Museum of Liberia **2:**240
National Party (Australia) **10:**1364

National Party (South Africa) **7:**907, 911, 931, 940, 945–946, 947, 948, 958, 974
  see also apartheid
National Provisional Ruling Council (Sierra Leone) **2:**274
National Theater (Ghana) **3:***378*
National Union for Democracy and Progress (Cameroon) **1:**54
National Union for the Total Independence of Angola *see* UNITA
National University of Benin **3:**343, 344
National Woodcutter's Rally-Democratic (Gabon) **1:**82, 84
National Youth Movement (Nigeria) **1:**101
Native Land Trust Board (Fiji) **8:**1043
natural gas *see* oil and natural gas
Nauru **8:**1074–1083
  art and architecture **8:**1080
  climate **8:**1019–1022, 1074
  cultural expression **8:**1080
  daily life **8:**1081
  economy **8:**1075, 1083
  family **8:**1081
  festivals and food **8:**1080
  flag **8:**1075
  flora and fauna **8:**1023–1025
  geography **8:**1014, 1016, 1074
  geology **8:**1017–1018
  government and political parties **8:**1075, 1078, 1079
  health, welfare, and education **8:**1081
  history
    chronology **8:**1077
    early **8:**1074
    modern **8:**1035, 1074, 1079
  independence **8:**1074, 1079, 1080
  languages **8:**1075, 1076, 1080
  literature **8:**1080
  music **8:**1080
  peoples **8:**1036, 1076, 1081
  population **8:**1075
  religion **8:**1076, 1081
  resources **8:**1014, 1074, 1079, 1083

transportation and communication **8:**1075, 1083

Tuvalu **9:**1279, 1284

Nauruan Independent Church **8:**1081

Nauruan language **8:**1037, 1080

Nauru Phosphate Corporation **8:**1079, 1083

Nazinon River **3:**292, 294

Ndadaye, Melchior **5:**638

Ndakarou *see* Dakar

Ndar Island **2:**170

N'Debeka, Maxime **5:**689

Ndebele (people) **7:**888, 893, 896, 900, 951, 957, 988, 994, 995, *996,* 997

uprising **7:**991

ZAPU supporters **7:**992, 993, 1000

Ndereba, Catherine **4:**528

Ndiaye, Iba **2:**258

Ndimurukundo-Kururu, Barbara **5:**636

Ndizeyeto, Charles *see* Ntare V, king of Burundi

Ndogo, Lake **1:**78

Ndola **6:**727, 857

Ndongo-Bidyogo, Donato **1:**74

Ndongo kingdom **5:**597, 599, 601, 602, 610

N'Dour, Youssou **2:**258

Ndwandwe (people) **7:**889, 895, 896

Negash, Ghirmai **4:**489

negritude movement **2:**257; **3:**417; **5:**653

Nelson (city) **9:**1160, 1184, 1221

Netherlands **1:**38–39; **9:**1180–1181, 1258, 1263

Angola **5:**601–602, 624

central African slave trade **5:**598, 601

Gold Coast **3:**313, 320–321, 324, 368, 377, 383

slave trade **2:**171, 250, 268, 280

West Africa **2:**170, 171, 172, 263

Western Pacific **8:**1032, 1033, 1034, 1038, 1103

see also Dutch East India Company

Neto, Agostinho **5:**617, 619, 621

Neves, José Maria Peira **2:**185

New Australian Poetry movement **10:**1373

New Britain **8:**1012, 1015, 1027, 1103, 1107, 1117

dance **8:**1109

religion **8:**1085

New Caledonia **8:**1084–1085; **9:**1164, 1174, 1290

flora and fauna **8:**1023–1025

geography **8:**1012, 1016, 1084

government **8:**1085

history 1026–1027; **8:**1033, 1034, 1084, 1141

Lapita site **8:**1026

peoples **8:**1036, 1037, 1085

Newcastle (Australia) **10:**1402, *1408,* 1413, 1415

history **10:**1347, 1350

Newcombe, John **10:**1382

New Georgia Island **8:**1027, *1124*

New Guinea *see* Papua New Guinea

New Guinea Company **8:**1103

New Hebrides *see* Vanuatu

New Hebrides Trench **8:**1012

New Ireland **8:**1015, 1027, 1033, 1103, 1107, 1110

dance **8:**1109

traditional art **8:**1106

New Plymouth **9:**1184, 1185

New South Wales **10:**1365, 1366, 1380, 1398, *1408,* 1411

Aboriginal Australians **10:**1355

climate **10:**1325

federation **10:**1388

geography **10:**1309, 1310, 1311

history **10:**1346, 1347, 1348, 1349, 1350, 1358, 1404

resources **10:**1385, 1409, 1411

rugby **10:**1382

theater **10:**1379

university **10:**1393

see also Canberra; Melbourne; Sydney

New Yam Festival (Nigeria) **1:**110

New Zealand **8:**1034, 1074, 1079; **9:**1179, 1210–1235

art and architecture **9:**1219, 1230

climate **9:**1166, 1167–1169, 1210

Cook Islands **9:**1194

cultural expression **9:**1218–1222

daily life **9:**1223–1227

economy **9:**1212, 1231–1235

family and society **9:**1224–1225

festivals and ceremonies **9:***1191, 1217,* 1221, 1222

flag **9:**1211

flora and fauna **9:**1170–1172, 1177, 1185

food and drink **9:**1222

geography **9:**1158–1160, 1210

geology **9:**1164–1166

government and political parties **9:**1185, 1212, 1214, 1216, 1217

health, welfare, and education **9:**1226–1227, 1233

history

chronology **9:**1213

early **9:**1174, 1177–1179, 1210

modern **9:**1179, 1180, 1181, 1182–1185, 1187, 1188, 1191, 1210, 1215–1217, 1231

independence **9:**1210, 1215, 1216, 1231

languages **9:**1189, 1218

literature **9:**1218

music **9:**1220

Niue **9:**1236

peoples **9:**1189, 1190, 1191, 1210, 1212, 1224, 1225

population **9:**1212

religion **9:**1123, 1182, 1184, 1189, 1212

resources **9:**1210, *1232,* 1233–1234

Samoa **9:**1240, 1245, 1252

Tokelau **9:**1256

transportation and communication **9:**1212, 1229, 1230, 1233, 1235

Tuvalu **9:**1274, 1279

New Zealand Association **9:**1183

New Zealand Company **9:**1184, 1228

New Zealand Wars **9:**1179, *1183,* 1184, 1185, 1209

Nfah-Abbenyi, Juliana **1:**58

Ngale, Ilongo Fritz **1:**58

Nganang, Patrice **1:**58

Ngando (Lomami-Tshibamba) **5:**671

Ngati Tumatakokiri (people) **9:**1180

Ngazargamo (Birni Gazargamo) **1:**29, 30

Ngendandumwe, Pierre **5:**634

Ngola a Hari *see* Felipe I

Ngola Mbandi, king of Ndongo **5:**599

Ngondo festival **1:**59

Ngoni (people) **6:**739, 744, 746, 747, 782, 852

Ngorongoro Conservation Area **6:**735

Ngorongoro Crater **6:**727, 843

Ngouabi, Marien **5:**688, 695

Ngozi, Chimamanda **1:**105

Ngubane, Jordan **7:**950

Nguema, Francisco Macias **1:**72, 73, 74, 76

Nguema, Teodoro Obiang **1:**68, 72, 73, 74

Nguema Madja, Fernando **1:**74

Ngugi wa Thiong'o **4:**526, 527

Ngulu *see* Barotseland

Ngunga troupe **5:**69

Nguni (people) **7:**887, 888, 892, 893, 896, 900, 980, 986, 995

Ngwane (people) *see* Swazi

Ngwane III, king of Swazi **7:**974

N'Hada, Sana Na **2:**224

Niari Valley **5:**584, 696

Nichol, Abioseh **2:**275

nickel **5:**643; **7:**912, 1002; **8:**1084

Niger **3:**336, 355

Niger-Bantu languages **5:**607

Niger-Benue Trough **1:**10, 19

Niger-Congo languages **3:**327–329; **5:**607, 609

Niger Delta **1:**8, 13, 20, 22, 23

militants **1:**127

oil fields **1:**104, 127

slave trade **1:**43

Niger Delta Basin **1:**13, 16, 17

Nigeria **1:**94–129; **2:**174, 176; **3:**322, 323, 325, 329, 396

art and architecture **1:**106–107, 119

Bakassi dispute **1:**56, 65

British Cameroon **1:**55

climate **1:**18–21, 94

cultural expression **1:**105–111, 129

economy **1:**97, 104, 125–129

education **1:**117, 120

family and society **1:**114–115

festivals and ceremonies **1:**110, *114*

flag **1:**94

flora and fauna **1:**22–25

food and drink **1:**111

geography **1:**8–14, 18, 19, 94

government and political parties **1:**97, 99, 101

military regimes **1:**103, 104, 116, 125, 126, 129

Nigeria (*continued*)
health and welfare **1**:116
history
Bakassi dispute **1**:56, 65
chronology **1**:98
colonial **1**:30, 42, 43–44, 100–101, 112, 120, 121, 122, 123
early **1**:27–32, 36–37
historic Benin Empire **3**:322, 330, 337
modern, **1**:100-104, 112
see also Nigerian Civil War
modern Benin **3**:336, 337
housing **1**:118
independence **1**:102–104
music **1**:108, 129
peoples **1**:31, 40–42, 47–49, 97, 101, 104, 114; **2**:176
population **1**:10, 97, 104
religion **1**:40, 41–42, 97, 112, 114, 121
resources **1**:94, 127
transportation and communication **1**:97, 120, 121, 126, 129
Nigerian Civil War **1**:48, *102*, 113, 119, 121, 124, 126
Nigerian National Democratic Party **1**:101
Nigerian National Mosque (Abuja) **1**:*113*, 119
Niger Plains **2**:152
Niger River **1**:8, 10, 12–13, 19, 27, 129; **2**:152, 168, 176, 216; **3**:306, 307, 311, 335, 336, 346
British trade **1**:43
early trade centers **3**:314
Northern Mossi **3**:316
trade route **1**:34, 43
W National Park **3**:306
Niger River Valley **3**:298, 325, 329
Nigussie, Yoftahe **4**:507
Nikashama, Ngandu **5**:672
Nile River **4**:239, 436, 438, 441,*441*, 454, 562; **5**:583
search for source **4**:458, 466
source **5**:582, 585, 603, *629*; **6**:744
see also Blue Nile River
Nilotic (people) **6**:739, 748
Nilotic language **4**:457, 468–469
Nimba, Mount **2**:151, 152–153, 162, 204, 216, 247; **3**:296
Nimba rebellion (1989) **2**:239
Nimrod Expedition (1907) **10**:1353, *1354*

Nine Saints (missionaries) **4**:455, *507*
Niokolo Koba National Park **2**:*260*
Niokolo region **2**:151
Nioro territory **2**:168
Niue **9**:1236–1237
climate **9**:1167
cyclone **9**:1168, 1236
geography **9**:1160, 1236
geology **9**:*1165*
history **9**:1174, 1188, 1215, 1236, 1258
independence **9**:1217, 1236
migrants to New Zealand **9**:1225, 1229, 1236
peoples **9**:1189, 1237
religion **9**:1189, 1237
Njembe (indigenous faith) **1**:88
Njimi **1**:28, 29
N'Kodia, Alain **5**:690
Nkomo, Joshua **7**:992, 995
Nkrumah, Kwame **3**:368, 372, 374, 375, 386, 388, 396
memorial and tomb **3**:*374*
Nkumbula, Harry **6**:844
Nkurunziza, Innocent **5**:706
No. 1 Ladies' Detective Agency (McCall-Smith) **7**:908
Nok culture **1**:26, 31, 106
Nokoué, Lake **3**:294, 339
Nolan, Sidney **10**:1375
Noli, António da **2**:169
Nollywood **1**:106, 129
Norfolk Island **9**:1188, 1238; **10**:1310, 1416–1417
first settlement **10**:1347, 1348
Noronha, Rui de **6**:807
Northern Cape Province **7**:872, 951, 971
Northern Mariana Islands **8**:1086–1087
climate **8**:1019–1022, 1086
flora and fauna **8**:1023–1025
geography **8**:1015, 1086
geology **8**:1017–1018
government **8**:1087
history
colonial **8**:1034–1035
early **8**:1029–1031, 1086
modern **8**:1034, 1069, 1086
peoples **8**:1037, 1087
Northern Rhodesia *see* Zambia
Northern Territory **10**:1318, 1350, 1396
Aboriginal Australians **10**:1359, *1386*, 1387

agriculture **10**:1411
climate **10**:1322–1323, 1324
geography **10**:1300, 1304, 1305, 1306, 1307
resources **10**:1409
see also Alice Springs
Northern War **9**:1185
North Island **9**:1158–1159, 1165, 1231, 1234
climate **9**:1166
flora and fauna **9**:1170, 1172
history **9**:1182, 1185
Maori **9**:1177, 1178, 1179, 1189
see also Auckland; Wellington
Northland **9**:1159, 1165, 1168, 1229
North-West Province **7**:872, 889, 957
nor'wester (wind) **9**:1168–1169
Note, Kessai Hesa **8**:*1058*, 1059
Notre Dame de Apotres Cathedral (Cotonou) **3**:*344*
Nouméa **8**:1016, 1084
Nsukka School (Nigerian arts) **1**:106
Ntamo **5**:677, 694
Ntare V, king of Burundi **5**:634
Ntaryamira, Cyprien **5**:635, 705
Nthunya, Mpho' M'atsepo **7**:920
Ntibantunganya, Sylvestre **5**:635
Ntombi, queen mother of Swazi **7**:979
Nubia **4**:454, 455
nuclear testing **8**:1059, 1060, 1063
Nuclear Victims Remembrance Day **8**:1060
Nujoma, Samuel **7**:930, 931
Nuku'alofa **9**:1160, 1174, *1258*, 1264, 1268, *1269*, 1270
riots **9**:1258, *1263*, 1264, 1270, 1271
Nukufetau Atoll **9**:1279
Nukuleka site **9**:1174
Nukunonu Atoll **9**:1161, 1256
Nukuoro **8**:1029, 1037, *1066*
Nullarbor Plain **10**:1304, 1306, *1317*, 1318
Nuna (people) **3**:311, *358*
Nuñez de Balboa, Vasco **8**:1031, *1033*
Nun River **1**:8
Nupe kingdom **1**:32, 112
nutmeg **8**:1032

Nyama, Jean Divassa **1**:85
Nyamwezi (people) **6**:739, 744, 746, 748, 835, 837
Nyamwezi language **6**:739, 744, 746, 748, 835, 837
Nyangoma, Nadine **2**:224
Nyanza **5**:703, 706, 712, 713
Nyasa, Lake *see* Malawi (Nyasa), Lake
Nyasaland *see* Malawi
Nyasaland African Congress **6**:778, 779
Nyeko, Monica Arac de **4**:562
Nyerere, Julius **4**:560; **6**:828, 833, 834, 840, 843
Nyobé, Ruben Um **1**:55
Nyonda, Vincent de Paul **1**:85
Nyos, Lake **1**:14, *16*, 17
Nzebi (people) **1**:48
Nzinga, Raymond Lema A'nsi **5**:672
Nzinga a Nkuwu *see* João I, king of Kongo
N'Zongo Soul **5**:690
Nzwani *see* Anjouan Island

O
Oba dynasty **1**:31
Obasanjo, Olusegen **1**:56, 103, 128
Obey, Commander Ebenezer **1**:108
Obock **4**:470, 475, 479
Obote, Milton **4**:554, 558, 559, 560, 561, 568
Obudu Plateau **1**:12, 24
Obunumankoma, king of Bono **3**:313
Oceania **10**:1300
oceanic faults **1**:17
Oceanic peoples **8**:1029, 1036
Odinga, Oginga **4**:468, 525
Odinga, Raila **4**:468, 525
Oduduwa (god) **1**:31, 32, 33
Oeno Island **9**:1163, 1238
offshore banking **8**:1079, 1083
offshore oil and gas *see* oil and natural gas
Ofori, Dominic **2**:275
Ogaden **4**:440, 444, 467, 502, 546
Ogaden War **4**:503, 504, 513, 514, 547, 552
Ogiso (rulers of the sky) **1**:33
Ogonga, Jimmy **4**:526–527
Ogoni (people) **1**:104
Ogooué River **1**:15, 45, 46
Ogot, Grace **4**:526
Ogun (god) **1**:42
Ogunde, Hubert **1**:105

oil and natural gas
  Angola **5:**582, 618, 622, 623, 625, 627
  Antarctica **10:**1431, 1432
  Australia **10:**1301, 1311, 1407, 1409, 1409–1410, 1410, 1414
  Benin **3:**347–348
  Botswana **7:**912
  Cameroon **1:**14, 17, 50, 56, 64–65, 65, 66, 67
  Congo, Republic of **5:**687, 688, 695, 696
  Equatorial Guinea **1:**15, 68, 73, 76, 77, 92
  Gabon **1:**15, 17, 78, 83, *85*, 90, 91, 92, 93
  Ghana **3:**388
  Gulf of Guinea **1:**135, 137
  Gulf of Papua **8:**1012
  Ivory Coast **3:**407
  Namibia **7:**936
  New Zealand **9:**1233
  Niger Delta Basin **1:**13
  Nigeria **1:**13, 17, 103, 104, 107, 121, 125, 126, 127, 129, 135
  Papua New Guinea **8:**1118, 1120
  Rwanda **5:**713
  São Tomé and Príncipe **1:**130, 135, 137
  Western Pacific **8:**1012
Ojukwu, Chukwuemeka **1:**103; **3:**396
Okavango Delta **7:**883, *904, 910*
Okavango River **7:**874
Okello, Tito **4:**560, 561
Okri, Ben **1:**105
Oktika **1:**27
Olaniyi, Taiwo **1:**106
Olumuyiwa, Oluwole **1:**107
Olurun (god) **1:**31
Olympic Games **4:**507; **7:**946; **10:**1382, 1401, 1405
Olympio, Gilchrist **3:**414, 416, 424
Olympio, Sylvanus **3:**414, 415, 416
Oman **4:**458, 459, 460, 518, 526, 527, 535, 536; **6:**741, 743, 744, 748, 828, 834
Omani Empire **4:**460–461
Omar Bongo University **1:**90
Ombwiri (indigenous faith) **1:**8
Omotic languages **4:**467, 468
Onabolu, Aina **1:**106
Ondongo, Nicolas **5:**689
Ondo State **1:**12
Onitsha **1:**8

Onitsha Market Literature **1:**105
Onka, Destin **5:***691*
On Trial for My Country (Samkange) **7:**994
OPEC (Organization of the Petroleum Exporting Countries) **5:**625
Operation Hijump Expedition **10:**1424
Ophir **4:**452
Opobo city-state **1:**43
Opoku Ware I, king of Ashanti **3:**314
Orange Free State **7:**893, 894, 898, 903, 940, 945, 962, 967
Orange River **7:**868, 870, 872, 874, 883, 891, 893, 897, 936
Oranmiyan, ruler of Benin **1:**33
Organization for the Victory of Islam **1:**113
Organization of African Unity *see* African Union
Oribi Gorge Nature Reserve **7:**883
Orisha (god) **1:***32*
Oromo (people) **4:**464, 467, 509
Orompoto, ruler of Yoruba **1:**32
Orthodox Christians **10:**1384, 1385
  see also Ethiopian Orthodox Church
Osei Bonsu, king of Ashanti **3:**313, 314
Osei Kwadwo, king of Ashanti **3:**314
Osei Tutu I, king Ashanti **3:**314, 385
Oshoffa, Samuel Bilehou **3:**341
Osogbo School (Nigerian arts) **1:**106
O'Sullivan, Vincent **9:**1218
Osun (spirit goddess) **1:**42
Otago **9:**1160, 1165, *1227*
  Gabriel's Gully **9:***1185*
  gold rush **9:**1184, 1185, 1215
  Presbyterian First Church **9:**1223
  wine production **9:***1235*
Ottamari (people) **3:**341
Ottoman Turks **4:**459, 462, 464, 482, 491, 540
Ouagadougou **3:**292, 353, 358, 367
  fairs and festivals **3:**357, 359, 363, 367

  history **3:**311, 316, 318, 326, 350, 355, 363
  markets **3:**361, 363
  population **3:**297, 353
  public buildings **3:***354*, 363
  rainfall **3:**303, 305
  universities **3:**362, 363
Ouatchi (people) **3:**420
Ouattara, Alassane **3:**396, 397
Oubangui-Shari **1:**46
Ouedraogo (Mossi legendary founder) **3:**311, 316
Ouedraogo, Dimdolobsom **3:**357
Ouedraogo, Idrissa **3:**358
Ouidah **3:**313, 321, *342*
Ouidah kingdom **3:**322, 330
Oupay, Mount **1:**11
Our Lady of Peace of Yamoussoukro Basilica **3:**396, 399, 404, *404*
Ovambo (people) **7:**889, 901, 926, 928, 932, 934
Ovimbundu (people) **5:**608, 612, 622
Ovonramwen, ruler of Benin **1:**35
Owen Falls Dam *see* Nalubaale Dam
Owen Stanley Range **8:**1015, *1123*
Owondo, Laurent **1:**85
Owu (people) **1:**317
Owusu, Martin **3:**377
Oyo **1:**31, 32, 42, 43, 106, 120
Oyo-Ile **1:**27
Oyo kingdom **3:**322, 345
Oyoko clan **3:**314
Oyono, Ferdinand **1:**57, 58
Ozolua the Conqueror, ruler of Benin **1:**34
ozone layer hole **10:**1339, 1418, 1425, 1430

P

Pacific Arts Festivals **8:**1080
Pacific Community **8:**1084
Pacific Forum **8:**1133; **9:**1264
Pacific Islanders **8:**1036; **9:**1224, 1225, 1226, 1228, 1268
Pacific Island groups **8:**1014
  see also United States Pacific Islands Territories; *specific islands*
Pacific Islands Company **9:**1203
Pacific Phosphate Company **8:**1079
Pacific Plate **8:**1014; **9:**1164, 1165

Pacific Ring **8:**1017
Páez, Pedro **4:**464
Pagan, Mount **8:**1015
Pago Pago **9:**1163, 1187, 1192
Paichuk **8:**1068, 1069
Palais des Sports de Treichville **3:***403*
Palau **8:**1088–1097
  art and architecture **8:**1094
  climate **8:**1019–1022, 1088
  cultural expression **8:**1094
  daily life **8:**1095
  economy **8:**1089, 1097
  festivals and food **8:**1094
  flag **8:**1089
  flora and fauna **8:**1023–1025
  geography **8:**1015, 1088
  geology **8:**1017–1018
  government **8:**1090, 1092
  history
    chronology **8:**1091
    colonial **8:**1034–1035
    early **8:**1029, 1031
    modern **8:**1034, 1069, 1088, 1093, 1094
  independence **8:**1093, 1097
  languages **8:**1090, 1094
  literature **8:**1094
  music **8:**1094
  peoples **8:**1036–1037, 1090
  population **8:**1088, 1095
  religion **8:**1090, 1093, 1095
  resources **8:**1088, 1097
  transportation and communication **8:**1090, 1097
Pallotine Order **1:**46
Palmer, Geoffrey **9:**1217
Palmer, Nathaniel **10:**1352
palm products **1:**43, 73; **2:**273, 280; **3:**323, 325, 344, 388, *408*
Palmyra Atoll **9:**1163, 1288
Pan-African Event **3:**300–301
Panafrican Film and Television Festival **3:**363, 367
Panafrican Music Festival **3:**358, 363
Pan-African orogeny **2:**154; **3:**300, 300–301
pandanus leaves **9:**1204, *1205*
Pangaea **10:**1320
pangolin (anteater) **5:**595
Papel (people) **2:**173, 226
Papua, Gulf of **8:**1012, 1015, 1107, 1117, 1118, 1120
Papua New Guinea **8:**1098–1123
  art and architecture **8:**1106–1107

Papua New Guinea (*continued*)
climate **8:**1019–1020, 1098, 1118
cultural expression **8:**1106–1110
daily life **8:**1111–1116
economy **8:**1100, 1118–1123
education **8:**1116
family and society **8:**1112–1113, 1115
festivals and ceremonies **8:**1108, 1109
flag **8:**1100
flora and fauna **8:**1023–1025, 1028
food and drink **8:**1110
geography **8:**1012, 1014–1015, 1016, 1098
geology **8:**1017–1018
government and political parties **8:**1100, 1102
health and welfare **8:**1114–1115
history
chronology **8:**1101
early **8:**1026, 1027, 1028, 1098
modern **8:**1033, 1034, 1035, 1098, 1103–1105, 1117, 1118, 1141
independence **8:**1098, 1105
languages **8:**1036, 1098, 1100, 1106, 1116
literature **8:**1106
music **8:**1108–1109
peoples **8:**1026, 1036–1037, 1100, 1106, 1112
population **8:**1098–1099
religion **8:**1100, 1111
resources **8:**1098, 1118, 1120–1121
transportation and communication **8:**1100, 1122
Papunya-Tulu movement **10:**1375
Paris Club **1:**56
Parr, Mike **10:**1375
parrots **10:**1333–1334
Party for Social Renewal (Guinea-Bissau) **2:**223
Pass Laws (South Africa) **7:**960
Patagonian toothfish **10:**1433
Patassé, Ange-Félix **5:**650, 652
Pate **6:**741, 743
Paterson, A. B. ("Banjo") **10:**1373
Pathé 'O (fashion designer) **3:**398

Paton, Alan **7:**950
Paul and Clara Gebauer Collection **1:**59
Peace Pole (Kumasi) **3:***379*
peanuts *see* groundnuts
Pearl Harbor attack (1941) **8:**1035
pearl oysters **4:**450
Pedro IV, king of Kongo **5:**598–599
Pedro VI, king of Kongo **5:**599
Peleliu, Battle of (1944) **8:**1093
Pelew Islands *see* Palau
pelicans **7:**883
Pellew, Sir Edward **10:**1300
Pemba **4:**460; **6:**726, 733, 748
history **6:**740, 741, 743, 834
penal colonies *see* convict settlements
Pene, Omar **2:**258
penguins
Antarctica **10:**1334, 1337–1338, *1337*, 1418, *1433*, *1435*
New Zealand **9:**1171, 1177
Pentecostal churches **3:**370, 380, 401; **4:**556, 565; **7:**905, 910, 942, 956, 982, 997; **8:**1071, 1111
Pentecost Island **8:**1143
People's Democratic Party (Nigeria) **1:**99
People's Movement for Democratic Change (Sierra Leone) **2:**272
People's Progressive Party (Gambia) **2:**196, 197
People's Redemption Council (Liberia) **2:**238, 247
Pereira, Aristides **2:**185
Pereira, Fernando **1:**135
Peringuey's adder **7:**884
Perth **10:**1324, 1387, 1403, 1415
geography **10:**1304–1305
history **10:**1357, 1358
Peters, Lenrie **2:**198
Petersen, Taliep **7:**953
petroglyphs **8:**1130
petroleum industry *see* oil and natural gas
Peuhl (people) **2:**211, 231
Philippines **8:**1033, 1034, 1035, 1064
Phillip, Arthur **10:**1346, 1347
Phoenix Islands *see* Kiribati
Phophonyane Falls **7:***975*
phosphate
Nauru **8:**1014, 1074, *1078*, 1079, 1080, 1081, 1083

New Zealand **9:**1203, 1208, 1209
Palau **8:**1093
Solomon Islands **8:**1134
Togo **3:**424, 427
Tuvalu **9:**1279, 1284
photography **10:**1375–1376
Pico do Cano **2:**153, 180
Pidgin English **8:**1106, 1116
Pidjiguiti massacre (1959) **2:**223, 225
Pietermaritzburg **7:**962, 964
Pilbara region **10:**1304, 1305
piracy **2:**169
Somalia **4:**475, 547, 553
Pitcairn **9:**1176, 1188, 1238–1239; **10:**1416
geography **9:**1163, 1238
population **9:**1191, 1238
plantain **5:**638, 643, 660
platypus **10:**1331–1332
Plenty, Bay of **9:**1159, 1165, 1185
Pliya, Jean **3:**338
Plymouth Company **9:**1184
Pohamba, Hifikepunye **7:**931
Pohnpei **8:**1016, 1019, 1064, 1069, 1070, 1072
Pohnpeian language **8:**1037, 1070, 1071
Pointe-Noire **5:**584, 658, 687, 690, 692, 693, 694, 695, 696, 697
Polish immigrants **10:**1388
polygamy **1:**60, 89, 114, 137; **2:**177, 200, 213, 226, 243, 261, 278; **3:**341, 361, 381, 402, 420; **4:**464, 530, 550, 565, 566; **6:**746, 756, 782
Polynesia **8:**1014
climate **9:**1166–1169
flora and fauna **9:**1170, 1172–1173, 1177
geography **9:**1158, *1159*, 1160, 1163
geology **9:**1164, 1165
see also French Polynesia; Tonga
Polynesian Blue airline **9:***153*
Polynesians (people) **8:**1030, 1036, 1037, 1074, 1130, 1132; **9:**1189–1192, 1229, 1280, 1284, 1291; **10:**1416
European contacts **9:**1181, 1186
migration **9:**1174–1176, 1177, 1180, 1189, 1196, 1198, 1240, 1256
Pomare II, king of Tahiti **9:**1186

Pomare V, king of Tahiti **9:**1186, 1196
Pongsona (typhoon) **8:***1021*, 1022
Popo kingdom **3:**345
Popular Movement for the Liberation of Angola *see* MPLA
Pore-Daka, Battle of (1896) **2:**167, 172
Poro (animists) **2:**243, 277
Porquet, Niangoran **3:**399
Port-aux-Français **10:**1315, 1434, 1435
Port Elizabeth **7:**870, 883, 951, 973
Port-Gentil **1:**15, *80*, 84, *85*, 87, 88, *89*, 90, *91*
oil industry **1:**92
Port Harcourt **1:**13, 127
Port Jackson *see* Sydney Harbour
Port Louis **6:**729, 745, 796, 797
Port Moresby **8:**1015, 1020, 1028, 1104, 1105, 1107, 1108, 1116, 1117
manufacturing **8:**1121
transportation and communication **8:**1122
urbanization **8:**1113
Port Natal *see* Durban
Porto-Novo **3:**294, 341, 344, 345
architecture **3:***337*, 338, 339
history **3:**322, 323, 325, 326, 330, 335, 345
Port Phillip Bay **10:**1311, 1347, 1400
ports
Angola **5:**580, 582, 583, *609*, 624
Australia **10:**1305, 1382, 1397, *1400*, 1401, 1402, 1404, 1405, 1415
Benin **3:**337, 346, 349
Burundi **5:**590, 642, 645
Cameroon **1:**63, 66, 67
Cape Verde **2:***182*, 185, 189, 190, 191
Central African Republic **5:**658, 661
Comoros **6:**758
Congo, Democratic Republic of **5:**583, 605, 645, 677, 681
Congo, Republic of **5:**584, 687, 692, 694, 695, 696, 697
Djibouti **4:**438, 465, 470, 479, 480, 481

Equatorial Guinea **1**:76, 77
Eritrea **4**:439, 465, 487
Fiji **8**:1049
Gambia **2**:201, 203
Ghana **3**:373, 383, 384, *386*, 389
Guinea **2**:214
Guinea-Bissau **2**:227
Ivory Coast **3**:395, 405
Kenya **4**:441, 535, 538
Liberia **2**:237, 246, 249
Madagascar **6**:728
Malawi **6**:780
Mauritius **6**:796
Mozambique **6**:726, 745, 785, 812
Namibia **7**:874, 935, 937
Nauru **8**:1080
New Zealand **9**:1159, *1210*, 1220, 1221, 1228, 1229, *1229*, 1230, 1235
Nigeria **1**:124, 129
Papua New Guinea **8**:1015, *1113*, 1117
Samoa **9**:*1246*, 1252
Senegal **2**:250, 255, 262, 263, 267
Seychelles **6**:726
Sierra Leone **2**:280, 283
Solomon Islands **8**:1133
Somalia **4**:440, 462, 551, 553
Somaliland **4**:544
South Africa **7**:870, 954, 963, 964, 966, 973
Swahili **4**:459
Tanzania **6**:726, 727, 839
Togo **3**:423, 427
Tonga **9**:1270
Vanuatu **8**:1141, 1145, 1147
Portugal **1**:34, 46, 68, 78
Angola **5**:583, 602, 603, 604, 610, 614, 615–616, 616, 617, 618, 619, 620, 621, 622, 624, 682
Cape Verde **2**:166, 169, 172, 173, 179, 180, 185, 186, 189, 190, 223
central West Africa exploration **3**:292, 313, 314–315, 319, 321, 330, 345, 368, 380
colonial expansion **2**:173
see also Cape Verde; Portuguese Guinea
colonial guerrilla insurrections **2**:223
dictatorship **2**:185, 223
eastern African coast **4**:518, 535, 536, 551

Ethiopia **4**:458, 459–460, 464, 496
Guinea **2**:210
Guinea-Bissau *see* Portuguese Guinea
Indian Ocean islands **6**:739, 741, 742, 745, 750, 774, 788, 816, 818, 828
Kongo kingdom **5**:598, 599, 600–602, 603, 608, 610, 674
Lagos **1**:38, 123
Pacific exploration **8**:1031, 1064, 1086
São Tomé and Príncipe **1**:26, 38, 49, 130, 135, 137, 138
slave trade **1**:38, 123; **2**:169, 204, 250, 263; **3**:324
slave trade ban **2**:172
southern Africa **7**:887, 889, 890, 896, 926, 938, 940, 986
West African coastal exploration **2**:165, 166, 169, 170, 171, 172, 192, 204, 227, 230, 246, 250, 268
Portuguese East Africa **6**:800, 812
see also Mozambique
Portuguese Guinea **2**:173, 180, 184, 185, 210, 222, 224–225, 228
formation **2**:223, 227
independence *see* Guinea-Bissau
Portuguese language **2**:186, 224; **5**:607, 612, 619
Portuguese West Africa *see* Angola
Port-Vila **8**:1140, 1141, 1143, 1144, 1145, 1146
art galleries **8**:1142
tourism **8**:1147
postage stamp sales **10**:1416
Potatau, king of Maori **9**:1185
Poto-Poto School (painting) **5**:689
pottery **5**:*599*
Angola **5**:619
Cape Verde **2**:186
Choiseul **8**:1130
Fiji **8**:1045
Gambia **2**:199
Lapita **9**:1174
Maori **9**:1219
Melanesia **8**:1026–1027, 1028, 1029
Micronesia **8**:1029, 1031
Namibia **7**:933

New Zealand **9**:1219
Rwanda **5**:706
Samoa **9**:1174
Pouka, Louis-Maraie **1**:57
Praed, Mrs. Campbell (Rosa) **10**:1372
Praia **2**:153, 159, 186–187, 189, 191
praise poetry **7**:952
prehistory *see* fossils
Pre-Latte period **8**:1030
Prempeh I, king of Ashanti **3**:326; **6**:823
Presbyterianism
Australia **10**:1384, 1385
Malawi **6**:776, 782
New Zealand **9**:1123, 1223
Vanuatu **8**:1138, 1143
Prester John **1**:38; **4**:456
Preston, Margaret **10**:1375
Pretoria **7**:871, 882, *893*, 951, 962
history **7**:899, 962
university **7**:961, 962
Pretoria Agreement (2005) **3**:397
Pretoria Minute (1990) **7**:948
Pretorius, Andries **7**:892, 962
Pretorius, Marthinus **7**:893, 962
Prichard, Katherine Susannah **10**:1373
Prince Charles Mountains **10**:1314, 1432
Prince Edward Islands **7**:868
Príncipe *see* São Tomé and Príncipe
Proença, Helder **2**:224
Progressive Alliance of Liberia **2**:238
Protea genus **7**:*885*
Protestantism
Angola **5**:612, 616, 622
Benin **3**:332, 341
Burkina Faso **3**:352, 360
Burundi **5**:639
Cameroon **1**:60
Cape Verde **2**:182, 188
Central African Republic **5**:648, 656
Congo, Democratic Republic of **5**:664, 674
Congo, Republic of **5**:684, 692
Equatorial Guinea **1**:75
Ethiopia **4**:498, 508
Gabon **1**:80, 88
Gambia **2**:194, 201
Ghana **3**:370, 380
Guinea **2**:213

Ivory Coast **3**:392, 401, 402, 403
Kenya **4**:520, 529
Liberia **2**:232, 243
Madagascar **6**:742, 763, 769
Mozambique **6**:810
Nigeria **1**:97, 112
Rwanda **5**:700, 709, 710
Senegal **2**:261
Tanzania **6**:830
Togo **3**:412, 420
Uganda **4**:565
West African coast **2**:174, 179
Zambia **6**:846, 853
see also specific denominations and sects
Pukapuka *see* Cook Islands
Pulaar (Pular) (people) **2**:161, 260
Puntland **4**:440, 544, 545, 547, 550, 552, 553
Puttkamer, Jesko von **1**:59
pygmies **5**:609
see also Twa

Q

Qadiriyyah (Islamic brotherhood) **2**:260
Qaeda, al- **4**:547
Qarshe, Abdillah **4**:549
qat (khat) **4**:*476*, 478, 553
Quakers **2**:235
Queen Maud Land **10**:1314, 1425
Queensland **8**:1034, 1104, 1141; **10**:1365, 1394, 1411, 1413
climate **10**:1322–1323, 1325
federation **10**:1388
geography **10**:1300, 1306, *1307*, 1309, 1310, 1318
history **10**:1347, 1349, 1350, 1351
indigenous peoples **10**:1300, 1355, 1387, 1398
resources **10**:1409, 1410, 1411
rugby **10**:1382
university **10**:1393
see also Brisbane; Gold Coast
Quelimane **6**:726, 741, 744
Quirós, Pedro Fernández de **8**:1033; **9**:1180

R

Rabaul **8**:1015, 1103, 1104, 1108, 1117
Rabearivelo, Jean-Joseph **6**:766

Rabemananjara, Charles **6:**_764_

Rabemananjara, Jacques **6:**766

Rabih az-Zubayr **1:**30

Rabi Island **8:**1047; **9:**1202

Rabuka, Sitiveni **8:**1044

racial segregation _see_ apartheid

Radama I, king of Madagascar **6:**742, 745, 771

Radama II, king of Madagascar **6:**742

raffia cloth **5:**597, 600

Rafohy, queen of Merina **6:**742

railroads
  Australia **10:**1305, 1401, 1402, _1413_, 1415
  Congo Basin **5:**582, 583, 687
  South Africa **7:**973
  Tanzania **6:**833, 838, 839, _840_
  Zambia **6:**859
  Zimbabwe **7:**1003

rainfall
  Australia **10:**1321–1322, 1324, 1325
  Congo Basin **5:**588, 589, 590–591
  eastern Africa **4:**444–445, 446, 447, 449

rain forest
  Burundi **5:**644
  central West Africa **3:**294, _302_, 306, 307–308, 310, 322
  Congo Basin **5:**583, _584_, _590_, 591, 592–595, 594, 596, 660, 678, 679, 695, 696
  Liberia **2:**248
  Nigeria and Gulf of Guinea **1:**13, 14, 17, 22, 23, 26, 57, _64_, 77
  Polynesia **9:**1173
  West Africa **2:**150
  Western Pacific **8:**1014, 1015, 1023, 1024

Rajoelina, André **6:**765

Raklura _see_ Stewart Island

Rakotoson, Michèle **6:**766

Ralaimongo, Jean **6:**765

Ralik and Ratak _see_ Marshall Islands

Ramaema, Elias Phisoana **7:**919

Ramanantsoa, Gabriel **6:**765

Ramaphosa, Cyril **7:**948

Ramgoolam, Navim **6:**793

Ramgoolam, Seewoosagur **6:**793

Rampontchombo, Antochouwé Kowe (Denis) **1:**45–46

RAMSI (Regional Assistance Mission to the Solomon Islands) **8:**1129, 1134

Ranaivo, Flavien **6:**766

Ranavalona I, queen of Madagascar **6:**742, 745, 765, 769, 771

Ranavalona III, queen of Madagascar **6:**742

Rand _see_ Witwatersrand

Rand Revolt (1922) **7:**965, 967

Rano (Hausa state) **1:**36

Rapanui **9:**1189, 1191

rape
  civil wars **2:**243, 278; **5:**640, 656, _670_
  spousal **5:**656

rapids **5:**583

Raponda Walker, André **1:**85

Rarotonga Island **9:**1160, 1169, 1194

Rashidi-Kabamba, Maguy **5:**672

Rastafarianism **4:**502, 513

Ras Tafari Makkonen _see_ Haile Selassie I

Ratana, Tahupotiki Wiremu **9:**1189, 1223

Ratana Church **9:**1189, 1223

Ratsimandrava, Richard **6:**765

Ratsiraka, Didier **6:**764, 765

Ravalomanana, Marc **6:**764, 765

Rawiri, George **1:**85

Rawlings, Jerry **3:**368, 372, 376, 386

razana (ancestor spirits) **6:**769–770
  Polynesia **9:**1186, 1189, 1190, 1191

Read, Gabriel **9:**_1185_

Rebmann, Johannes **6:**744

recording industry **8:**1108–1109, 1131, 1143

Redda, Tewelde **4:**490

Red Sea **4:**449, 452, 453, 454, 459, 462, 465, 475, 479, 480, 487
  fish resources **4:**481

Red Terror (Ethiopia) **4:**512

Red Volta **3:**292, 294, 355

Reed Dance Day (Swaziland) **7:**981, 983

Reeves, William Pember **9:**1215, 1218

Reid, George **10:**1365

Remeliik, Haruo I. **8:**1093

Remengesau, Thomas Esang, Jr. **8:**_1093_

Renamo (Mozambican National Resistance) **6:**800, 804, 806, 810, 812, 813

René, France-Albert **6:**822, 823

reptiles **4:**448; **9:**1171

Reunification Monument (Yaoundé) **1:**_58_, 63

Reunion **6:**731, 737, 748, 816–817

Revolutionary United Front (Sierra Leone) **2:**274, 278, 281

Rey, Jacobus de la **7:**899

rhinoceros **4:**448; **5:**592; **7:**882, 883

Rhodes, Cecil **6:**745, 844, 849; **7:**893, 896, 898, 907, 967

Rhodesia **7:**896, 992, 999, 1000, 1003 _see also_ Zambia; Zimbabwe; Southern Rhodesia

Rhodes Memorial **7:**951

rhumba style **7:**995–996

Riale (Mandé hunter) **3:**311

rias (flooded river valleys) **2:**150

Ribeira Grande _see_ Cidade Velha

rice **2:**148, 150, 277, 282; **6:**726, _772_, 776

Richardson, Henry Handel **10:**1373

Richard Toll (city) **2:**148

Riebeeck, Jan van **7:**890

rift system **1:**16; **4:**438, 439, 443, 448

Rift Valley **6:**724, 726, 727, 731, 738

Rima River **1:**10

Rimbaud, Arthur **4:**476

Rio Muni _see_ Mbini

Rivonia trial **7:**947

Roba, Fatuma **4:**507

Robert, Shabaan **6:**835

Roberto, Holden **5:**617

Roberts, Joseph Jenkins **2:**236, _236_

Roberts, Lord **7:**898–899

Roberts, Tom **10:**1374

Rocado Zulu Théâtre **5:**690

Rocha de Serpa Pinto, Alexandre Alberto da **5:**603

rock art **4:**526; **7:**_976_
  Aboriginal Australians **10:**1318, 1374, 1413
  Botswana **7:**_904_, 908, _908_
  Lesotho **7:**920, 921
  Namibia **7:**933, _933_

San people **7:**_889_, _904_, 921, 933, _933_, 951, 995
  South Africa **7:**951
  Zimbabwe **7:**995

rock-hewn churches **4:**456, _456_, 506, 517

Rock Islands **8:**1015, 1031, _1090_

Rodrigues Island **6:**729, 792

Roggeveen, Jacob **9:**1180–1181, 1186; **10:**1346

Roggeveld Mountains **7:**871

Roha _see_ Lalibela

Roman Catholicism **1:**49; **3:**319, 324; **6:**747, 748
  Angola **5:**612, 620, 621, 622, 623, 624
  Australia **10:**1350, 1362, 1384, 1385, 1401
  Benin **3:**332, 335, 338, 339, 341, 344
  Botswana **7:**905, 910
  Burkina Faso **3:**352, 360, 363
  Burundi **5:**630, 634, 638, 639, 642
  Cameroon **1:**52, 60, 62, 63
  Cape Verde **2:**179, 182, 188
  Central African Republic **5:**648, 651, 654, 656
  Congo, Democratic Republic of **5:**664, 667, 674
  Congo, Republic of **5:**684, 692, 694
  Djibouti **4:**478
  Equatorial Guinea **1:**70, 73, 75
  Eritrea **4:**491, 492
  Fiji **8:**1040, _1044_, 1047
  Gabon **1:**80, 88, 90
  Gambia **2:**194, 200, 201
  Ghana **3:**370, 380, 384
  Guam **8:**1053
  Guinea **2:**206, 213
  Guinea-Bissau **2:**226
  Ivory Coast **3:**392, 396, 398–399, 401, 402, 403, _404_
  Kenya **4:**520, 529
  Kirbati **9:**1200, 1206, 1207
  Kongo kingdom **5:**598, 599, 600, 674
  Lesotho **7:**916, 921, 922, 923
  Liberia **2:**232, 243
  Madagascar **6:**763, 769, 771
  Malawi **6:**779, 782
  Marshall islands **8:**1056, 1061
  Mauritius **6:**790, 793, 795, 796
  Micronesia **8:**1066, 1071
  Mozambique **6:**802, _808_, 809, 810

Namibia **7:**928
Nauru **8:**1081
New Caledonia **8:**1085
New Zealand **9:**1182, 1186, 1189, 1212, 1223
Nigeria **1:**97, 112
Northern Mariana Islands **8:**1086, 1087
Palau **8:**1090, 1093, 1095
Papua New Guinea **8:**1100, 1103, 1104, 1111
Portugal **4:**459, 464
Reunion **6:**748, 817
Rwanda **5:**700, 704, 709, 710, 711, 712
Samoa **9:**1242, 1249
São Tomé and Príncipe **1:**132, 137, 138
Senegal **2:**252, 257, 261, *263*
Seychelles **6:**748, 820, 824, 825, 826
Solomon Islands **8:**1126, 1132
South Africa **7:**943, 956
Swaziland **7:**976, 982
Tanzania **6:**830, 837
Togo **3:**412, 419, 420, 423
Tonga **9:**1260, 1268
Uganda **4:**469, 556, 565
Vanuatu **8:**1138, 1143
Wallis and Futuna **9:**1291
Zambia **6:**846, 851, 853
Zimbabwe **7:**988, 997
Roman Empire **4:**454, 455
Roman Uniate Catholics **4:**484
Ronne-Filchner Ice Shelf **10:**1313
Rooiberg Mountains **7:**889
Roos, Nico **7:**933
Roosevelt, Theodore **2:**236
Roots (Haley book and TV series) **2:**198
Roots Festival (Gambia) **2:**198, 199, 203
Ross, James Clark **10:**1352
Ross, Mount **10:**1315
Ross Ice Shelf **10:**1313, 1353
Ross Island **10:**1314, *1419*, 1429, 1433
Ross Sea **10:**1312, 1313, 1320, 1432
Rotini, Ola **1:**105
Rousseau, Jean-Jacques **9:**1181
Rova palace complex **6:**771
Royal Drummmers of Burundi **5:***636*, 637
Royal Flying Doctor Service **10:**1390–1391
Royal Niger Company **1:**35, 43

Royal Palace of Bassar **3:***420*
Ruanda *see* Rwanda
Ruanda kingdom **5:**698, 703, 706, 711, 712, 713
Ruanda-Urundi **5:**604, 609, 628, 633, 642, 698, 703, 706, 712, 713
rubber
  Congo Basin **5:**606, 651, 687
  Liberia **2:***160*, 237, 247, 248, 249
Rudd, Kevin **10:**1371
Rufiji Valley **6:**726, 842
Rufisque **2:**263
Rugamba, Cyprien **5:**706, 707
rugby **7:**954; **8:**1048; **9:**1220, 1221, 1229, *1246*; **10:**1382
Rugyendo, Mukotani **4:**562
Rui, Manuel **5:**619
Rundi language **5:**609, 630, 636
running, long-distance **4:**489, *505*, 507, 528
Russell, John Peter **10:**1374
rutile **2:**281, 283
Ruwenzori Mountains **4:**439, 441, 442, 446, 571; **5:***583*, 585, 587
Rwagasore, Louis **5:**634, 638
Rwanda **4:**561; **5:**698–715, 700, 709
  art and architecture **5:**706
  Burundi **5:**642, 643, 645
  climate **5:**589, 590, *591*, 698
  cultural expression **5:**706–708
  daily life **5:**709–711
  economy **5:**699–700, 713–715
  education **5:***709*, 711
  family and society **5:**710–711
  festivals and ceremonies **5:**707–708
  flag **5:**699
  flora and fauna **5:**592–595
  food and drink **5:**708
  geography **5:**580, 582, 585, 698, 713
  geology **5:**586–587
  government and political parties **5:**700, 702
  health and welfare **5:**711
  history
    chronology **5:**701
    colonial *see* Ruanda-Urundi
    Congo Wars **5:**670, 678, 705
    modern **5:**618, 670, 698, 703–705, 709
    precolonial **5:**599

    independence **5:**698, 703, 704, 708, 709, 712, 713
  languages **5:**700, 705, 706
  music **5:**706–707
  peoples **5:**607, 609, 698, 700
    see also Hutu; Tutsi
  population **5:**699, 713
  religion **5:**700, 707–708, 709–710
  resources **5:**698, 713–714
  transportation and communication **5:**700, 715
Rwanda language *see* Kinyarwanda language
Rwandan genocide **5:**607, 609, 670, 698, 703, *704*, 705, 706, 707
  deaths **5:**709, 712
  economic effects **5:**713
  memorials **5:***704*, 708, 712
Rwandan Patriotic Front **5:**698, 702, 704, 705, 708, 709, 712, 715

S

Saba (Arabia) **4:**452, 453, 454
Sadji, Abdoulaye **2:**257
Sahara Desert **2:**150, 156, 158; **5:**590
  caravan trade **2:**164, 165–166, 169
Said, Abdulkadir Ahmed **4:**549
Sa'id, Al Bu **6:**741, 743
Saint Allouam, François-Alesno **10:**1346
Saint Anne Basilica **5:**690, 694
Saint Charles's Church Regent **2:**276
Saint George's Cathedral **2:**276, 280; **4:**513, *513*
Saint Helena **7:**938
  climate **7:**880, 938
  flag **7:**938
  flora and fauna **7:**885
  geography **7:**872, 938
  geology **7:**877
  population **7:**938
Saint Joseph's Cathedral **4:***491*
Saint-Louis **2:**148, 150, *250*, 258
  festival **2:**259
  history **2:**170, 171, 172, *173*, 250, 263
Saint Mary of Zion Church **4:**452, 508
Saint Mary's Catholic Cathedral **10:***1384*
Saint Mary's Island **2:**150, 173, 201

Saint Paul River **2:**152, 246, 248
Saint Vincent, Gulf of **10:**1308, 1397
Saipan **8:**1029, 1035
Sakassou kingdom **3:**390
Saker, Alfred **1:**46
Sakyi, Kwabena **3:**377
Salama, Abba **4:**505
Salazar, António de Oliveira **2:**185; **5:**615
Salii, Lazarus E. **8:**1093
Salik of Debre **4:**505
Salim, Aboucar Said **6:**756
Salisbury *see* Harare
Salisbury, Lord (Robert Cecil) **7:**999
Sal Island **2:**153, 191
Salonga National Park **5:**592
Salote Topou III, queen of Tonga **9:**1263
Saloum River **2:**150
salt lakes **10:**1306, 1309
salt mines **1:**28; **2:***151*; **5:**597
Sambi, Ahmed Abdallah Mohamed **6:**754
Samkange, Stanlake **7:**994
Sammy-Mackfoy, Pierre **5:**654
Samo (people) **3:**318
Samoa **8:**1026–1027, 1034, 1124, 1129; **9:**1240–1255
  art and architecture **9:**1246–1247
  climate **9:**1166, 1167, 1240
  cultural tradition **9:**1246–1248
  daily life **9:**1249–1251
  economy **9:**1240–1241, 1253–1255
  family and society **9:**1249–1251
  festivals and ceremonies **9:**1247–1248
  flag **9:**1242
  flora and fauna **9:**1170, 1173
  food and drink **9:**1248
  geography **9:**1162–1163, 1240
  geology **9:**1165
  government and political parties **9:**1190, 1241, 1244, 1253
  health and education **9:**1251
  history
    chronology **9:**1243
    early **9:**1174, 1175, 1176, 1180, 1240
    modern **9:**1187, 1240, 1245, 1252
  independence **9:**1244, 1245
  languages **9:**1190, 1242, 1246

Samoa (*continued*)
  literature **9:**1246
  music **9:**1247
  natural disasters **9:**1168, 1253
  partition **9:**1187
  peoples **9:**1180, 1189–1190, 1191, 1242, 1249
  population **9:**1240
  religion **9:**1190, 1242, 1249
  resources **9:**1240, 1254
  transportation and communication **9:**1242, 1255
  see also American Samoa; German Samoa; Western Samoa
Samori Ture (Samoury Touré) **2:**209, 168, 172, 173; **3:**326
Samputu, Jean-Paul **5:**707
Samy, Domingas **2:**224
San (people) **7:**901
  musical bow **7:**952
  rock art **7:***889, 904*, 921, 933, *933*, 951, 995
Sanaga River **1:**12, 65
Sanaga Valley **1:**14, 15
sandalwood **8:**1034, 1038, 1084, 1136, 1146
sand art **2:***259*; **8:**1142; **10:**1374
sand dunes **3:**298–299, *303*
  Hadejia-Nguru **1:**11
Sande (animists) **2:**243, 277
Sandhills Region **2:**150
Sand River Convention **7:**893
sandstone **10:**1310, 1318, 1319, 1320, *1342*
  rock formation **10:**1413
Sangha River **5:**604, 661
Sangho language **5:**607, 608, 648, 651, 653
Sanha, Malam Bacai **2:**223
Sanjane, Eusébio **6:**807
Sankara, Thomas **3:**355–356, 357, 359, 364
Sankawulo, Wilson **2:**240
Sankoh, Foday **2:**274
Santa Cruz Islands **8:**1016, 1130
Santiago (São Tiago) Island **2:**153, 169, 189, 190, 191
Santo Antão Island **2:**153, 190
Santos, Arnaldo **5:**619
Santos, José Eduardo dos **5:**614, 617, 618
Sanwi kingdom **3:**390
Sao (people) **1:**27, 29, 50
São Nicolau Island **2:**153, 190

São Paulo de Luanda *see* Luanda
São Tomé (city) **1:**15, 138
São Tomé and Príncipe **1:**130–139
  art and architecture **1:**136
  climate **1:**18, 21, 130
  cultural expression **1:**136
  daily life **1:**137
  economy **1:**132, 139
  education **1:**137
  flag **1:**131
  flora and fauna **1:**22, 25
  geography **1:**10, 15, 130
  geology **1:**17
  government and political parties **1:**130, 132, 134, 135
  history
    chronology **1:**133
    modern **1:**135
    Portuguese settlement **1:**26, 38, 49, 130, 135, 137, 138
  independence **1:**130, 135
  literature **1:**136
  music **1:**136
  peoples **1:**47, 49, 132, 138
  population **1:**130
  religion **1:**132
  resources **1:**92, 130, 139
  transportation and communication **1:**132, 138
São Tomé Island **5:**598, 602
São Vincente Island **2:**153, *180*, 185, *188*, 189, *190*, 191
sapphires **6:**773
Sargeson, Frank **9:**1218
Sarki Babari, Gobir ruler **1:**37
Saro-Wiwa, Ken **1:**105
Sassine, Williams **2:**211
Sassou-Nguesso, Denis **5:***686*, 688
Saudeleur dynasty **8:**1031
Saunana, John **8:**1130
Savage, Michael **9:**1216, 1231
Savai'i Island **9:**1162–1163, 1240, *1250*, 1252
savanna
  Akan people **3:**314
  Central African Republic **5:***646*, 660
  coastal **3:**308
  Congo Basin and Angola **5:**583, 584, 585, 592, *594*, 595
  Congo, Republic of **5:***684*
  eastern Africa **4:**448–449, 451
  eastern Central Africa **6:**726, *730*, 735, *736*, 738

  eastern South Africa **7:**870, 874, *875*, *987*
  Ghana **3:**380
  Guinea **1:**23–24
  Nigeria **1:**10, 11, 22, 23–24
  Sahel **1:**24
  southern Africa **7:**870, 874, *875*
  sub-Sahara **3:**294, *295*, 297–298, 306–307, 310
  Sudan **1:**24
  termite mounds **2:**218
  West African coast **2:**150, 151, *161*, 162–163
  Western Pacific **8:**1024
  Zimbabwe **7:***987*
savanna snakes **4:**448
Savimbi, Jonas **5:**617, 618
Sawa (people) **1:**57, 59
Sayfawa dynasty **1:**28, 29, 30, 36
Sayf ibn Dhi Yazan, ruler of Yemen **1:**28
Sayyid Sa'id ibn Sultan **6:**741, 743
schistosomiasis **3:**342, 381, 421
Schools of the Air **10:**1393
Schouten, Willem **8:**1033; **9:**1180
Schweitzer, Albert **1:**87
scientific bases, Antarctic **10:**1418, 1419, 1424, 1425, 1428–1429, 1430, 1434, 1435
scientific exploration, Western Pacific **8:**1033
Scott, Robert **10:**1314, 1353, *1354*, 1424
"scramble for Africa" **2:**172, 173; **3:**325–326; **4:**465, 501; **5:**602, 603, 604, 605, 615; **6:**743
Scullin, James **10:**1367
sculpture **6:**748
  Australia **10:**1375, *1376*
  Ivory Coast **3:**398
  Mozambique **6:**807–808
  Tanzania **6:**835
  Togo **3:**418
  Zambia **6:**851
  see also carving; wood carving
scurvy **9:**1181
sea level rise *see* climate change
seals **10:**1302, 1338–1339, *1338*, 1348, 1352, 1418, 1426, 1430, *1434*
sea mounts (submarine mountains) **1:**17

  eastern South Africa **7:**870, 874, *875*, *987*
Sea Shepherd (organization) **10:***1433*
SEATO (South East Asian Treaty Organization) **9:**1216
Seck, Idrissa **2:**256
Second Anglo-Boer War **7:**894, 898–899, 940, 945, 962, 965, 967, 979
Second Angolan Civil War **7:**931
Second Congo War **5:**618, 662, 666, 671; **6:**673; **7:**931
  deaths **5:**670, 678, 705
  economic effects **5:**678, 680, 681
Second Liberian Civil War **2:**239
Seddon, Richard John **9:**1215
segaba tradition **7:**909
Ségou (city) **3:**323
Ségou kingdom **2:**168
Seifu, Debebe **4:**506
Seke (people) **1:**46
Sekondi **3:**373
Sékou Touré, Ahmed **2:**204, 209, 210, 211, 212, 215, 255; **3:**396
Seku Amadu **3:**323
Selassie, Hiruy Wolde **4:**505
semba (Angolan music genre) **5:**620
Sembène, Ousmane **2:**257, 258
Semedo, Odete **2:**224
Semitic languages **4:**453, 467, 468
Senegal **2:**250–267; **3:**329, 335, 395, 417
  art and architecture **2:**257–258, 259, *265*
  chronology **2:**252
  climate **2:**156–157, 159, 250, *260*
  cultural expression **2:**257–259, 275; **5:**653
  daily life **2:**260–261
  economy **2:**252, 264–267
  education **2:***256*, 260, 262
  family and society **2:**261–262
  festivals and ceremonies **2:**258–259
  flag **2:**252
  flora and fauna **2:**160–163
  food and drink **2:**259
  geography **2:**148–151, 250
  geology **2:**154
  government and political parties **2:**252, 254
  health and welfare **2:**262

history
early **2:**164–168, 250, 263
French rule **2:**172–173,
209, 250, 255, 257, 263,
264
modern **2:**250, 255–256
independence **2:**250, 255
literature **2:**257; **3:**417
music **2:**258, 259
peoples **2:**176, 177, 178, 179,
252, 257, 258, 260, 261
population **2:**252, 261
religion **2:**250, 252, 257,
259, 260–261
resources **2:**250, 265
transportation and
communication **2:**252,
263, 267
Senegalese Democratic Bloc
2:255
Senegalese Democratic Party
2:256
Senegal River **2:**148, 150, 164,
165, 250
exploration **2:**169, 170
flooding **2:**148, 150
French settlement **2:**172,
263
Senegambia Confederation
2:192, 197, 250, 256
Senghor, Léopold Sédar **2:**250,
255–256, *255*, 257, 264,
275; **3:**395, 417; **5:**653
Senhaja Berbers **2:**164
Sentinel Peak **7:***873*
Senufo (people) **3:**323, 328,
360, 398
Senufo language **3:**357, 398
Sepamia, Sipho **7:**950
Sepik art **8:**1106, 1107, *1111*
Sepik River **8:**1015, 1107
Serengeti National Park **6:**735,
834, 843
service sector *see* industry and
services
Sese Seko *see* Mobutu Sese
Seko
Setlhako, Ratsie **7:**909
Seventh-Day Adventists
8:1040, 1047, 1138, 1143
Sewell, Henry **9:**1185
Sex Discrimination Act (1984,
Australia) **10:**1389
Seychelles **6:**818–827
climate **6:**732–733, 818
cultural expression **6:**824
daily life **6:**825
economy **6:**819, 827
family and society **6:**825
festivals and food **6:**824

flag **6:**820
flora and fauna **6:**736, *818*
geography **6:**724, 729, 818
geology **6:**730, 731
government and political
parties **6:**819–820, 822, 823
health and education **6:**825
history
chronology **6:**821
modern **6:**745, 748, 818,
823
independence **6:**749, 818, 823
literature **6:**824
music **6:**824
peoples **6:**820, 825
population **6:**818–819
religion **6:**820, 825
resources **6:**818, 827
transportation **6:**820, 827
Seydou, Chris **3:**398
Seydou Nourou Tall mosque
2:*257*
Shaba *see* Katanga province
Shabaab, al (Somali militant
organization) **4:**545
Shabeelle River **4:**440, 515,
553
Shackleton, Ernest **10:**1314,
1353, 1354, 1428
Shackleton Range **10:**1313
Shadbolt, Maurice **9:**1218
Shag Island **10:**1426
Shaka, king of Zulu **6:**744
Shaka kaSenzangakhona, king
of Zulu **7:**892, 895, 896,
900, 920, 964
shantytowns
Angola **5:**620, 622, 624
Burundi **5:**642
Congo, Democratic Republic
of **5:**677
Mozambique **6:**810, 812
Rwanda **5:**706
South Africa **7:***957*
Zambia **6:**855
Zimbabwe **7:**999
Sharia (Islamic law) **1:**36, 40,
41, 104, 112, 114, 121;
4:545, 547
Sharp, Granville **2:**174, 280
Sharpeville massacre (1960)
7:946, 954
Sheba, queen of **4:**452, 463,
464, 468, 502, 505
sheep raising **9:**1160, 1231,
1233, 1234; **10:**1348,
1406, 1410–1411, *1411*
shell necklace **8:***1028*
Shepstone, Theophilus **7:**896
Sherbro Island **2:**171

Shermarke, Abdirashid Ali
4:547
Shimbra Kure, Battle of (1529)
4:462, 464
Shipley, Jenny **9:**1217
Shirazi dynasties **6:**740–741
Shire River **6:**736, 744
Shire Valley **6:**727, 734, 739
Shityuwete, Helao **7:**932
Shiva (Hindu god) **6:**794, *795*
Shoa kingdom **4:**456, 501
Shona (people) **7:**886,
900–901, 988, 992, 994,
995, 996, 997
Short Chronology Model
8:1029
Siad Barre, Muhammad **4:**540,
544, 545, 547, 548, 550
SIAO (International Art and
Craft Fair) **3:**357, 359,
363, 367
Siaosi Tupou V, king of Tonga
9:1264–1265, 1268, 1272
Siegu, Pierre Monsard **1:**85
Sierra Leone **1:**38, 43, 73;
2:268–283; **3:**315
art and architecture **2:**186,
275–276, 280
chronology **2:**271
climate **2:**157–158, 268
cultural expression **2:**186,
275–277
daily life **2:**278–279
economy **2:**270, 281–283
education **2:**273, 279
family and society **2:**278
festivals and ceremonies
2:277
flag **2:**269
food and drink **2:**277
founding **2:**174–175, 176, 179
geography **2:**148, 152–153,
268
geology **2:**154
government and political
parties **2:**270, 272, *273*
health and welfare **2:**278, 279
history
British rule **2:**173,
174–175, 179, 268, 273,
275, 280, 281
civil war **2:**239, 268, 273,
274, 278, 279, 280, 281,
282, 283
early **2:**172, 268
founding **2:**174–175, 176,
179
modern **2:**268, 273–274
independence **2:**268, 272,
273, 280, 281

Liberia **2:**239, 240, 268
literature **2:**275
music **2:**276–277
peoples **2:**176, 177–178, 270,
275, 278
population **2:**269
religion **2:**174, 270, 277, 278
resources **2:**268, 281–282
transportation and
communication **2:**270,
280, 283
Sierra Leone Company **2:**173,
174–175, 268, 280
Sierra Leone Peninsula **2:**152,
169
Sierra Leone People's Party
2:272, 273, 274
Sierra Leone Selection Trust
2:282
Sierra Leone Truth and
Reconciliation
Commission **2:**274
Sigave **9:**1162, 1186, 1290
Sila, Abdulai **2:**224
Silva, João Carlos **1:**136
Simangaliso Wetlands Park
7:883
Simango, Daviz **6:**804
Simina, Wesley **8:***1068*
Simon, Paul **7:**953
Simpson Desert **10:**1306
Sine kingdom **2:**172
Singavi, Mount **9:**1162
Singh, Vijay **8:**1048
Sinyangwe, Binwell **6:**851
Sipolo, Jully **8:**1130
Sithole, Lucas **7:**951
Sithole, Ndabaningi **7:**992
Skate, Bill **8:**1119
Slater, Ransford **3:**373
Slave, The (Couchoro) **3:**338
Slave Coast **3:**321, 322, 325
slavery
Cape Verde **2:**186
Liberia **2:**237
São Tomé and Príncipe **1:**38,
130, 135, 137, 138
southern Africa **7:**890–891,
901, 963
see also freed slave
settlements
slave trade
abolition **2:**172, 180;
3:322–323, 324, 325;
5:602, 603, 604, 615
Benin **1:**34, 35
British ban **1:**35, 42, 45, 46,
68, 76; **2:**172, 173, 192,
197, 268, 273; **3:**322–323,
324, 325; **6:**744

slave trade (*continued*)
Cape Verde **2**:179, 180, 185, 186
Central African Republic **5**:646
central West Africa **3**:313, 314, 315, 318, 319, 320, 345, 383
Congo **5**:605, 675, *684*; **6**:682
Danhome kingdom **3**:321, 322, 324, 328, 330
Douala **1**:63
Dutch Republic **2**:171, 250, 268, 280
eastern Central Africa **6**:739, 740, 741, 743, 744–745, 748, 821
embarkation sites **2**:198, 250, 263
Gabon **1**:45, 46
Gambia **2**:192, 197, 198
Gorée **2**:171, 250, 263
Guinea **2**:204
Guinea-Bissau **2**:218, 227
Gulf of Guinea **1**:39, 42
Hausa states **1**:36
Kongo **5**:590, 597, 598, 599, *600*, 601
Lagos **1**:38, 123
Mali Empire **2**:166
Mauritius **6**:788, 796
Nigeria **1**:38–39, *39*, 45, 46
Niger River Delta **1**:43
peak years **3**:321
Portugal **5**:598, 599, 601, 602, 615, 624
Seychelles **6**:821
Sierra Leone **2**:268, 280
Togo **3**:410
West Africa **2**:166, 169, 170, 171, 176, 204
Yoruba **1**:32
Slave Trade Act (1807, Britain) **1**:45, 46
sleeping sickness **3**:307, 343, 381, 403
smallpox **9**:1181; **10**:1344
Smith, Ian **7**:992, 995
Smith, William **10**:1352
smuggling **5**:681; **7**:1002
Smuts, Jan **7**:945, 946
Snowy Mountains **10**:1309, 1311, 1406
Snowy River Project **10**:1368, 1410
soapstone-carved birds **7**:995
Sobhuza II, king of Swazi **7**:974, 978, 979, 981, 984

soccer **1**:62, *74*, *110*; **3**:*342*, *360*, *381*, 384, *419*; **4**:491, 507; **5**:*619*, *691*; **10**:1382
see also World Cup
Social Democratic Convergence (Equatorial Guinea) **1**:72
Social Democratic Front (Cameroon) **1**:54, 56
Socialist Party (Senegal) **2**:254, 255, 256
Socialist Realist style **5**:690
Society Islands **9**:175, 1163, 1176
history **9**:1181, 1186, 1196
Sofala *see* Beira
Soglo, Nicéphore **3**:336, 346–347
Soilihi, Ali **6**:756
Sokoto **1**:10, 20, 30, 37, 40, 41–42, 45, 47, *96*, 101; **2**:167; **3**:329
Sokoto Plains **1**:10, 20
Sokoto River **1**:10
Solomon, King (biblical) **4**:452, 463, 464, 468, 502, 505
Solomon Basin **8**:1012
Solomonic dynasty **4**:456, 463–464, 468, 501–502
founding legend **4**:505
Solomon Islands **8**:1124–1135; **9**:1174, 1187, 1245
art and architecture **8**:1130–1131
climate **8**:1019–1022, 1124
cultural expression **8**:1130–1131
daily life **8**:1132
economy **8**:1125, 1134–1135
family and society **8**:1132
festivals, food, and drink **8**:1131
flag **8**:1126
flora and fauna **8**:1023–1025
geography **8**:1012, 1015, 1016, 1124
geology **8**:1017–1018
government and political parties **8**:1125, 1128
health, welfare, and education **8**:1132
history
chronology **8**:1127
early **8**:1027, 1032, 1033, 1124
modern **8**:1034, 1035, 1103, 1124, 1129, 1133, 1134, 1141
independence **8**:1124, 1129, 1131

languages **8**:1126, 1130, 1133
literature **8**:1130
music **8**:1131
peoples **8**:1036, 1124, 1126, 1129, 1130, 1134
population **8**:1125
provinces **8**:1126, 1128
religion **8**:1126, 1132
resources **8**:1124, 1134
transportation and communication **8**:1126, 1135
Solomon Sea **8**:1012
Solomon Trench **8**:1012
Somali (people) **4**:464, 465, 467, 470, 474, 475, 476, 529, 540, 542, 546
clans **4**:550
see also Issa
Somalia **4**:540–553
art and architecture **4**:548
climate **4**:444, 446, 447, 540
cultural expression **4**:548–549
daily life **4**:550
economy **4**:542, 552–553
as failed state **4**:540, 545, 546, 547, 553
family and society **4**:550
festivals and ceremonies **4**:549
flag **4**:541
flora and fauna **4**:448–451
food and drink **4**:549
geography **4**:436, 440, 442–443, 540
government **4**:540, 542, 544, 545
history
chronology **4**:543
colonial *see* British Somaliland; Italian Somaliland
early **4**:459, 462–463, 464, 540
Ethiopian war *see* Ogaden
modern **4**:487, 546–547, 552
independence **4**:440, 540, 546, 547, 551
literature **4**:548
music **4**:549
peoples **4**:462, 467, 542, 546, 550
population **4**:541–542
religion **4**:464, 467, 540, 542, 545, 550
resources **4**:540, *552*, 553
transportation and communication **4**:542, 553

Somalian immigrants **10**:1389
Somaliland **4**:464, 465, 466, 544, 550
autonomy **4**:544, 545, 547, 549, 552
economy **4**:544, 553
flag **4**:544
government **4**:545
Somali language **4**:472, 476, 542, 548
Somare, Michael **8**:*1102*, 1105
Somba (people) **3**:338–339
Songhai empire **1**:27, 29, 36; **2**:166; **3**:312, *327*
Soninke (people) **2**:164, 178, 258
Sonni Ali (Songhai king) **3**:312
Sopi Coalition (Senegal) **2**:256
Soro, Guillaume **3**:394, 397, 406
Soshangane (Ngoni leader) **6**:739, 747
Sosseh, Laba **2**:199
Sotavento Islands **2**:153
Sotho (people) *see* Basotho
Souaré, Ahmed Tidiane **2**:210
Soul Makossa (song) **1**:59
Sousou (Susu) (people) **2**:178, 204, 211, 212, 213, 214
South Africa **3**:396; **7**:940–973
art and architecture **7**:951, 966
chronology **7**:943
climate **7**:878, 879, 880, 881, 940
cultural expression **7**:950–955
daily life **7**:956–961
economy **7**:936, 942, 949, 967–973
education **7**:961, 968, 970
family and society **7**:957–958, 970
festivals and ceremonies **7**:954
flag **7**:942
flora and fauna **7**:882–885
food and drink **7**:955
formation **7**:907, 940
geography **5**:583, 589; **7**:868–873, 940
geology **7**:876–877
government and political parties **7**:942, 944, 949
new democratic era **7**:940, 947, 948–949, 954, 969–970
health and welfare **7**:959–960, 970

history
Angolan Civil War **5**:617,
625
Congo War **5**:670
European settlers
7:890–896, 898–899, 940
modern **7**:940, 945–949,
967
languages **7**:943, 950, 957,
961
literature **7**:950
music **7**:952–953
peoples **7**:900, 901, 902, 942,
945, 946, 952, 957–958
population **7**:942
religion **7**:942–943, 954,
956, 958
resources **7**:893, 940, 962,
967, 971
transportation and
communication **7**:942,
966, 971, 972, 973
South African Republic *see*
Transvaal
South African Truth and
Reconciliation
Commission **7**:749
South Asians **6**:748, 833, 834
Malawi **6**:783
Mauritius **6**:788, 794, 795,
796
Reunion. **6**:816
South Africa **7**:892, 901, 947,
952, 956, 957, 958, 964,
967
Tanzania **6**:833, 834
see also Indo-Fijians
South Australia **10**:1308,
1309, 1365
climate **10**:1322, 1324
federation **10**:1388
history **10**:1348, 1349, 1350,
1358
resources **10**:1409
see also Adelaide
South East Asian Treaty
Organization **9**:1216
Southern African Customs
Union **7**:936, 985
Southern African Development
Community **6**:859
Southern Alps **9**:1159, 1160,
1165, 1166, 1168, 1170,
1172
Southern Ocean **10**:1302,
1313, 1320, 1339, 1424,
1425, 1430
climate of islands **10**:1328
fisheries **10**:1432–1433
islands' climate **10**:1328

Southern Rhodesia **7**:896, 986,
991, 991–993, 993, 994,
997, 999, 1000
see also Zimbabwe
South Georgia **10**:1315, 1328,
1337, 1338, 1339, 1423,
1426, 1430
exploration **10**:1354
South Island **9**:1158,
1159–1160, *1162*, 1165,
1228, 1229, 1231
agriculture **9**:1234
architecture **9**:1219
climate **9**:1166, 1168
flora and fauna **9**:1170, 1171
history **9**:1180, 1182, 1185,
1191
lifetyle **9**:1225
Maori settlement **9**:1177,
1178–1179
see also Christchurch
South Luangwa National Park
6:859
South Orkney Islands **10**:1313,
1315, 1337
South Pacific Arts Society
9:1246
South Pacific Forum **9**:1264
South Pole **10**:1313, 1320,
1336, 1352, 1353, *1354,*
1423, 1424, 1425, 1433
Amundsen-Scott Station
10:1326, 1328, *1429*
South Sandwich Islands
10:1313, 1315, 1337, 1423,
1426
South Sandwich Trench
10:1302
South Sea Evangelical Mission
8:1132
South Shetland Islands
10:1315, 1337
South West Africa *see* Namibia
Soviet Union
Angola **5**:617, 618, 625
Congo, Democratic Republic
of **5**:668
Congo, Republic of **5**:687,
690
Ethiopia **4**:503–504, 514
Guinea **2**:204, 209, 210, 217
Guinea-Bissau **2**:223, 228
Katanga secession **5**:668
Namibia **7**:931
Somalia **4**:547
see also Cold War
Sow, Ousmane **2**:258
Soweto **7**:*956*, 957, 965, 966
Soweto uprising (1976) **7**:947,
954, 966

Soyinka, Wole **1**:105
Spain
Dutch war **5**:601
Equatorial Guinea **1**:72, 73,
75
maritime exploration
1:38–39, 46; **2**:170
Western Pacific **8**:1032–1033,
1034–1035, 1052, 1054,
1059, 1064, 1069, 1086,
1093, 1095
Spanish-American War
8:1034–1035, 1052, 1093
Spanish Guinea **1**:68, 72, 73,
75, 76
Spanish language **1**:70, 75
Speight, George **8**:1044
Speke, John Hanning **4**:466;
5:603; **6**:744
spices **6**:726, 743, 756, 842;
8:1032
Spinola, António de **2**:223
Stairs, William Grant
5:605–606
stamps, Tuvalu **9**:1279
Stanley, Henry Morton
5:603–604, 605, 677
Stanley Falls *see* Boyoma Falls
Stanley Pool *see* Malebo Pool
Stanleyville *see* Kisangani
Stead, Christina, (Australian
writer) **10**:1373
Stead, C. K. (New Zealand
writer) **9**:1218
stelae **4**:454, 455, 506
Stele of Aksum **4**:*455*
Stellaland republic **7**:896
Stellenbosch University **7**:961
Stellenbosch Valley **7**:*967*
Stern, Irma **7**:951
Stevens, Jimmy **8**:1141
Stevens, Siaka **2**:272, 274
Stewart, Harold **10**:1373
Stewart Island **9**:1158, 1231
Steyn, Marthinus Theunis
7:898
Stirling **10**:1403
Stirling, James **10**:1347
Stirling Mountains **10**:1305
"Stolen Generation"
(Aboriginal children)
10:1356, 1371, 1373, 1388
stone carving **7**:995
stone complexes, Great
Zimbabwe **7**:*886*, 887,
986, *994*, 995
story-boards (Palau) **8**:1094
Strasser, Valentine **2**:274
Streeton, Arthur **10**:1374
Strijdom, Johannes G. **7**:946

Strzelecki, Paul **10**:1311
Stuart, John McDouall
10:1350
Sturt, Charles **10**:1348
Sturt Stony Desert **10**:1309
sub-Antarctic territories
10:1302, 1315, 1423,
1424, 1426–1427
climate **10**:1326
tourism **10**:1433
see also French Southern
Territories
subtropical forest **10**:1399
Sudan **4**:453, 454, 455, 459,
465, 496
geology **5**:586–587
history, modern **5**:652
linguistic groups **4**:457
Mahdi **4**:487, 501
Uganda **4**:561
Suez Canal **4**:465, 470, 479,
501, 546; **6**:796, 816
Sufism **2**:167, 177, 257, 260,
262; **4**:477, 508, 548,
550
Somalian music **4**:549
sugar plantations **1**:130, 138;
7:985; **8**:1086
Australia **10**:1388, 1411
eastern Central Africa **6**:729,
748, 793, 797, 816
Fiji **8**:1037, 1038, *1042*,
1043, 1047, 1050
slave labor **5**:598, 601, 602
Sukuma (people) **6**:739, 746,
747, 748, 837
Sukuna, Lala **8**:1043
Suleyman, mansa of Mali
2:165
sulu (Fijian garment) **8**:1045
Sunni Muslims *see* Islam
Sunset Boys **2**:241
Sunshine Coast (Australia)
10:1310, 1413
Surfers Paradise (Australia)
10:1399
Susenyos, emperor of Ethiopia
4:464
Suso, Foday Musa **2**:199
Susu (people) *see* Sousou
Sutherland, Afua **3**:377
Sutherland, Joan **10**:1378
Suva **8**:1016, 1045, 1049
Swahili (people) **4**:457–458,
459, *460*, 466, 469; **6**:739,
740, 741, 742, 743, 746,
747, 748, 750, 756, 760,
835, 837
art and architecture **4**:526,
527

Swahili language **4**:458, 467, 526, 556, 562; **5**:607, 664, 671; **6**:739, 740, 741, 742, 743, 746, 747, 748, 750, 756, 760, 835, 837

Swakopmund **7**:932, 933, 937

Swan River colony **10**:1347, 1358, 1403

SWAPO (South West Africa People's Organization) **7**:926, 930, 931, 947

Swazi (people) **7**:889, 895, 900, 974, 976, 980, 982

Swaziland **7**:974–985

art and architecture **7**:980

climate **7**:878, 879, 974

cultural expression **7**:980–981

daily life **7**:982

economy **7**:936, 975, 984–985

family and society **7**:982

festivals, food, and drink **7**:981, 983

flag **7**:976

flora and fauna **7**:882–885, *984*

geography **7**:870, 974

geology **7**:876

government and political parties **7**:974, 975, 978, 979, 984

health, welfare, and education **7**:*979*, 982

history

chronology **7**:977

modern **7**:907, 974, 979, 983

precolonial **7**:888–889, 896

independence **7**:974, 978, 979, 983

languages **7**:976, 980

literature **7**:980

music **7**:980–981

peoples **7**:900, 976, 980, 982

population **7**:975

religion **7**:976, 982

resources **7**:974, 985

transportation and communication **7**:976, 985

Sweden, Gold Coast **3**:320, 324, 368, 383

Swedish Lutheran Mission **4**:492

sweet potato **8**:1028, 1110

Sydney **10**:1310–1311, 1366, 1395, 1398, 1404–1405, 1415

art and architecture **10**:1374, 1376

festivals **10**:1381

history **10**:1344, 1347, 1348, 1349, 1350, 1357, 1372, 1401, 1404–1405

housing **10**:1394

population **10**:1311, 1404

religion **10**:1384

universities **10**:1393, 1405

Sydney, Viscount (Thomas Townshend) **10**:1404

Sydney Cove **10**:1380, 1387

Sydney Harbour **10**:1311, 1344, 1347, 1372, *1381*, 1404

Sydney Harbour Bridge **10**:*1404*, 1405

Sydney Opera House **10**:1376, *1376*, 1378, 1379, *1404*, 1405

syncretic religions **7**:988, 997

T

Taal, Omar Foutiyou **2**:199

Tabai, Jeremia **9**:1203

Table Bay **7**:890

Table Mountain **7**:*871*, 872, 885, 963

Rhodes Memorial **7**:951

taboos *see tapu*

Tadjo, Véronique **3**:398

Tadjoura **4**:*471*, 475, 476, 479

Tadjoura, Gulf of **4**:438, 479

Tadjoura sultanate **4**:465, 470, 475, 479

Tagbaladougou Falls **3**:298

Tahiti **9**:1163, 1165, 1166

flora and fauna **9**:1173

history **9**:1181, 1186, 1196

peoples **9**:1189, 1191

Takoradi **3**:373, 389

Takrur (early state) **2**:164–165

Talansan, Battle of **2**:167

Tamale **3**:304, 305, *381*

Tamatave *see* Toamasina

Tana, Lake **4**:*439*, 451, *515*

Tanami Desert **10**:1306

Tananarive *see* Antananarivo

Tanga **6**:726, 837

Tanganyika *see* Tanzania

Tanganyika, Lake **5**:580, 585, 642, 643; **6**:727, 731, 736, 746

British explorers **5**:603

European explorers **6**:744

fishing **5**:*628*, 638, 644; **6**:842, 858

German railroad line **6**:833, 838, 839

Tange, Kenzo **1**:119

Tanna Island **8**:1016, *1137*, 1141, 1143

Tansi, Sony Labou **5**:689, 690

TANU (Tanganyika African National Union) **6**:832, 833, 834, 836

Tanyi-Tang, Anne **1**:58

Tanzania **4**:466, 523; **5**:586–587, 645, 681; **6**:828–843

art and architecture **6**:835, 839

Burundi refugees **5**:*638*, 641, 643, 645

climate **6**:732–734, 828

cultural expression **6**:756, 835–836

daily life **6**:837

economy **6**:830, 840–843

family life **6**:837

festivals and food **6**:836

flag **6**:830

flora and fauna **6**:735–736

geography **6**:724, 726–727, 736, 828

geology **6**:730, 731

government and political parties **6**:830, 832

health and education **6**:837

history

chronology **6**:831

modern **6**:744, 745, 828, 833–834, 838, 839, 849–850

precolonial **6**:739, 740–741, 747, 828

independence **6**:828, 833, 839

Kenya **4**:535, 538

lingua franca **6**:748

literature **6**:835

music **6**:836

peoples **6**:744, 746, 747–748, 830, 837; **7**:896

population **6**:829, 834

religion **6**:830, 837

resources **6**:828, 841

Rwanda **5**:705

transportation and communication **6**:830, *840*, 843, 859

Uganda **4**:560, 568

Tanzanian Craton **4**:442

tanzanite (gemstone) **6**:841

Taoué River **2**:148

tapa (bark cloth) **8**:1107, 1130; **9**:1247, 1265–1266, *1280*

tapu (Maori taboos) **9**:1179, 1182, 1223

Taranaki **9**:1159, 1184, 1185, 1221, 1233

Taranaki War **9**:1185

Tarawa, Battle of **9**:1198, 1203

Tarawa Atoll **9**:1161, 1203, 1204, 1205, 1206, 1207, 1279, 1284

taro **8**:*1031*, 1110

Tasman, Abel Janszoon **8**:1033; **9**:1180, 1209; **10**:1300, 1345

Tasman Bay **9**:1160

Tasman Glacier **9**:1159, 1165

Tasmania **10**:1304, 1309, 1311, 1381, 1400

Aboriginal Australians **10**:1343, 1355

climate **10**:1323, 1329

federation **10**:1388

flora and fauna **10**:1334

history **10**:1345, 1346, 1347, 1348, 1349, 1387

resources **10**:1410, 1411

university **10**:1393

Tasman Sea **9**:1166

tattoos **4**:526; **8**:1130; **9**:1247, 1266

Taufa'ahau Tupou IV, king of Tonga **9**:1264, *1269*

Ta'u Island **9**:1163, *1168*

Taupo, Lake **9**:1159, 1165

Tauranga **9**:1159, 1221, 1229, 1235

Tavares, Eugénio **2**:186, 187

Tavurvur, Mount **8**:*1018*, *1100*, *1123*

Tawhiao, king of Maori **9**:1185

tax haven **8**:1145, 1147

Tayali, Henry **6**:851

Taylor, Charles **2**:239; **3**:396

Taytu, empress of Ethiopia **4**:512

Tchicaya, Gérald Félix **5**:653

Tchicaya U Tam'si **5**:689

Tchichellé Tchivela **5**:689

tectonic plates **4**:442, 443; **8**:1017

Teixeira de Sousa, Henrique **2**:186

Te Kanawa, Kiri **9**:1220

Téké (people) **5**:599, 689–690, 692, 694

Tekle, Afework **4**:506

Tem (people) **3**:419

Tema **3**:294, 383, 384, *386*, 389

Temne (people) **2**:172, 173, 174, 177–178, 273, 275, 278

Tench, Watkin **10**:1372

Tenkodogo kingdom **3**:311, 316, 350

tennis **10**:1382
Tenreiro, José Francisco **1**:136
Te Rauparaha (Maori chief) **9**:1179
Terra Australis **9**:1180, 1181; **10**:1346, 1352, 1418
Terra Nova Expedition **10**:1353, *1354*
terra nullius concept **10**:1348
terrorism
    Kenya **4**:537, 538
    Uganda **4**:560, 561, 565
Tesfai, Alemseged **4**:489
Teso language **4**:562
Têtes Brulées, Les (music group) **1**:59
Teuila festival **9**:1248
Te Wherowhero (Maori king) **9**:1185
textile dyes
    Gambia **2**:199
    Guinea **2**:212
    Senegal **2**:258
    Sierra Leone **2**:276
textiles
    Burkina Faso **3**:363, 367
    Congo Basin **5**:597
    Ghana **3**:378, 385, 389
    Ivory Coast **3**:398
    Northern Marianas **8**:1086
Thaman, Konai Helu **9**:1265
Thatcher, Margaret **7**:992
Théâtre d l'Éclair **5**:690
Theodore II, emperor of Ethiopia **4**:496, 501, 505
Thias, Limamu Laye **2**:260
Thomas, Rover **10**:1375
Thorpe, Ian **10**:1382
Thukela River **7**:895, 896
Thuli Parks and Wildlife Land **7**:*986*
Thuwayn, sultan **6**:743
thylacine (marsupial) **10**:1334
Tidjani Tall, caliph **2**:168
Tieba Traore **2**:168
Tiendrébéogo, Marie Bernadette **2**:211
Tigray **4**:453, 454, 464, 468, 501, 504
    religion **4**:508
Tigrayan People's Liberation Front **4**:503, 504, 509
Tigré (people) **4**:468, 490, 491
Tigré language **4**:468, 489, 491, 492
Tigrinya (people) **4**:492, 493
Tigrinya language **4**:468, 489
Tijaniyya (Islamic brotherhood) **2**:260

Timbo **2**:167, 172
Timbuktu **1**:8; **2**:168
tin **5**:583, 633, 643, 662, 679, 713; **7**:936
Tingatinga, Edward Saidi **6**:835
Tinkisso Falls **2**:151
Tintenpalast **7**:*930, 931*, 932, 935
Tio (Tyo) kingdom **5**:599, 602, 682, 694
Tippu Tib (Arab trader) **5**:599, 605
Tito, Teburoro **9**:1203
Tjapaltjarri, Clifford Possum **10**:1375
Toamasina **6**:728, 742, 745
tobacco **6**:785, 786
Todd, Judith **7**:995
Togo **1**:49; **3**:410–427; **5**:618
    art and architecture **3**:417–418
    Benin border dispute **3**:336
    climate **3**:302–305, 410
    cultural expression **3**:417–419
    daily life **3**:420–422
    economy **3**:344, 411, 424–427
    education **3**:422, 425
    family and society **3**:420–421
    festivals and ceremonies **3**:419
    flag **3**:411
    flora and fauna **3**:306–309
    food and drink **3**:419
    geography **3**:292–299, 410
    geology **3**:300–301
    government and political parties **3**:411, 414, 415–416
    health and welfare **3**:421–422, 425
    history
        chronology **3**:413
        colonial *see* Togoland
        early **3**:321
        modern **3**:410, 415–416, 424
    independence **3**:410, 415, 419, 423
    literature **3**:417
    music **3**:419
    peoples **3**:327–329, 410, 412, 417, 420, 421, 423
    population **3**:410–411
    religion **3**:412, 419, 420, 421
    resources **3**:410, 425–426
    transportation and communication **3**:412, 423, 427

Togo-Atakora Mountains **3**:294, 295
Togoland **3**:*324*, 325, 326
    British-French partition **3**:373, 410, 415
    French region **3**:415–416, 417, 423, 424
Toihiri, Mohamed **6**:756
Tokelau **9**:1256–1257
    climate change **9**:1169, 1256
    geography **9**:1161, 1256
    geology **9**:1165
    peoples **9**:1189, 1257
Tok Pisin (Pidgin English) **8**:1106, 1116
Tol'Ande, Mweya **5**:672
Tolbert, William R., Jr. **2**:230, 238, 247; **3**:396
Tombo Island **2**:152, 214
Tombouctou **3**:311, 312
Tomeing, Litokwa **8**:1058
Tonga **8**:1026–1027; **9**:1258–1273
    art and architecture **9**:1265
    climate **9**:1167, 1258
    cultural expression **9**:1265–1267
    cyclone **9**:1168, 1271
    daily life **9**:1268–1269
    economy **9**:1258–1259, 1271–1273
    family and society **9**:1268
    festivals, food, and drink **9**:1267
    flag **9**:1260
    flora and fauna **9**:1173
    geography **9**:1160, 1258
    geology **9**:1165
    government and political parties **9**:1260, 1262, 1272
    health, welfare, and education **9**:1268–1269
    history
        chronology **9**:1261
        early **9**:1174, 1175, 1176, 1180, *1188*, 1258
        modern **9**:1180, 1181, 1186–1187, 1258, 1263–1264
    independence **9**:1258, 1263, 1271
    language **9**:1260, 1265
    literature **9**:1265
    music **9**:*1259*, 1265, 1266–1267
    New Zealand **9**:1229
    peoples **9**:1174, 1180, 1189, 1190, 1258, 1260, 1268
    population **9**:1259

    religion **9**:1186, 1190, 1260, 1268
    resources **9**:1258, 1272
    transportation and communication **9**:1260, 1273
Tonga (people) **6**:746–747, 853
Tongareva Island **9**:1160
Tongatapu Island **9**:1165, 1180, 1258, 1264, *1266*, 1267
Tordesillas, Treaty of (1494) **1**:38; **2**:170; **3**:320
Toribiong, Johnson **8**:*1092*
Toro kingdom **4**:558, 562
Torrens River **10**:1397
Torres, Luís Vaz de **8**:1033; **10**:1344
Torres Strait **8**:1033; **10**:1300, 1310, 1342, 1344, 1345
Torres Strait Islanders **10**:1355–1356, 1362, 1387, 1388, 1390
tortoise, giant **6**:736, *818*
Torwa kingdom **7**:887
totem, clan **8**:1071
Touba **2**:260, *262*
Toucouleur Empire **2**:167–168, 172; **3**:323
Touré, Ahmed Sékou *see* Sékou Touré, Ahmed
Touré Samoury *see* Samori Ture
Toure Kunda (music group) **2**:258
Townshend, Thomas, Viscount Sydney **10**:1404
trade
    ancient **4**:452–453, 454, 455–456, 457–458, 469
    Angola **5**:612, 627
    Arab **4**:459–461, 465, 523, 535, 536
    Australia **10**:1406–1407, 1408, 1414–1415
    Benin **3**:331, 337, 344, 349
    Benin Kingdom **1**:34–35
    Botswana **7**:913
    Burkina Faso **3**:367
    Burundi **5**:630, 642, 643, 644, 645
    Cameroon **1**:45, 63, 67
    Cape Verde **2**:181, 189, 190, 191
    Central African Republic **5**:647, 659, 661
    colonial **5**:602, 606
    colonial European rivalry **3**:321, 324–325
    Comoros **6**:759
    Congo, Democratic Republic of **5**:664, 681

trade *(continued)*
 Congo, Republic of **5:**684, 694, 695, 697
 Djibouti **4:**479, 480, 481
 early European **1:**38–39, 43; **2:**169, 170, 176; **3:**313, 314, 315, 319, 320–321, 323; **4:**459–461, 465, 523, 535, 536; **8:**1032–1033, 1034, 1038, 1074
 Eritrea **4:**495
 Ethiopia **4:**438, 479, 480, 514–515, 517
 Fiji **8:**1039, 1051
 Gabon **1:**93
 Gambia **2:**193, 203
 Ghana **3:**383, 389
 Guinea **2:**206, 216, 217
 Guinea-Bissau **2:**220
 Hausa states **1:**36, 37
 Indian Ocean routes **6:**740, 741, 743, 748
 Ivory Coast **3:**406, 409
 Kenya **4:**538–539
 Kiribati **9:**1209
 Lesotho **7:**925
 Liberia **2:**247, 249
 lingua franca **4:**467
 Madagascar **6:**773
 Malawi **6:**775, 785, 786, 787
 Marshall Islands **8:**1056, 1063
 Mauritius **6:**797
 Mayotte **6:**798
 Micronesia **8:**1065, 1073
 Mossi Empire **3:**311, 317
 Mozambique **6:**812, 815
 Namibia **7:**937
 Nauru **8:**1083
 New Zealand **9:**1184, 1215, 1231, 1234, 1235
 Nigeria **1:**122, 129
 Niger River **1:**34, 43; **3:**314
 Papua New Guinea **8:**1120, 1121, 1122
 Polynesia **9:**1180, 1181, 1183, 1185
 precolonial Congo Basin 99, 600–601
 Rwanda **5:**700, 714, 715
 Samoa **9:**1241, 1255
 São Tomé and Príncipe **1:**139
 Senegal **2:**252, 255, 263, 264, 267
 Sierra Leone **2:**273, 280, 281, 282, 283
 Solomon Islands **8:**1133, 1135
 Somalia **4:**551, 553

 South Africa **7:**964, 971, 972–973
 southern Africa **7:**886–887, 889
 Swaziland **7:**985
 Tanzania **6:**748, 828
 Togo **3:**344, 423, 424, 426, 427
 Tonga **9:**1264, 1271, 1273
 trans-Sahara **1:**28, 29, 30, 32; **2:**164, 165–166, 169
 Tuvalu **9:**1285
 Uganda **4:**571
 Vanuatu **8:**1147
 Yoruba **1:**32
 Zambia **6:**843, 859
 Zimbabwe **7:**1003
 see also slave trade
traditional medicine **5:**692, 693; **6:**810
Trans-Antarctic Expedition **10:**1425
Transantarctic Mountains **10:**1313, 1318, 1320
transatlantic slave trade *see* slave trade
Transkei **7:**947
Transvaal **7:**893, 894, 895, 896, 903, 907, 940, 945, 962, 964, 965, 967
 Second Anglo-Boer War **7:**898–899, 940, 962
 Swaziland **7:**974, 979
Traoré, Diarra **2:**210
Traoré, Mahama Johnson **2:**258
tree frogs **10:**1333
Treich-Lapène, Marcel **3:**325
trekboere see Afrikaaners
Triangular Trade **1:**39; **2:**171
Tristan da Cunha Islands **7:**872, 877, 880, 938
Trobriand Islands **8:**1015, 1104, 1109, 1113
Tromelin Island **6:**762; **10:**1434
tropical cyclones *see* cyclones
tropical forest *see* rain forest
Trotha, Lothar von **7:**897
Trovoada, Miguel **1:**135
Trovoada, Patrice **1:**135
True Whig Party (Liberia) **2:**237
Truk *see* Chuuk lagoon
Trust Territory of the Pacific Islands *see* United States Pacific Islands Territories
Truth and Reconciliation Commission (Sierra Leone) **2:**274

Truth and Reconciliation Commission (South Africa) **7:**949
tsetse fly **5:**637, 660, 679, 696; **6:**738
Tshombe, Moïse **5:**668, 669
Tsiolkas, Christos **10:**1373
Tsirana, Philibert **6:**765
Tsodilo Hills **7:***904*, 908, *908*
Tsonga (people) **6:**746, 747, 810
tsunami **6:**826; **9:***1166*, 1245, 1253
Tsvangirai, Morgan **7:**990, 993, 1001
Tswana (people) **7:**872–873, 888–889, 896, 900, 902, 906, 908, 909, 910, 911, 957
Tuamotu Archipelago **9:**1163, 1180, 1181, 1186
Tuareg (people) **2:**164, 168; **3:**317
tuatara reptile **9:**1171
Tubman, William **2:**238, 240, 241, 247
Tubuai **9:**1163
Tucker, Albert **10:**1375
Tu'i Kanokupolu dynasty **9:**1263
Tu'i Tonga dynasty **9:**1258, 1263, *1266*
Tulagi **8:**1129, 1133
Tumba, Lake **5:**583
Tumbuka (people) **6:**781, 782
tungsten **7:**936
Tupou dynasty **9:**1186–1187, 1258, 1262, 1270
Tupua Tamasese Meaole, Samoan chief of state **9:**1245
Ture, Samori *see* Samori Ture
Turkana, Lake **4:**439, 441, 451, 453, 469, 537
Tutsi (people) **5:**599, 628, 630, 632, 711, 713, 714
 Burundi violence **5:**634–635, 638, 639, 642, 643, 644
 colonial policies **5:**609, 633, 642, 703, 709, 711
 Congo Wars **5:**670
 cultural expression **5:**636, 637, 706
 percentage in Rwanda **5:**706, 709
 Ruanda kingdom **5:**698, 703, 711
 Rwandan genocide **5:**670, 698, 704–705, 709, 712
 Rwandan government **5:**702, 708, 712

Tutuila Island **9:**1163, 1174, 1187, 1192
Tutuola, Amos **1:**105, 106
Tuvalu **9:**1274–1285
 art and architecture **9:**1280
 climate **9:**1274
 climate change danger **9:**1162, 1169, 1274, *1276*, 1279, 1284
 cultural expression **9:**1280–1281
 daily life **9:**1282
 economy **9:**1275, 1284–1285
 family, health, and education **9:**1282
 festivals, food, and drink **9:**1281
 flora and fauna **9:**1173
 geography **9:**1161–1162, 1274
 geology **9:**1165
 government **9:**1275, 1278
 history
  chronology **9:**1277
  modern **9:**1180, 1181, 1188, 1203, 1274, 1279
  independence **9:**1274, 1279, 1284
 languages **9:**1276, 1280
 literature **9:**1280
 music **9:**1281
 peoples **9:**1189, 1190, *1191*, 1276, 1280
 religion **9:**1276, 1280, 1281, 1282
 resources **9:**1274, 1284
 transportation and communication **9:**1276, 1285
Tuvaluans (people) **8:**1047, 1081
Tuvalu Maritime Training Institute **9:**1282, 1285
Tuvalu Trust Fund **9:**1284
Tuwhare, Hone **9:**1218
Twa (people) **5:***608*, 609, 630, 639, 674, 692, 705, 709
Tyo kingdom *see* Tio (Tyo) kingdom
typhoons **8:**1021, 1022; **9:**1236

U

Ubangi Plateau **5:**583
Ubangi River **5:**583, 651, 658, 660, 661
Ubangi-Shari **5:**646, 651–652, 653, 658, 659, 687, 694
Uganda **4:**554–571; **5:**670, 698
 Angola **5:**618
 art and architecture **4:**562

Central African Republic
  5:652
climate 4:444, 446–447, 554
cultural expression 4:562–564
daily life 4:565
economy 4:535, 536, 556,
  568–571
education 4:566, 568
family and society
  4:565–566
flag 4:555
flora and fauna 4:448–451
food and drink 4:564
geography 4:436, 440, 441,
  554
geology 4:442–443
government and political
  parties 4:556, 558, 561
health and welfare 4:566,
  569
history
  chronology 4:556
  colonial 4:457–458, 466,
    523, 559, 562, 566, 567
  modern 4:554, 559–561,
    568
independence 4:554, 559,
  568
literature 4:562
music 4:562–563
peoples 4:457–458, 468, 469,
  556, 559, 563–564, 565
population 4:556
religion 4:469, 556, 565
resources 4:554, 569, 570
transportation and
  communication 4:556,
  567, 571
Tutsi exiles 5:703, 704, 705,
  708, 709
Uganda Railroad 4:523, 533,
  535, 536, 539, 559, 562,
  568, 571
UGTAN (Guinea) 2:209
Uhuru Park 4:533, 534
Ujamaa villages policy 6:834,
  840
uKhahlamba-Drakensberg
  Park 7:882, 951
Ulithian language 8:1037
Uluru (Ayers Rock) 10:1307,
  1413, 1418
Umar, sultan of Kanemiyin 1:30
Umar ibn Idris, ruler of Kanuri
  1:29
Umar Tall, caliph 2:167–168,
  172, 260; 3:323
Umbundu (people) 5:607, 608
Umbundu language 5:608,
  612, 619

Union Buildings 7:951, 962
Union Islands see Tokelau
Union of Gabonese People
  1:82, 84
Union of South Africa see
  South Africa
Union of the Peoples of
  Cameroon 1:55, 56
UNITA (National Union for the
  Total Independence of
  Angola) 5:610, 614, 616,
  617, 618, 625, 670
United Africa Company 1:43;
  3:415, 424
United Australia Party 10:1367
United Kingdom see Great
  Britain
United Nations 3:375, 415
  Angola 5:617, 618
  Australia 10:1368, 1389
  Benin 3:342
  Burundi 5:628, 633
  Cameroon 1:50, 55
  Congo, Democratic Republic
    of 5:670
  Eritrea 4:482, 488, 493, 495,
    502, 504
  Ethiopia 4:513
  Human Development Index
    5:656
  Ivory Coast peacekeeping
    3:397, 406
  Katanga secession 5:668, 669
  Liberia 2:237, 239, 247
  Namibia 7:926, 931
  New Zealand 9:1216
  Rwanda 5:698, 712
  Samoa 9:1240, 1253–1254
  Sierra Leone 2:268, 274,
    278, 281
  Somalia 4:533, 546, 547,
    551
  South Africa 7:947
  Western Pacific 8:1035, 1059,
    1064, 1069, 1073, 1079,
    1093, 1097, 1105, 1118
  Zimbabwe 7:986
United States 9:1186, 1187,
  1216, 1217
  Angolan Civil War 5:617, 625
  Antarctica 10:1423, 1424,
    1425, 1429, 1430, 1432
  Australia 10:1369, 1370
  Liberia 2:234–236, 237, 238
  Western Pacific
    8:1034–1035, 1052, 1054,
    1058, 1060, 1063, 1064,
    1069, 1071, 1093, 1094,
    1095
  see also American Samoa

United States Exploring
  Expedition 10:1352
United States Pacific Islands
  Territories 8:1035, 1054,
    1059, 1064, 1069,
    1086–1087, 1093, 1097,
    1098; 9:1286–1289
  geography 9:1163, 1263,
    1286–1289
United States Pacific Remote
  Islands National Wildlife
  Refuge 9:1161, 1286
Uniting Church in Australia
  10:1384
Unity and Progress Party
  (Guinea) 2:210
Unity Party (Liberia) 2:234
Universidade Católica de
  Angola 5:623
Universidade Lusiada de São
  Tomé and Príncipe 1:137
Universidad Nacional de
  Educación 1:75
Universidad Nacional de Guinea
  Ecuatorial 1:75, 76
Université Omar Bongo 1:88
University Collage (Ibadan)
  1:107
University of Bangui 5:657,
  658
University of Burundi 5:641,
  642
University of Ibadan 1:120
University of Otago 9:1227
University of Papua New
  Guinea 8:1106, 1116,
  1117
University of the South Pacific
  8:1045, 1048, 1049, 1130,
  1132, 1144; 9:1204, 1246,
  1265, 1282
Unnuth, Abhimanyu 6:794
Upolu Island 9:1162, 1163,
  1187, 1240, 1241, 1242
Upper Senegal-Niger (French
  colony) 3:350, 355, 363
Upper Volta 3:326, 350, 355,
  357, 360, 363, 364
  Mossi system 3:318, 350
  see also Burkina Faso
uranium 5:583, 626, 643
  Central African Republic
    5:652, 659
  Congo, Democratic Republic
    of 5:662, 668, 679
  Congo, Republic of 5:696
  Namibia 7:936
Urban, Keith 10:1378
Urban Grooves (popular
  music) 7:996

Urewera National Park 9:1172
Urundi see Burundi
Usman dan Fodio, caliph of
  Sokoto 1:30, 37, 40,
    41–42, 45, 47, 112
Usumbura see Bujumbura
Uvéa 9:1162, 1174, 1186, 1290
Uwilinglyamana, Agathe 5:705
Uys, Pieter-Dirk 7:953

V
Vaal River 7:868, 870, 883,
  888, 893, 896
Vai (people) 2:178, 240, 241
Vaiaku 9:1279, 1280, 1283
Vailele site 9:1174
Vaitupu Atoll 9:1279, 1281,
  1285
Vali, Justin 6:768
Van Diemen's Land see
  Tasmania
vanilla 6:776, 798
Vanuatu 8:1136–1147
  art and architecture
    8:1142–1143
  climate 8:1019–1022, 1136
  cultural expression
    8:1142–1143
  daily life 8:1144
  economy 8:1137, 1146–1147
  family and society 8:1144
  festivals, food, and drink
    8:1143
  flag 8:1137
  flora and fauna 8:1023–1025
  geography 8:1012, 1014,
    1016, 1136
  geology 8:1017–1018
  government and political
    parties 8:1138, 1140
  health, welfare, and
    education 8:1144
  history
    chronology 8:1139
    early 8:1026–1027, 1033
    modern 8:1136, 1141, 1145
  independence 8:1136, 1140,
    1141, 1145, 1146
  languages 8:1036, 1138,
    1142
  literature 8:1142
  music 8:1143
  peoples 8:1036, 1138, 1142,
    1144
  population 8:1137
  religion 8:1138, 1144
  resources 8:1136, 1146
  transportation and
    communication 8:1138,
    1147

Vasco da Gama Church **4:***458*
Vaughan-Richards, Alan **1:**107
Veiga, Carlos **2:**185
Vella Lavella **8:**1130
Venda (people) **7:**889, 947
Vera, Yvonne **7:**994
Veramo, Joseph **8:**1045
Vereeniging **7:**868, 871
Versailles, Treaty of (1919) **2:**237
Verwoerd, Hendrik **7:**946, 947
Vichy France **1:**83, 90; **4:**475, 479
Victoria (Australian state) **10:**1311, 1365, 1382, 1411
  bushfires **10:**1324, 1408
  federation **10:**1388
  history **10:**1311, 1348, 1349, 1350, 1358, 1385, 1400, 1405, 1406
  resources **10:**1410
  see also Melbourne
Victoria (Malawi city) **6:**729, 733, *823*, 826
Victoria, Lake **4:**436, 438, 439, 441, 446, 451, 467, 468, 469, 559; **5:**603, *642*; **6:**727, 736, 738, 739
  European explorers **6:**744
  fishing **6:**842
  Kenya **4:**523, 528, 537–538
  as Nile source **4:**466
  Uganda **4:**562, 564, 567, 570, 571
Victoria Falls **6:**724, *726*, 727, 744, 855, 859; **7:**875
Victoria Land **10:**1314, *1315*
video industry, Nigeria **1:**109
vidomegon practice **3:**341–342
Vieira, João Bernardo **2:**222, 223, 228
Vietnam War **10:**1369, 1370, 1380
Vieyra, Paulin Soumanou **2:**258
Villa Ki-Yi (arts training center) **3:**400
vineyards **7:**872; **10:**1308, *1410*, 1411
  see also wine
Vinson, Mount **10:**1314
Virunga Mountains **5:**585, 587, *593*, 714
Virunga National Park **5:***591*, 715
Viti Levu **8:**1016, *1038*, *1042*, 1047, 1049, 1050
Vlamingh, Willem de **10:**1344, 1403
Vogelsang, Heinrich **7:**897

Vohou-Vohou movement **3:**398
Volans, Kevin **7:**953
volcanic activity
  Antarctica **10:**1320
  Cameroon **1:**50
  Comoros **6:***751*
  East Africa **4:**439, *440*, 443
  eastern Central Africa **6:**729, 731, 736
  Gulf of Guinea **1:**15, 17, *17*, *19*
  Mauritius **6:***790*
  New Zealand and Polynesia **9:**1158, 1159, *1159*, 1160, 1162, 1163, 1164, 1165; **10:**1320
  Saint Helena **7:**872, 877, 938
  São Tomé and Príncipe **1:***131*, *132*
  southern Africa **7:**872, 877, 938
  West African coastal islands **2:**153, 155, 190
  Western Pacific **8:**1014, 1015, 1016, 1017, *1018*, *1123*, *1137*
Volta, Lake **3:**292, 294, 295, 305, 375, *376*, 381, *382*, 388
Voltaian Basin **3:**294–295, 300, 328
Voltaic languages **3:**328
Voltaic Republic **3:**355
Volta River **3:**292, 294, 295, *298*, *299*, 307, 312, 388
Voortrekker Monument **7:***893*, 962
Voortrekkers *see* Afrikaaners
Vorster, John **7:**947
Vostok Station **10:**1326–1327, 1429
voting rights
  Australia **10:**1388, 1389
  New Zealand **9:**1185, 1215, 1224, 1245
Voudoun **3:**339, 341, 418, 419, 420

W

Waberi, Abdourahman A. **4:**476
Wade, Abdoulaye **2:***254*, 256
Wagadougou (Wagadugu) kingdom **3:**311, 316, 318, 326, 350, 360, 363
Waigani **8:**1116, 1117
Waikato **9:**1165, 1185, 1233
Waikato River **9:**1159
Wainaina, Binyavanga **4:**526
Wairau Affray (1841) **9:**1184

Waitangi, Treaty of (1840) **9:**1179, 1183, 1184, 1209, 1217
Waitangi Day **9:***1217*, 1221
Waitemata Harbour **9:**1229
Wakefield, Edward Gibbon **9:**1184; **10:**1348
Wakefield System **9:**1184
Wake Island **9:**1286, *1288*
  geography **9:**1163, 1289
wallabies **10:**1332, 1410
Wallabies (rugby team) **10:**1382
Wallas Players **5:**690
Wallis, Samuel **9:**1181, *1181*, 1186; **10:**1346
Wallis and Futuna **9:**1290–1291
  geography **9:**1162, 1290
  history **9:**1174, 1180, 1186, 1290
  peoples **9:**1191, 1291
Wall of Names (Rwanda) **5:***704*
wall paintings **4:**506
Walter Lini Day (Vanuatu) **8:**1143
"Waltzing Matilda" (song) **10:**1373
Walukumbu-Bene, Withankenge **5:**672
Walvis Bay **7:**874, 881, 926, 931, 937
  population **7:**935
Wangboje, Solomon **1:**106
war crimes
  Liberia **2:**239
  Sierra Leone **2:**274
Ward, Joseph **9:**1216
Wassoulou Empire **2:**168, 172; **3:**326
Wassu stone circle **2:***199*
Waterberg, Battle of **7:**897
Waterberg Plateau **7:**872
waterfalls **5:***585*
water hyacinths **4:**570, 571
water scarcity
  southern Africa **7:**878, 912, 936
  Tuvalu **9:**1284–1285
  see also drought
Watson, John Christian ("Chris") **10:**1365
Watt, Emmanuel **8:**1142
wattlebird **9:**1171
Weah, George **2:**234, 239
weaving
  Central African Republic **5:***654*
  Ghana **3:**378, 389
  Lesotho **7:**920, *921*

  Madagascar **6:**767
  Samoa **9:**1246
  Tonga **9:**1265
  Tuvalu **9:**1280
  see also basketry; textiles
Weddell, John **10:**1352
Weddell Sea **10:***1312*, 1313, 1314, 1327, 1352
Wegbaja, king of Abomey **3:**322
Weir, Peter **10:**1379
Welamo *see* Wolayta
Wellesley, Arthur, duke of Wellington **9:**1228
Wellesley Islands **10:**1300
Wellington **9:**1159, 1228, 1229, 1235
  architecture **9:**1219
  Arts Festival **9:**1221
  churches **9:**1223
  history **9:**1184, 1185, 1228
  immigrant population **9:**1225, 1228
Wellington Harbour **9:**1159, 1228
welwitschia (desert plant) **7:**884
Wemba, Papa **5:**673
Wendt, Albert **9:**1246
Wenger, Susanne **1:**106
Werrason (singer-songwriter) **5:**673
Wertenbaker, Timberlake **10:**1379
Wesleyan Methodist Missionary Society **8:**1103
Wesleyan Methodists *see* Methodism
West African coast
  climate **2:**156–159
  colonial division **2:**172–173, 250
  early states **2:**164–168
  first European intervention **2:**169–171, 250
  flora and fauna **2:**160–163
  freed slave settlements **2:**174–175
  geography 148–153
  geology **2:**154–155
  peoples **2:**176–179
  slave trade **2:**171, 180, 250
West African craton **1:**16
West African Frontier Force **1:**44
West African manatee **2:**163
West African Shield **2:**154; **3:**300, 301
West Antarctic Ice Sheet **10:**1312, 1313, 1425

West Antarctic Mountains **10**:1314

West Atlantic languages **1**:47; **2**:176, 177

West Cameroon *see* British Cameroon

Western Australia **10**:1304, 1305, 1365, 1393, 1409, 1411

    Aboriginal Australians **10**:1355, 1356

    federation **10**:1388

    history **10**:1347, 1349, 1350, 1351, 1358, 1387, 1406

    resources **10**:1306, 1409–1410, 1411

    see also Perth

Western Australian Shield **10**:1316–1317

Western Cape Province **7**:871, 951, 955, 958, *967*, 971, 972

Western Desert Language **10**:1356

Western Pacific, colonial history **8**:1034–1035

Western Plateau **10**:1304, 1305, 1306

Western Rift Valley **5**:585, *586*

Western Samoa **9**:1187, 1216, 1217, 1240, 1245

    see also Samoa

Westland **9**:1160, 1166

Westland Tai Poutini National Park **9**:1172

Westminster, Statute of **9**:1210, 1216, 1231; **10**:1358

wetlands **1**:24; **3**:307

whale, southern **7**:885

whaling **8**:1033; **10**:1302, 1339, 1348, 1352, 1430, 1432, *1433*

wheat *see* grain

White, Eduardo **6**:807

White, Patrick **10**:1373, 1379

"White Australia" policy **10**:1350, 1357, 1368, 1370, 1385, 1388

White Fathers (missionaries) **5**:709, 710; **6**:851

Whiteley, Brett **10**:1375

White Nile River **4**:*441*

white rhinoceros **5**:592

White Volta 292; **3**:294, 316, 355

Whitlam, Gough **10**:1369, 1370

Whydah *see* Ouidah kingdom

Wichale, Treaty of (1889) **4**:465, 501–502

wildlife reserves **6**:726, *729*; **7**:883, 885; **9**:1163, 1172, 1286, *1288*; **10**:1335, 1413

    Zambia **6**:843, 859

    Zimbabwe **7**:*984, 986*

Wilhelm, Mount **8**:1015

Wilkes, Charles **10**:1352

Wilkes Land coast **10**:1429

Willaumez, Bouet **1**:45–46

Williamson, David **10**:1379

Williamson, James Cassius **10**:1379

Willis, William John **10**:1350

Willis Islets **10**:1310

Wilson, Edward **10**:1353, *1354*

Windhoek **7**:874, 897, 933, 934, 935

    architecture **7**:*930, 931*, 932, *934*

winds **9**:1168–1169

    Antarctica **10**:*1326*, 1327, 1336

    see also harmattan wind

wine

    Australia **10**:1411

    New Zealand **9**:1222, *1235*

    South Africa **7**:872, 955, *967*, 971

Winton, Francis de **5**:605

Winton, Tim **10**:1373

Wiriyamu Massacre **6**:806

Wissmann, Herman von **5**:604

Witwatersrand **7**:871, 876, 961, 962, 964, 965, 966

    gold field **7**:893, 898, 965, 967, 971

Witwatersrand University **7**:961, 966

W National Park **3**:306

Woide, Mamo **4**:507

Wolayta (people) **4**:468

Wollemia **10**:1331, *1332*

Wolof (people) **2**:176, 177, *178*, 198, 200, 201, 252, 256, 257, 258, 259, 261

Wolof kingdoms **2**:164, 165–166, 169, 171, 172

Wolseley, Garnet **3**:315, 324

wool **9**:1184, 1231; **10**:1406, 1410, 1411

Worku, Dagnachew **4**:505

World Bank

    Benin **3**:336

    Burkina Faso **3**:364–365

    Burundi **5**:643

    Cameroon **1**:50, 64

    Central African Republic **5**:659–660

    Congo, Democratic Republic of **5**:679

    Congo, Republic of **5**:695

    Ghana **3**:386, 388

    Guinea **2**:216

    Kenya **4**:536, 537

    Nigeria **1**:125

    Rwanda **5**:713

    São Tomé and Príncipe **1**:135

    Senegal **2**:264

    Sierra Leone **2**:281, 282

    Uganda **4**:561

World Conservation Society **1**:84

World Cup **7**:949, 954, 970, 972, *973*; **10**:1382

World Food Programme **2**:*247*; **4**:531

World Health Organization **1**:89

world music **2**:199; **5**:707; **7**:953

World Trade Organization **2**:190

World War I

    Australia **10**:1358, 1366–1367, 1380, 1396

    Cameroon **1**:44, 46, 55, 60, 62, 63, 83

    Fiji **8**:1035, 1038, 1043

    Gabon **1**:83

    Ghana **3**:373

    Liberia **2**:237

    Marshall Islands **8**:1054, 1059

    Micronesia **8**:1064, 1069

    Nauru **8**:1074, 1079

    New Zealand **9**:1210, 1215–1216, 1221

    Nigeria **1**:44

    Northern Mariana Islands **8**:1086

    Papua New Guinea **8**:1098, 1104, 1117

    Polynesia **9**:1187

    postwar trusteeships *see* League of Nations

    Samoa **9**:1240, 1245, 1252

    Togo **3**:410, 415, 423

World War II **9**:1186, *1288, 1289*

    Australia **10**:1358, 1367, 1368, 1380, 1396, 1398, 1402, 1406

    Cameroon **1**:50, 55

    Coral Sea battle **8**:1104; **10**:1367

    Eritrea **4**:482, 487, *488*, 489, 494

    Ethiopia **4**:496

    Fiji **8**:1043, 1049

    Freetown **2**:280

    French Somaliland **4**:475, 479

    Gabon civil war **1**:83, 90

    Gambia **2**:197

    Guadalcanal battle **8**:*1034*, 1035, 1124, 1129, 1133

    Guam **8**:1052

    Ivory Coast **3**:374

    Kiribati **9**:1198, 1203, 1208, 1209

    Liberia **2**:237

    Marshall Islands **8**:1054, 1059

    Micronesia **8**:1064, 1069, 1073

    Nauru **8**:1074, 1079

    New Guinea **8**:1098, *1105*, 1117, 1118

    New Zealand **9**:1191, 1210, 1216, 1231

    Nigeria **1**:101

    Norfolk Island **10**:1416

    Northern Mariana Islands **8**:1086

    Pearl Harbor attack **8**:1035

    Peleliu battle **8**:1093

    Samoa **9**:1245, 1252

    Solomon Islands **8**:1124, 1129, 1131, 1133, 1134

    Somalia **4**:540, 546, 551

    Tarawa, Battle of (1943) **9**:1198, 1203

    Tonga **9**:1263, 1270

    Tuvalu **9**:1274, 1279

    Vanuatu **8**:1141, 1143, 1145

Wright, Judith **10**:1373

Wuteve, Mount **2**:153

X

Xhosa (people) **7**:888, *889*, 891, 894, 900, 920, 922, 957, 982

X-ray art **10**:1374

xylophone orchestras **6**:808

Y

Yakoma (people) **5**:651, 652, 656

Yaméogo, Maurice **3**:355

Yamoussoukro **3**:297, 396, 404, 405

    public buildings **3**:396, 399, *400*, 403

yams **3**:310, 379, 400

Yao (people) **6**:746, 747, 782, 807

Yaoundé **1**:14, *58*, 59, 60, 62, *67*

Yap (island) **8**:1029, 1064, 1069, 1070, 1071

Yapese Empire **8**:1031

Yapese language **8**:1037, 1070, 1071

WORLD AND ITS PEOPLES

ATLANTIC OCEAN

Turks and Caicos Islands

Haiti

Dominican Republic

U.S. Virgin Islands

British Virgin Islands

Puerto Rico

Anguilla

Saint Kitts-Nevis

Antigua and Barbuda

Montserrat

Guadeloupe

Dominica

Martinique

CARIBBEAN SEA

Saint Lucia

Barbados

Netherlands Antilles

Saint Vincent and the Grenadines

Grenada

Trinidad and Tobago

Venezuela

Greenland

Canada

United States

Saint-Pierre and Miquelon

ATLANTIC OCEAN

Bermuda

Hawaiian Islands

Mexico

Honduras

Belize

Bahamas

Cuba

Jamaica

Seneg

Cape Ver

Gambia

Guatemala

El Salvador

Costa Rica

Nicaragua

PACIFIC OCEAN

Guinea-

Guinea

Sierra

Leone

Guyana

Panama

Venezuela

Suriname

French Guiana

Colombia

Ecuador

Peru

Brazil

Bolivia

Paraguay

Chile

Uruguay

Argentina

ISLANDS OF THE PACIFIC

Northern Mariana Islands

Guam

Marshall Islands

PACIFIC OCEAN

Palau

Micronesia

Gilbert Islands

Nauru

Kiribati

Papua New Guinea

Solomon Islands

Tuvalu

Tokelau

Wallis and Futuna

Samoa

American Samoa

Vanuatu

Fiji

Tonga

Cook Islands

French Polynesia

New Caledonia

Pitcairn

Australia

Natick High School
Library